Learning Disabilities and Employment

Learning Disabilities and Employment

Edited by

Paul J. Gerber
Dale S. Brown

pro·ed

8700 Shoal Creek Boulevard
Austin, Texas 78757-6897

pro·ed

© 1997 by PRO-ED, Inc.
8700 Shoal Creek Boulevard
Austin, Texas 78757-6897

Library of Congress Cataloging-in-Publication Data

Learning disabilities and employment / Paul J. Gerber, Dale S. Brown.
    p.   cm.
    Includes bibliographical references and index.
    ISBN 0-89079-717-X (pbk. : alk. paper)
    1. Learning disabled—Employment—United States. 2. Learning
disabled—Services for—United States. I. Gerber, Paul Jay.
  II. Brown, Dale S.
HD7256.U5L43 1997
331.5'9—dc21   96-45338
                                           CIP

This book is designed in Palatino.

Production Manager: Alan Grimes
Production Coordinators: Tad Gaither, Karen Swain
Managing Editor: Tracy Sergo
Art Director: Thomas Barkley
Reprints Buyer: Alicia Woods
Editor: Robert Griffin
Editorial Assistant: Claudette Landry
Editorial Assistant: Suzi Hunn

Printed in the United States of America

1 2 3 4 5 6 7 8 9 10   00 99 98 97

Dedication

*To my mother Helen Dillon Gerber, and
my dear aunt Florence "R" Dillon—PJG.*

*To my parents; Joy Gilman and Bertram S. Brown
and my other ancestors—DSB.*

Contents

· · · · · · · · · · · · · · · · ·Part III· · · · · · · · · · · · · · · · · ·
Workplace Issues

· · · · · · · · · · · · · · · · ·Part IV· · · · · · · · · · · · · · · · · ·
Experiences in the Workplace

Contributors

Michele L. Anderson
Special Education Teacher
South Middle School District
Arlington Heights, Illinois

Ernest F. Biller, Ph.D.
Associate Professor of Education
University of Idaho
Moscow, Idaho

Jose Blackorby, Ph.D.
Education and Human Services
  Research Program
SRI International
Palo Alto, California

Loring C. Brinckerhoff, Ph.D.
Adjunct Assistant Professor
Tufts University
Boston, Massachusetts

Dale S. Brown, B.S.
National Network of Learning
  Disabled Adults
Washington, DC

Paul J. Gerber, Ph.D.
Professor of Education
Virginia Commonwealth University
Richmond, Virginia

Thomas Grayson, Ph.D.
Associate Director
Transition Research Institute
University of Illinois
Champaign, Illinois

Thomas M. Holub, Ph.D.
Transition Facilitator
Madison Metropolitan School
  District
Madison, Wisconsin

Patricia Horan Latham, J.D.
Attorney
Latham and Latham
Washington, DC

Peter S. Latham, J.D.
Attorney
Latham and Latham
Washington, DC

Richard G. Luecking, Ph.D.
President
TransCen, Inc.
Rockville, Maryland

Joan M. McGuire, Ph.D.
Director, Program for College
  Students with Learning
  Disabilities
University of Connecticut
Storrs, Connecticut

Nancie Payne, M.S.
Learning Disabilities Consultant
Payne and Associates
Olympia, Washington

Craig A. Michaels, Ph.D.
Director, Research and Training
    Institute
National Center for Disability
    Services
Albertson, New York

Lynda Price, Ph.D.
Assistant Professor of Education
State University of New York at
    Potsdam
Potsdam, New York

Rhonda Rapp, M.Ed.
Learning Disabilities Specialist
St. Philip's College
San Antonio, Texas

Marshall Raskind, Ph.D.
Director of Research
Frostig Center
Pasadena, California

Stephen Reder, Ph.D.
Assistant Professor of Psychology
Portland State University
Portland, Oregon

Henry B. Reiff, Ph.D.
Associate Professor of Education
Western Maryland College
Westminster, Maryland

Susan A. Vogel, Ph.D.
Professor of Special Education
Northern Illinois University
DeKalb, Illinois

Mary Wagner, Ph.D.
Education and Human Services
    Research Program
SRI International
Palo Alto, California

Thomas R. Wermuth, Ph.D.
Visiting Assistant Professor of
    Vocational Education
University of Illinois
Champaign, Illinois

Thomas G. West
President
Visualization Research Institute, Inc.
Washington, DC

PART I

Employment of People with Learning Disabilities: The Big Picture

CHAPTER 1

Life After School:
Challenges in the Workplace

Paul J. Gerber

Beyond school, there is a world unlike anything experienced by individuals with learning disabilities during their school-age years. It is a world that holds many challenges not previously confronted and, oftentimes, not anticipated by the most well–thought-out transition plans. It is a complicated and complex world predicated on profit and efficiency. Without question, the private and public sectors differ in terms of goals and objectives, but share a common concern for watching the bottom line and being accountable to those they serve.

Therefore because of the nature of learning disabilities, the vast majority of those who are learning disabled can compete for employment. A key question emerges at this time: How do people with learning disabilities "fit in" when it comes to employment? Beyond the rhetoric and lip service paid to such notions as diversity and equal employment practices, the contemporary workplace is, in theory, a learning disability-friendly environment in which hopes and dreams are realized. It can also harbor frustration, agony, and misplaced goals and ambitions. Now, 5 years after full implementation of the Americans with Disabilities Act of 1990 (ADA), the workplace has changed for the better for individuals with learning disabilities. Yet individuals with learning disabilities still experience higher rates of unemployment and struggle with the phenomenon of underemployment. Conversely, popular media and learning disabilities research literature carry more and more stories of those who became successful despite the odds. Less frequently, the names of Albert Einstein, Thomas Edison, Nelson Rockefeller, and Winston Churchill are evoked, for the new exemplars are our neighbors, colleagues, and fellow community members who have become role models for those who are learning disabled.

The Cultures of School and the Workplace

Ever since the passage of the Education for All Handicapped Children Act of 1975, the culture of the nation's public schools has become attuned to the notion of disability. Without question, a great amount of sophistication has developed around this issue as the years have progressed. Serious efforts have been mounted to provide appropriate and effective programs for all students with disabilities, including those in the high-incidence category of learning disabilities. Attitudes have been adjusted, expectations recalibrated, and systems changed. Most noteworthy is that school professionals have learned how to think about students with learning disabilities, how to interact with them, and how to relate to them appropriately. Disability is part of the culture of schools, and individuals with learning disabilities now live and learn with professionals and peers who are accustomed to dealing with the learning disabled experience.

In contrast, the workplace culture is still adjusting to the concept of disability, particularly the invisible nature of learning disabilities. The workplace is a microcosm of society, with disability largely misunderstood and attitudes and feelings occurring along a continuum from acceptance to rejection. Unfortunately, studies indicate that some people still equate learning disabilities with mental retardation; this causes confusion in the workplace. Moreover, invisibility causes the nature of learning disabilities to appear abstract. Unlike individuals who use wheelchairs, canes, or hearing aids, those who have functional limitations in such areas as sequencing and organization, auditory processing, or dyslexia appear to be nondisabled. If what cannot be seen cannot be readily understood, then employees with learning disabilities have additional burdens to carry in the world of work.

A shift toward greater personal responsibility occurs when an individual with learning disabilities moves from the culture of school to the culture of work. Whereas self-advocacy is a goal of school-age programming for students with learning disabilities, schools still have a child-and-youth focus that does not necessarily cultivate self-direction. In order for a person who is learning disabled to navigate in the workplace, self-direction as well as self-advocacy is a must. After all, employment settings may not include an advocate for individuals with disabilities or a professional charged with determining how disability interferes with overall functioning. Thus, there is a shift in responsibility—the responsibility ascribed to all adults in the work world. This is consistent with the goal of empowerment that was a hallmark of the disabilities movement in the 1990s. Also, it is in line with the paradigm shift in disability policy articulated through legislation and public policy during the Bush administration (1988–1992). Now, people with disabilities are expected to move from the paternalism of yesteryear to independence and self-reliance for the future.

More About the Workplace Culture

At the outset of the Americans with Disabilities Act era, Gerber (1992b) studied the ways in which business and industry were preparing for a workplace that would include more individuals with learning disabilities. Many of the findings of that time still hold true for the learning disabled population. To this day, the workplace is still adjusting to the influx of individuals with disabilities and to those already in the workforce.

Diversity in the workforce is a persistent issue in the public and private sector. Whereas the term usually signals considerations of race and gender, it also includes the issue of disabilities. Thus, beyond resolving problems of architectural barriers and accessibility, managers and supervisors are learning to work alongside individuals with learning disabilities.

Hiring individuals with learning disabilities is not automatic. Business and industry human resources specialists know full well that the intent of the Americans with Disabilities Act is not affirmative action but equal employment opportunity. At job entry, managers are not obliged to hire persons with learning disabilities; they are expected to give them an equal chance in the employee selection process. Therefore, when evaluating their applicant pool, managers always seek a prospective employee who will contribute the most to their corporate mission, whether nondisabled or learning disabled; they know that they have the right to hire someone who is not disabled. Competitive employment is full of chief executive officers (CEOs) who aspire to be good corporate citizens. They feel comfortable about hiring "a good fit," but believe they can only go so far without becoming a "social service organization" (Gerber, 1992b).

Learning disabilities are not easily understood in the workplace. Policymakers within many larger companies have tried valiantly to understand learning disabilities and their multifaceted manifestations. Yet learning disabilities may be grouped with other categories such as developmental disabilities, mental retardation, and sensory disabilities (Emily Hall Tremaine Foundation, 1995). Even when employers have a general notion about learning disabilities, they may be confused regarding problems in attention span, language, and so forth. Even more disconcerting is that underestimated potential and value may lead to underemployment, lack of job advancement opportunities, and negative job satisfaction for the employee.

Self-advocacy becomes crucial to employment success. Self-disclosure is only a beginning. Individuals with learning disabilities must be conversant in the exact nature of their learning disabilities, in how they manifest themselves in the workplace, and in ways to bypass temporary problems. Accordingly, they must clearly articulate strengths and weaknesses in work style and contribute suggestions and ideas regarding reasonable accommodations on an ongoing basis.

Because companies rely on training in order to be efficient and thus competitive, their training procedures are constantly under review and regularly updated. An important focus is designing business and industrial training consistent with the ways all individuals learn, including persons with learning disabilities. Training is not useful when employees are unable to perform their job duties. This results in lower productivity for the organization. Moreover, the worst-case scenario for any business organization is one in which it invests human and capital resources in an employee only to lose him or her to attrition.

The expectations of those who are learning disabled and those who employ them must be realistic for productive outcomes. That means that all involved need to be flexible in employment settings. Change is inevitable when systems adapt to individuals with learning disabilities and when the individuals, in turn, adapt. Time is a key variable. New ways of thinking and doing create new patterns of behavior that settle in after transition periods. Patience is important in the process, as well, from the onset of employment and beyond.

Employment: The Big Picture

In order to understand learning disabilities in the full context of the workplace, it is important to view larger employment trends. Currently, individuals with learning disabilities enter or already work in a dynamic economy fluctuating with downsizing, mergers, restructurings, and advanced technology. There is instability and lack of job security. Without question, lifetime guarantees no longer exist when it comes to work. There is a notion that employees need to be more self-reliant to be competitive. That means keeping up by developing new skills and being ready to take advantage of job opportunities when they arise.

Amidst these business trends, the economy cycles from full employment to relatively high levels of unemployment. When the economy is near, or at, full employment, opportunity in the work force improves for learning disabled and nondisabled people alike. Conversely, at times of economic recession, jobs become more scarce and the pool of potential workers grows larger for every available job. This negatively impacts individuals with learning disabilities, particularly at job entry. The chances of being chosen from among a qualified applicant pool are far slimmer. Moreover, a group of individuals in the economy has acquired the moniker *structurally unemployed*. These people are permanently unemployed under all economic conditions, whether from giving up the quest for a job or from lacking skills to fit into any job available. It is not known how many of these individuals are learning disabled, but recent reports of the United States Department of Labor (1991) and the Inspector General of the United States Department of Health and Human Services (1992) reflected a high incidence of learning disabilities in low-income, poor, and welfare-recipient populations.

Employment: The Learning Disabilities Picture

Numerous studies of late have been designed to uncover the employment situation within the learning disabled population. In the field, the mantra recited for several years now is *unemployed and underemployed*. A look at the actual studies tells a more detailed story.

Mixed results emerge when postschool follow-up studies are examined. Peraino (1990) reviewed 11 follow-up studies of individuals with learning disabilities in the late 1980s. He found the average unemployment rate to be 70% with a range of 57 to 89%. In addition, six other studies were done to measure unemployment rate. The average rate was 21% with 15% unemployed in rural localities. When these studies were done, the national unemployment rate for persons 18 through 24 years of age was 13% and the country was in a recession.

In New Mexico, Haring, Lovett, and Smith (1990) surveyed former students with learning disabilities who had been in self-contained classes. They found that their subjects had an unemployment rate of 31%, more than twice the national average for those who were 16 through 24 years of age (13%). In the Canadian province of Ontario, 80 adults who were deemed learning disabled were studied by Malcolm, Polatajko, and Simons (1990). Of the group they followed, 24.4% were still students, while 38.5% were employed and 34.6% unemployed. The unemployment figures for the general population at that time was 4 to 5.5%. Also in 1990, Sitlington and Frank studied 911 randomly selected students with learning disabilities in the state of Iowa and found that only 77% of graduates were working either part- or full-time with 9% "otherwise meaningfully engaged" (p. 45). Moreover, 15% more males than females were employed, and the males earned on the average over one dollar more an hour than the females.

Employment research yields more favorable reports. Bruck (1985) studied employment of former high school students with learning disabilities, using their siblings as a control group. The rate of unemployment was very similar for this middle-class group. Moreover, individuals in both groups held a variety of jobs and very few worked in unskilled occupations. D'Amico (1991) found that time was one important factor in judging the employment situation of former students. At the outset of the study, the employment rate for former students with learning disabilities was 58% and a comparison group of nondisabled students was 61%. Yet over a two-year period of the study (1987–1989), the employment rate for the individuals with learning disabilities jumped from 62.7% to 75.8%.

Other studies found that the more time individuals with learning disabilities spent in the job market, the better the employment figures. Edgar, Levine, Levine, and Dubney (1988) studied employment outcomes of individuals with learning disabilities in Washington State. They found the employment rate to be 65% after six months and 75% after two years. De Bettencourt, Zigmond, and Thornton (1989) found that the employment rate of individuals with learning disabilities improved to 89% in a rural study after 1½ years, while Scuccimarra and Speece (1990) found employment rates to be as high as 89% after 5 years of study.

There are other interesting findings as well. Most notably, Peraino (1992) found that the wages for those students with learning disabilities who dropped out of school and those who left school with a certificate of completion (as opposed to a high school diploma) were about the same. From his work, it does not appear that "sticking it out" made any measurable difference. Somewhat related is the notion of underemployment. In addition, White (1992), in a review of research of postschool adjustment of individuals with learning disabilities, found underemployment to be a hidden issue. He observed in vocational outcome studies, that the jobs persons with learning disabilities held were low-level service, laborer, production, and helper occupations. He went on to compare a learning-disabled sample and non–learning-disabled sample of adults in the workforce and found those with learning disabilities to have significantly less job status than their nondisabled peers.

Focusing on the learning disabilities and employment data in isolation can be misleading. It is important to digest the data with full knowledge of the context. All too often researchers declare improvement, success, or failure from the latest study on employment, employment outcomes, and employment attainment. As one can see in this section alone, geography has had a bearing on employment as well as the time frame in which employment was studied. Variables to be considered include health of the national economy, urban versus rural settings, agriculture versus manufacturing versus service jobs, and community infrastructure to support the job market. Greater macroeconomic trends affect all persons who work or want to work, including individuals with learning disabilities.

In addition, it is crucial to consider what stage of the employment process is being studied. Currently, the research in learning disabilities and employment does not go very much farther than job entry. Hence, only a small part of the total story is being told. There are vast differences between job entry and other points along the employment continuum. As noted earlier, it is not uncommon that the longer one stays in the workforce the greater success one experiences in keeping a job and becoming eligible for job advancement opportunities.

The Americans with Disabilities Act era is upon us. Passed in 1990, partially implemented in 1992, and fully implemented in 1994, the law presents a new factor in employment studies. Much of the data on employment and learning disabilities predate, or exist concurrent to the very beginning of, the ADA. It is safe to say that the precepts of the law have created greater opportunity for those with learning disabilities. The notion of nondiscrimination and reasonable accommodation alone may lead one to believe that the employment situation has gotten better. Administrative and case law attests to the ongoing work of resolving employment issues, and to the workplace response to the letter and spirit of the ADA.

The Workplace *in vivo*

To date, much of what we know about the workplace comes from studies that have investigated workplace adjustment or success relative to some external standard, typically with quantitative methodology. Those data are useful to the field of learning disabilities and help in setting policies and strategies on "what to do next." However, another body of knowledge affords a view of the workplace through the eyes of working people with learning disabilities. What they have revealed in their stories is valuable and has had an impact on the thinking of researchers, writers, and service providers. One example is the two-year follow-along study by Gerber (1992a, in press) of TJ, a neophyte teacher with learning disabilities who taught a class of students with learning disabilities.

TJ is an adult with learning disabilities whose life is marked by perseverance, triumph, and frustration. After having a less-than-satisfactory experience as a student with a learning disability during his school-age years, he began working in the mid 1980s for his city's biggest employer—a shipbuilding company. In an effort to accommodate his epilepsy, the management transferred him from one position to another; he finally ended up in a clerical job at the shipyard. After some time he left his job and contacted vocational rehabilitation services for help in finding employment. He went to scores of interviews and was never offered a job. (He attributes this to the fact that his prospective employers knew he was learning disabled.) He was encouraged to attend a nearby university on a full-time basis. He did so because, in his thinking, the only other alternative was to kill himself. (In his interpretation, things were at a point of desperation.) After doing satisfactorily in his early years in college, he decided to major in special education and become certified to teach students with learning disabilities. While in his program, he frequently used the university's office for students with disabilities and accessed many of the accommodations available, including nonstandard testing, in-class academic adjustments, and some course-requirement modifications. In addition, he became a campus voice for those who were disabled. Upon receiving his bachelor's degree, he interviewed for several teaching positions, was offered several, and chose the one most fitting for him.

His choice was predicated on several factors. They all stemmed from a clear sense of where he could succeed and under what conditions. He chose a primary school that would not tax his higher-level reading, writing, and math skills. His school assignment was in a rural setting; this kept him out of the fast pace of urban and suburban school systems. Moreover, he sensed that the principal and special education colleagues would be supportive of him in his position because, among other things, his disclosure that he was learning disabled did not bother them in the least. TJ's first year was a successful one. It was marked with a lot of personal pressure and many instances where his learning disability provided tough challenges. His first teaching experience did have its ups and downs. As TJ said:

> My experiences have really helped me with my students. If I had to do it all over again, I'd do it all over again. Because when I'm with my students and things are clicking—that's the greatest high—the greatest high I can think of. Because when they get it I appreciate it more than a regular or special education teacher. I know what they had to do to get there. (p. 224)

TJ provided a credible learning-disabilities resource program in which his students progressed, in which more students were served than ever before, and in which some students transitioned into regular classroom settings. He was a force to contend with in his advocacy of students with learning disabilities. TJ passed a state-mandated beginning teacher assessment program requirement and received favorable teaching reviews from his principal. Anyone who knew him would have declared his career a success (even after a year). Certainly the prognosis was quite favorable for a remarkable teaching career. But the whims and vagaries of the workplace always necessitate vigilance and capacity to change. TJ's case was no different. At the end of TJ's first year, Gerber wrote:

> His accomplishments in year one portend the beginnings of a productive and successful career, but year two may not be any easier, nor any year after that. This may be the fate of one who has a learning disability. It does not, even in the smallest way, diminish the competence, talent or qualifications TJ has shown in his first year of teaching. (p. 230)

Year 2 of TJ's teaching was far from "deja vu all over again." It was as if he had gotten another job. The ingredients from his first year to the next changed dramatically. He had a new principal, his special education colleagues had transferred, and the students he taught were many more in number and far more challenging in nature. A lot of what he had developed for his class during the first year could not be used again. One got the idea that he would not have taken this job if it were offered to him at job entry. The challenges of his disability grew even more challenging. The support he had sought and enjoyed his first year came in different forms and at various times was not present at all. Stress and ambivalence about his job became pervasive themes, and it seemed at times that the situation would be too much of a burden for TJ to overcome. Because, for him it was like "starting all over again" (p. 36). He did not draw strength and pride from the earlier set of success experiences. TJ put his second year in perspective:

> This year was worse than last. I learned to work with the teachers, and I matured a lot. Last year they doubted me. Now more teachers are asking for hints for the learning problems of their students . . . But now I have more problems with my supervisor, things are up in the air with my principal, the size of my class is worse, and the behavior of the class is worse. I had none of that last year. (p. 49)

TJ did have a successful, albeit "rocky" second year—perhaps more successful than his first year because of what he had to deal with to teach his students, and what he had to do to carry out a creditable program. Much had changed. Some similarities were noted in his 2 years' experience, but not enough for generalizing. There is a postscript to this story. In Year 3 of his teaching, TJ found that "things have not really gotten better—much the same like Year 2." (p. 55) He then decided to leave his position and took a similar one in a school division that is more urbanized and where many aspects of the job were more fast-paced and complex. Year 4 was a transition for him and his performance was judged as marginal. In Year 5, he was transferred to another school and did not make it through the year. Currently, he is out of teaching—probably never to return.

TJ's story is characterized by success and failure. His beginning years of teaching showed promise; his last years were filled with unfortunate failure. Much can be learned from TJ's triumphs and tribulations in the workplace. First, that a smooth transition from school to work does not automatically ensure employment success. Second, the workplace is a dynamic setting with continued changes and new adjustments to be made. The key to employment success is flexibility and introspection when it comes to change. The lifespan of work encompasses unpredictable peaks and valleys. People with learning disabilities are as likely to experience those times as are their nondisabled peers, but the degree of challenge and the resulting duration of stress can be far greater. In essence, they may be always at risk in employment, no matter how long they have been working.

Employment Strata: Adults with Learning Disabilities

Other research allows specialists in the field to discover in retrospect the experiences of adults with learning disabilities (Gerber & Reiff, 1991). In an ethnographic study, the lives of nine adults with learning disabilities, ages 19 to 55, were chronicled in a variety of domains, including employment. The clusters of occupations were highly successful: attorney, dentist, assistant dean; moderately successful: electrician, office worker, office worker/driver; and marginally successful/unsuccessful: truck driver, office helper (unemployed), and odd-jobs helper (mostly unemployed). They represented a range of occupations typical of individuals with learning disabilities in the workplace.

In the highly successful group, individuals were determined to use their verbal skills despite weakness in reading and writing. This necessitated the use of elaborate support systems. Most noteworthy, these individuals shared a set of realistic notions of how their learning disabilities affected job performance generally as well as component tasks. This allowed them to know under what conditions they needed to compensate, and when they needed to delegate responsibility to others.

In addition, all individuals displayed a lot of confidence in performing their roles. They remained and advanced in their chosen careers, reporting significant satisfaction in what they were doing and indicating they liked the idea of being in professions that helped other people.

Characteristic of the moderately successful adults with learning disabilities was a distinct openness about learning disabilities. All had revealed their disabilities to their employers, who had helped them find workable job accommodations. (Note: This was prior to the Americans with Disabilities Act era.) These individuals were easygoing and upbeat. They had very good social skills, which enhanced their adjustment to jobs. All aspired to job advancement, and there was already some evidence that this was beginning to happen. The dominant theme in this group was a sense of future and an optimism that they were "going to make it" in the world of work. They readily anticipated success and job satisfaction beyond their current positions.

The last group evidenced a history of spotty employment and, for the most part, job failure. Because of their assorted problems in the world of work, they were apprehensive about the future and lacked plans for how to proceed. They seemed unsure of how to compete in the workplace. All seemed to lack self-confidence and had problems in the area of social skills and fitting in with the mainstream of society. Because they had experienced very little success in employment, they did not know how to think about work and all that it encompassed. They had no future vocational plans or even the slightest idea of how to succeed in the workplace. Each and every one of them evidenced dependency on others (usually on parents or spouses), particularly for financial support.

Of the six individuals who were succeeding in the workplace, all learned to compensate in their jobs in order to achieve. They knew full well the dimensions of their disabilities and accepted them, never losing confidence in themselves although at times losing confidence in their skills and abilities. The group that had experienced limited or no success in the workplace presented a striking contrast. The wherewithal to deal with their disability was lacking, and their potential for making changes, either vocationally or generally, seemed limited. In placing work amongst the broader perspective of adult functioning, it is easy to envision how the effects of vocational success, or the lack of it, can have a significant impact on all other aspects of the quality of adult lives.

When Adults with Learning Disabilities Succeed

For many years, we have heard the tales of those who were learning disabled and became successful. In the learning disability community, the names of Einstein, Edison, Churchill, and Rockefeller have often been invoked to show the world and the field that individuals can make it "in spite of the odds." Curiously, researchers in the field of learning disabilities did not embark on an effort to study successful adults with learning disabilities before the Gerber and Reiff study cited earlier. Several attempts undertaken to investigate the success of people with disabilities excluded those with learning disabilities. This left some to wonder if learning disability was perceived as a deficit model despite the conventional wisdom that it was always important to accentuate strengths while mitigating weaknesses.

The work of Gerber, Ginsberg, and Reiff (1992) and Reiff, Gerber, and Ginsberg (in press) provided extensive information regarding success in the workplace and how that success is achieved. From extensive interviews conducted within a conceptual framework of employment success came numerous discoveries. Among them were:

1. Those with advanced degrees became successful, but that alone did not guarantee success. There were individuals who completed high school only, or did not complete college, who have done quite well in the world of work.

2. Individuals with learning disabilities are in all areas of employment including the professions, business and industry, and public service. Some of them are exemplars in their field, garnering the highest awards and being the most-watched and quoted regarding their work.

3. A significant number of very successful entrepreneurs are learning disabled. In some cases, they have become the leaders in their respective fields and in their business organizations for their creativity and problem-solving abilities.

4. Success has come at a cost. Residual feelings associated with their learning disabilities are still with them despite their success (i.e.,

impostor syndrome, issues of low self-esteem, pain of early failures, feelings of not being "whole").

5. For them, learning disability meant fitting into the "normal" world
by adapting to it—or making it adapt to them. Yet all of their successes occurred prior to the Americans with Disabilities Act era.

6. Many successful adults with learning disabilities have opened
doors in the workplace for other individuals with learning disabilities. They have shown they can perform and achieve at high levels,
making hiring persons with learning disabilities less risky. Some
successful adults with learning disabilities even have taken high
profiles in their work and communities as avocational speakers. In
essence, they have done much to change attitudes and create new
opportunities.

Gerber et al. (1992) found that an interactionist approach had led to
employment success. Thus, it was not only those internal processes,
such as desire and goal setting, that fostered success. It was the inter-
facing of those attributes with adaptive capabilities such as finding the
right "'fit," creative problem solving, and using social support systems.
In composite, these elements helped provide the ecological wherewithal
to maintain and ensure control, which is the key to success. The linchpin of the entire system, however, was an internal process called reframing: introspective positive thinking about one's learning disability that
frames a productive response to the challenges of everyday life.

Those Who Are Not Successful in the Workplace

Earlier and ongoing research into learning disabilities and their manifestations provides more and more evidence of heterogeneity. As with other
disabilities, there is a continuum of functioning, in school and workplace, from high to low levels of adaptability, and a continuum of severity, as well, from mild to severe. Such is true in the area of employment.

Data have shown a wide diversity of employment outcomes for
nearly two decades (Rogan & Hartman, 1976). But the classification of
those who are learning disabled as low-income and poor has recently
become an important issue in the field of learning disabilities, especially
as it becomes part of public policy debate. The low-income and poor
group of individuals with learning disabilities has been invisible. At the
beginning of this decade, two federal reports framed the issues regarding
low-income populations and learning disabilities. *The Learning Disabled in*

Employment and Training Programs (U.S. Department of Labor, 1991) and *Functional Impairments of AFDC Clients* (Inspector General of the U.S. Department of Health and Human Services, 1992) stated that as many as 40 to 50% of Aid to Families with Dependent Children/Job Opportunities and Basic Skills (AFDC/JOBS) clients may have undiagnosed learning disabilities. In addition to these major findings, the U.S. Department of Labor (1991) also found that 15–23% of Jobs Training Partnership Act (JTPA) Title IIA participants may be learning disabled. Moreover, learning disabilities impact clients' efforts to become employed and have a large bearing on acquisition of life skills required for self-sufficiency.

Currently, several national and regional efforts, as well as many local efforts, address this important issue. A majority of these efforts are occurring through the work of literacy centers (and, to a lesser extent, Adult Basic Education [ABE] programs) in large metropolitan areas and in rural settings. Literacy is the objective, but staff members work to impart skills to help individuals obtain jobs, gain proficiency, or advance. Moreover, general equivalency diploma (GED) attainment or greater reading proficiency is not always the goal. Equally important is the notion of accommodation to enhance the many facets of adult functioning, including the concept of reasonable accommodation, to make the workplace more employee-friendly.

Conclusion

Effective advocacy of meaningful, long-term employment of people with learning disabilities is the next significant step that professionals in the field must take to ensure that hopes and dreams are fulfilled and talents and capabilities are not wasted. The field of learning disabilities has come a long way in a relatively short period of time. (Current opportunities and services have not come a moment too soon, however.) There was a time, prior to 1975, when students with learning disabilities wondered how they would get a quality education, and at what price. There was a time prior to the 1980s (when the concept of transition was introduced), when students with learning disabilities were educated without a clear notion of "educated for what." Until the early 1990s, individuals with learning disabilities entered the workplace without guarantees of fundamental rights enabling them to compete on an "even footing" with their nondisabled peers.

Those days are in the past, but perhaps the most difficult days lie ahead. Tracking employment takes specialists from the field into an unfamiliar area. But their knowledge of learning disabilities compels them to sound a clarion call for positive employment outcomes. This is a crucial signal, because much that happens in the workplace is key to the fulfillment of adult life. Work, for so many, is the touchstone for self-esteem, self-fulfillment, and self actualization. What comes next, after the school years, for adults with learning disabilities? Researchers, teachers, and mentors who monitor their progress will learn firsthand whether the world of work yet offers the promise of inclusion and the experience of normalization.

References

Americans with Disabilities Act of 1990, 42 U.S.C. 12101 *et seq.*

D'Amico, R. (1991). The working world awaits: Employment experiences during and shortly after school. In M. Wagner, *Youth with disabilities: How are they doing? The first comprehensive report from the national longitudinal transition study of special education students.* Menlo Park, CA: SRI International.

deBettencourt, L., Zigmond, N., & Thorton, H. (1989). Follow-up of postsecondary-age rural learning disabled graduates and dropouts. *Exceptional Children, 56*(1), 40–49.

Edgar, E., Levine, P., Levine, R., & Dubney, M. (1988). *Washington state follow-along studies 1983–1987: Students in transition* (final report). Unpublished manuscript.

Education for All Handicapped Children Act of 1975, 20 U.S.C. 1400 *et seq.*

Emily Hall Tremaine Foundation (1995). *Learning disabilities and the American public: A look at Americans' awareness and knowledge.* Washington, DC: Author.

Gerber, P. J. (1992a). Being learning disabled and a beginning teacher and teaching a class of students with learning disabilities. *Exceptionality 3*(4), 213–232.

Gerber, P. J. (1992b). Personal perspective. At first glance: Employment for people with learning disabilities at the beginning of the Americans with Disabilities Act era. *Learning Disability Quarterly, 15,* 330–332.

Gerber, P. J. (in press). Trials and tribulations in the workplace: An adult with learning disabilities through two years of employment. In R. Anderson, C. Keller & J. Karp (Eds.), *Enhancing diversity: Educators with disabilities in the educational enterprise.* Washington, DC: Gallaudet University Press.

Gerber, P. J., Ginsberg, R., & Reiff, H. B. (1992). Identifying alterable patterns in employment success for highly successful adults with learning disabilities. *Journal of Learning Disabilities, 25,* 475–487.

Gerber, P. J. & Reiff, H. B. (1991). *Speaking for themselves: Ethnographic interviews with adults with learning disabilities.* Ann Arbor, MI: The University of Michigan Press.

Haring, K. A., Lovett, D., & Smith, D. D. (1990). A follow-up study of recent special education graduates in learning disabilities programs. *Journal of Learning Disabilities, 23*(2), 108–113.

Individuals with Disabilities Education Act of 1990, 20 U.S.C. 1400 *et seq.*

Individuals with Disabilities Education Act Amendments of 1991, 20 U.S.C. 1400 *et seq.*

Inspector General of the U.S. Department of Health and Human services (1993). *Functional impairments of AFDC clients.* Washington, DC: Author.

Malcolm, C. B., Polatajko, H. J., & Simons, J. (1990). A descriptive study of adults with suspected learning disabilities. *Journal of Learning Disabilities, 23*(8), 518–520.

Peraino, J. M. (1992). Post–21 follow-up studies: How do special education students fare? In P. Wehman (Ed.), *Life beyond the classroom.* Baltimore: Paul Brookes Publishing.

Reiff, H. B., Gerber, P. J., & Ginsberg, R. (in press). *Exceeding expectations: Highly successful adults with learning disabilities.* Austin; TX: PRO-ED.

Rogan, L. & Hartman, L. (1976). *A follow-up study of learning disabled children as adults.* Final report (Project No. 443CH600100, Grant No. OEG-0-74-7453), Washington, DC: Bureau of the Education of the Handicapped, U.S. Department of Health, Education and Welfare.

Scuccimarra, D., & Speece, D. (1990). Employment outcomes and social integration of students with mild handicaps: The quality of life two years after high school. *Journal of Learning Disabilities, 23*(4), 213–219.

Sitlington, P. L., & Frank, A. R. (1990). Are adolescents with learning disabilities successfully crossing the bridge into adult life? *Learning Disability Quarterly, 13,* 97–111.

U.S. Department of Labor, Office of Strategic Planning and Policy Development, Employment and Training Administration. (1991). *The learning disabled in employment and training programs.* Washington, DC: Author.

White, W. J. (1992). The postschool adjustment of persons with learning disabilities: Current status and future projections. *Journal of Learning Disabilities, 25*(7), 448 456.

CHAPTER 2

The New Economy in the 21st Century: Implications for Individuals with Learning Disabilities

Dale S. Brown

T he coming millennium holds challenges for all citizens of the world. The workplace is changing dramatically. The old model of "9-to-5 'til 65" is a fantasy for today's young people, and even middle-aged people, in the workplace. Many of the old rules of the game have been transformed or have disappeared. These changes present challenges for people with learning disabilities, offering more freedom and opportunity to use their strengths—or increased unemployment. The purpose of this chapter is to provide for readers a map to this new world so they can help people with learning disabilities deploy their strengths strategically. If people with learning disabilities prepare for the world of yesterday and spend their lives frantically trying to catch up, the nation will be deprived of their potential contributions. If, on the other hand, they are able to accurately assess their own strengths, weaknesses, and disabilities and find creative ways to prepare for the world of tomorrow, the United States will be a better country because of what they have to offer.

Technology: Automating the Brain

To understand the impact of technology on learning disabilities, consider the impact of inexpensive calculators. The calculator has replaced the cognitive skills involved in adding or multiplying accurately in one's head. People who were once valued for having and honing these skills have found the economic need for mental calculation automated away. Yet there is another way to look at this development. A person with dyscalculia now can use the calculator for routine mathematical tasks. A machine that is easily available, inexpensive, and ubiquitous has compensated for one portion of that functional limitation.

Technology has in other ways modified the economic worth of specific skills. In agricultural societies, muscle power and endurance were valued. Learning disabilities were not so apparent in the days before literacy. The industrial revolution caused farmers to leave the land (Drucker, 1995) and go to the factory. No matter how strong a man's body, he could not replace the backhoe. As machines became more complicated and presses made the printed word a major means of communication for the masses, inability to learn to read emerged as a disability. The information revolution we are engineering today is often compared to the industrial revolution (Dent, 1995). The technological changes of the information revolution will have a dramatic impact on workers with learning disabilities.

A look at the swift improvements in computer power shows the extent of the change caused by the information revolution. According to T. J. Rodgers, chief executive officer of Cypress[1] and co-author of *No Excuses Management* (Rodgers, Taylor, & Forman, 1992) ". . . . if automobiles had advanced since 1960 at the same rate as computer chips, we would all be commuting to work in cars that cost a penny, went 2,000 miles an hour and got great gas mileage—about 1,000 miles to the ounce" (p. 1). Highly noticeable results include the growth of the Internet and the World Wide Web. Speed doubles and price declines every 18 months, according to the "rule of microprocessors" (Society of Human Resources Management, 1995, p. 1). The change wrought by computers has just begun.

The results for people with learning disabilities are positive and negative. On the positive side, computers are mechanizing the routine tasks of many white-collar jobs, eliminating challenges for people with dyslexia or other language-related problems. Grammar-checking functions, for example, have reduced some repetitive aspects of editors' jobs, leaving them with more time for the creative tasks. Spell-checking programs have resolved many typing and spelling problems. Creative writers with severe dyslexia have been freed, and within that freedom undoubtedly will flourish. In some companies, computer programs enable employees to see when their operations vary from company rules and regulations, lessening the need for the worker to remember all of the details. Personal information management programs are making it easier for people whose memory is poor to keep track of their daily schedules and to have the information they need right at their fingertips.

On the negative side, using the technology often requires compensating for one's learning disabilities. Voice mail demands that the user

---

[1]Cypress Semiconductor, located in the Silicon Valley area, produces some of the world's most powerful microprocessors.

write down the messages, requiring accurate auditory perception, particularly when a telephone number and address are included. Even business cards are more complicated, carrying home, work, and car telephone numbers, pager numbers, Teletypewriter for the deaf (TTD) numbers for people who are deaf, facsimile (FAX) numbers for home and office, and one or more E-mail addresses. A business card with one number is almost old-fashioned. However, as software gets more sophisticated, it becomes more user-friendly. Speed dialing, which requires a person to punch one or two letters, is an example of the simplification of the future.

Customers: Crucial Concern of Corporations

Clearly, technology has changed the nature of many jobs. Dent, author of *Job Shock* (1995), depicts Linda, a telephone salesperson, at work with a computer:

> A mail order customer is calling. While the phone is ringing, a micro-computer is at work behind the scenes analyzing the number to decide if the caller is a past customer. If he or she is, the computer will access the customer's summarized file of age, income, past buying history, credit approval levels, ages and birth dates for the entire family, comments about past preferences, experiences with this caller, credit card numbers, and so on. The file will pop up to the sales representative as he or she answers the phone. And if it's not a past customer, the computer will determine the exact address or at least the calling area code from the phone number and access an on-line marketing database to pull up an approximate demographic and lifestyle file on the caller—age and income, life-style preferences, propensity to buy, and so on. (p. 69)

Linda is looking at a computer screen with written words on it throughout this interaction. This could be a barrier if she has dyslexia, cannot read, and has previously relied on her "gift of gab." On the other hand, voice-output software could allow the computer to "talk" to her, equalizing her productivity with that of her reading peers. Linda's vignette also shows the increased customer orientation of today's business. A person who is able to skillfully assess a paying customer's needs and show the company how to meet them will more easily find employment in tomorrow's economy.

Customers have more power than ever before (Hammer, 1993). In the mass-production phase between World War II and the oil crisis of

1973, goods were highly standardized and mass-marketed. Customers bought what was available. Growing families of the immediate postwar period and baby boom were eager buyers of scare U.S.-made consumer items. In the ensuing decades, the Japanese and other foreign competitors flooded United States markets with higher-quality products, thus raising consumers' expectations. Today, few shortages occur. Consumers demand products tailored to their individual needs quickly and cheaply. To meet these demands, retooled assembly lines allow customizing. The design of Steelcase[2] factories provides for variations in the crafting of each ergonomic chair according to the buyer's choice of features and fabrics. Numerous fast-food shops now allow the customer to select bread, fillings, spread, and other options for a sandwich. Of course, this customization also requires changes in staff structure.

Empowerment of consumers and expansion of product choices have assisted people with special needs in many ways. The range of type fonts in computer software offers helpful options to many people with visual perception disabilities. A person can choose an appliance designed to accommodate for perceptual and motor disabilities. And, of course, in some settings, the customer can select the salesperson. Perceptive sales and service personnel who can master information about a product line, "stand in the customer's shoes," and persuade them to buy will always be in demand. A person who brings to a company a group of loyal clients will have tremendous bargaining power regarding salary and benefits.

The World Is Our Village: Globalization of Business

People who are able to serve customers from many cultures will be in particularly high demand as the global village becomes a reality. Multinational corporations have risen in power. The world is becoming one marketplace. Europe and North America have consolidated their economies through the European Economic Community and the North American Free Trade Agreement. Higher quality telephone connections and the Internet have made communication with people in other countries significantly easier.

Some individuals with learning disabilities may be ideally suited for the challenge of participating in international business. They have developed unusually strong diplomatic skills to get what they need to accommodate their life challenges. For them, the effort to fit in and communi-

---

[2]Steelcase, headquartered in Grand Rapids, Michigan, designs and manufactures a large proportion of the world's office furniture.

cate with people who are different is a finely honed skill used each day. Those people who learn to do this effectively and grow from the experience are likely to be particularly skilled in working in cultures other than their own. This may help them in the international environment that demands more thoughtfulness and adaptability to different customs.

How Organizations Have Changed

People with learning disabilities have always had a hard time fitting into the neat boxes of bureaucracy. Their disabilities often made it difficult for them to conform. For the most part, they were not "organization men." They did not adapt well to a mass-market society that educated students by forcing them to sit at desks in rows and passively learn. The industrial past demanded many people who came in on time, filled out forms well, and obeyed orders. People with dyslexia often did not make the grade.

Those unable to meet such demands will have an opportunity to profit from current organizational changes. The needs of the "ever more picky" customer, improving technology, and heightened competition have led to a breakdown of large hierarchical organizations into smaller units (Dent, 1995; Drucker, 1995; Frank & Cook, 1995; Hammer & Champy, 1993; Kotter, 1995; Rodgers, 1992; Ross, 1994). Within the past 10 years, the proportion of the workforce employed by the Fortune 500 companies has fallen from 30% to 13% (Drucker, 1995). The business literature is close to unanimous regarding the trend toward smaller units and more autonomy, although the descriptions vary. Many books speak of going from hierarchies to networks. The "molecular organization" (Ross, 1994) is described as an atom with the boss at the center, the employees as the electrons, and values and vision holding the group together. Another analyst (Dent, 1995) likens the old model of organization to a whale and the new model to a school of minnows. The whale turns slowly, the school of minnows turns quickly. Each minnow feels the same forces the others detect and turns with them. The school can also divide and subdivide—unlike a whale.

The eight-hour day job, with a set starting time, is being replaced by other ways of organizing work. This is good news for people with temporal perceptual problems or biological rhythms that differ from the norm. Corporations are shedding employees and "contracting out" or "outsourcing." The number of temporary employment agencies doubled between 1989 and 1994 (Drucker, 1995). Manpower Inc., the largest temporary agency, has 600,000 people on its payroll—outnumbering

General Motors by 200,000 (Fierman, 1994). Many contractors are Single Owner, Home Office (SOHOs) with a responsibility to do the job, but no obligations to socially conform to an office code or work within sight of a supervisor.

Drucker (1995) says that within the next ten to fifteen years, organizations may outsource all work that is support rather than revenue producing. "Even more important," he states, "is the trend towards *alliances* as the vehicles for business growth. . . . the largely unreported growth of relationships that are not based on ownership but on partnership; joint ventures; minority investments cementing a joint-marketing agreement or an agreement to do joint research; and semiformal alliances of all sorts" (p. 69).

This means that managers have a new role—organizing work without necessarily having power over people by controlling their major source of income. For example, a team member may see the manager as one of 10 customers and, perhaps, not even a key customer. This means that managers need to inspire and persuade people to become part of a joint vision rather than implementing the traditional skills of planning, organizing, controlling, and monitoring (Manz & Sims, 1993). The old-style autocratic boss is disappearing, being replaced by a "coach" or an "internal consultant." Employees with learning disabilities may be able to use the climate of empowerment and flexibility to be productive, to self-accommodate their disabilities, and to work their own way. In addition, managers, deprived of the traditional power over subordinates' paychecks, must communicate more effectively and adjust to various interpersonal and work styles.

Impact on the Individual Worker

Work Is Faster

People who are hyperactive may find themselves better adapted to the high speed that will be required in tomorrow's world. Organizations are changing so they can accelerate production. Thus, individual workers must work swiftly to meet the goals of their leadership. Schor (1991) calculated the work time of employees during the past 20 years and has shown an increase of 163 hours a year between 1969 and 1987—approximately a full extra month. In the past decade, paid time off such as holidays and sick time has decreased by three and a half days.

Technology has made us more productive, but it also increases time pressure. The FAX machine has bought us convenience and has also removed the relaxing few days it once took for documents to reach their destination. Voice mail has doubled and tripled the number of phone calls for many workers. The ability to send information quickly puts pressure on the provider of that information to send it immediately. Customers want it now!

To take a peek in the future, read this description of life at Netscape, a high technology company (Steinert-Threlkeld, 1995): "Jamie Zawinski was fried. He had fallen into the habit of working two days straight, sleeping for six hours, then beginning another two-day shift (p. 86) . . . Netscape turned from an office to a dormitory. Programmers crashed in their cubicles, or if they needed 'real' rest, in the futon room. Jamie Zawinski's 130 hour weeks became the norm. Mike Barbarino, who worked on the Windows version of the Navigator (and who, now 35, is an old man by Netscape standards), spent seven days a week at the office and slept on a futon only three or four hours a night"(p. 89).

Teamwork Is More Important

The change from hierarchy to networks makes social skills more critical than ever. Under the traditional chain-of-command structure, a person with a learning disability generally had one key relationship: the relationship with the boss. If they were successful in getting along with their direct superior, communication with co-workers, customers, and subordinates was helpful but not necessarily crucial to getting the job done. On a team, the worker has a myriad of relationships to juggle. The contacts are so close that the usual recommendation to disclose one's disability only to one's supervisor and the human resources staff may be unrealistic. Team members may be involved in accommodation issues formerly contained within the old key relationship.

Governmental organizations, companies, and non-profit entities are reorganizing their employees into teams in order to keep up with the demands of customers and competition. Some teams are "self-managed," organizing their own breaks, handling machinery and equipment repair, making job assignments and training new group members. *Businesses without Bosses*, a book about self-managed teams, in a chapter titled "Tyrannosaurus Rex: The Boss as Corporate Dinosaur," explains what is repeated in much of the business literature, "Bosses limit, control, and too often waste the potential of employees; teams, in contrast, unleash it"

(p. 1). Manz and Sims (1993) estimated that by the 21st century, "40–50% of the U.S. workforce may be employed in some kind of empowered teams" (p. 12). Hundreds of books have been written for managers and employees alike describing the phenomena.

O'Brien (1995), in a book fairly typical of the genre, gives examples of new abilities needed for team membership and delineates the following roles: The summarizer, who urges the group to work toward consensus and decision; the orienter, who keeps the team on track; the fact seeker, who tests reality through researching or requesting information; the harmonizer, who calls team members' attention to conflict and helps resolve it; the analyzer, who watches for changes in the vital signs of the team and alerts colleagues; and the encourager, who shows support for people's ideas, efforts, and communication (p. 51). Of course, for those people with learning disabilities whose social skills are finely honed, a team can be a nurturing group. Some people who have skills that are highly valued by the team find other members cheerfully pitching in to the parts of the job that give them trouble.

Workers Are More Empowered

The shift to team structure is one of many changes empowering workers. Technological innovations that make individuals more productive enable them to add more value to corporations. Creativity, increasingly regarded as a corporate virtue, gives crucial strategic advantage to the higher-functioning segment of the learning-disabled population. In addition, companies are expanding the scope of jobs, even those traditionally simple and routinized. For example, Texas Instruments in Malaysia has placed its machine operators in self-managing work teams and instituted "total productive maintenance." According to Cheny, Sims, and Manz (1993):

> Several steps are required to set up this concept. First, machine operators learn to clean their machines using standard cleaning procedures. Next, they learn to adjust the machine when something goes wrong. Previously they were instructed to stop a machine with even small maladjustments and tell their supervisor. The supervisor then filled out a maintenance request order, which was sent to Maintenance and answered perhaps the next day (or later!). Although many seasoned operators knew how to perform these minor adjustments, they were not permitted to do so.
>
> In the next step, workers learn to clean and oil their machines. Then they become responsible for total inspection of the machine operation

using the manual, which is followed by preventive maintenance. They learn in detail how each machine operation affects the quality of their product. Finally, each operator becomes responsible for total preventive maintenance. Generally the full process takes three years. (p. 162)

This exemplifies job-activities change, making work more complicated and substantive. In *Reengineering the Corporation*, Michael Hammer and James Champy (1993) reported that the content of jobs changes after reengineering. "When a process is reengineered, jobs evolve from narrow and task-oriented to multidimensional. People who once did as they were instructed now make choices and decisions on their own instead. Assembly-line work disappears. Functional departments lose their reasons for being. Managers stop acting like supervisors and behave more like coaches. . . . Practically every aspect of the organization is transformed, often beyond recognition" (p. 65).

Workers Are Released from the Office

Organizations are also transforming their physical space. Offices will change beyond recognition—and fewer people will occupy them. The most recent conversion in many work places, from private offices to open space, has been extremely challenging for professionals who are distractible or hyperactive. Many legitimately need quiet and privacy to do their jobs.

However, technology has broken the link between the work to be done and a specific place to do it (Hammer, 1993). Telecommuting has allowed many employees to work at home part of the time. According to the Society for Human Resource Management (1995), "In 1994, close to 9 million people did some or all of their work from home—a 20% increase over the 7.6 million telecommuters in 1993. Link Resources, an information industry research firm, expects this number to exceed 13 million by 1998." (p. 2) This trend is widely perceived as a response to family needs, environmental concerns, and the bottom line. Corporate expenditures for office space are high (Handy, 1995). LEXIS-NEXIS has closed many field offices and required its displaced representatives to work at home—at their own expense for air conditioning, heating, and electricity during weekday hours.

Some businesses, in a new concept called "hoteling" or "hot-desking", require workers who need an office and a desk to reserve in advance. Thomas W. Hubbs, vice president and chief of staff of VeriFone, Inc. sets up his "virtual office" wherever he is—even if it means using pliers, screwdrivers, and alligator clips to attach his modem and computer to a face plate or handset (Mitchell, 1994). More than 13 million people work at home for themselves rather than for a company or at company head-quarters (Cheney, 1996).

What Does All This Mean for Employees with Learning Disabilities?

Trends toward worker empowerment, teamwork, lessening of the requirement to be in the office, and the phasing-out of the oppressive "boss" are positive outcomes for people with learning disabilities. People who identify their strengths and create or find jobs to match those strengths will have more bargaining power to seek accommodations for their working styles. Expectations that workers should stay at their desks, spell words correctly, fill out forms accurately, and obey petty commands from superiors, are gradually being phased out because of their negative impact on productivity, particularly for knowledge workers.

The modernizing, democratizing trends may not favor the person with a learning disability who has a low-average to average IQ and lacks clearly salable strengths or access to remediation. Old-fashioned manufacturing and service jobs that did not require literacy are disappearing. In addition, new immigrants and welfare recipients are competing for entry-level jobs. Technology, which can be helpful, is also used to monitor workers, catching and recording errors as they happen.

These problems are partially mitigated by the Americans with Disabilities Act of 1990, which makes it illegal for a company to deny reasonable accommodation unless it represents an undue hardship. Unfortunately, as organizations cut costs, they may be more hesitant to pay even the minor expenses of accommodation. More troubling is the trend towards smaller organizations and subcontracting which may muddy the waters when one is trying to confirm a violation of the ADA. The employment section of the Americans with Disabilities Act does not cover employers with less than fifteen employees.

The act covers employees who are qualified and able to perform the essential functions of a job. The flexibility required of an individual on a team of workers may make determining essential functions more difficult. In addition, many corporations are broadening their job descriptions or expecting employees who they hire to be ready for frequent transfers within the company.

As the authors of *Reengineering the Corporation* explain (Hammer & Champy, 1993); "If jobs are more satisfying, they are also more challenging and difficult. Much of the old, routine work is eliminated and automated. If the old model was simple tasks for simple people, the new one is complex jobs for smart people, which raises the bar for entry into the workforce. Few simple, routine, unskilled jobs are to be found in a reengineered environment." (p. 70) At worst, the information age could lead to more unemployment if machines displace people rather than empower them (Rifkin, 1995).

Although the exit of the "boss" helps the person with a learning disability, the thinning of middle-management ranks means that each supervisor has more people to supervise and less time for each person. This can lessen training time and the myriad of informal accommodations that supervisors often provided their productive learning disabled employees. The increase in working hours is still another problem.

The greatest challenge to people with learning disabilities is the same one that each and every worker must face in today's world and the world of tomorrow. Change is now continuous and competition from other workers and other companies is very tough. To find ways of handling the current situation, it may be helpful to review a study of the Harvard Business School class of 1974, a group of top achievers who have competed hard and won.

The Harvard Business School Class of 1974

John Kotter (1995) followed the careers of Harvard Business School graduates and reported his findings in the book *The New Rules*. This summary of changes in the workplace since the 1970s is useful for those who are contemplating their careers or providing services to help improve employment opportunities for underrepresented groups such as minorities, women, and people with disabilities—particularly people with learning disabilities. They are:

> *New Rule # 1* The location of opportunities is shifting. Succeeding at work today demands strategies and career paths that are often different from mid-20th century norms. Increasingly, the new rule is: beware of the conventional and traditional. In a time of rapid change, the unconventional often wins. (p. 36).

> *New Rule #2* The globalization of markets and competition is creating enormous change. The new rule is: to succeed, one must capitalize on the opportunities available in the faster-moving and more competitive

business environment while avoiding the many hazards inherent in such an environment. (p. 57).

New Rule #3 Increasingly, success is going to the small and entrepreneurial, not the big and bureaucratic. The new rule is: people who found and grow small organizations are often receiving both more job satisfaction and more income than most of those in traditional large organizations (p. 79).

New Rule #4 Huge and inwardly focused hierarchies perform poorly in fast-moving and competitive environments. As a result, big organizations everywhere are being forced to slim down, become less bureaucratic, and form closer relationships with customers and suppliers. This trend offers great opportunities—for small distributors, suppliers, and especially business consultants. (p. 97).

New Rule #5 Success in managerial jobs increasingly requires leadership, not just good management. Even at lower levels in firms, the inability to lead is hurting both corporate performance and individual careers. Organizations that stifle leadership from employees are no longer winning. (p. 115).

New Rule #6 Today's global business environment offers huge opportunities for financially oriented deal makers. The new rule is: deal if you can, but be careful. Some of those opportunities are not in anyone's best interests except the deal maker's. Because some people are capitalizing on those socially questionable possibilities, the public is increasingly looking at all financial deal makers (and, to a lesser degree, all business people) with suspicion and contempt. (p. 135).

New Rule #7 In the increasingly competitive and fast-moving global business environment, winners reap big rewards while those who are unable or unwilling to compete can encounter huge problems. The new rule is: you have got to be an able competitor. Effective competition requires many things, especially high standards and a strong desire to win. (p. 158).

New Rule #8 In a rapidly changing and competitive environment, formal K–12-university education is very important, but insufficient. Success at work demands huge growth after a terminal degree to learn new approaches, skills, techniques, and more. A turbulent environment offers many opportunities for growth for those willing to take some risks and to reflect honestly on their experiences. (p. 173).

Recommendations for Individuals with Learning Disabilities

Professionals who consult the following recommendations in helping people with learning disabilities should ask themselves how they can influence their clients to consider these ideas, develop an inner locus of control, and actualize themselves. These suggestions, written for people with learning disabilities who are confronting career issues, are based on the trends discussed in this chapter.

1. Know your strengths. A study of highly successful adults with learning disabilities (Gerber, Ginsberg & Reiff, 1992) showed that "goodness of fit" between the person and the job is one of the key indicators for success. The experience of the writer of this chapter in the self-help movement has reinforced this lesson. Many people who continue struggling to remediate their weaknesses fail. Those who find their strengths and sell their skills best succeed. (See New Rules 4 and 7.)

    Many career books recommend exercises for discovering your strengths. Find one and use it. Counseling is worthwhile. Some good indicators of strength may be found by answering the following questions:

    a. What do you like to do?

    b. What brings you compliments?

    c. What are your major past successes?

2. Consider writing a "mission statement" for your life. This step is recommended by Covey (1989) and other experts in motivation. Developing your goal in life and putting it in writing gives you a sense of purpose that will help you overcome obstacles. People with learning disabilities must often spend extra time self-accommodating their disabilities, particularly early in their careers. In addition, those whose learning disabilities are known in the community may have to fight prejudice and discrimination.

3. Determine who might pay for your strengths and enable you to achieve your life mission. After determining your abilities, the next step is sorting out how these strengths can be marketed. Ask yourself:

    a. Where do people get paid for this?

    b. Who might pay me to do this if they knew I possessed these skills?

      c. Who needs this? Of those who need it, who has financial resources to pay me?

You may find these questions answered in the context of a traditional job. Or you may find yourself selling your services as an independent contractor or freelance expert. (See New Rule 4.)

4. Network and make friends. Develop a support community. This can be a challenge for someone whose disability affects social skills. Nevertheless, determining who will pay for your strengths requires talking to others and selling your talents. Use your coping skills. For example, you may have to consciously memorize and practice statements explaining your strengths to be able to say them spontaneously at interviews and sales meetings. You may need to attend business networking events where the people are not customers for your services. Rehearsals prepare you for later interactions with your potential customers. Networking books and materials abound.

5. Learn to work as a member of a team and try different roles on various teams. If you have the opportunity to join a team in your current job, volunteer. If you are athletic, consider joining sports teams as they provide many lessons and metaphors for success at work. Self-help groups have provided good experiences in teamwork for many people with learning disabilities. Consider joining or forming one in your area. If you have a business idea, form a group to make it happen. Two skills are particularly important to practice:

      a. communicating your strengths.

      b. effectively requesting what you need in order to be productive. In some cases, you will request accommodations for your learning disabilities.

6. Be yourself. The need to conform to rigid norms is less important than ever before. You no longer have to try to fit into the same mold as everyone else. Having a personality that is unique may not be as difficult as in the old days of "the organization man." For example, many companies allow workers to vary their starting times. You may be able to work at home some or all of the time. (See New Rule 1.)

7. Feel free to change jobs. It is no longer stigmatizing to change jobs laterally. It can help you find or create the role that best fits your unique profile of strengths and weaknesses. And as a person with a learning disability, you want a culture where getting whatever

accommodation you need is easy and natural. Avoid situations where you must fight for your rights! (See New Rule 1.)

8. Consider small businesses as places to work. They require long hours, but give you the opportunity to take on more responsibility. During the current period, they are projected to produce most of the new jobs for the future. They also have a high failure rate. Study the business, particularly its financial condition, before accepting a job offer. (See New Rules 1, 3, and 4.)

9. Prepare for lifelong learning; it is particularly critical to learn about technology. Learning goes on forever. Get yourself on the information highway no matter how unsympathetic your computer is with your dyslexia. Fifty-five business leaders cited the following skills as those most needed for the 21st century in a study conducted by the American Association of School Administrators (1996):

   a. Use of math, logic, and reasoning skills; functional and operational literacy; and an understanding of statistics

   b. critical interpersonal skills, including speaking, listening, and being a part of a team

   c. effective information accessing and processing skills, using technology.

   d. writing skills

   e. knowledge of U.S. history and government

   f. scientific knowledge base, including applied science

   g. multicultural understanding

   h. knowledge of foreign languages

   i. knowledge of world geography

   Adult education is more flexible and empowering than the education you experienced in high school and college. Find or create situations where you can learn needed skills. (See New Rules 7 and 8.)

10. Become a global citizen. Learn a foreign language; your disability may present an extra challenge, but this is worth the effort. If an opportunity comes up to work in another country or to serve on an international team, take it. Meanwhile, extend your interpersonal skills to get to know people from other countries and cultures. (See New Rule 2.)

Implications for the Field
of Learning Disabilities

These recommendations follow a common theme: Individuals must continuously work to understand and improve themselves. In the same way, governments are being "reinvented" and corporations are being "reengineered." The field of learning disabilities and its network of service providers will have to change significantly to assure that the next generation of students with learning disabilities is ready to face and enter the world of work.

The issue of consumer empowerment is more than a civil rights issue. Consumer empowerment is the only way placement providers can be effective in helping their clients find work. People with learning disabilities must be self-directed in order to survive and thrive in the future. Within the old paradigm, "placing" a person in a job emphasized passive conformity. The structure of the new paradigm is helping the prospective employer, as consumer, "create" a job.

Educational methodology must advance to the point at which students with learning disabilities are accommodated so they can meet ever-higher academic standards. Basic literacy is essential, but for most jobs, it is not nearly enough. Auditory literacy—the ability to understand complicated verbal directions and concepts—should be taught. Many work settings require employees to catch and process complex communication while one or both parties is rushing or performing some other task.

Long before they enter the job market, people with learning disabilities need clear information about their disabilities and about options for remediation and compensation. They should learn about their marketable areas of excellence. Information on how to disclose their disability and ask for accommodation also is vital.

In the future, social skills training, including intercultural information, will be even more important. Cooperative learning, with students working in teams and pairs as they will in the workplace, should be seriously considered. Training in organizational and self-management skills, including software programs, will help students work more quickly and finish tasks at the expected speed. Tomorrow's economy will be less patient with those who "go at their own pace" if that pace is slow.

In the future, workers will have more freedom in terms of approaching daily tasks. More employees will be able to work at home and schedule their breaks as they wish, and may find themselves working for a customer rather than a boss. The remaining jobs in traditional workplaces are becoming more intellectually demanding and fulfilling.

The new millennium brings both potential problems and promise. If people with learning disabilities receive appropriate education, transition services, and career guidance, their disabilities need not constitute a barrier to performance. People with learning disabilities can make strong contributions to the global economy. They can share their strengths and become part of the team. It is hoped that readers of this chapter take seriously the challenge of the future and their roles in equipping people with learning disabilities to excel in the new reality.

Suggested Readings

The author would like to acknowledge three seminal books that have particularly influenced this chapter. They are:

Drucker, P. F. (1995). *Managing in a Time of Great Change.* New York: Truman Talley Books.

Peter Drucker is among the best-known management writers in the United States. For more than 50 years, he has taught, advised, and written about organizations and their structure. He has written 26 books since his first, *The Concept of a Corporation.* This book covers current management challenges, the information-based organization, types of teams, the world economy, and the role of non-profit and government sectors.

Kotter, J. P. (1995). *The New Rules.* New York: The Free Press.

Kotter developed these rules by carefully following 115 MBA students from the Harvard Business School's class of 1974 and showing how their careers differed from those of the generation before. He sent them yearly questionnaires, which nine out of ten of them returned. He found that the "rules" he drew from this talented group of individuals were consistent with the results of six other studies he conducted with a more diverse group of individuals (Kotter, 1995). These rules are presented to the reader for serious consideration by and for people with learning disabilities.

Hammer, M., & Champy, J. (1993). *Reengineering the Corporation.* New York: Harper Collins Publishers.

This book has spawned numerous other books and has been used as a bible for change by hundreds of corporations and consulting firms.

Although some say reengineering is a management fad (Davenport), the concepts and processes described in this book are integral to current production practices, and the changes described in the workplace are well-documented by many authors

References

American Association of School Administrators. (1996, January 30). *Ethics, communication, technology, and cultural understanding: Top list of knowledge, skills, behaviors needed for life in the 21st Century.* (Press release, pp. 4–6). Arlington, VA: Author.

Americans with Disabilities Act of 1990, 42 U.S.C. 12101 *et seq.*

Cheney, A. B., Sims, H. P. & Manz, C. (1993). Teams and total quality management: An international application. In C. Manz & H. Sims (Eds.), *Business without bosses: How self-managing teams are building high-performing companies.* New York: John Wiley & Sons, Inc.

Cheney, K. (1996, March). You can make six figures working at home. *Money, 25*(3), 74–87.

Covey, S. R. (1989). *The seven habits of highly effective people.* New York: Simon and Schuster.

Davenport, T. (1995). Why reengineering failed and what comes next: The fad that forgot people. *Fast company, 1*(1), 69–74.

Dent, H. S. (1995). *Job shock.* New York: St. Martin's Press.

Drucker, P. (1995). *Managing in a time of great change.* New York: Truman Talley Books/ Dutton.

Fierman, H. (1994, January 14). The contingency work force. *Fortune, 129*(2), 30–36.

Frank, R. H. & Cook P. J. (1995). *The winner take all society.* New York: Martin Kessler Books, The Free Press.

Gerber, P. J., Ginsberg, R. & Reiff, H. B. (1992). Identifying alterable patterns in employment success for highly successful adults with learning disabilities. *Journal of Learning Disabilities, 25,* 475–487.

Hammer, M. & Champy, J. (1993). *Reengineering the corporation.* New York: Harper Business.

Handy, C. (1995, May-June). Trust and the virtual organization. *Harvard Business Review, 173,* 40–50.

Kotter, J. (1995). *The new rules: How to succeed in today's post-corporate world.* New York: The Free Press.

Manz, C. & Sims, H. (Eds.) (1993). *Businesses without bosses: How self-managing teams are building high-performing companies.* New York: John Wiley & Sons, Inc.

Mitchell, R. (1994, October 17). Virtual worker: Anyplace I hang my modem is home. *Business Week, 3394,* 96.

O'Brien, M. (1995). *Who's got the ball? And other nagging questions about team life.* San Francisco: Jossey–Bass Inc.

Rifkin, J. (1995). *The end of work.* New York: Putnam Books.

Rodgers, T. J., Taylor, W., & Forman, R. (1992). *No excuses management.* New York: Doubleday.

Ross, G. & Kay, M. (1994). *Toppling the pyramids. Redefining the way companies are run.* New York: Times Books.

Schor, J. B. (1991). *The overworked American.* New York: Basic Books.

Society for Human Resources Management. (1995, September-October). *Issues in HR.* Alexandria, VA: Society for Human Resources Management.

Steinert-Threlkeld, T. (1995). Can you work in netscape time? *Fast Company, 1*(1), 86–96.

CHAPTER 3

Legal Rights of Adults with Learning Disabilities in Employment

Patricia H. Latham
Peter S. Latham

The basic concepts of due process and equal protection of the law are reflected in the 5th and 14th amendments to the Constitution. Two important federal statutes apply these concepts to protect the rights of individuals with disabilities, including specific learning disabilities

The first is the Rehabilitation Act of 1973 (RA).[1] It made discrimination against individuals with disabilities unlawful in three areas: (a) employment by the executive branch of the federal government, (b) employment by most federal government contractors and (c) activities funded by federal subsidies or grants. This latter category includes all public elementary and secondary schools and most postsecondary institutions. The statutory section prohibiting discrimination in grants was numbered § 504 in the original legislation, and the RA is often referred to simply as "Section 504". Other sections of the RA, for example, create a limited requirement for affirmative action in the hiring of individuals with disabilities by the executive branch of the federal government and most federal government contractors.

The second federal statute is the Americans with Disabilities Act of 1990 (ADA).[2] This Act extended the concepts of Section 504 to (a) employers with 15 or more employees (Title I), (b) all activities of state and local governments, including but not limited to employment and education (Title II) and (c) virtually all places which offer goods and services to the public, termed "places of public accommodation" (Title III). In addition, the ADA extended the anti-discrimination provisions of the RA to employment by the Congress.

A third federal statute bears upon the rights of individuals with learning disabilities in employment because it contains the basic definition of specific learning disabilities and is sometimes referenced in employment cases. That statute is the Individuals with Disabilities Education Act (IDEA).[3] It was initially enacted in 1975 and was titled the Education for All Handicapped Children Act. It provided funds to state and local elementary and secondary schools for public education, including the education of children with specific learning disabilities.

Basic Legal Principles

The RA and ADA have collectively created the right to be free from discrimination based on one's disability. The protections of these laws extend to those who (a) are individuals with disabilities under the law, (b) are otherwise qualified, with or without a reasonable accommodation; (c) are being excluded from employment, promotion or other benefit solely by reason of their disability; and (d) are covered by applicable law.

What Is a Disability?

The protections of the RA and ADA apply only to an "individual with a disability" which is any person who:

(i) has a physical or mental impairment which substantially limits one or more of such person's major life activities,

(ii) has a record of such an impairment, or

(iii) is regarded as having such an impairment.[4]

The second and third definitions are intended to protect individuals who (a) previously had a disability but do not now and (b) are treated as though they had a disability but do not. For our purposes, the most important category is the first. It covers specific learning disabilities, as discussed below. The ADA contains definitions "equivalent" to those contained in the RA. Unless otherwise specified, the following discussion applies to both statutes. In some instances, cases will be discussed that do not themselves involve learning disabilities. These cases are included because they establish principles that are applicable to persons with various disabilities, including learning disabilities.

Specific Learning Disabilities Are Covered Impairments

The definition of a "physical or mental impairment" includes: "any mental or psychological disorder, such as mental retardation, organic brain syndrome, emotional or mental illness, and specific learning disabilities."[5]

Note that "specific learning disabilities" are expressly covered by the regulations. Courts have indicated that they will utilize the definition of a "specific learning disability" as it appears in the IDEA, when construing this regulation.[6]

The IDEA provides the following definition of a specific learning disability:

> The term "children with specific learning disabilities" means those children who have a disorder in one or more of the basic psychological processes involved in understanding or in using language, spoken or written, which disorder may manifest itself in imperfect ability to listen, think, speak, read, write, spell, or do mathematical calculations. Such disorders include such conditions as perceptual disabilities, brain injury, minimal brain dysfunction, dyslexia, and developmental aphasia. Such term does not include children who have learning problems which are primarily the result of visual, hearing, or motor disabilities, of mental retardation, of emotional disturbance, or of environmental, cultural, or economic disadvantage.[7]

Attention-Deficit/hyperactivity disorder (ADHD, or ADD as it is still popularly called), frequently coexisting with learning disabilities and considered by some to be a form of learning disability, is not specifically mentioned in the regulations. ADD has been recognized as a "mental or psychological disorder." The Gaston County School District of North Carolina (which received federal funding) failed to identify, evaluate, and provide the complainant's ADD child with a free public education appropriate to his disorder and thereby violated the RA.[8] There are similar holdings under the ADA. The discussion in this chapter of legal principles pertaining to specific learning disabilities would also apply to ADD.

Thus, the RA and ADA potentially apply to individuals with specific learning disabilities. However, the specific learning disability in question must also substantially limit a major life activity.

'Substantially limits'

The impact of the specific learning disability must be severe enough to result in an actual limitation of performance. The regulations provide that the term "substantially limits" means **either** that an individual is (a) "[u]nable to perform a major life activity that the average person in the general population can perform" or (b) is "[s]ignificantly restricted as to the condition, manner or duration" of the major life activity in question, when measured against the abilities of the "average person in the general population."[9]

Learning disabilities have been found to be disabilities. For example, a firefighter with dyslexia was found to have shown a prima facie case of discrimination, as a qualified individual with a disability, under a state's fair employment practices statute. The finding was based on testimony that his supervisor had said that the firefighter should not be promoted because he had a reading disability.[10]

Note that an individual with considerable achievements may nevertheless be substantially limited in a major life activity. For example, a law student with dyslexia may be substantially limited in learning even though she successfully completed college. Suppose the student has put in three times the time spent by fellow classmates to master the subject matter. The right to receive accommodations as a person with an impairment—dyslexia—that substantially limits a major life activity has been upheld by the courts.[11]

Major Life Activities

An impairment must substantially limit a major life activity before it can be considered a "disability" under the law. The major life activities have been recognized to be "caring for oneself, performing manual tasks, walking, seeing, hearing, speaking, breathing, learning, and working."[12] In March, 1995, The Equal Employment Opportunity Commission (EEOC), which has responsibility for enforcing Title I of the ADA, released guidance: *Compliance Manual Section 902: Definition of the Term Disability.* This guidance adds to the list of major life activities mental and emotional processes such as thinking, concentration and interacting with others.

Note that working is treated differently from all other major life activities for purposes of considering whether an individual with an impairment is substantially limited. In order to determine whether a substantial limitation on working exists, the individual's impairment must bar him or her from significant classes of jobs, and not just a particular job. Only disabilities with the former (and broader) impact are considered substantially to limit working. For example, an individual with limited use of her right arm was found not to have a substantial limitation of the major life activity of working. While she was unable to perform her job because it required some lifting she was not considered significantly restricted in overall employment opportunities.[13]

Who Is "Otherwise Qualified"?

Under both the RA and ADA, an "individual with a disability" must be one who is "otherwise qualified." An "otherwise qualified" individual is one who, though possessed of a disability, would be eligible for the job, education, or program benefit, with or without a reasonable accommodation. The institution or employer must either provide the accommodation or justify in detail the refusal to provide it.[14]

A disability may have such impact that it renders the individual not qualified for a particular job. In one case, the court upheld the termination of a draftsman with visual learning impairments. The termination was found not to violate the ADA because the employer had provided reasonable accommodations in allowing the employee almost two years to master the job functions.[15] In another case, an individual was found to be qualified. A federal court in California held that the termination of an employee with epilepsy, who wandered away from his worksite during a seizure, violated the ADA. The court found that, while poor attendance may render an employee not otherwise qualified, missing one day due to a seizure would not be sufficient to establish that he could not perform the essential functions of his job.[16]

When Is Job-Related Testing Discriminatory?

Entry level employment involves testing. Sometimes promotion does, too. Testing modifications and accommodations are, therefore, of central importance to individuals with specific learning disabilities.

Discriminatory testing is prohibited under both the RA and ADA. There are four further questions to be answered in deciding whether a test (employment or otherwise) is discriminatory:

- Does the test measure a relevant job-related skill or an irrelevant disability?

- If the test results **may** reflect the existence of a disability is the measured skill one that is **essential** to the job offered?

- Are there alternative methods of measuring an essential job-related skill?

- Is the process of providing alternatives unreasonably expensive, given the employer's resources?

Testing accommodations are required for individuals with disabilities unless the accommodations would alter the essential nature of the job or create an undue hardship.

What Is a Job?

At the outset, it is important to consider just what is meant by job requirements. Most job "requirements" fall into at least five separate categories. These are (a) academic qualifications, (b) required on-the-job experience, (c) competence in the work itself, (d) general standards of cooperativeness in the work situation and (e) compliance with "good citizenship" rules—e.g. being on time, no unauthorized absences, etc. Moreover, interpretation of requirements c–e becomes increasingly subjective as the seniority and pay of the positions increase. All of these factors must be considered in selecting a job and deciding whether and how to deal with a disability.

A couple of case studies pertaining to disabilities in general may be helpful. In *Duzey v. Department of the Air Force*,[17] a GS-12 auditor was removed in major part for using abusive language in the office. She suffered from mood changes caused by manic depression and an "apparently irrational dislike for her supervisor." Her psychiatrist prescribed lithium and prozac and testified that the treatment would prevent bizarre disruptive behavior if the auditor returned to the workplace even without accommodations. However, the auditor displayed some of these symptoms at the trial notwithstanding medication. The administrative judge found that she had not shown that medication provided a sufficient solution. Accordingly, the judge found that she "could not perform the essential functions of her position because such essential functions included not engaging in the bizarre behavior previously engaged in, and getting along with her supervisor." Clearly, having the (a) academic qualifications, (b) required on-the-job experience, and (c) competence in the work itself, while failing to meet general standards of cooperativeness in the work situation and compliance with "good citizenship" rules, was not sufficient.

In *Mancini v. General Electric Co.*,[18] the court held that an employee with a disability who had developed a personality conflict with his supervisor resulting in a failure to comply with the supervisor's directions to work in particular places which made him uncomfortable—was properly discharged under the Vermont Fair Employment Practices Act (similar to the RA and ADA). The court held that the employer had no obligation to transfer the employee in order to avoid a conflict with the supervisor. In so ruling, the court said that "[E]mployees must be present and willing to obey their supervisors to perform the essential functions of their job."[19] Had the employee identified himself as an individual with a disability and employed appropriate strategies, it is entirely possible that the work situation would not have deteriorated to the point of disobedience and firing.

What Are the Essential Functions of a Job?

An individual with a disability is required to perform the essential functions of a job with or without a reasonable accommodation. All job functions that are not essential are considered marginal, and therefore capable of being restructured as a reasonable accommodation.

Each of the five job elements discussed earlier may be considered essential to job performance. As noted above, meeting general standards and rules becomes increasingly important as the seniority of the position increases. However, definition and interpretation of these elements can be highly subjective, and in some cases, can serve as a pretext for discrimination. The regulations and *EEOC Interpretive Guidance* analyze the essential features of a job by considering primarily the role the job plays in the **employer's** operations rather than the **individual skills** necessary to perform the job. However, the case law suggests that the broader factors considered in this section also apply.

Many jobs involve several sets of duties. It may be necessary to decide whether all of these sets of duties should be considered essential requirements of a single job. Compare the following cases.

In *Fitzgerald v. Green Valley Area Education Agency*,[20] the Court held that a school district's requirement that all teachers take turns driving school buses was not an essential part of the teaching function. Accordingly, the school district was required to restructure its job requirements to permit the hiring of a qualified teacher whose dyslexia and other impairments prevented him from driving a school bus.

In *DiPompo v. West Point Military Academy*,[21] the Court held that dispatcher duties which were required of all firemen on a rotational basis and involved the use of computers were an essential part of the work of a fireman and refused to order job restructuring. The United States Court of Appeals for the Second Circuit affirmed the trial court's decision.

What Are Some Examples of Reasonable Accommodations?

Reasonable accommodations are of three general types: (a) those required to ensure equal opportunity in the job application process, (b) those which enable the individual with a disability to perform the essential features of a job, and (c) those which enable individuals with disabilities to enjoy the same benefits and privileges as those available to individuals without disabilities.[22] Reasonable accommodations for specific learning disabilities can include any of the following:

- providing or modifying equipment or devices
- job restructuring
- part-time or modified work schedules
- reassignment to a vacant position
- adjusting or modifying examinations, training materials, or policies
- providing readers or interpreters
- making the workplace readily accessible to, and usable by people with disabilities.[23]

Despite this sweeping description, the accommodations actually required for individuals with ADD and LD are generally neither extensive nor expensive. The President's Committee on Employment of People with Disabilities has pointed out:

- Thirty-one percent of accommodations cost nothing.
- Fifty percent cost less than $50
- Sixty-nine percent cost less than $500
- Eighty-eight percent cost less than $1,000.[24]

The bar against employment discrimination covers all employment activities of the firms to which it applies. These include recruitment, advertising and job application procedures, hiring, upgrading, promotion, award of tenure, demotion, transfer, layoff, termination, right of return from layoff, rehiring, rates of pay, compensation, changes in compensation, job assignments, job classifications, organizational structures, position descriptions, lines of progression, seniority lists, leaves of absence, sick leave, other leaves, fringe benefits, selection and financial support for training (including apprenticeships, professional meetings, conferences, and other related activities), selection for leaves of absence to pursue training, activities sponsored by a covered entity including social and recreational programs and any other term, condition, or privilege of employment.[25] The potential number of reasonable accommodations is as broad as the range of activities to which the ban on discrimination applies.

The President's Committee gave these examples which may be helpful.

Problem: A person with a learning disability worked in the mail room and had difficulty remembering which streets belonged to which zip codes.

Solution: A rolodex card system was filed by street name alphabetically with the zip code. This helped him to increase his output. ($150)

Problem: An individual with dyslexia who worked as a police officer spent hours filling out forms at the end of each day.

Solution: He was provided with a tape recorder. A secretary typed out his reports from dictation, while she typed others from handwritten copy. This accommodation allowed him to keep his job. ($69)[26]

The EEOC recommends a four-step process in determining whether a reasonable accommodation is required.

1. Analyze the particular job involved and determine its purpose and essential functions.

2. Consult the individual with a disability to ascertain the precise job-related limitations imposed by the individual's disability and how those limitations could be overcome with a reasonable accommodation.

3. In consultation with the individual to be accommodated, identify potential accommodations and assess the effectiveness each would have in enabling the individual to perform the essential functions of the position.

4. Consider the preference of the individual to be accommodated and select and implement the accommodation that is most appropriate for both the employee and employer.[27]

Note the central role played by the definition of the essential features of the job in the following case discussions.

Many jobs (such as writing a book) need not be performed during a specific eight-hour period. Others (such as police officer) must be. Often it is necessary to decide whether the essential requirements of a job preclude the use of flexible schedules. Compare the following cases.

In *Lynch v. Department of Education*,[28] a GS-13 trial attorney was dismissed for unsatisfactory work and excessive absences due to an epileptic condition that was treatable with medication. The medication, however, affected her memory and ability to concentrate. As a reasonable accommodation she requested (a) training in legal drafting, (b) specific structured assignments including clear written assignment instructions and increased supervisory assistance and (c) the opportunity to make up hours missed by late arrivals. These accommodations were found to be reasonable, in our view, because they increased only marginally (if at all) the burden on the employer. Specifically, the agency needed legal drafting done. Further, it already had in place supervisors whose very purpose was to make sure that work flowed smoothly. Finally, the opportunity to make up missed work functioned very much like the flex-time program many employers (including the agency) already had in place. As a result, the individual was found to be a "qualified handicapped person" under the RA. Her proposed accommodation was deemed reasonable; and she was ordered reinstated to her position.

In *Guice-Mills v. Derwinski*,[29] a nurse who suffered from depression and took sedating medication that required her to report two hours late was not judged to be an otherwise qualified person. Whether changes in schedule or job description are regarded as reasonable accommodations depends on the facts.

Generally speaking, an employer is entitled to enforce rules designed to reduce workplace friction by requiring polite behavior on the job. This behavior is generally considered an essential feature of a job, with compliance required. Compare the following cases.

Ross v. Beaumont Hospital,[30] a hospital terminated the privileges of a surgeon who suffered from narcolepsy despite the fact that her narcolepsy was largely controlled through medication. However, the surgeon also engaged in verbal abuse of nurses over a seven year period. There was no evidence that the abuse was related to the narcolepsy. Accordingly, the termination was held to be lawful under the RA because it was based in major part on her unacceptable conduct.

In *Schartle v. Motorola, Inc.*,[31] a dyslexic security guard who had difficulty writing reports and who was insubordinate was properly fired for insubordination. The anti-insubordination policy was uniformly applied. No evidence indicated that the policy was applied as a result of a request for an accommodation.

What Is Reasonable?

A "reasonable accommodation" is one that does not create an "undue hardship." A proposed accommodation creates an "undue hardship" and need not be made if it either (a) alters the essential nature of a job or (b) results in "significant difficulty or expense" to the employer.[32]

In judging whether a proposed accommodation creates an "undue hardship," the particular circumstances of the employer's situation must be considered. An undue hardship for one employer may not be an undue hardship for another. The EEOC gives, as an example, the case of an individual with a disabling visual impairment that makes it extremely difficult to see in dim lighting. If such an individual were to seek employment as a waiter in a nightclub, the club would not be required to provide bright lighting for the dining and lounge areas even though it would involve nothing more than turning up the lights. The nightclub relies on dim lighting to create an "ambiance" that attracts customers, and bright lighting would destroy the nightclub's trade. Providing it would be an undue hardship.[33]

Disclosure

There is no duty to disclose a disability and none to accommodate a disability which has not been disclosed. Unless pre-employment test accommodations are needed, generally disclosure of a disability need not be made until after the offer of employment. Even then, there may be no need to disclose unless accommodations are to be requested. However, some individuals with specific learning disabilities have difficulty with the social aspects of the workplace. If individuals have trouble picking up on subtle cues, they may be the last to see that their jobs are in jeopardy. Disclosing when termination is imminent and feelings are running high often is ineffective. Thus, the matter of when to disclose the disability is an individual matter that should take account of the individual characteristics. There can be another reason for disclosure. Mandatory drug testing which is justified by business necessity and is uniformly administered is lawful. Mandatory drug tests may identify drugs such as Ritalin or Dexedrine. If so, disclosure that these drugs are prescribed medications would be appropriate.

Documentation

Most documentation involves three steps: **diagnosis, evaluation of impact,** and **recommendation.** Diagnosis establishes the existence of a disability. Evaluation of impact details how that disability impacts upon the individual in a particular setting. The recommendation should set forth specific reasonable accommodations to be provided by the employer.

How much documentation is enough? The ADA addresses the question of documentation in connection with academic and license testing. The *Preamble to Regulation on Nondiscrimination on the Basis of Disability by Public Accommodations and in Commercial Facilities,* which provides guidance on the proper interpretation of the ADA and its implementing regulations, provides that (a) "requests for documentation must be reasonable," (b) "must be limited to the need for the documentation or aid requested," and (c) the "applicant may be required to bear the cost of providing such documentation . . . ."[34]

A principal purpose of documentation is the establishment of an individual's entitlement to reasonable accommodations in the workplace. With few exceptions, the "requirements" for documentation are really dictated by the rules governing burden of proof in a civil action. Here is what we mean: If you assert a claim for reasonable accommodation based on your disability, your employer can do one of two things: accept your claim or reject it. Some employers will recognize and accommodate disabilities generously. If you are dealing with such an employer, the amount of documentation required may be minimal. You will reach agreement quickly. However, if you do not reach agreement with an employer and the employer resists your claim, then you may face the necessity of advocating or proving your claim to a third party. This may be conducted informally, in a mediation or arbitration proceeding, or by an EEOC or other federal compliance officer, or in an administrative proceeding, or formally in a court proceeding.

In asserting your claim during a proceeding, you will act as a plaintiff or claimant. In that case, you will be required to prove your claim by a **preponderance of the evidence.** That is legal language that means your evidence must be substantially more convincing and persuasive than that of your opponent. In other words, most of the convincing evidence must support your claim.

As a practical matter then, you must "document" your disability by either (a) presenting that amount of evidence necessary to **persuade** the employer with which you are dealing or (b) **proving** your entitlement by a preponderance of the evidence. Since you can never know for certain whether or when you will be called on to prove your case, your documentation should be developed with care in the event that you may one day need to provide proof.

Confidentiality

Pre-employment Inquiries

Several sources of requirements define when, and on what terms, confidential information must be shared with others.

The rules governing pre-employment inquiries concerning disabilities are quite definite. A prospective employer who is subject to the ADA "shall not conduct a medical examination or make inquiries of a job applicant as to whether such applicant is an individual with a disability or as to the nature or severity of such disability."[35] The prospective employer may, however, "make preemployment inquiries into the ability of an applicant to perform job-related functions."[36]

After a prospective employer makes an offer, but before the start of employment, he may require an "employment entrance examination" if (a) "all entering employees are subjected to such an examination regardless of disability" and (b) certain confidentiality restrictions (discussed below) are observed and (c) the "results of such examination" are used only in accordance with the ADA.[37]

The confidentiality restrictions are worth considering at some length. The post-offer, pre-employment medical examination must meet the requirement that information obtained regarding the medical condition or history of the applicant is collected and maintained on separate forms and in separate medical files and is treated as a confidential medical record, except that:

- "supervisors and managers" may be "informed regarding necessary restrictions on the work duties of the employee and necessary accommodations. . . ."

- first aid and safety personnel "may be informed, when appropriate, if the disability might require emergency treatment."

- government officials may have access to the information for the purpose of ensuring compliance with the ADA.

- state workers' compensation offices may be provided with the medical information.

- insurance companies providing coverage for the firm may require medical examinations before providing health or life insurance to employees.[38]

The legitimate scope of the medical examination is not defined, but if it is the standard medical examination given to all employees, it will not necessarily elicit information about specific learning disabilities. However, it will almost certainly require discussion of one's medication. In the case of most individuals with adult ADD, the examination will require disclosure of that condition, even if no disability is claimed.

Job Accommodation Information

An employer may require a medical examination to confirm the existence of a claimed disability, and the appropriateness of a proposed reasonable accommodation. An employer also may be entitled to require a medical examination if an employee is unable to perform his or her job effectively.[39]

Advocating for Legal Rights

Advocacy Steps

Advocating for your legal rights does not necessarily mean filing a suit in court. Many steps precede that action. In fact, many individuals are able to accomplish all of their objectives, including obtaining needed accommodations, without any adversarial process.

The basic advocacy steps are: communication, negotiation, mediation, arbitration, and more formal proceedings.

Communication

Often, an employer wishes to be fair but simply doesn't understand a disability and resulting need for accommodation. In such situations, it is important to educate the employer concerning the disability, how it impacts upon you, and what accommodations will enable you to perform your job. Point out that the requested accommodations will be relatively easy for the employer to provide and that they will increase your productivity. Documenting your disability may be an important part of this process.

Negotiation

If communication concerning your disability and needs does not achieve a positive result, then negotiation is usually the next step. The employer may disagree as to whether you have a disability, what accommodations you need, or whether your requested accommodations are reasonable. Negotiation will provide the opportunity to address concerns and issues and to seek to persuade your employer. You, your medical/psychological professional, or your attorney may negotiate with your employer.

Alternative Dispute Resolution

If, after negotiation, areas of disagreement remain, alternative dispute resolution (ADR) may be the next step. ADR includes mediation and arbitration. ADR is encouraged under the ADA. Mediation is a voluntary process in which the mediator seeks to facilitate resolution of the dispute. When mediation works, it has the added benefit that both parties agreed to, and therefore are satisfied with, the result. Arbitration is a more informal and more expeditious alternative to court. It is an adversary proceeding in which the arbitrator will hear testimony and review documentary evidence and make a decision that is binding upon the parties.

Formal Proceedings

Formal proceedings include filing a complaint with the Equal Employment Opportunity Commission (EEOC) and initiating litigation in court. Individuals may recover attorneys' fees in appropriate cases. The ADA enforcement mechanisms include, in addition, actions by the EEOC and the Department of Justice.

Summary

Individuals with specific learning disabilities are considered individuals with disabilities under federal law when their conditions substantially limit a major life activity such as learning, concentrating, thinking, interacting with others, and working.

Two important federal laws are the Rehabilitation Act of 1973 and the Americans with Disabilities Act of 1990. Qualified individuals with these disabilities enjoy the right to be free from discrimination in the workplace. The bar against discrimination covers all employment activities, including recruitment, advertising and job application procedures, hiring, upgrading, promotion, award of tenure, demotion, transfer, layoff, termination, rehiring, job assignments, seniority lists, leaves, and activities.

Qualified persons with disabilities may be entitled to reasonable accommodations in the workplace. A reasonable accommodation is one that does not alter the essential nature of the job and does not result in significant difficulty or expense to the employer.

Persons with disabilities are not required to disclose their disabilities. They may decide if, when, and how to disclose the disability to an employer. However, employers are not required to accommodate an undisclosed disability. If disclosure is made, the individual may be called upon to document the disability. Documentation is provided by a qualified professional and involves diagnosis, evaluation of how the impairment impacts upon the individual in learning or working, and specific recommendations.

The Americans with Disabilities Act of 1990 provides for confidentiality of medical information. Such information is to be maintained in separate files, and specific provisions govern access to confidential information.

Advocating for legal rights in the workplace does not necessarily mean filing a lawsuit. The basic advocacy steps are: communication, negotiation, alternative dispute resolution, and more formal proceedings.

With reasonable work accommodations and the use of appropriate strategies, individuals with learning disabilities may be well positioned to succeed in the workplace.

References

1 Rehabilitation Act of 1973, 29 U.S.C.A. § 701 *et seq.* (1995).

2 Americans with Disabilities Act of 1990, 42 U.S.C.A. § 12101 *et seq.* (1995).

3 Individuals with Disabilities Education Act of 1990, 20 U.S.C.A. § 1400 *et seq.* (1995).

4 29 U.S.C.A. § 706(8)(B) (1995).

5 29 C.F.R. § 1613.702(b)(2) (1995).

6 Argen v. New York State Bd. of Law Examiners, 860 F. Supp. 84 (W. D. N. Y. 1994).

7 20 U.S.C.A. § 1401(a)(15) (1995).

8 Letter of Findings (LOF) OCR Docket No. 04-90-1617, 17 Sep 90; Gaston County School District.

9 29 C.F.R. §§ 1630.2(j)(1)(i)–(ii) (1995).

10 Gallipo v. City of Rutland, 656 A.2d 635 (Vt. 1994).

11 Weintraub v. Board of Bar Examiners, SJC, No OE-0087 (Mass. 1992).

12 29 C.F.R. § 1630.2(i) (1995).

13 Taylor v. Albertson's, Inc., 886 F. Supp. 819 (W.D. Okla. 1995), aff'd, 1996 WL 10931 (10th Cir. 1996).

14 Fitzgerald v. Green Valley Area Educ. Agency, 589 F. Supp. 1130 (S.D. Iowa 1984).

15 Riblett v. Boeing Co., 1995 WL 580053 (D. Kan. 1995).

16 Sunkett v. Olsten Temporary Services, 1996 WL 61154 (N.D. Cal. 1995).

17 Dazey v. Department of Air Force, 54 M. S. P. R. 658 (M. S. P. B. 1992).

18 Mancini v. General Elec Co., 820 F. Supp. 141 (D. Vt. 1993).

19 *Mancini v. General Elec. Co.*, p. 147.

20 Fitzgerald v. Green Valley Area Educ. Agency, 589 F. Supp. 1130 (S.D. Iowa 1984).

21 DiPompo v. West Point Military Academy, 960 F.2d 326 (2nd Cir. 1992).

22 U.S. Equal Employment Opportunity Commission. *Interpretative Guidance.* Author. p. 408.

23 U.S. Equal Employment Opportunity Commission. (1991) *The Americans with Disabilities Act: Your Rights as an Individual with a Disability.* (EEOC-BK-18, Author, p. 3.

24 President's Committee on Employment of People with Disabilities. (1993, October). *Job Accommodation Ideas.* Author.

25 29 C.F.R. §§ 1630.4 (a)–(i) (1995).

26 *Job Accommodation Ideas.*

27 *Interpretive Guidance*, p. 415.

28 Lynch v. Department of Educ., 52 M. S. P. R. 541 (M. S. P. B. 1992).

29 Guice-Mills v. Derwinski, 967 F.2d 794 (2nd Cir. 1992).

30 Ross v. Beaumont Hosp., 687 F. Supp. 1115 (E.D. Mich. 1988).

31 Schartle v. Motorola, Inc., 1994 WL 323281 (N.D. Ill. 1994).

32 *Interpretive Guidance*, p. 409.

33 *Interpretive Guidance*, p. 409.

34 28 C. F. R. § 36, App. B; *Preamble to Regulation on Nondiscrimination on the Basis of Disability by Public Accommodations and in Commercial Facilities.* (p. 626). (Emphasis added)

35 42 U.S.C.A. § 12112(d)(2)(A) (1995).

36 42 U.S.C.A. § 12112(d)(2)(B) (1995).

37 42 U.S.C.A. § 12112(d) (1995).

38 U.S. Equal Employment Opportunity Commission. *A Technical Assistance Manual on the Employment Provisions (Title I) of the Americans with Disabilities Act.* Author, pp. VI–12.

39 *A Technical Assistance Manual*, pp. VI–13–14.

CHAPTER 4

The Employment Outcomes of Youth with Learning Disabilities: A Review of Findings from the National Longitudinal Transition Study of Special Education Students

Jose Blackorby
Mary M. Wagner

A desire to improve outcomes for children and families drives much of the current effort to reform systems of education and human services in this country. In the education context, the consensus that has emerged over the past decade regarding the importance of attending to outcomes is perhaps most clearly embodied in the national education goals, codified in Goals 2000: Educate America Act (P.L. 103-227). By addressing issues such as increasing graduation rates and achieving world-class standards in core subject areas, national education goals focus attention on the contribution of positive student outcomes to our nation's future well-being.[1]

The need for a comprehensive look at outcomes also has been recognized for students with disabilities. Outcome studies in several states reported that many students with disabilities were not finishing high school and were achieving only limited success as young adults.[2] But these state studies provided an insufficient basis for federal policy making to improve outcomes for students with disabilities; national data were needed to make national policy.

To fill this need for information, Congress directed the Secretary of Education to conduct a longitudinal study of "the educational progress of students with disabilities while in special education" and "the occupational, educational, and independent living status of students with disabilities after graduating from secondary school or otherwise leaving special education" [U.S.C. sec. 1418(3)(2(A)]. In 1985, under contract to the Office of Special Education Programs (OSEP) of the U.S. Department of Education, SRI International began to develop the design, sample, and data collection instruments for the National Longitudinal Transi tion Study of Special Education Students (NLTS). SRI initiated the study in 1987 and completed it in 1994.

The NLTS has compiled a longitudinal database that includes more than 8,000 young people with disabilities who were ages 13 through 21 and special education students in the 1985–86 school year in more than 300 school districts nationwide. It is a nationally representative sample[3] that permits generalizations to young people with disabilities as a whole and to those in each federal special education disability category. Data were collected from telephone interviews with parents and with young people with disabilities when they were able to respond to questions for themselves. The researchers obtained school records for students' high school years and surveyed principals at their schools and teachers who served them.[4]

Among the numerous analyses generated by the NLTS since 1989, there is no single story to tell about outcomes of students with disabilities. Young people with different kinds of disabilities differed more from one another than they did from the general population of youth, and the outcomes they were able to achieve reflected those sizable differences. Some youth, such as those with sensory impairments, progressed through postsecondary schools at virtually the same rate as youth in the general population, but fared less well in the labor market. In contrast, youth with learning disabilities—the focus of this chapter—enjoyed better success in the labor market, but rarely furthered their education or training after high school. Thus, it is important to examine the experiences of students who share specific disability characteristics.

Throughout our work, while compelling arguments have signalled a need for diversity of outcomes to include socialization and self-determination, interest in the labor market experiences of young people with disabilities—particularly those with learning disabilities—has been particularly high. This is due in part to the central role employment fills regarding participation in the economy. However, it is also true that many other important outcomes (e.g., residential independence) are largely dependent on success in the labor market.

This chapter uses NLTS data to spotlight several facets of the employment outcomes of students with learning disabilities in the early years after secondary school. The probability of their finding work, the intensity of work, the stability of employment, and the wages they received are described. High school programs and performance of young people with learning disabilities are then analyzed in a search for clues to contributors to the pattern of outcomes of such youth and to opportunities to improve those outcomes in the future. We present descriptive data that compare outcomes for youth with learning disabilities to those for the general youth population and multivariate analyses comparing students with learning disabilities to other youth with disabilities.

Characteristics of Students with Learning Disabilities

Understanding the characteristics of students with learning disabilities is important in interpreting the outcomes they achieved. Students with learning disabilities represented the largest group of students receiving special education services (56%). They differed from the general population in ways other than disability. Students with disabilities in general, and those with learning disabilities in particular, were significantly more likely than students as a whole to be male and African American, and to experience a constellation of factors associated with economic disadvantage (see Table 4.1). For example, 22% of high school students with learning disabilities were African American, even though African American students constituted only 14% of the general population of students of similar age. Some contend that this over-representation of African American students among those with "discretionary disabilities," such as learning disabilities, results from schools' intolerance for behaviors more characteristic of the African American culture than mainstream white society.[5] However, similar proportions of African American students were found among those who were deaf (24%), visually impaired (26%), or orthopedically impaired (19%)—categories for which staff discretion in identifying students as having disabilities was minimal. This suggests that poverty may be the contributing factor to African American students' appearing disproportionately in all categories of disability, rather than primarily school policy or practice.

Table 4.1 demonstrates that poverty was pervasive among students with learning disabilities. In 1987, nearly one-third of students with learning disabilities came from households with an annual income of less than $12,000; only 18% of students in the general population did so. Thirty-four percent of students with learning disabilities came from single-parent

TABLE 4.1
Demographic Characteristics of Youth with Learning Disabilities
and Youth Generally

Demographic Characteristics	Percentage of Youth	
	With LD	In the general population
Male	73.4	51.4[a]
Ethnicity:		
White	67.2	73.0[a]
African American	21.6	14.0
Hispanic	8.4	6.2
Other	2.8	6.9
Annual household income (1986):		
Under $12,000	31.1	18.2[b]
$12,000 to $24,999	34.3	20.6
$25,000 to $37,000	17.6	25.4
$38,000 or more	17.0	35.8
Education level attained by head of household:		
Some high school	37.8	22.3[b]
High school graduate	39.1	38.8
Some college/2-year degree	14.5	17.8
4-year degree or more	8.6	21.1
Single-parent household	34.3	25.6[b]
Community:		
Urban	28.2	22.3[c]
Suburban	35.8	47.9
Rural	36.1	28.7

[a]The gender and ethnicity data in column 3 are from *National Longitudinal Survey of Youth,* (NLSY) by U.S. Department of Labor, 1979–1983, unpublished. Data are for youth ages 15–20 who were in secondary school or had been in secondary school in the current or previous school years.

[b]The income and education data in column 3 are from U.S. Bureau of the Census, 1988a. Data refer to youth ages 12–17 living with at least one parent in March 1987. Note that categorical boundaries are $12,500, $25,000, and $40,000 rather than the $12,000, $25,000, and $38,000 used in the National Longitudinal Transition Study of Special Education Students (NLTS).

[c]The community data in column 3 are from *High School and Beyond 1980 sophomore cohost third follow-up (1986),* vol. 1 (p. 8.1.2), by Center for Education Statistics, 1987, Washington, DC: U.S. Department of Education.

Note: The range of subsamples corresponding to variables was 846–994.

NLTS source: parent interviews.

households, compared with about one-fourth of the general population of students. Furthermore, students with learning disabilities were signifi- cantly more likely to reside in homes where the head of household did not complete high school. This picture of learning disability, significant eco- nomic disadvantage, and low family educational attainment is the back- drop against which to view the employment outcomes of students with learning disabilities.

Postschool Goals of Young People with Disabilities

In interpreting the outcomes of young people with learning disabilities experienced during their early postschool years, it is important to have an understanding of what they had hoped to achieve. What goals did they have?[6] When we examine their intended postschool paths, we have an appropriate yardstick against which to assess the outcomes they achieved.

The majority of high school students with learning disabilities intended to enter the workforce upon leaving school (Table 4.2).[7] In many ways, high school was a difficult academic environment for stu- dents with learning disabilities, and the world of work may have offered them a wider variety of activities in which they could succeed. Among 12th-graders with learning disabilities, more than half (58%) indicated they had a goal of finding competitive employment after leaving high school, and 4% had a goal of obtaining supported employment.[8] Even among those who did not intend to go to work immediately, training for

TABLE 4.2
Transition Goals of Students with Learning Disabilities

Type of transition goal	Percent
Competitive employment	58.6
Sheltered employment	0
Supported employment	3.5
Postsecondary education (academic)	27.8
Postsecondary education (vocational)	32.4

Note: Correspondence of subsamples to variables was 177.

Note: From parent interviews and surveys of teachers of 12th grade NLTS sample members.

work dominated over academic pursuits. Nearly one-third of 12th-graders with learning disabilities (32%) had a goal of postsecondary vocational training, compared with 28% citing college attendance as their postsecondary goal. Given the prevalence of employment-oriented goals, one would expect to see students with learning disabilities pursuing vocational programs with greater emphasis than college-preparatory academic programs, an expectation not borne out in the course-taking experiences of many high school students with learning disabilities.

Employment Outcomes

In the United States, many have expressed increasing concern about the quality of high school graduates and their ability to help the country compete in a global economy. The School-To-Work Transition Act of 1994 (P.L. 103-239) reflects the country's commitment to support students in acquiring high-end vocational skills and in transitioning to the kinds of jobs needed in an increasingly information-based economy. Provisions in that legislation explicitly require states to include students with disabilities in the plans they develop for school-to-work programs.

In this section, we describe the outcomes of students with learning disabilities as they transition from high school to the important adult domain of employment. Where we have data to do so, we also compare outcomes of youth with learning disabilities to a national sample of youth in the general population that has been adjusted to reflect the same overrepresentation—of students who were male, African American, poor, and with heads of households who were not high school graduates—as existed among students with learning disabilities.[9]

Probability of Employment

This inclusion of students with disabilities in employment-related transition programs reflects both an understanding of the difficult time many of them have finding a place in the workforce after high school and observations during 10 years' experience in transition programming in special education and related services.[10] When youth with learning disabilities had been out of high school between 3 and 5 years, 71% were working competitively (Table 4.3) and the majority (57%) were doing so full-time. Just under a third of youth with learning disabilities were not working (29%); a minority (14%) was not looking for work. These rates of participation in the workplace parallel and, in the case of full-time employment, exceed those of non-disabled peers: 69% of youth in the general population were employed when they had been out of secondary school 3 to 5 years (p<.001); only 46% did so full-time.

This degree of success in employment is unique among categories of youth with disabilities. Only youth with speech impairments began to approach the employment rates of youth with learning disabilities. Successes also were most apparent for those who had finished high school. Three in 4 graduates with learning disabilities (76%) were employed competitively 3 to 5 years after high school compared with only 59% of dropouts. Three to 5 years after high school, employment also was significantly more common for young men with learning disabilities than for young women (76% vs. 53%; p<.001) and for white youth with learning

TABLE 4.3

Employment Outcomes of Youth with Learning Disabilities,
and Youth in the General Population

Employment	Youth	
	With LD	*In the general population*
Currently competitively employed when out of high school 3 to 5 years	70.8	69.4
Employed full-time	56.7	46.1
Comparing employment when out of school up to 2 years and 3 to 5 years, percentage who were:		
Employed at both times	47.2	46.1
Employed at neither time	17.5	
Lost employment	12.4	
Gained employment	22.9	
Earning more than $6 per hour when out of high school 3 to 5 years	39.8	

Note: The range of subsamples corresponding to variables was 44–534.

Other than voter registration rates, data for the general population come from the 1979–83 National Longitudinal Survey of Youth. The analysis includes a nationally representative sample of youth who were 15 to 20 years old and out of high school an average of 8 months. Data on voter registration rates for the general population come from the *High School and Beyond* study of the class of 1980. Center for Education Statistics, *High School and Beyond 1980 sophomore cohort third follow-up (1986), volume 1, data file users manual.* Washington, DC: U.S. Department of Education, 1987. NLTS source: parent/youth interviews. Data for the general population are from the 1979–83 National Longitudinal Survey of Youth, and from *NLS Handbook: 1988: The National Longitudinal Surveys of Labor Market Experience,* by Center for Human Resource Research, Ohio State University, 1988.

disabilities than for their African American or Hispanic peers (74% vs. 62% and 63%; p<.05).

Job Stability

Early job market experiences are often characterized as unstable as youth gain experience and responsibility. Many youth experience "spells" of unemployment between jobs. Data from the NLTS show that many youth with learning disabilities enjoyed relatively stable employment in the early years after high school. When the employment status for youth out of school up to 2 years was compared with their employment status 3 years later, young people with learning disabilities were more likely than youth with any disability to have been employed at both times, and were less likely to have lost jobs or to have been employed at neither time than youth with any disability (Table 4.3). Nearly half of students with learning disabilities were employed at both data collection points. Furthermore, 22% of these youth gained employment over time, a figure twice the magnitude of those who lost employment over the same period of time. Thus, according to a number of different measures, students with learning disabilities adjusted comparatively well to the world of work in the early years after high school.

Wages Earned

This relatively successful level of labor force participation did not necessarily translate into financial independence for youth with learning disabilities. The mean hourly wage for working youth with learning disabilities was $6.45 3 to 5 years after high school (1990), and only 40% of working youth with learning disabilities were earning more than $6 per hour. Thus, students with learning disabilities working full-time and year-round had annual incomes less than $12,000. While low wages are common for all youth, such comparatively low wages are bound to negatively influence students' abilities to achieve other goals, such as residential independence. Almost twice as many young men as women with learning disabilities were earning more than $6 per hour (44% vs. 23%; p<.05), and more than three times as many white working youth as African American youth were earning that much (46% vs. 14%; p<.001). Although graduates with learning disabilities were significantly more likely than dropouts to have found jobs, they were not significantly more likely to be earning more than $6 per hour (46% vs. 41%).

Possible Contributing Factors

Although this discussion has demonstrated that many young people with learning disabilities experienced some success in the labor market, there remains much room for improvement if students are to attain independence and self-determination outcomes. Descriptive and multivariate analyses from the NLTS have identified several factors that relate to significantly better postschool outcomes. We relied on multivariate analyses that focus on clusters of disability categories. The mild cluster is comprised of youth with learning disabilities, emotional disturbances, and speech impairments. We compared the results of this cluster to youth with disabilities as a whole, and to youth in clusters of sensory and physical disabilities. The range of these potentially beneficial factors illustrated that there is no single locus of responsibility for improving outcomes for youth with learning disabilities; parents, schools, and other community organizations all can contribute to that end.

Curriculum Mismatch

The majority of 12th graders with learning disabilities (58%) were reported to have a postschool goal of finding competitive employment; only 28% had a goal of college attendance. Despite the nonacademic nature of their goals, academic course-taking dominated their high school programs, particularly in 9th and 10th grades, when 3 of the average of 5 credits earned were in academic courses (see Table 4.4). About 80% of students took their academic courses in regular education classes. Unfortunately, regular academic classes are precisely the environments where students with learning disabilities were most likely to fail classes, and to start a cycle of negative academic experiences that often lead to the failure to complete high school. If they managed to stay in high school until the upper grades, the emphasis on academic course-taking diminished somewhat and students with learning disabilities took occupationally oriented vocational education courses with greater frequency, in line with their employment goals. The vast majority of vocational courses were in regular education. Thus, the students with learning disabilities had postschool goals that were vocational in nature, yet the education provided to them was largely academic. NLTS data

TABLE 4.4
Characteristics of Secondary School Programs
of Students with Disabilities

	Students	
	With LD	*With any disability*
Percentage of students whose proportion of time in regular education classes was:		
0%	2.0	3.4
1% to 25%	3.3	6.8
26% to 50%	13.4	16.3
51% to 75%	22.1	21.3
76% to 99%	39.0	31.0
100%	20.2	21.3
Average percentage of class time spent in regular education classes over four high school grade levels	74.6	69.6
Average academic credits earned in:		
9th grade	3.2	3.2
10th grade	3.1	3.0
11th grade	2.6	2.7
12th grade	2.2	2.2
Percentage taking occupationally oriented vocational education in:		
9th grade	63.0	58.1
10th grade	73.9	69.5
11th grade	81.6	79.0
12th grade	85.2	83.1

Note: The range of subsamples corresponding to variables was 399 (with LD); 474–3,283 (with any disability).

Data are from students' school records and surveys of teachers of 12th grade NLTS sample members.

suggest that dropout prevention and vocational education are two keys to employment success after school.

Dropping Out of High School

Almost one out of three students with learning disabilities did not receive a high school diploma—a rate substantially higher than dropping out or failing at that of their peers in the general population.

Dropouts with disabilities had consistently poorer postschool outcomes than their peers who persisted in school (independent of other differences between them). Dropouts with learning disabilities were less likely to enroll in postsecondary vocational programs (a 14 percentage-point difference compared with nondropouts) and academic programs (a 12 percentage-point difference), particularly among youth with mild disabilities, those most likely to have dropped out (a 14 percentage-point difference). A pattern of negative, though weak, relationships was found between dropping out of secondary school and employment outcomes for youth with learning disabilities as a group when other factors in the analyses were controlled. These findings underscore the importance of successful completion of secondary school as a platform for success in adulthood. School policies and programs that contribute to positive school performance and school completion for students with disabilities also help set the stage for their success in their early postschool years.

Vocational Course-taking

Permitting flexibility in course-taking so that students with learning disabilities can pursue their vocational interests opens an important option. Students with learning disabilities who took occupationally oriented vocational courses in high school were significantly less likely to drop out than nonvocational students with learning disabilities (controlling for other differences between them). Yet widespread efforts to increase academic course requirements for high school graduation have had the effect of limiting, rather than expanding, curricular options for students who do not have academic postschool goals.

The intention of vocational education is to benefit youth both in finding postschool employment and in the wages they earn. Table 4.5 depicts the effects of two different levels of participation in vocational education for youth with learning or other mild disabilities in comparison to youth with disabilities as a whole, youth with sensory disabilities, and youth with physical disabilities. Both surveys (one of students taking fewer than four related vocational education courses and concentrated vocational training, the other of students taking four or more related vocational education courses) gave strong positive support to the probability of competitive employment (20 and 19 percentage-point high probabilities for vocational students). Although both choices contributed to higher employment rates in this analysis, additional NLTS analyses have suggested that employment gains grew over time for youth taking a concentration of courses, whereas the employment rate was fairly stable

TABLE 4.5

Estimated Difference in Outcomes Associated with High School
Vocational Education and Work Experience Programs

Program participation/outcomes	Type of Disability[a]			
	All Youth	Mild	Sensory	Physical[b]
Comparing youth with unrelated vocational education **survey courses** in high school with nonvocational or prevocational students, the estimated difference in:				
The percentage enrolled in post-secondary vocational programs	10.4	9.5	4.8	—
The percentage competitively employed	19.8*	35.6**	16.6	—
The total dollar compensation earned from employment	$1,097	$3,993*	$1,021	—
Comparing youth who **concentrated in vocational education**[c] in high school with nonvocational or prevocational students, the estimated difference in:				
The percentage enrolled in post-secondary vocational programs	10.3	13.6	4.6	–1.8
The percentage competitively employed	19.0*	39.9***	15.3	–5.3
The total dollar compensation earned from employment	$1,851	$6,247***	$1,071	$2,009*
Comparing youth who had taken a high school **work experience program** with those who had not, the estimated difference in:				
The percentage enrolled in post-secondary vocational programs	5.6	1.1	3.6	2.7
The percentage competitively employed	–2.0	10.4	–11.3	32.6*
The total dollar compensation earned from employment	$542	$1,379	–$697	$4,196***

[a]There were no consistent or significant relationships between vocational education experiences and postschool outcomes for youth with severe disabilities; they are included in "all youth," but relationships are not reported for them separately.

[b]The distribution of vocational education variables for the physical disability cluster did not allow the inclusion of both variables. Thus, for this cluster, models included only concentration in vocational education.

[c]A concentration is at least 4 semesters of vocational education in the same content area (e.g., trade and industry, office occupations).

*$p<.05$; **$p<.01$; ***$p<.001$

over time for those taking unrelated survey courses, suggesting greater long-term benefits of concentrated vocational training.

Furthermore, taking a concentration of vocational classes was related to larger incomes; concentrators were estimated to earn $1,851 more than nonvocational or prevocational students. Again, wage gaps increased over time for those taking a concentration of vocational education. These postschool benefits of vocational education encored the positive outcomes associated with such training while students were still in secondary school.

The largest benefits for both kinds of vocational course-taking accrued to youth with learning and other mild disabilities, as expected, among whom vocational students had a probability of competitive employment almost 40 percentage points greater than students without vocational experiences in secondary school, independent of other differences between them. Further, for those youth with learning and other mild disabilities, a concentration in vocational education was especially lucrative; concentrators were estimated to earn $6,247 more annually than nonvocational or prevocational students. Youth with learning or other mild disabilities who took survey vocational courses also earned more—nearly $4,000 per year—than peers who took none.

Contrary to expectations, Table 4.5 shows that, when other variables were included in the analyses, work experience was positively and significantly associated with employment for youth with physical impairments and, to a lesser extent, those with learning and other mild disabilities. This contrasts with the finding that work experience did not make a significant added contribution to any outcomes for youth with disabilities as a group. It is likely that the skills and foci of work experience programs and vocational education in general were similar and the two factors were confounded when we consider the two factors simultaneously.

Placement Options

Choices among placement options also can influence the postschool success of students with learning disabilities. The NLTS surveyors found that regular education placements had significant, but mixed, relationships to student outcomes. Social goals that students, parents, and schools might have for placing students with disabilities in regular education classes appear to be furthered by those placements. However, spending more time in regular-education academic classes was powerfully associated with a higher rate of course failure for students with learning disabilities (independent of disability and other factors), and a high failure rate, in turn, was among the strongest predictors of students dropping out of school.

If students with disabilities as a group were successful enough to have stayed in school, however, their regular education and academic course experiences appear to have benefited them in their later years. Controlling for other differences between youth, the researchers noted that more time spent in general education classrooms was positively related to employment (Table 4.6). For example, youth who spent all of the school day during secondary school in regular education settings were 11 percentage points more likely than peers who spent half of their time there to be competitively employed and were estimated to have higher earnings ($2,095 more per year). However, these employment advantages accrued only to youth with sensory or physical disabilities, not to youth with learning disabilities and other mild disabilities. This difference in impacts supports the notion that regular education disproportionately benefits youth whose disabilities are not cognitive in nature. The benefits of regular education placements for youth with learning and other mild disabil-

TABLE 4.6
Estimated Difference in Outcomes
Associated with Amount of Time
Spent in Regular Education Classes

	Type of Disability[a]			
	All Youth	Mild[a]	Sensory	Physical
Comparing youth who spent all of their class time in regular education classes with those who spent half of their time there, the estimated difference in:				
The percentage enrolled in post-secondary vocational programs	3.2	10.4**	−4.0	15.0
The percentage competitively employed	11.2**	1.9	15.0*	43.2**
The total dollar compensation earned from employment	2,095***	683	1,550**	1,664*

[a]There were no consistent or statistically significant relationships between regular education placement and postschool outcomes for youth with severe disabilities; they are included in "all youth," but relationships are not reported for them separately.
*p<.05; **p<.01; ***p<.001

ities were much weaker. On the other hand, time spent in regular education also was associated with a greater likelihood of postsecondary vocational enrollment for youth with mild disabilities (10 percentage points).

Two caveats must be offered in interpreting these findings. First, one should not interpret these relationships as implying that regular education necessarily caused variations in outcomes; rather, it is possible that unmeasured competencies of youth themselves contributed to their positive outcomes. In other words, it is possible that youth who were more competent in ways not measured by the skills scales and disability-related variables in the NLTS were more involved in regular education and achieved better post-school outcomes. Second, the importance of the fact that the other variables in the model are held constant at their means cannot be overemphasized. The average of the dichotomous dropout variable in the unweighed sample included in these analyses was approximately 25%; the proportion of high school graduates was approximately 75%. Thus, these analyses reflect in large measure the experiences of youth who had succeeded in regular education classrooms sufficiently to graduate from high school. But many students with learning disabilities did not do well enough in regular education classes to graduate. Findings from other NLTS research showed that spending more time in regular education was associated with a higher likelihood of course failure, which in turn contributed greatly to a higher likelihood of students' dropping out of school. Those who did not succeed in regular education settings and dropped out experienced negative postschool outcomes, as described above. Thus, regular education appears to confer advantages on those who succeed within it and become graduates, but the negative effects of dropping out dominate the experiences of those who do not succeed in regular education settings.

Parent Involvement

Findings regarding young people with learning disabilities confirmed what we know about the importance of parents in the lives of all young people. Key factors in student success, in general, are the extent to which the family encourages learning, expresses high expectations for children, and becomes involved in their school and community life.[11] Consistent with this, students with disabilities whose parents were more involved in supporting their educations while in high school (e.g., monitoring students' progress in school, helping with homework) were estimated to miss five fewer days of school per year and to be 25 percentage points less likely to fail a class than their peers with less-involved parents, independent of socioeconomic and other differences between them. Controlling for demographic and school program differences, the NLTS team noted that youth with disabilities whose parents were more involved in their education during high school were significantly more likely to go on to postsecondary schools than were other youth with disabilities. Similarly, youth with disabilities whose parents had high expectations for their postschool outcomes were significantly more likely to have achieved those outcomes than were other youth (independent of other differences between them in demographics or school programs). These findings support the current federal initiatives to increase parental participation in the process of developing both the individualized education plans and individualized transition plans for students with disabilities.

Social Integration

Schools also can support the social integration of students with disabilities into the life of the school. Multivariate NLTS analyses revealed that, independent of other differences between them, students with learning and other mild disabilities who belonged to social, sports, hobby, or other kinds of groups while in high school missed significantly less school and had significantly lower probabilities of failing courses and dropping out than students who were not affiliated with groups while in school.[12] Schools can encourage the development of a wide range of options for group affiliations that will appeal to the interests of a wide variety of students and actively instruct students with learning disabilities in the skills needed to succeed in such groups.

Collaboration and Transition Planning

Although these opportunities for improving outcomes for students with learning disabilities are available to most schools, the tendency to focus on the traditional school activities of coursework and student interactions often persists, resulting in neglect of the vocational needs of students and the constellation of family-related stresses common to students with learning disabilities. Schools are unlikely to be able to address these complex and multifaceted issues alone; collaboration with employment and social service agencies is required to construct "wrap-around" services that can meet the multiple needs of many students with learning disabilities and their families. Today, many promising model programs address the transition needs of students with disabilities. The legislated mandate for transition planning will bring further innovation to this area of special education. It is interesting to note, however, that even when special educators encourage "embracing a more expansive understanding of collaborative relationships,"[13] the encouraged collaboration is generally between elements of the school community—regular and special educators, vocational and academic educators, preservice teacher trainers of different disciplines—and between schools and parents, but not explicitly with agencies outside the school.

Data such as those provided by the NLTS have sounded a "wake-up call" to policymakers, educators, other human service practitioners, parents, and students, about the outcomes experienced by many students with learning disabilities. Their successes in the employment arena are often achieved without support from school curricula and bring them earnings so low as to make the attainment of long-term independence difficult. There is no way to measure those personal costs.

Much can be done to help students with disabilities achieve their employment related transition goals. Collaborative efforts between schools, parents, transition programs, and the business community are most likely to bring positive results. Continued assessment of the outcomes of students with learning disabilities will indicate whether school reform efforts, and the program improvement initiatives undertaken to improve them, meet that important goal.

Notes

[1]National Education Goals Panel. *The national goals report: Building a nation of learners.* Washington, DC: US Government Printing Office, 1991.

[2]Mithaug, D. E., and Horiuchi, C. N. *Colorado statewide followup survey of special education students.* Denver, CO: Colorado Department of Education, 1983. Hasazi, S. B., Gordon, L. R., and Roe, C. A. Factors associated with the employment status of handicapped youth exiting high school from 1979–1983. *Exceptional children* (1985), 51:455–469. Edgar, E., Levine, P., and Maddox, M. *Washington state followup data of former secondary special education students.* Seattle, WA: University of Washington, 1985.

[3]Details of the NLTS sample and weighting are found in Javitz, H., and Wagner, M. *The National Longitudinal Transition Study of Special Education Students: Report on sample design and limitations, wave 1 (1987).* Menlo Park, CA: SRI International, 1990; and Javitz, H., and Wagner, M. *The National Longitudinal Transition Study of Special Education Students: Sample characteristics and procedures, wave 2 (1990).* Menlo Park, CA: SRI International, 1993. Note that the statistics reported from the NLTS are weighted population estimates for the entire population of students with disabilities and for the LD category specifically; they are not percentages of the NLTS sample.

[4]Details of data collection for the NLTS are found in Wagner, M., Newman, L., and Shaver, D. *The National Longitudinal Transition Study of Special Education Students: Report on procedures for the first wave of data collection (1987).* Menlo Park, CA: SRI International, 1989; and Marder, C., Habina, K., and Prince, N. *The National Longitudinal Transition Study of Special Education Students. Report on procedures for the second wave of data collection (1990).* Menlo Park, CA: SRI International, 1992.

[5]Harry, B. *Cultural diversity, families, and the special education system: Communication for empowerment.* New York: Teachers College Press, 1992.

[6]Postschool goals were reported in written questionnaires completed by teachers of 12th-grade students with disabilities who were familiar with their school programs and transition plans.

[7]Cameto, R. Support services provided by secondary schools. In Wagner, M. (Ed.). *The secondary school programs of students with disabilities. A report from the National Longitudinal Transition Study of Special Education Students.* Menlo Park, CA: SRI International, 1993.

[8]Supported employment often involves working in competitive jobs, but with the wages earned being subsidized by public funds in order to provide an incentive to employers to hire persons with disabilities. Those in supported employment also may receive support services from an employment "coach" or counselor, such as job training or supervision or advocacy on behalf of the person with disabilities in relationships with other workers or supervisors. Sheltered employment is work in settings in which most or all other workers have disabilities; wages are generally below those earned in competitive jobs.

[9]The NLTS methodology for constructing this "adjusted" sample of youth from the general population is described in Marder, C., and D'Amico, R., *How well are youth with disabilities really doing? A comparison of youth with disabilities and youth in general.* Menlo Park, CA: SRI International, 1992. Center for Human Resource Research. (1988). *NLS Handbook: The National Longitudinal Surveys of Labor Market Experience.* Columbus, OH: Ohio State University, Author.

[10]D'Amico, R. The working world awaits: Employment experiences during and shortly after secondary school. In Wagner, M., Newman, L., D'Amico, R., Jay E. D., Butler-Nalin, P., Marder, C., and Cox, R. *Youth with disabilities: How are they doing? The first comprehensive report from the National Longitudinal Transition Study of Special Education Students.* Menlo Park, CA: SRI International. 1991.

[11]Henderson, A. *A new generation of evidence: The family is critical to student achievement.* Washington, DC: National Committee for Citizens in Education, 1994.

[12]Wagner, M., Blackorby, J., Cameto, R., & Newman, L. What makes a difference? Influences on postschool outcomes of youth with disabilities. *The third comprehensive report from the National Longitudinal Transition Study of Special Education Students.* Menlo Park, CA: SRI International, 1993.

[13]Johnson, L. J., and Pugach, M. C., Continuing the dialogue: Embracing a more expansive understanding of collaborative relationships. In Stainback, W., and Stainback, S., (Eds.), *Controversial issues confronting special education. Divergent perspectives.* Boston: Allyn and Bacon, 1992.

PART II

Training Persons with Learning Disabilities for Employment

Effective Practices of Transition from School to Work for People with Learning Disabilities

Thomas E. Grayson
Thomas R. Wermuth
Thomas M. Holub
Michele L. Anderson

T he transition from high school to adult life can mean many things to individuals with learning disabilities. Some youths and young adults with learning disabilities leave high school with the necessary academic, vocational, interpersonal, and social skills to successfully continue their education in postsecondary settings or enter the world of work. Others exit secondary school, some before graduating, only to experience, as Halpern (1992) has described, "a period of floundering that occurs for at least the first several years after leaving school as adolescents attempt to assume a variety of adult roles in their communities" (p. 203). It is our premise that the goal of secondary-level educational programs designed for individuals with learning disabilities should attempt to minimize the "period of floundering" described by Halpern (1992) by offering a vocationally-oriented secondary school curriculum that evolves from the transition planning process.

A number of follow-up studies describe the outcomes of students formerly enrolled in special education programs after exiting secondary schools. Most of these studies report high dropout rates for individuals with learning disabilities, high rates of unemployment or underemployment, and low rates of enrollment in postsecondary education (Edgar & Levine, 1986; Harnisch, Wermuth, & Zheng, 1992; Hasazi, Gordon, & Roe, 1985; Mithaug, Horiuchi, & Fanning, 1985; Sitlington, Frank, & Cooper, 1989; Wagner, 1989; Zigmond & Thornton, 1985). Results of these studies do not flatter secondary special education programs. Rather, a picture has emerged—of poor academic preparation and a lack of marketable vocational skills—among students served by those supposedly "special" programs.

Follow-up studies suggest that approximately 15% to 28% of students who were diagnosed with learning disabilities and completed high school subsequently attended postsecondary institutions (e.g., community colleges, junior colleges, or four-year colleges or universities) on either a full-time or part-time basis (Edgar & Levine, 1986; Harnisch et al., 1992; Sitlington et al., 1989; Wagner, 1989) Although several model demonstration projects have been designed to facilitate the transition of students with learning disabilities from school to various forms of postsecondary education (Aune, 1991; Bursuck, 1987; Bursuck & Rose, 1992; Zigmond, 1990; Zigmond & Miller, 1992) or help them succeed at the postsecondary level (Association on Handicapped Student Service Programs in Postsecondary Education, 1987; Gajar, 1986; Vogel, 1990), we can expect that only a small percentage of students with learning disabilities will benefit from what these initiatives have taught. We know that the majority of individuals diagnosed with learning disabilities in school seek employment after exiting high school, but fail to obtain work. However, few model programs have been designed and implemented with a specific focus on facilitating the transition of youths with learning disabilities from high school to careers.

Employment Outcomes

Many follow-up studies have verified that the majority of individuals diagnosed with learning disabilities seek employment after exiting high school (Edgar & Levine, 1986; Harnisch et al., 1992; Sitlington et al., 1989). The percentage of high school graduates diagnosed with learning disabilities entering either full-time or part-time employment immediately after exiting high school in these studies ranges from 57% to 77% (Sitlington et al., 1989; Wagner, 1989). In addition, some students with learning disabilities enter other formal training programs after leaving the secondary setting, including: the military, private vocational training, apprenticeships, or adult basic education (Sitlington et al., 1989). Tragically, but not surprisingly, the percentage of high school dropouts with learning disabilities who successfully obtain employment, further education, or training after dropping out is significantly lower than the percentage of high school graduates with learning disabilities (Edgar, 1987; Sitlington et al., 1989; Wagner, 1989).

Individuals with learning disabilities who obtain employment after leaving high school often work in positions that offer little opportunity for advancement, pay the minimum wage or slightly above, and do not include benefits such as health insurance (Edgar, 1987; Harnisch et al.,

1992; Sitlington et al., 1989; Wagner, 1989). Edgar (1987) noted that secondary-level students diagnosed with learning disabilities.

> . . . are not profiting from the remedial academic approach of most secondary special education programs, they appear to be disenchanted with them (they tend to leave them), and even though they have the best employment rates of all special education students they earn paltry salaries. (p. 558)

It seems that most youths and young adults with learning disabilities use a "family-friend network," initially identified by Hasazi et al. (1985), as the primary source of help in finding employment. Sitlington, et al. (1989) reported in their follow-up study, conducted in Iowa, that most graduates with learning disabilities found employment through their own resourcefulness (43.3%) or with the assistance of family or friends (39.9%). Additionally, Hasazi et al. (1985) found that working for pay while in high school, whether as part of a school program or not, is strongly associated with post-school employment. Edgar (1987) believes that the importance of non-school contacts in finding employment tends to further minimize the influence of secondary educational programs in the post-school lives of individuals with learning disabilities.

Most secondary programs that serve individuals with learning disabilities focus on remedial academic instruction designed to increase basic skills (Okolo & Sitlington, 1986). These remediation-oriented programs appear to have little impact on the eventual postschool adjustment of students with learning disabilities (Edgar, 1987). Corroborating these findings, Zigmond (1990) has observed that: "Many students with learning disabilities enter the ninth grade barely literate and leave high school after 1, 2, 3, or 4 years with literacy skills virtually unchanged" (p. 5). The marginal statistics on dropout rates, academic achievement, and employment status of former special education students has led Edgar (1987) to question the utility of most secondary special education programs and conclude that

> The only solution is a radical (no namby-pamby modification or cosmetic addition to existing programs) shift in focus of secondary curriculum away from academics to functional, vocational, independent living tasks. (p. 560)

This chapter addresses secondary-level transition models designed to facilitate the movement of students with learning disabilities from high school to employment. The discussion is divided into four sections. First, previous secondary models for students with learning disabilities are detailed; second, a proposed theoretical vocationally-oriented model is postulated; third, an existing comprehensive transition program implemented at West High School in Madison, Wisconsin, is described; and finally, particular transition challenges for students with learning disabilities are discussed.

Previous Secondary Models

Zigmond (1990) believes that effective secondary special education programs for individuals with learning disabilities should have the following four program components:

1. intensive instruction in reading and mathematics

2. explicit instruction in survival skills

3. core instruction courses required for high school graduation

4. an explicit student plan for life after high school (p. 6)

Zigmond and her colleagues designed two models to serve students with learning disabilities based on these four components (Zigmond, 1990; Zigmond & Miller, 1992). The first model, titled "Less but Very Special Education," is intended for students with learning disabilities planning to enroll for postsecondary education after graduation from high school (Zigmond, 1990; Zigmond & Miller, 1992) and would serve approximately 15% to 30% of secondary students with learning disabilities (Edgar, 1987; Edgar & Levine, 1986; Harnisch et al., 1992; Hasazi et al., 1985; Mithaug et al., 1985; Sitlington et al., 1989; Wagner, 1989; Zigmond & Thornton, 1985).

The second model, titled "More Special Education," is designed for the majority of students with learning disabilities (70% to 85%) who would enter work immediately after finishing high school (Zigmond, 1990; Zigmond & Miller, 1992). This model has five distinctive features:

1. Basic skills are taught by special educators and these basic skills are linked to transition planning.

2. Required core instruction areas are taught by special educators.

3. Vocational education is provided in mainstream settings and coordinated with transition planning within special education.

4. All ninth grade students are required to take a course on survival skills taught by a special educator.

5. Students' schedules would reflect a light academic load through-out the ninth grade to ensure successful completion of the first year of high school. (pp. 18–19)

Although this "More" model is vocationally oriented and includes mainstream vocational education courses that are coordinated with transition planning (Zigmond, 1990), it also relies on pull-out classrooms (e.g., resource rooms or specific courses for students with learning disabilities) that focus on remedial academic and basic skills instruction taught primarily by special education teachers. This model appears to be an attempt to replicate the high school education experienced by most individuals without disabilities rather than providing an alternative curriculum aimed specifically at individuals with learning disabilities. A special education curriculum that parallels the regular or general education curriculum may force students, parents, and teachers to choose between academic programs provided in segregated school settings and community-based vocational activities, such as job placement experiences, that may be more applicable to individual students' futures.

Okolo and Sitlington (1986) also developed a secondary model designed to assist individuals with learning disabilities make the transition from school to work. Their model describes six types of vocationally relevant activities that should be part of secondary special education programs serving individuals with learning disabilities:

1. occupational awareness, exploration, and basic work experience

2. in-depth career/vocational assessment

3. instruction in job-related academic skills

4. instruction in job-related interpersonal skills

5. support services to other disciplines involved in vocational programming

6. postschool placement and follow-up (p. 292)

The models described above may alter the content of secondary special education for some students. However, it does not seem to us that those alterations would be dramatic enough to reform the structure and content of high school programs serving individuals with learning disabilities and, consequently, to influence the postschool outcomes those individuals would attain as adults. An alternative educational option is overdue; it should incorporate the salient characteristics from both the Okolo and Sitlington (1986) and Zigmond (1990) models, offer an entirely vocational orientation, and use special education as the primary provider of job placement, training, and follow-along services before and after students complete high school, and allow for flexible re-entry into the secondary school, when necessary, after graduation.

A Proposed Vocationally Oriented Model

Based on the interpretation by DeStefano & Wermuth (1992) of federal transition requirements, needed reforms of secondary special education programs must include:

1. development of linkages between school personnel and others involved in the provision of transition services

2. broadening the scope of secondary special education curricula and programs

3. changing the roles and skill requirements of secondary-level special education personnel (p. 538)

These suggested reforms would require secondary-level special education programs to move away from a narrow focus on remedial instruction, designed to parallel regular education, to more integrated and vocationally relevant environments of the school and community. This section describes such an approach, a vocationally oriented model of transition services.

A vocationally oriented model such as the one Stefano and Wermuth propose would reflect the following principles: (a) Basic skills instruction, survival skills instruction, academic strategies instruction, and job-related skills must be taught in a vocationally relevant manner; (b) subject matter (content area) must be integrated with the vocational education curriculum; (c) in-school mainstream vocational education courses and community-based job experiences must begin in the ninth grade and continue throughout high school; (d) special educators must be responsible for job placement, training, and follow-along before students exit high school; (e) multiple high school re-entry points must be available to all youths with learning disabilities, whether they have been graduated from high school or not, until they reach age 21. These components call for dramatic changes in the roles and skill requirements of special education professionals, and in the secondary special education curriculum now offered to most students with learning disabilities. Discussion of each component in greater detail follows.

Basic skills instruction, survival skills instruction, academic strategies instruction, and job-related skills must be taught in a vocationally relevant manner.

Secondary-level special education programs for individuals with learning disabilities often provide students with instruction regarding strategies designed to assist them to "survive" in regular education classrooms such as study skills strategies, time management strategies, inter- and intra-personal skills strategies, appropriate means of conflict resolution, note-taking strategies, and basic skills instruction (Bos & Vaughn, 1988). All of the strategies just listed, along with job-related strategies such as locating, obtaining, and maintaining employment, should be provided in vocational education environments, both in school and in the community. For example, basic skills instruction (e.g., reading and math skills), academic strategy instruction (e.g., problem-solving and note-taking strategies), and conflict resolution should be provided in formats that students may encounter while working or as part of job placement experiences, such as reading operation manuals and employee handbooks (i.e., reading-to-do activities), working on applied math problems associated with measuring or finances, or positively dealing with constructive criticism from an employer.

Subject matter (i.e., content area) must be integrated with the vocational education curriculum.

All social studies, language arts, math, and science instruction should be applied to vocational problems and should be taught in an integrated manner with vocational education courses, materials, and work experiences. An example of an entirely integrated curriculum exists in Chicago at the Vocational Agriculture High School. Every subject in this school, including electives such as music and art, has an agricultural theme. By explicitly bringing the vocational relevance of content-area subjects into the forefront of instruction, the curriculum will better enable students to make the connection between activities they are working on in school to future employment and how those activities apply in the "real world." This link or connection between skills learned in school and application of those skills in real-world settings should be overt rather than covert; that is, students need to be shown the reason for learning a particular skill and how that skill will become an essential component of their future lives.

Both in-school mainstream vocational education courses and community-based job experiences must begin in the ninth grade and continue throughout high school.

Recent research has suggested that vocational education and employment experiences early in high school appears to reduce the dropout rate of students at risk, including individuals with learning disabilities (Wagner, 1991). Providing mainstream vocational education options early in high school, and coupling that instruction with community-based job experiences that are monitored closely by school personnel, will help students to understand the expectations and skills needed to become successfully employed. Additionally, these experiences should help ninth and tenth graders explore various vocational options and provide eleventh and twelfth graders specific experiences that will be valuable to them as they transition from job try-out activities to specific job placement and training.

Special educators must be responsible for job placement, training, and follow-along before students exit high school.

Across the United States, adult service providers of post-high school assistance to students with disabilities are in short supply (Edgar, 1987). Therefore, it is reasonable to expect special education teachers to provide a rationale for all learning tasks explicitly connecting school activities with skills students will need to be successful as adults. Special education teachers must be involved in job development, placement, and training activities for students with learning disabilities. These activities will require that special education teachers at the secondary level have schedules that allow them the flexibility to spend part or all of the school day working with students and employers in the community. Additionally, special education teachers must follow former students along for at least the first 2 years after they exit high school, in an attempt to provide additional job placement and training or other pertinent services if or when needed. Making job placement, training, and follow-along a major goal and function of secondary special education will directly influence the outcomes attained by young adults with learning disabilities after they exit high school.

Multiple high school re-entry points must be accessible to all youths with learning disabilities, whether they have graduated from high school or not, until they reach age 21.

Special education programs must continue providing academic and vocational instruction to all students with diagnosed learning disabilities until they reach the age of 21. This will provide a safety net for students who wish to enhance their academic skills before entering postsecondary education, or for students who desire additional vocational training or job placement and training once they have exited high school. As the primary service providers for youths and young adults with learning disabilities until the age when the educational system's legal responsibility ends, special education professionals would be in a position to assist students and graduates with additional academic or vocational training by decompressing the time an individual transitions from high school to adult life.

Implementation of this vocationally oriented model will require many changes in the roles and responsibilities of secondary special educators. Collaboration with vocational educators and employers is the cornerstone of the proposed model. Additionally, the setting in which instruction is provided will expand to include vocational education classrooms and community-based work sites, and the time frame that constitutes a normal school day (9:00 a.m. to 3:30 p.m.) or school year (September to June) may no longer be applicable.

Parts of this theoretical model exist and have been successful in some states (e.g., Madison, Wisconsin; San Francisco, California; Seattle, Washington; and South Burlington, Vermont). It is time for students with learning disabilities to gain the option of enrolling in a completely vocationally-oriented secondary program. A change in the form and function of secondary special education programs to a completely vocationally oriented curriculum is one possible solution to the current practices associated with poor adult outcomes attained by individuals with learning disabilities.

The next section describes The Pathways to Satisfaction (PTS) Model at West High School, Madison, Wisconsin. Although this program does not contain all components of the proposed model described above, it is considered to be a model that others may wish to explore and replicate.

The Pathways to Satisfaction Model

Since the mid 1980s, secondary-level students with learning disabilities attending West High School in Madison, Wisconsin have had the opportunity to participate in a comprehensive program designed to facilitate their transition from school to adult life. The program, formally titled Pathways To Satisfaction, was developed by Thomas M. Holub in 1990 and is currently being implemented, in part or whole, in over 30 school districts located in Wisconsin, Illinois, and Minnesota. The PTS program has five interrelated phases through which students progress based on their individual needs, interests, and goals for the future. The phases are designed to follow a sequential order; however, they are dynamic in nature, allowing individual students the ability to move between phases flexibly, based on their own contextual and life-orienting experiences in educational settings or the community.

The term *transition* was initially defined as the movement from school to work (Will, 1984). However, more recent definitions tend to illuminate the transition process in broader developmental parameters rather than in a series of narrowly defined discrete activities and outcomes. Wehman (1992) defines this broad process as follows:

> Transition from school to adulthood may be defined as the life changes, adjustments, and cumulative experiences that occur in the lives of young adults as they move from school environments to more independent living and work environments. (p. 5)

The PTS program is developmental in nature, starting before students enter the high school setting, and is designed to evolve as they progress towards adulthood. Further, the program continues beyond the point in time when students exit high school and enter their next stage of life.

Each phase in the PTS program is student-centered and student-driven. The transition specialists employed by the Madison Metropolitan School District receive continuous inservice training and are provided the option to receive training through Preparing Transition Leadership Cadres for Wisconsin—a program offered throughout the state by the University of Wisconsin–Madison (Hanley-Maxwell, 1993). Although trained transition specialists work specifically with students with learning disabilities at Madison West High School, students and their parents are expected to be the primary actors throughout the transition process, self-advocating to ensure their desires are programmatically implemented and managing their own transition plans. Students and their parents receive instruction, prior to and throughout the transition period, on becoming their own case managers, connecting with postsecondary institutions and agencies, and overcoming common barriers inhibiting successful transitions.

The PTS program is grounded in the philosophical belief that all students should be educated with their chronologically-aged peers and be included to the greatest extent possible in the regular or general education environment. If general education courses and programs offer instructional opportunities for students enrolled in the PTS program, enrollment in those options is explored rather than creating a separate parallel system serving only students with learning disabilities. If general education opportunities need to be supported by special education teachers in order to meet the educational needs of students enrolled in the PTS program, collaborative instruction involving the general education teacher and special education teacher is implemented. Reasonable instructional accommodations are made for students in such inclusive environments. The accommodations, made with relative ease due to collaborative instruction, include special methodological practices, adaptations for strategy implementation, and alterations of expectations. Regular education staff members involved in the collaborative efforts routinely request that PTS strategies be implemented for all enrollees in fully included classes and parental requests for such participation has been common for students in all grades. The PTS program encourages flexibility and the use of currently available resources and staff to meet the diverse needs of individual students.

The five phases in the PTS program include: (a) focus, (b) synthesis, (c) exploration, (d) connection, and (e) evaluation. Taken together, the phases extend from when students are nearing the end of their middle school or junior high school experience and are gathering information about potential high school options or pathways, until after the students have successfully exited from high school. Formal and informal activities and resources made available within each of the phases are initiated based on the interests and needs of the students and their parents.

Focus

The focus phase begins when students enroll in the seventh and eighth grades. In the focus phase, students work in small groups or individually with a transition specialist on activities geared toward awareness of secondary school options, including: college preparation and vocational education programs, identifying individual learning styles, identifying academic strengths and weaknesses, self-actualization, and goal setting for high school and beyond. Other activities conducted during the focus phase include: parent conferences with the transition team, course scheduling for ninth grade, visitations to the high school, peer mentoring with older high school students, and general information sessions regarding academic and social high school survival skills.

During the focus phase, the transition specialist provides students and their parents with general information about high school and initiates discussions between each student and his or her parents about the future. Initiating these activities and discussions early, before students enter high school, provides students and their parents time to absorb information and reflect about issues that will need to be addressed during transition planning throughout high school. Additionally, providing advance knowledge about high school options allows parents and students to think about and discuss the advantages and limitations of various programmatic choices before they are expected to make any final decisions.

Synthesis

During the synthesis phase, which occurs while students are enrolled in the ninth and 10th grades, individuals work independently or on a one-to-one basis with a transition specialist to organize information that will help them throughout the transition process. Students gather and synthesize information about the types of postsecondary education programs that may interest them, employment options available, current and future labor market needs in the greater Madison area, the independent living skills they need to obtain before they move out "on their own," and recreational outlets that exist in the community.

A key component of the synthesis phase includes a comprehensive vocational assessment for each student. The assessment provides formal and informal measures of leisure interests, career interests, work behaviors, medical conditions, functional skills, basic academic skills, life skills, learning styles, social skills, and values clarification. Each student receives formal feedback from the transition specialist regarding the mesh between the student's goals and his or her current level of functioning in each of the assessment areas.

Multidisciplinary staff conduct assessment in special and regular education courses. The special education courses *Life and Work Choices, Careers,* and *Transition Life Planning* offer the most comprehensive assessment activities. By design, course activities are developed and conducted in the community context. In Madison, for example, life skills are assessed in the university credit union and the YMCA. Students, staff, and mentors implement PTS activities and collect information to ascertain the level of functioning in a particular skill cluster. In more inclusive environments, standardized tests of interest, attitude, and aptitude (e.g., COPS[1], COPES[2],

---

[1]Comprehensive Occupational Preference Survey

[2]Career Orientation Placement and Evaluation Survey

CAPS[3]—Edits Corporation, San Diego, CA) are used. In addition, regular education environments offer assessment through the curriculum. For example, an essay written in an English class might identify where a student hopes to live after high school and what his or her life expectations are. In all cases, assessment information is discussed in groups and in most instances, during transition planning meetings. Scheduled interventions are completed within the semester.

At the end of the synthesis phase, each student and his or her parents are provided with a description of the student's strengths and areas needing improvement, and strategies to remove potential barriers. The student, working in a triad with his or her parents and the school staff members, develops and implements goals to eliminate potential barriers. Activities in the synthesis phase promote realistic and attainable goal-setting by all of the individuals involved in the transition planning process.

Exploration

In the exploration phase, students pursue areas of interest they have identified during the previous two phases. Exploration takes place while students are enrolled in the ninth, 10th, and 11th grades and encompasses a wide array of activities, including: checking credits obtained for graduation; scheduling appointments with guidance counselors and in the high school career/college center, writing or calling postsecondary schools of interest for information; planning to take and enrolling in courses needed to enter desired programs; attending college and career fairs; exploring living arrangements available away from home, financial aid opportunities, and apprenticeship programs; visiting educational programs and employment opportunities of interest; exploring entrance requirements for various programs of interest; and job-shadowing experiences. (In the latter, students may work with and "shadow" members of the Retired Senior Volunteer Program, for example, and continuously evaluate the volunteers' actions in a formative manner.) The exploration phase is developed individually for each student based on his or her identified future areas of interest.

Connection

In the connection phase, students are assisted in making formal connections with various post-school institutions and organizations. Activities

---

[3]Career Aptitude Placement Survey

in this phase include scheduling apprenticeship interviews with trade union representatives, attending conferences with community college and university admissions officers, seeking acceptance to postsecondary vocational education programs, enlisting in the military, and completing high school. The connection phase takes place when students are in the 11th and 12th grades and is different for each individual in the PTS program based on their individual goals and the steps they have taken to achieve those goals.

If desired connections cannot be made, the student, his or her parents, and school personnel meet in order to re-assess and re-evaluate post-secondary options. This process allows students opportunities to alter their goals and to ensure that the secondary school will assist students in achieving revised or newly developed goals. Because of information gathering, sharing, and discussions that occur throughout the PTS program, few students are unable to access and attain appropriate postsecondary-level options.

Students generally are graduated from high school at the conclusion of the connection phase. Each student involved in the PTS program receives an assessment and information portfolio before leaving Madison West High School. The portfolio contains a variety of information, including each student's educational assessment data, vocational assessment information, record of vocational experiences, postsecondary planning, and contact information for community resources and postsecondary educational programs. The portfolio becomes a traveling resource guide for students and has practical value after they exit the secondary setting.

Evaluation

The PTS evaluation phase centers around follow-along activities conducted by school staff specialists with each student in order to track their successes and emerging concerns. Telephone contacts from the school to program graduates, scheduled at regular intervals during the first two years after graduation allow transition specialists from the high school to remain involved with former students, intervening and providing additional information or resources if necessary. This ongoing follow-along evaluation meets the intent of the Individuals with Disabilities Education Act of 1990 (IDEA) (Public Law 101-476) mandate requiring that the educational agency be responsible for reconvening the Individualized Educational Planning (IEP) team if transition-related goals and objectives have not been met.

The five phases, approximate grade levels, and a sample of the potential activities associated with implementation of each phase in the PTS program are summarized in Table 5.1.

Case Example Illustrating the PTS Model

Mark is a bright college freshman with a mild learning disability. A year ago, when Mark's high school education was coming to an end, his parents were worried about whether he would be successful at the postsecondary level. Fortunately, Mark and his parents had been involved in the PTS program since Mark was in the eighth grade and had developed a positive working relationship with the transition specialist. The following chronological anecdote illustrates the implementation of PTS program phases around Mark's interests, abilities, needs, and goals for the future.

Focusing on the Future

During the eighth grade, Mark was interviewed by the transition specialist at his middle school. The initial interview was followed by a series of informal small-group meetings with some of Mark's peers who had similar interests and concerns about high school programs and beyond. The small group generated a list of potential postsecondary goals and plans to reach those goals. Mark's parents were integrally involved in assisting him with decisions he needed to make regarding his high school education. During the middle of Mark's eighth-grade year, he selected a high school to attend and made course selections for ninth grade. The high school he chose, Madison West, offered the best blend of technological expertise and academic rigor. In this school, classes with technological orientation could be provided with shoulder-to-shoulder, highly integrated math instruction and an emphasis on technical writing. The remainder of eighth grade was spent preparing Mark and his parents for the academic challenges high school would present.

Synthesizing Information

During ninth and 10th grade, Mark and his parents were provided with numerous formal and informal vocational assessment opportunities. Because Mark had no definite postsecondary plans, it was important that he take part in assessment activities that would allow him to explore potential options and discuss the positives and negatives of each option.

TABLE 5.1
Phases of the Pathways to Satisfaction Model

Phase	Approximate grade level	Sample of potential activities
1. Focus	7th and 8th	a) high school scheduling b) secondary survival skills c) learning styles inventory d) academic skills inventory
2. Synthesis	9th and 10th	a) discussions regarding postsecondary education options b) discussions regarding potential employment options c) vocational assessment
3. Exploration	9th through 11th	a) credit checks for graduation b) job shadowing experiences c) visit postsecondary education institutions d) contact apprenticeship programs
4. Connection	11th and 12th	a) schedule apprenticeship interviews b) admissions conferences with colleges and universities c) conferences with military recruiters d) graduation from high school
5. Evaluation	Post-high school	a) telephone contact with student b) telephone contact with home c) telephone contact with university personnel d) face-to-face contact with an employer

Some of the assessment activities included a situational assessment of learning style, a community-based volunteer job-shadowing experience, numerous formal and informal interest inventories, and the State of Wisconsin Gateway Vocational Assessment.

Mark enjoyed his work in the technology education courses he elected to take; however, he also enjoyed writing and wanted to pursue a career in journalism. Based on these two areas of interest, Mark, along with the transition specialist, was able to gather information about the specifics of careers in both journalism and technology. By the end of 10th grade, Mark had decided to work towards a career in journalism and to maintain his interest in technology as a hobby.

Exploration and Connection

In the 11th grade, Mark explored the specifics of a number of postsecondary schools. Mark determined how far away from home he was willing to move, the admissions requirements for a number of schools, the cost of attending college (including financial-aid possibilities), and support services available to students with learning disabilities at several colleges. Mark and the transition specialist made visits to four postsecondary schools within Wisconsin. Mark applied to three of the four schools visited and was accepted at two institutions.

During 12th grade, Mark chose to attend one of the institutions where he was accepted and worked with the transition specialist and a student support services representative from that campus to develop a list of competencies he would need in order to achieve long-term success at the postsecondary level. Mark spent a large part of his senior year refining notetaking, study skills, and test-taking strategies that would help him succeed in college. Mark worked with the transition specialist and resource teacher on implementing these strategies in his general education classes.

Evaluation

During the fall and spring semesters of Mark's freshman year in college, the transition specialist remained in contact with Mark, his parents, and the college's student support services facilitator through quarterly telephone contacts. Although Mark did not need any additional direct services from the transition specialist, ongoing communication was maintained to monitor his progress and provide him with support. Both Mark and his parents appreciated the involvement and encouragement of the transition specialist.

Mark recently completed his first year at college. He received a B average and wrote a few short articles for the school paper. Most of the journalism classes in which Mark enrolled were challenging, and reasonable accommodations were made by the college staff upon Mark's request. The self-awareness component of PTS and self-advocacy skills Mark acquired helped him to be self-determined and confident in requesting accommodations when necessary. Both Mark and his parents realize that many emergent issues must be addressed as he progresses through college; however, they are all satisfied with his current successes. Mark is advancing toward his career goal and he is satisfied with the educational choice he has made for his baccalaureate degree.

Conclusions Regarding the PTS Model

The PTS program has several unique features distinguishing it from traditional high school programs serving students with learning disabilities. The activities that make up the phases in the PTS program are often generated by students' or their parents' questions about the future and informational needs. Additionally, the transition specialist spends a large portion of the day networking with individuals and agencies outside the school setting rather than providing direct service to students. Extensive networking in the community allows the transition specialist to develop a truly individualized transition program for each student.

Flexibility is also a landmark of the PTS program. To call the PTS a true program may be erroneous, because it is not a typical educational program through which a group of students runs from start to finish. Rather, the PTS program differs with each student, and its phases tend to blend together as students progress through high school. The transition specialist maintains a flexible schedule rather than the usual seven- or eight-period school day routine. This flexibility facilitates communication between key stakeholders in the transition process.

Continuity and long-term support are also unique aspects of the PTS program. Students and their parents are in contact with the transition specialist from seventh grade until after students exit the secondary-level setting. This intensity and duration of involvement allows students and their parents the opportunity to develop long-term relationships with the transition specialist. The development of this relationship enhances and fosters communication between the student, home, and school. This communication becomes the key not only to the success of the PTS program, but also to the success of students as they move from school to adult life.

Transition Challenges

The Individuals with Disabilities Education Act (Public Law 101-476), has, for the first time, provided a definition of transition services within the federal special education legislation in an attempt to assist all students with disabilities to successfully move from school to various roles that comprise adult life. The IDEA defines "transition services" as follows:

> The term transition services means a coordinated set of activities for a student, designed within an outcome oriented process, which promotes movement from school to post-school activities, including postsecondary education, vocational training, integrated employment (including supported employment), continuing and adult education, adult services, independent living, and/or community participation. (Section 602(a)(19))

According to Section 300.18 of the IDEA regulations, the list of adult outcomes included in the definition of transition services is designed only to provide appropriate examples and is not exhaustive. The IDEA requires that transition-related objectives be included on the Individualized Educational Plan (IEP) developed for all students receiving special education, beginning at age 16 and annually thereafter (Section 602(a)(20)(D)). The IDEA also requires educational agencies to take the lead in planning and monitoring the provision of transition services provided not only by the school but also by individuals and agencies outside of education, such as vocational rehabilitation facilities.

These mandates provide a springboard for the development, implementation, and evaluation of alternative modes of providing special educational services to individuals with learning disabilities at the secondary level. Edgar (1987) has stated that "there are not (and never will be) adequate community-based programs to serve all special education students who leave school" (p. 560). If secondary-level special education is to have lasting effects on the lives of the students served in those programs, those programs must ensure that students exit high school employed and carrying knowledge of independent living and community integration options, including recreation outlets, that exist in their local communities. Without ensuring success before a student leaves high school, secondary special education programs will continue to be judged as failing entities based on the results of future follow-up studies.

Although the benefits of a vocationally-oriented high school curriculum may be advantageous for a number of students, a program that dramatically alters common (i.e., status quo) practice will be difficult to implement, due to a number of constraints. Zigmond (1990) identified two categories of issues that may work against implementation of her "More" special education model, including: a) issues related to staffing and personnel preparation; and b) issues, related to policies and regulations, that also may work against the implementation of the proposed vocationally-oriented model. Additionally, the issue of "tracking" students into careers early in their high school careers may also constrain the implementation of the proposed model. The model's safety-net feature would allow students to re-enter the secondary school as postgraduates to receive additional or different training accounts for this potential barrier.

Staffing the proposed vocationally-oriented model would require special educators to change their current roles and responsibilities, working exclusively in vocational education and community-based settings. All instruction would be provided in the vocational arena and special educators would be required to plan collaboratively with vocational educators and employers in order to integrate basic skills instruction and content-area instruction into vocationally relevant activities and experiences.

In order to adequately staff vocationally-oriented programs at the secondary level, both preservice and inservice teacher training would have to be altered. In their discussion of personnel preparation for individuals providing transition services, Asselin, Hanley-Maxwell, and Szymanski (1992) state that:

> To function successfully it is imperative that professionals from the fields of special and vocational education and rehabilitation personnel preparation be based on a transdisciplinary model that develops cooperation, collaboration, and general understanding of specific roles and responsibilities. (p. 265)

Implementation of the proposed model would require that personnel preparation and inservice training assist educators to become proficient in a variety of new skills and instructional methodologies that exploit the potential value of vocational activities.

At the policy level, the sequence of courses and community-based activities that would make up the curriculum in the vocationally-oriented model may not meet local or state educational agency graduation requirements. Zigmond (1990) suggests that waivers be used in order to count alternative courses towards high school graduation. A waiver system may also be a viable option for courses offered through the proposed vocationally oriented model. For example, it may be appropriate to grant mathematics credit to students involved in a job experience that requires the application of a number of math skills and concepts, such as measurement of ingredients for recipes, or for purchasing an appropriate amount of building materials for a construction project. Local educational agencies and school boards will have to develop policies to ensure that students enrolled in vocationally oriented models fulfill all graduation requirements prescribed within local and state policies.

Finally, the issue of tracking or guiding students into specific career paths early in their high school years may be problematic. Edgar (1987) contemplates the positives and negatives associated with the tracking issue by stating:

> What a dilemma—two *equally* appalling alternatives; integrated main-streaming in a nonfunctional curriculum which results in horrendous outcomes (few jobs, high dropout rate) or separate, segregated programs for an already devalued group, a repugnant thought in a democratic society. (p. 560)

The proposed model does not advocate tracking or a segregated educational program. Rather, existing vocational education programs and cooperative education opportunities would become crucial components of the model and would be enhanced through involvement by special education professionals. Additionally, administrators adapting the model would be encouraged to accommodate individual student needs and to make individualized educational planning recommendations.

The current educational system appears not to be working, based on the high dropout rates and poor postschool outcomes that individuals with learning disabilities attain as young adults. It appears that the currently available secondary-level programmatic options lead students into adult life ill prepared to be anything but second-class citizens. It is time to move from discussing alternative programs to implementing options that may appear radically different than current programs that produce marginally effective outcomes.

References

Asselin, S. B., Hanley-Maxwell, C., & Szymanski, E. M. (1992). Transdisciplinary personnel preparation. In F. R. Rusch, L. DeStefano, J. Chadsey-Rusch, L. A. Phelps, & E. Szymanski (Eds.), *Transition from school to adult life: Models, linkages, and policy* (pp. 265–283). Sycamore, IL: Sycamore Publishing Company.

Association on Handicapped Student Service Programs in Postsecondary Education. (1987). *Making the transition to postsecondary education.* Columbus, OH: Author.

Aune, E. (1991). A transition model for postsecondary-bound students with learning disabilities. *Learning Disabilities Research and Practice, 6,* 177–187.

Bos, C. S., & Vaughn, S. (1988). *Strategies for teaching students with learning and behavior problems.* Boston, MA: Allyn and Bacon.

Bursuck, W. D. (1987, October). *Transition planning for adolescents with learning disabilities: An analysis of student IEPs.* Paper presented at the annual conference of the Council for Learning Disabilities, San Diego, CA.

Bursuck, W. D., & Rose, E. (1992). Community college options for students with mild disabilities. In F. R. Rusch, L. DeStefano, J. Chadsey-Rusch, L. A. Phelps, & E. Szymanski (Eds.), *Transition from school to adult life: Models, linkages, and policy* (pp. 71–91). Sycamore, IL: Sycamore Publishing Company.

DeStefano, L., & Wermuth, T. R. (1992). IDEA (P.L. 101-476): Defining a second generation of transition services. In F. R. Rusch, L. DeStefano, J. Chadsey-Rusch, L. A. Phelps, & E. Szymanski (Eds.), *Transition from school to adult life: Models, linkages, and policy* (pp. 537–549). Sycamore, IL: Sycamore Publishing Company.

Edgar, E. (1987). Secondary programs in special education: Are many of them justifiable? *Exceptional Children, 53*, 555–561.

Edgar, E., & Levine, P. (1986). *Washington State follow-up studies of post-secondary special education students.* Seattle, WA: University of Washington.

Gajar, A. H. (1986). *Assisting the learning disabled: A program development and service delivery guide for university diagnosticians, tutors, counselors, and learning disabled students.* Columbus, OH: Association on Handicapped Student Service Programs in Postsecondary Education.

Halpern, A. S. (1992). Transition: Old wine in new bottles. *Exceptional Children, 58*(3), 202–211.

Hanley-Maxwell, C. (1993). *Preparing transition leadership cadres in Wisconsin.* Madison, WI: University of Wisconsin–Madison, The Center on Education and Work.

Harnisch, D. L., Wermuth, T. R., & Zheng, P. (1992, January). *Identification and validation of transition quality indicators: Implications for educational reform.* Paper presented at the third international conference of the Division on Mental Retardation of the Council for Exceptional Children, Honolulu, HI.

Hasazi, S., Gordon, L., & Roe, C. (1985). Factors associated with the employment status of handicapped youth exiting high school from 1979 to 1983. *Exceptional Children, 51*, 455–469.

Mithaug, D. E., Horiuchi, C. M., & Fanning, P. N. (1985). A report on the Colorado statewide follow-up survey of special education students. *Exceptional Children, 55*, 397–404.

Okolo, C. M., & Sitlington, P. (1986). The role of special education in LD adolescents' transition from school to work. *Learning Disability Quarterly, 11*, 292–306.

Sitlington, P. L., Frank, A. R., & Cooper, L. (1989). *Iowa statewide follow-up study: Adult adjustment of individuals with learning disabilities one year after leaving high school.* Des Moines, IA: Iowa Department of Education.

Vogel, S. A. (1990). *College students with learning disabilities: A handbook* (3rd ed.). Pittsburgh, PA: ACLD Bookstore.

Wagner, M. (1989). *The transition experiences of youth with disabilities: A report from the national longitudinal transition study.* Menlo Park, CA: SRI International.

Wagner, M. (1991). *The benefits associated with secondary vocational education for young people with disabilities.* Menlo Park, CA: SRI International.

Wehman, P. (1992). *Life beyond the classroom: Transition strategies for young people with disabilities.* Baltimore, MD: Paul H. Brookes.

Will, M. (1984). *OSERS programming for the transition of youth with disabilities: Bridges from school to working life.* Washington, DC: U.S. Department of Education, Office of Special Education and Rehabilitative Services.

Zigmond, N. (1990). Rethinking secondary school programs for students with learning disabilities, *Focus on Exceptional Children, 23*, 1–22.

Zigmond, N., & Miller, S. E. (1992). Improving high school programs for students with learning disabilities: A matter of substance as well as form. In F. R. Rusch, L. DeStefano, J. Chadsey-Rusch, L. A. Phelps, & E. Szymanski (Eds.), *Transition from school to adult life: Models, linkages, and policy* (pp. 17–31). Sycamore, IL: Sycamore Publishing Company.

Zigmond, N., & Thornton, H. S. (1985). Follow-up of post-secondary age LD graduates and dropouts. *Learning Disabilities Research, 1*, 50–55.

CHAPTER 6

Community College Programs: Their Role in Preparing Students with Learning Disabilities for Employment

Rhonda H. Rapp

From their inception, community colleges, often referred to as the "people's colleges" (American Association of Community and Junior Colleges [AACJC], 1988) or "democracy's college" (Cohen & Brawer, 1987), have stirred an egalitarian zeal among their constituents. The open-door policy has been pursued with an intensity and dedication comparable to that shown by those who championed the populist, the civil rights, and feminist movements. While more elitist institutions may define excellence as exclusion, community colleges have sought excellence in service to the many. Moreover, while traditional institutions too often have been isolated islands, community colleges have built connections within and beyond the campus (AACJC, 1988; Trachtenberg, 1992; Myran, 1978; Long, 1989; Cohen & Brawer, 1987; Laanan, 1995). The community college's connectedness, its open-door policy, diverse educational offerings, expanded support services for students with disabilities, federal laws that bar discrimination, and better preparation at the secondary level have brought an influx of students with learning disabilities into the two-year colleges. (Hawkins, 1992; Nolting, 1991).

What role do community colleges and their programs really play in preparing students with learning disabilities for employment? This chapter represents an attempt to answer the question by outlining the role of community colleges in transitioning students with learning disabilities from college to the world of work.

Community Colleges: An Overview

The term community college is fairly young, having been coined in the 1950s. It refers to comprehensive, public, two-year institutions that are accredited to award "certificates of completion" in vocational (career) or technical areas or both as well as associate of art or science degrees as its highest degrees (Cohen & Brawer, 1982). Community colleges have filled, and continue to fill, an important role in the postsecondary formula. As O'Banion (1989) states:

> The community collage as an institution is one of the most important innovations in the history of higher education. A distinctly American social invention, the public, comprehensive community college is unique in purpose, scope, and design. At no other time, and in no other place, has such a cultural experiment been attempted. The driving premise of the community college—higher education for everyone—is a pivotal educational innovation not just for America, but for the world. (p. 1)

As the name implies, community colleges are not merely institutions located within the geographical parameters of their respective communities but are, in fact, organizations that have, since their beginnings, focused their programs and services on the constantly changing needs of those communities. The characteristics of a community-based college can be divided into two main categories: (a) connections beyond the campus and (b) innovative program offerings within the institution. Examples of connections beyond the campus include, but are not limited to, partnerships with business and industry, corroborative programs with elementary and secondary schools, partnerships with government units, coordinated programs with community groups, specialized programs for specific populations, and coordinated planning with other community agencies. Participatory learning experiences as well as cognitive ones, the wide range of ages, abilities, and life goals represented in its student body, the alternative instructional approaches it arranges to make learning accessible to various community groups (Myran, 1978), flexibility in program content, use of off-campus (in-the-community) sites, and specific outreach and recruitment efforts (Walsh, 1979) are just of few of the characteristic innovative program and service offerings to be found within the community college.

Education for work has been a key component of the community college mandate from the first. Early in this century, L.V. Koos described work preparation as a singular contribution of the movement. The importance of preparation for work was also stressed by the 1948 Truman Commission report on higher education (AACJC, 1988). In their book *The American Community College* (1982), Cohen and Brawer (1987) go so far as to state that two-year colleges are expected to solve the problems of unemployment in their communities by preparing students for jobs. In 1988, the American Association of Community and Junior Colleges reported that two-thirds of all community college students were enrolled in career and technical studies and that only about 25% of the associate degrees awarded were in liberal arts. In fact, the largest number of students (in 1988 and still today) pursue studies in health, business, and engineering fields. This emphasis on vocational (career) and technical programs and the trend toward high enrollments in these programs is not surprising, since most vocational/technical areas of study (i.e., licensed vocational nursing, physical therapy, accounting technology, interior design, and others) offered at community colleges are, in fact, terminal degrees (or certificates of completion) signifying that the graduates are ready for immediate employment and/or pursuit of higher postsecondary degrees. Put simply, in as little as two years, graduates of the nation's community colleges could go straight to work. Many of those who graduate with degrees or certification in allied health or nursing fields could earn salaries comparable to or higher than those of newly graduated students with bachelors degrees in fields such as education or business.

These enrollment trends in the vocational and technical fields, coupled with the reality that most graduates of two-year institutions are ready to join the workforce, place community colleges in a unique position to respond directly to work-based and school-based learning and connecting activities (Laanan, 1995). Hence, the corroborative partnerships between community colleges, tech-prep programs and school-to-work initiatives were formed to move students from secondary schools to postsecondary institutions and into the workforce seamlessly (School-to-Work Opportunities Act of 1994; U.S. Department of Education 1994a). These partnership initiatives were also fueled by projections that, by the year 2000, an estimated 75% of jobs will require post-high school education or training but will not require four-year college degrees (American Association for Community Colleges [AACC], 1993; Brown, Asselin, Hoerner, Daines, & Clowes, 1991). Therefore, the characteristics that set community colleges apart from traditional senior, research universities in combination with the employment trends of the future have "provided a spark of hope" for adults with learning disabilities. Numerous recent studies have found that community colleges are frequently the vehicle of choice by which students with learning disabilities move from high school to the workforce (Hawkins, 1992). In fact, Henderson (1995) found that 55% of students with disabilities attend a two-year college.

The Student with Learning Disabilities
and Work Preparation

Community colleges are experiencing a substantial increase in the enrollment of students with learning disabilities. Improved special education in
elementary schools, middle schools, and high schools has helped students
with learning disabilities to graduate (Nolting, 1991; Brinckerhoff, Shaw,
& McGuire, 1993). In the 1995 report, *College Freshman with Disabilities:
A Triennial Statistical Profile,* Henderson reported that, among freshman
with disabilities, about 1 in 3 (32%) reported a learning disability. In 1988,
the comparable proportion was 15%. The most recent edition of the American Association of Community Colleges' *Directory of Disability Support
Services in Community Colleges* (1992) listed more than 500 institutions providing services for students with disabilities in the United States. However, among the institutions reporting data, learning disabilities constituted by far the largest single category (about 34%) of disability served by
the community college's support office for disabled students. With the
spotlight on school-to-work initiatives, the availability of support services
for students with learning disabilities, the choice of vocational/technical
(terminal) degrees or associate of art or science degrees, and the abun-
dance of career-related programs offered through community colleges,
indications are that the enrollment of students with learning disabilities
will continue its meteoric rise well into the 21st century.

Students with Learning Disabilities

A learning disability is a permanent disorder intrinsic to the individual—
one that affects the manner in which the individual takes in, retains, or
expresses information (Warner, 1988). Commonly recognized deficits in
adults with learning disabilities manifest themselves in one or more of
these general areas: processing written material, written expression, oral
expression, mathematical computation and/or comprehension, reasoning, and/or memory (Hawkins, 1992; Nolting, 1991). Specific functional
limitations of these general learning disability areas which are characteristic of students attending community colleges include, but are not limited to, difficulty with time/money management, difficulty following
directions (oral and/or written), difficulty reading new words, slow reading rate, poor comprehension, problems organizing written papers, frequent and inconsistent spelling errors, difficulty with basic math operations, difficulty with reasoning, difficulty reading and comprehending

word problems, poor vocabulary, difficulty with word retrieval, and problems with grammar. With these characteristics in mind, one turns to how community colleges' unique position in the postsecondary education realm and its community connection meets the job preparation needs of individuals with learning disabilities.

Job Preparation Needs

Development of vocational options and job skills are often seen as critical links in the process of maturing toward adulthood for adults with learning disabilities. Before discussing how community colleges meet the challenge of preparing students with learning disabilities for the world of work, however, one must first delineate "work preparation needs" for adults in general and of this population of students in particular.

Just as there is a movement among K–12 educators to develop standards for what students need to know and be able to do, there is a parallel movement to develop skills standards for the workplace. Since 1991, the U.S. Department of Labor has issued several reports from the Secretary's Commission on Achieving the Necessary Skills (SCANS). To prepare workers for the workplace, the SCANS reports focus on "generic" duties or tasks that job-training programs and employers most want in their employees (National Council on Adult Literacy, 1995).

The SCANS reports documented that the skills most frequently cited as desirable were to be able to learn; read, write and compute; think creatively and solve problems; possess good oral communication and listening skills; have good personal management skills (i.e., self-esteem, goal-setting, time management, motivation); have well-developed group effectiveness (interpersonal) skills; and possess organizational effectiveness and leadership skills. While these are the skills most desired by employers of all employees, they are only the basic job preparation building blocks for adults with learning disabilities attending any college or university.

Adults with learning disabilities are faced with other numerous and complex job preparation needs that are unique to their segment of the larger population with disabilities. In their article titled "Learning Disabilities, Employment Discrimination, and the ADA," Anderson, Kazmierski, and Cronin (1995) compiled a list of skills and competencies from a variety of works in the field that they felt should be the focus of both classroom and community programming as well as an integral part of the Individualized Education Program (IEP)/Individual Transition Plan (ITP). These skills/competencies included:

- demonstrating self-advocacy/self determination/empowerment skills

- articulating strengths and weaknesses

- being able to anticipate difficult tasks and solutions for them

- understanding ADA requirements and rights under the law

- being aware of appropriate modifications for various types of job tasks

- accepting and acting on suggestions for improvement in performing work tasks

- using negotiation skills appropriately

- being able to locate employment/advocacy resources in the community

- demonstrating good general work habits

- participating fully in transitional planning at the secondary level

- participating in paid employment or training situations prior to exiting from secondary programs

As extensive as this and the preceding list of work preparation skills/competencies are, they still fail to address some of the basic job preparation needs of adults/students with learning disabilities. Other studies in the field have indicated that, in fact, students with learning disabilities have employment/career problems due to career naïveté or career immaturity or both; insufficient or nonexistent career/vocational planning; erratic employment history, unemployment, and underemployment; and inadequate attention to social, vocational, and interpersonal skills development as they pertain to independent living and adulthood (Dowdy, Carter, & Smith, 1990). Couple the job preparation needs of students with learning disabilities with the knowledge that secondary schools across the nation are moving away from "special" classes for the disabled and toward inclusion in regular classrooms, and consider also the trend in many schools of ARDing (the process of: Admission, Review, and Dismissal) students with learning disabilities out of high school and into postsecondary education at 18 years of age instead of at 21 years of age (as outlined in the Education for All Handicapped Children Act of 1975, PL 94-142), and one finds a large gap in the school-to-work transition.

Enter the local community college, with its ability to change its programs and services to meet the changing needs of the community and its ability to close some education "gaps" in the community. Community colleges, with their connections to secondary schools, senior universities, rehabilitation services, businesses, and industries, are able to fill the gaps in a multitude of ways. The following discussion highlights those properties/programs/services found in the majority of community colleges.

First, many community colleges have developed transition programs that focus on career exploration including job shadowing and job mentoring, self-advocacy/self-determination, social skills, career search skills, and postsecondary education options (including on-the-job training such as apprenticeships, internships, job shadowing, certificates of completion, associate, and higher degrees, analysis of strengths and weaknesses, resource discovery and development, exploration of compensatory skills transferrable from school to work, and vocational assessments). Many of the nation's transition programs do, in fact, begin while the student with learning disabilities is still in high school. These same transition programs also usually contain some type of a "bridge" program held at the college as the culminating component of the program, providing the student with an opportunity to "get comfortable" with the college environment before actually starting college-level course work (Serebreni, Rumrill, Mullins, & Gordon, 1993; Dowdy, Carter, & Smith, 1990; Samberg, Barr, Hartman, & Murray, 1994).

Second, those at community colleges who provide services for students with disabilities also frequently attend the ARD meetings at high schools within their service areas. Thereby, if they actively participate in the meetings, they provide more on-target advice and information about postsecondary options.

Third, because of the nature of program offerings at community colleges, students with learning disabilities have options to participate in programs of study that are purely vocational (career) or technical in nature with little or no general education course work required. Some of these programs are offered through the college's continuing education department (without any general education requirements) and the rest through regular college courses. Since portions of the vocational/technical course work offered through regular college courses are transferable to upper-division senior colleges, this allows students to decide to pursue a terminal degree only or a degree that will prepare them for the workforce immediately and also transfer to a senior college or university as the first two years' credit for a bachelor's degree.

Fourth, community colleges also serve as connectors from high schools to upper-division universities for students who are not pursuing vocational/technical education but are underprepared for postsecondary course work (Cohen & Brawer, 1987). For these students, the community college offers courses to improve their basic educational skills in reading, mathematico, English, and study skills and provides needed training/ support in self-advocacy/self-determination development and in career exploration.

Fifth, because community colleges are frequently smaller than senior universities, they are able to offer much smaller instructor-to-student ratios in the classroom and more time for one-on-one work with an instructor. Related to this is the heightened (psychological) approachability felt between the student and the community college instructor. Also in many cases, instructors are content specialists and have been practitioners in their field while maintaining close ties to other practitioners within the community. This equips them to provide up-to-the-minute information about the status of job availability and how to best implement accommodations for specific learning disabilities into the workplace.

Sixth, many community colleges offer specialized classes and programs for students with learning disabilities. These range from study skills classes to job exploration sessions, résumé writing, job skills training, and support groups (AACC, 1993; Enright, 1994).

Seventh, many community colleges offer students the option of career training outside the college environment through apprenticeships, internships, (Laanan, 1995; Long, 1989) job-shadowing agreements, volunteer opportunities, and other on-the-job training options.

Eighth, many community colleges offer academic and vocational assessments to their students free of charge. These assessments make it possible for students to learn more about themselves and determine which careers might be their best options, considering the functional impact of their disabilities.

Finally, and possibly most important, community colleges have more flexibility to change program requirements and delivery systems as needed and to develop new programs or expand programs to match the needs of their constituencies in the community.

Job Preparation: Best Practices

Historically, services for students with learning disabilities have focused on relatively short-term immediate academic goals. At many postsecondary institutions, the focus of support services for adults with learning disabilities has consisted of the implementation of reasonable accommodations in the academic setting, the availability of auxiliary aids and services (taped textbooks, note takers, reader/scribes), and training in self-advocacy. However, in the past few years, many service providers from the realm of the disabled student services offices have come to realize that something more is needed to assist students with learning disabilities to attain their career goals than just the successful completion of their academic courses of study. They have come to understand that the interconnections already in place between the community college and the community need to be more fully utilized to develop programs and assistance with more long-term effects for students with learning disabilities. Included here are programs that provide vocational, psychological, and social exploration and growth. While numerous community colleges have taken up this cause and have developed and implemented very successful programs (AACC, 1993), a sampling of a variety of programs that typify the "best practices" in the field will help delineate the qualities of an exemplary program. A list of several such programs follows, with short descriptions of the main components of each. (See resource list for additional information.) While most programs listed provide services for all students with disabilities, it should be remembered that in these examples the largest population receiving services in the programs is that of students with learning disabilities.

- Center for Assessment and Training of the Handicapped (CAT): CAT took shape within the Disability Support Services Office of Valencia Community College in Florida. Its founders focused on providing comprehensive academic and other support services in order to increase the retention of students with disabilities and improve their subsequent employment outcomes.

  With the guidance of an advisory council of people from business and community social service agencies, CAT recruited students, assisted them in developing realistic career goals, and encouraged them to use the various support services offered as part of a comprehensive program. Staff members developed a work evaluation program to assess students' personalities, interests, and aptitudes. They also developed job readiness and employability programs with workshops on résumé writing, effective interviewing, and job search strategies (Samberg et al., 1994).

- Career Empowerment Opportunities Project (C.E.O.): Developed by the Indian River Community College (IRCC) in Florida, the CEO project staff works with IRCC Disabled Student Services, as well as community-based resources, to coordinate an individualized program of services for the unique needs of each student with a disability.

  Students are encouraged to become their own "C.E.O.s" by taking responsibility for directing their lives and careers. Specific services available include individual or group counseling to identify realistic career goals, linkages with available support services on- and off-campus, campus- or community-based job internship experiences, identification of students' preferred learning styles, assistance in identifying and requesting reasonable accommodations for their functional limitations, employability skills training, and interagency transition coordination with local community resources (Indian River Community College, 1994).

- Project ACCESS: Located on the Flathead Reservation in north-western Montana, Salish Kootenai College (SKC) is one of 24 trib-ally controlled colleges in the United States. Designers of this model program serving community college students with disabili-ties sought to reflect the role of tribal colleges and characteristics of Indian culture.

  The project relied on extensive coordination among a variety of service agencies already working with the Salish Kootenai commu-nity. Goals of the collaboration were to develop a comprehensive support program encouraging students with disabilities to enroll, then enabling them to complete their two-year educational pro-grams and transfer to a four-year institution or enter the job market (Samberg et al., 1994).

- WorkAbility: Making Careers more Accessible for Students with Disabilities: A program coordinated by the Metropolitan Com-munity Colleges of Kansas City, the WorkAbility Program seeks to increase the employability of students with disabilities by addressing their unique needs for career counseling, mentoring, job search skills, preparations, and career-related work experi-ences. WorkAbility is the first attempt to coordinate efforts between the district's three colleges to provide career services for students with disabilities. A special needs counselor and placement professional from each campus, along with commu-nity Rehabilitation Representatives, were involved in the pro-gram design (Metropolitan Community Colleges, personal com-munication, July 6, 1994).

- The Learning Disabilities Consortium: The consortium consisted of three institutions in two adjacent states: Central Piedmont Commu-nity College in North Carolina, University of North Carolina, and York Technical College in South Carolina. Central Piedmont coordi-nated the effort between the participating colleges. The goal of the project was to improve the transition from high school to further education and employment for students with learning disabilities. Outreach to the local school system was a main component of the Learning Disabilities Consortium. Its project staff conducted many

developmental activities, including workshops on career exploration, self-advocacy, study skills, and transition to college. High
school students also attended workshops about the college search
process, and the consortium recruited students for the summer
transition to college program (Samberg et al., 1994).

Many services and accommodations offered by the programs just
identified fall under the heading of "academic" support services. However, the main purpose for attending college, for many students, is to gain
or increase skills that will lead to initial employment or to getting a better job (Greenbaum, Graham, & Sacks, 1995). Thus, career exploration
and career development become integral facets of the educational experience, as do the vocational/technical programs, psychological services,
and resource linking available through community colleges. These services play an important role in helping students with learning disabilities
to work through the particular transition challenges they face as they
move from the programs of the community college to the next step of
individual evolution.

Job Preparation: Transition Challenges

Job preparation at the community college level is multifaceted and covers
everything from career exploration to skills analysis, academic and vocational development, and—finally—transitioning from community college
to the next step of the career development ladder, whether into the job
market or further postsecondary education. Adults with learning disabilities moving into the workforce face many transition challenges as they
complete programs of study and earn degrees from the community college (Serebreni et al., 1993). Most of these challenges are linked directly or
indirectly to the job preparation needs outlined earlier in this chapter.
Those needs/challenges include being their own advocates in both academic settings and in the workforce; building and maintaining job search
resources; deciding whether, how, and when to disclose their disabilities;
knowing enough about a disability to be able to inform others about it as
well as about their abilities; knowing their rights under section 504 of the
Rehabilitation Act of 1973 and the Americans with Disabilities Act of
1990; being knowledgeable about reasonable accommodations; being able
to learn required job skills; and being flexible about implementing suggestions for improvement in performance of work tasks.

Many of the transition challenges that students need to address
while moving into the workforce are also important, in the long-run, for
those who decide that their next step in job preparation is to further

their education and train at an upper-division senior university or college. However, these are not the only challenges facing the student with learning disabilities who chooses this route. For this student, knowing what support services are available at the university or college to which he or she is transferring and how to establish links with those services heads the list of transition challenges, especially if the university or college of choice is in another part of the state or in a totally different state. The student who decides to continue his or her postsecondary education will also face the challenge of deciding which university or college is best for his or her career interests and support needs. This student must also be able to evaluate what course(s) will transfer to the new institution and whom to see to confirm articulation agreements.[1] While funding for education may not have been an issue at the community college, it may be of considerable importance at the next postsecondary institution, especially if the student is moving away from home and into a dormitory or apartment. While many students with learning disabilities at the community college level opt to attend school only part-time, attendance in some upper-division universities and colleges may require full-time course work. Therefore, individuals will have to decide if they can continue to be successful academically as full-time students. And finally, the student with learning disabilities who decides to transfer to a university or college outside the home community will have to be able to establish a new support system at the institution that will aid him or her in realizing and achieving educational and career goals.

Summary

From their inception, community colleges have focused their programs and services around the constantly changing needs of the communities in which they are located. The characteristics that set the American community college apart from upper-division universities or colleges are the same characteristics that make it the vehicle of choice by which the majority of students with learning disabilities move from high school into the workforce.

---

[1]Essentially, an "articulation agreement" is a contract between two educational entities that guarantees the transferability of course work credit based upon pre-determined and pre-approved books, curriculum content, syllabi, and essential elements. Articulation agreements may exist between high schools and colleges or universities, between two-year and four-year institutions, between two-year and other two-year institutions, etc.

A key component of the community college mandate has been preparation of students for the world of work. For students with learning disabilities, this preparation continues to include programs that transition the student from high school to college and from college to the next step of a career development scheme. These include self-advocacy skill development, social skills development, resource development and maintenance, career exploration, job search skills, and job training outside the campus through apprenticeships, internships, job shadowing, volunteer opportunities, and other on-the-job training options.

Historically, services for students with learning disabilities have focused on relatively short-term academic goals. However, innovators at many community colleges have realized the need for assistance and services with more long-reaching effects for students with learning disabilities. The best programs in the field are varied, but most include career-related services as well as academic services, counseling services, and bridges that interlink the three.

A student's postsecondary career comprises many challenges and needs as he or she moves away from secondary education towards the workforce. Community colleges are recognized for their open career pathways and for their connections to community services, business and industry, and senior universities. They are also known for their ability to adapt programs and services to meet the needs and challenges of communities and populations they serve. Currently, 55% of students with disabilities attend community colleges in the United States. As these colleges continue to develop and expand their service and program offerings, so, too, will the population of students with learning disabilities continue to grow. For these students, who only a few years ago would never have considered attending a postsecondary institution of any kind, the community college has truly become the "people's college."

Resources

Center for Assessment and Training of the Handicapped (CAT)
Contact: Margaret Edmonds   Number served: 700
          Valencia Community College
          P.O. Box 3028
          Orlando, FL 32802
          (407) 299-5000

Career Empowerment Opportunities Project (C.E.O.)
Contact: Vocational Transition Center   Number served
        Indian River Community College   per year: 150
        3209 Virginia Avenue
        Fort Pierce, FL 34981
        (407) 462-4736

Project ACCESS
Contact: Mike Hermanson   Number Served: 133
        Salish Kootenai College
        Box 117
        Pablo, MT 59885
        (406) 675-4800

Workability: Making Careers More Accessible for Students with Disabilities
Contact: Metropolitan Community College   Number served
        Joanie Friend   per year: 100
        Workability Office
        3200 Broadway
        Kansas City, MO 64111
        (816) 759-4154

The Learning Disabilities Consortium
Contact: Jane Rochester   Number served: 240+
        Office of Disability Services
        University of North Carolina
        Charlotte, NC 28223
        (704) 547-4354

Note: All projects listed here were funded by grants from the U.S. Department of Education Office of Special Education and Rehabilitative Services (OSERS).

References

American Association of Community and Junior Colleges. (1988). *Building communities: A vision for a new century.* Washington, DC: National Center for Higher Education.

American Association for Community Colleges. (1993). *The critical link: Community colleges and the workforce.* Washington DC: American Association for Community Colleges.

Americans with Disabilities Act of 1990, 42 U.S.C. 12101 *et seq.*

Anderson, P. L., Kazmierski, S., & Cronin, M. E. (1995). Learning disabilities, employ-ment discrimination, and the ADA. *Journal of Learning Disabilities, 28*(4), 196–204.

Barnett, L. (Ed.). (1992). *Directory of disability support services in community colleges.* Wash-ington, DC: American Association of Community Colleges.

Brinckerhoff, L. C., Shaw, S. F., & McGuire, J. M. (1993). *Promoting postsecondary education for students with learning disabilities.* Austin, TX: PRO-ED.

Brown, J. M., Asselin, S. B., Hoerner, J. L., Daines, J., & Clowes, D. A. (1992). Should spe-cial needs learners have access to tech prep programs? *The Journal for Vocational Special Needs Education, 14.*

Cohen, A. M., & Brawer, F. B. (1982). *The American community college.* San Francisco: Jossey–Bass.

Cohen, A. M., & Brawer, F. B. (1987). *The collegiate function of community colleges.* San Francisco: Jossey–Bass.

Department of Education (1994a). *Goals 2000 and school-to-work opportunities information bulletin.* Washington, DC: U.S. Department of Education.

Dowdy, C. A., Carter, J. K., & Smith, T. E. C. (1990). Difference in transitional needs of high school students with and without learning disabilties. *Journal of Learning Disabilities, 23*(6), 343–348.

Education for All Handicapped Children Act of 1975, 25 U.S.C. 1400 *et. seq.*

Enright, M. S. (1994). *Career development of college students with disabilities: Results from a national survey of 2-year colleges.* Madison, WI: University of Wisconsin–Madison.

Greenbaum, B., Graham, S., & Scales, W. (1995). Adults with learning disabilities: Educa-tional and social experiences during college. *Exceptional children, 61*(5), 460–471.

Hawkins, B. D. (1992). CCs keep pace with enrollment growth by meeting the needs of the learning-disabled. *Community College Week, 5*(3).

Henderson, C. (1995). *College freshman with disabilities: A triennial statistical profile.* Wash-ington, DC: HEATH Resource Center.

Indian River Community College. (1994). *Career Empowerment Opportunities Project.* Fort Pierce, FL.

Koos, L. V. (1925). *The junior college movement.* Boston, MA: Ginn and Company.

Laanan, F. S. (1995). Community colleges as facilitators of school-to-work. *ERIC digest.* Los Angeles: ERIC Clearinghouse for Community Colleges.

Long, J. P. (1989). The college/private sector connection: Boom or bust? In T. O'Banion (Ed.), *Innovation in the community college* (pp. 159–167). New York: Macmillan.

Myran, G. A. (1978). Antecedents: Evolution of the community-based college. *New Direc-tions for Community Colleges, 6*(1), 1–6.

National Institute for Literacy (1995). *What works? Literacy training in the workplace.* Philadelphia, PA: National Institute for Literacy.

Nolting, P. D. (1991). *Math and the learning disabled student.* Pompano Beach, FL: Aca-demic Success Press, Inc..

O'Banion, T. (1989). The renaissance of innovation. In T. O'Banion (Ed.), *Innovation in the community college.* (p. 1). New York: Macmillan.

Rehabilitation Act of 1973, 29 U.S.C. 701 *et seq.*

Samberg, L., Barr, V., Hartman, R., & Murray, T. (1994). *Educating students with disabilities on campus: Strategies of successful projects.* Washington, DC: HEATH Resource Center.

School to Work Opportunities Act, (1994). Public Law No. 103-239, 108 Stat. 568 (1994).

Serebreni, R., Rumrill, P. D., Mullins, J. A., & Gordon, S. E. (1993). Project Excel: A demonstration of the higher education transition model for high-achieving students with disabilities. *Journal of Postsecondary Education and Disability, 10*(3), 15–23.

Tech prep and school-to-work opportunities information bulletin. Washington DC: U.S. Department of Education, 1994a.

Trachtenberg, S. J. (1992). Educating, training and retraining the American work force for the next decade. *Vital Speeches, 57*(9), 277–280.

Walsh, P. A. (1979). Directions for the Future. *New Directions for Community Colleges, 7*(3), 87–89.

Warner, C. (1988). *Understanding your learning disability.* Newark, Ohio: The Ohio State University at Newark.

CHAPTER 7

Four-Year College Programs: Effective Practices for Developing Employment Skills

Joan M. McGuire

It has been 25 years since the first full-time college support program for students with learning disabilities (LD) was initiated by Gertrude Webb at Curry College in Massachusetts (Brinckerhoff, Shaw, & McGuire, 1993). With the implementation of Section 504 regulations of the Rehabilitation Act of 1973, the increased awareness of the feasibility of college study among high school students and their parents, and the requirement for transition planning at the secondary level, two- and four-year colleges and universities have responded to the needs of students with LD by developing support services ranging from minimal compliance to comprehensive programs.

Nearly 1,000 institutions stated that services are available in the most recent edition of *Peterson's Colleges with Programs for Students with Learning Disabilities* (Mangrum & Strichart, 1992). Learning disabilities unequivocally constitute the largest single category of disabilities represented among full-time, first-time college freshmen (Information from HEATH, 1995). How to assist these adults with LD in preparing for the transition from postsecondary education to employment is a question addressed in this chapter. A review of the literature to examine adult outcomes is followed by a discussion of interventions that colleges may wish to implement as they strive to better prepare their potential graduates for the challenging and changing employment scene.

Outcomes for Adults with Learning Disabilities Participating in Postsecondary Education

Because the phenomenon of enrollment in postsecondary education by adults with learning disabilities is relatively recent, there is a dearth of research regarding outcomes for college graduates or individuals who have completed some postsecondary training. Vogel (1993) stated that, in general, reading rate, spelling, and the mechanics of writing are the most frequently occurring deficits in adults with learning disabilities, while problems with organization, time management, and self-esteem are often evident. In a study by Adelman and Vogel (1990) of 36 college graduates who had participated in a highly coordinated learning disability support program at a small, private midwestern college, responses indicated that processing difficulties (e.g., retention, organization, amount of time required to complete work tasks) were the most frequently cited effects of the LD in the employment setting. Language-related problems such as spelling, writing, and reading comprehension were the second-highest rated area of difficulty. Interestingly, only 4% of the responses referenced social/emotional difficulties while 7% indicated *positive* effects of the learning disability on work. The authors suggested that work success was explained in part by graduates' insight regarding the impact of their LD on their job and their understanding of ways to compensate.

Rogan and Hartman (1990) reported on their longitudinal investigation among adults between the ages of 30 and 40 who had attended a private school for children with LD during their elementary and middle school years. Twenty-eight college graduates responded, providing outcome data that appeared essentially very favorable. Eighty percent had obtained B.S. or B.A. degrees, while six had also earned advanced degrees. Seventy-nine percent reported full-time employment with 75% expressing highly positive job satisfaction. Most (79%) were living independently, with 68% rating their life satisfaction as highly positive. Qualitative comments underscored several themes: the presence of a personal perspective on, and acceptance of, their learning disabilities, as well as positive self-confidence and self-esteem. Rogan and Hartman speculated that successful outcomes were quite possibly related to factors such as supportive families and professionals, including teachers; the age at which the disability was identified; and the nature and intensity of remediation.

The work of Gerber and Reiff (1991), Reiff, Gerber, and Ginsberg (1992), and Reiff, Ginsberg, and Gerber (1995) offers some of the most provocative and illustrative evidence that successful adults with LD can contribute to our understanding of variables that promote positive outcomes. The authors have approached the question of effective practices by employing qualitative methods and eliciting retrospective comments from highly successful adults with LD. Nominations of successful adults were solicited from a variety of sources such as the Orton Dyslexia Society and the Association for Children and Adults with Learning Disabilities (now Learning Disabilities Association of America). Extensive telephone interviews were conducted to gather demographic information and data regarding their occupations and recognition in their fields as well as their job satisfaction. The overriding theme that characterized the lives of the highly successful participants was control, which many noted as the key to their success. Control meant "making conscious decisions to take charge of one's life (i.e., internal decisions) and making adaptations in order to move ahead (i.e., external manifestations)" (Reiff, Gerber, & Ginsberg, 1992, p. 14). Table 7.1 summarizes the variables articulated by 46 adults identified as highly successful.

Although research on postschool outcomes for high school graduates with LD raises serious concerns (McGuire & Apthorp, 1995; Shapiro &

TABLE 7.1
Factors Contributing to Outcomes for Highly Successful Adults
with Learning Disabilities (Reiff, Gerber, & Ginsberg, 199?)

Variable	Definition
Overall Theme:	
Control	• Making conscious decisions to take charge of one's life and to adapt in order to attain goals
Internal Variables:	
Desire	• Having an inner sense and determination to make it and be successful
Goal Orientation	• Having a focus or direction and willingness to change in order to pursue a goal
Reframing	• Reinterpreting one's learning disabilities experience to focus on abilities
External Variables:	
Persistence	• Working longer and harder than others with an ability to deal with failure by not giving up
Goodness-of-Fit	• Choosing work environments and jobs that allow for maximizing strengths and compensating for weaknesses
Learned Creativity	• Developing divergent ways to solve problems by capitalizing on strengths
Social Ecologies	• Seeking and utilizing assistance through supportive people

Lentz, 1991; Siegel, Robert, Waxman, & Gaylord-Ross, 1992; White, 1996), emerging evidence documents successful outcomes for adults with LD who have enrolled in four-year college programs. Because of the relative recency of postsecondary pursuits by this population, a body of knowledge about the relationship between postsecondary support services and subsequent adult outcomes does not exist. Yet there is the opportunity for college personnel to proactively plan for students' next transition: from college to employment. Using an inductive approach, we can extrapolate from what we do know through the limited follow-up studies cited in this section to plan effective interventions at the postsecondary level.

Postsecondary Education: A Bridge to Employment

Employment is a highly desirable adult outcome (Halpern, 1985; Will, 1984), and a logical next step following college, yet few studies have investigated the relationship between postsecondary training and adult adjustment including vocational success. Until empirical investigations are conducted to validate postsecondary program variables that are associated with employment, specialists in the field are left to speculate about effective interventions.

Kohler and Rusch (1995) articulated cautions that pertain to "best practices" associated with positive employment outcomes.

> Program evaluation has focused typically on outcomes achieved by program participants, but in many cases has overlooked specific documentation of the intervention or levels of the intervention, that can be used to assess particular program elements in relation to participant outcomes. (p. 33)

It is premature to render judgment on "best practices" in college support programs until longitudinal studies are conducted to examine several variables, including specific components of postsecondary support services, student characteristics including their degree of utilization of college LD support services, socioeconomic status, and subsequent employment and adult outcomes. Without carefully designed experimental studies, conclusions about effective practices must be cautious in light of the distinction between causation and correlation. Gajar (1996) recommended the use of alternative methodologies, including qualitative and single-subject designs that would add to our understanding of adults with learning disabilities given the heterogeneous nature of this population.

Nevertheless, given the escalation of LD services on college campuses nationwide, it is reasonable to consider program components that have the potential of contributing to successful transition into employment. The next sections illustrate elements that should characterize service delivery systems that will enhance adult outcomes for college students with learning disabilities.

Self-Determination: The Foundation for Support Services

Chickering (1978) described the developmental nature of the progression from adolescence to adulthood to include the following components: achieving competence, managing emotions, becoming autonomous, establishing identity, freeing interpersonal relationships (i.e., developing the capacity to interact with a wider range of persons), clarifying purposes, and developing integrity. Using this framework in juxtaposition with the insights of successful adults with learning disabilities and the construct of self-determination offers a dynamic backdrop against which to consider postsecondary practices and interventions that will enhance employment skills.

Colleges comprise a natural "laboratory" setting where the principle of self-determination should receive paramount priority. Autonomy, the quality of self-regulation, is implied in an environment where student decision-making is valued. Over the past decade, greater emphasis has been placed on the importance of self-determination for persons with disabilities. Ward (1988) spoke of the many facets of self-determination, including self-advocacy, creativity, assertiveness, independence, and self-actualization. Halpern (1994) has emphasized that successful transition must be based upon students' gaining a sense of empowerment. Support services at the postsecondary level should reflect a philosophical grounding in the construct of self-determination. Field and Hoffman (1994) have proposed a model of self-determination that mirrors the observations of the successful adults in previous studies (Adelman & Vogel, 1990; Gerber & Reiff, 1991; Reiff et al., 1992; Reiff et al., 1995; Rogan & Hartman, 1990; Spekman et al., 1992). Figure 7.1 illustrates this model, one that is consistent with an overall mission of higher education: to promote the emergence of adulthood. As portrayed in the figure, the ability to articulate goals that are based upon self-knowledge and valuing, pursue those goals, evaluate the "goodness of fit" between goals and outcomes, and refine or revise goals, are elements that comprise the act of self-determination. A powerful paradigm with relevance to the field of postsecondary disability support services emerges from

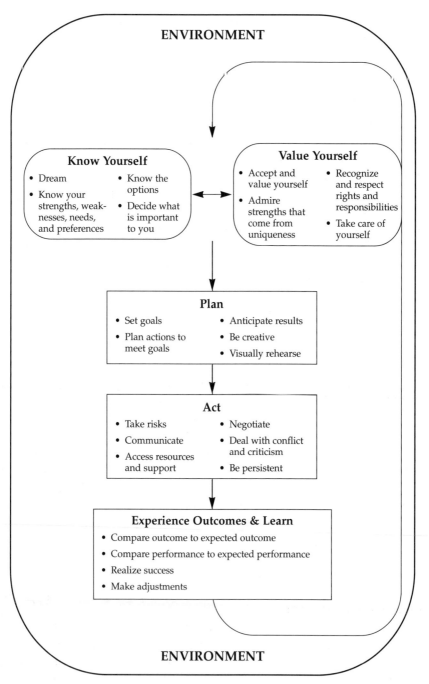

FIGURE 7.1. Model of self-determination. From S. Field & A. Hoffman, 1994. Development of a model of self-determination. *Career Development for Exceptional Individuals, 17,* 159–169. Reprinted with permission.

the synthesis of Field and Hoffman's (1994) model and the themes that characterize the successful adults with learning disabilities in the work of Gerber, Reiff, and Ginsberg (1991, 1992, 1995).

Articulating a Program Philosophy

Vogel (1993) noted that colleges and universities vary in their responses to meeting their legal responsibilities to students with learning disabilities as specified in the regulations for Section 504 of the Rehabilitation Act of 1973. Although no comprehensive survey has been conducted recently at the national level to examine components of postsecondary support services, Bursuck, Rose, Cowen, and Yahaya (1989) suggested three categories: 504 access services, special services with staff who are trained in the field of learning disabilities, and remedial services. Brinckerhoff et al. (1993) pointed out that "no single model or approach will fit every institution, given the diversity that is a hallmark of the American system of higher education" (p. 170).

Regardless of the types of services offered on a campus, they afford the opportunity to incorporate a philosophy promoting student independence and self-determination. The mission of LD services that is consistent with the overall institutional mission should be articulated in a clear, concise manner. By engaging students in a dialogue about their strengths, weaknesses, and need for services (including accommodations from their initial contact with personnel who staff support offices), the framework for all that follows can be established. Emphasis should be placed on student responsibility, self-advocacy, and decision-making. Using Field and Hoffman's (1994) model and reflecting on the patterns articulated by the adults in the work of Gerber et al. (1992), providers will find a powerful context for developing a statement of philosophy.

Operationalizing a Program Philosophy

Figure 7.2 portrays an example of a clearly defined program model and philosophy. At the University of Connecticut, a three-step Continuum of Services (Litt & McGuire, 1989) has been implemented to promote independence and foster success as students with learning disabilities pursue their studies in the standard university curriculum. At the *Direct Instruction* level, students may receive one to three hours of individual service per week. Sessions are structured on a one-to-one basis. The focus of these sessions is on understanding individual strengths and weaknesses, acquiring self-advocacy skills, learning strategies and

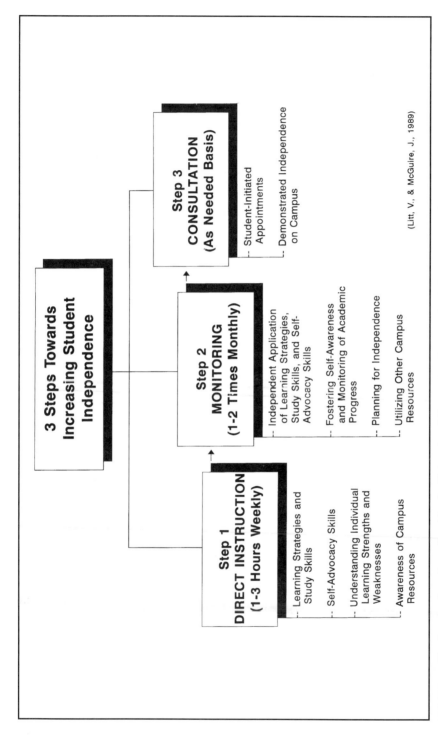

FIGURE 7.2. Continuum of services offered by the University of Connecticut Program for College Students with Learning Disabilities (UPLD). From A. V. Litt & J. M. McGuire, 1989. *Continuum of Services.* Storrs: University of Connecticut, A. J. Pappanikou Center on Special Education and Rehabilitation. Reprinted with permission.

study skills, and gaining an awareness of additional campus resources (i.e., recognizing the presence of effective support systems). At the *Monitoring* level, students receive one to two hours per month of services, reflecting increased independence. Emphasis is on continued independent application of learning strategies, self-awareness and self-advocacy. At the *Consultation* level, students initiate contact with the program when necessary, while independently monitoring their academic progress and accessing other campus resources as needed. Providers of LD program services are trained learning specialists who are graduate students pursuing master's or doctoral programs. Extensive staff training is provided, including a two-day workshop prior to the beginning of the academic year and weekly seminars. Each learning specialist is trained in systematic data collection procedures, and a comprehensive manual contains standardized data collection forms as well as uniform procedures for gathering data (McGuire & Litt, 1992). Students access the Continuum of Services at a level they believe will meet their needs, and they are actively involved in decision-making about their progression to the next level of service.

Results of an exploratory study designed to determine whether students could become increasingly independent while maintaining academic success confirmed that, in fact, students were able to progress along the Continuum of Services and reduce their need for LD support while maintaining a grade point average at or above the minimum university requirement (McGuire, Litt, Silver, Hatzes, & Madaus, 1995). Records of 37 students who elected to begin support services at the *Direct Instruction* level (> six hours of support services per month) were examined. The independent variable was category of students: Cohort 1 (n=27) consisted of those students who received one to two semesters of *Direct Instruction,* then progressed into Levels 2 and 3 of the Continuum of Services; Cohort 2 (n=10) received three to four semesters of *Direct Instruction* and then moved along the Continuum of Services. All subjects were undergraduates; 14 were female; 23 were male; seven were transfer students. Seven were diagnosed as having LD during college, while the remaining 30 had been diagnosed either in elementary or high school. All subjects scored within or above the average range of intelligence on an individual IQ test. Areas in which the LD manifested itself included auditory and visual short-term memory, simultaneous sequencing, rate of processing, and long-term memory. All subjects were full-time students who were enrolled in the standard university curriculum. In addition to receiving support services, students were eligible for reasonable accommodations (e.g., extended time on tests, use of a tape recorder in lectures, and taking tests in a different location) that were provided for those courses in which students and LD program staff members determined a need existed.

Systematic data collection is an integral component of the LD support program at this university. Monthly summaries compiled by each learning specialist detail the number of hours of service provided for each student. A university mainframe database program was used to record extensive information (e.g., demographic, diagnostic, family history, accommodations and LD support services history) on every student. Data from two additional on-campus databases (admissions and the registrar) are imported into the LD database.

Using the extensive records compiled for each student, the number of hours of services per semester for each student was calculated and students' grade point averages at the end of each semester were examined to determine whether the program's goals of increased independence and academic success were being met. Data from fall 1989 through spring 1994 were included. Students' progress was tracked, beginning with their first semester of accessing *Direct Instruction* through each subsequent semester. The enrollment status of students participating in the program was also examined to determine student retention. Descriptive data, including means, ranges, and percentages, were calculated and graphed.

For both cohorts, strong evidence indicated that most students reduced their need for LD support services while maintaining satisfactory academic performances. Figures 7.3 and 7.4 depict these results for Cohort 1 and Cohort 2. The decrease in the number of students in each cohort across the eight semesters of this study can be attributed to the following: (a) students completing their degree programs; (b) students currently enrolled who vary according to their semester standing; (c) students who transferred; and (d) students who were academically dismissed.

As portrayed in Figure 7.3, the average number of support service hours for the 27 students receiving *Direct Instruction* during their first semester of participation in the LD program was 17.6. By their second semester, these students averaged 10.7 hours per semester of *Direct Instruction*. The mean grade point averages for Cohort 1 during their first two semesters were 2.46 and 2.41, respectively.

For Cohort 2 (i.e., students who received three to four semesters of *Direct Instruction*), the average number of service hours for their first two semesters was 20 and 17.5, respectively. As depicted in Figure 7.4, students' mean grade point averages during these two semesters were 2.02 and 2.24.

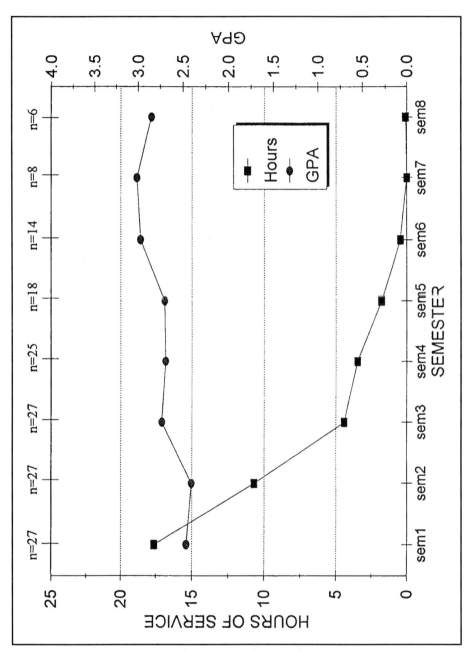

FIGURE 7.3. Service hours and GPA for Cohort 1 over eight semesters (n=27).

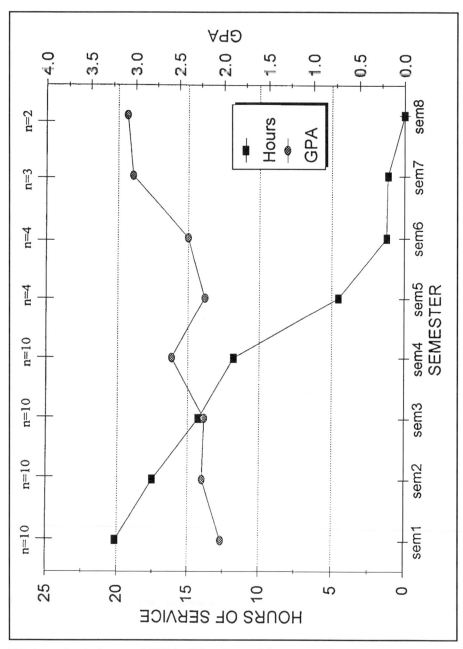

FIGURE 7.4. Service hours and GPA for Cohort 2 over eight semesters (n=10).

Both cohorts demonstrated a trend toward decreasing support service needs while performing at a satisfactory academic level. At no point across the eight semesters did the average GPA for both groups fall below the minimum satisfactory level of 2.0. There was a range, however, of total GPAs (i.e., the average GPA across all semesters of the student's enrollment): for Cohort 1, the range was 1.36–3.84; for Cohort 2, 1.47–3.48.

As indicated in Table 7.2, the majority of students in both cohorts had been graduated (81.1%) or were currently enrolled (8.1%) as of the end of the fall 1995 semester. Three students of the 37 were dismissed for academic reasons; one transferred to a smaller college. For the total sample of 37, the academic dismissal rate was 8.1%. For undergraduates without LD at this university, retention into the fourth year has ranged from 69% to 75.7% over the past five years (*University of Connecticut Fact Book: 1992–93*). It is apparent that the retention rate for students with LD compares very favorably with these figures.

Additional information shown in Table 7.3 demonstrates the importance of systematic data collection to document postsecondary academic outcomes of students with learning disabilities who receive LD support services. To date, 80% of all students participating in the Continuum of Services have either succeeded in their goal of attaining a degree or are pursuing that goal (McGuire, 1995). An academic dismissal rate of 6.3% attests to the success of students in a very academically competitive environment. Exit interviews with students who have transferred or withdrawn indicate the most frequent reason to be the level of difficulty of the university curriculum. Initiatives to survey graduates to determine post-college outcomes including employment are in progress.

TABLE 7.2
Enrollment Status Acording to Cohort

	Enrollment Status			
	G	*CE*	*T*	*AD*
Cohort 1 (n=27)	22 (81.5%)	2 (7.4%)	1 (3.7%)	2 (7.4%)
Cohort 2 (n=10)	8 (80%)	1 (10%)	0	1 (10%)
Total (n=37)	30 (81.1%)	3 (8.1%)	1 (2.7%)	3 (8.1%)

Note. G = graduated; CE = currently enrolled; T = transferred; AD = academically dismissed.

TABLE 7.3
Academic Status of University of Connecticut Students
with Learning Disabilities (n=334)

Status	Number (%)
Currently Enrolled	140 (41.9)
Awarded Degree	128 (38.3)
Academically Dismissed	21 (6.3)
Transferred	14 (4.2)
Withdrew	17 (5.1)
Status Unknown	14 (4.2)

Awareness of Legal Rights and Responsibilities

Regardless of the model or approach to service delivery, students must be familiar with the legal foundations that support equal opportunity if they are to be effective self-advocates. The linchpin for equal access, whether it be in educational or employment settings, is legislation that protects the civil rights of persons with learning disabilities. Although the Americans with Disabilities Act of 1990 has been the focus of discussion and debate since its passage (Anderson, Kazmierski, & Cronin, 1995), Section 504 and its regulations have been, and continue to be, the most relevant for post-secondary settings. Postsecondary service providers should prepare students not only to understand their rights and responsibilities under Section 504 while in college, but also to inform themselves about the legal rights and responsibilities of employers and employees with learning disabilities under the ADA.

Brinckerhoff (1994) described one approach to promoting knowledge of pertinent legislation: a college-based self-advocacy curriculum for high school graduates that includes a series of seminars offered during a six-week summer transition program. The content of one of the 90-minute topical workshops addressed the rights of individuals with learning disabilities by a brief overview of the Individuals with Disabilities Education Act of 1990 (IDEA), P.L. 101-476, Section 504, and the ADA. Students examined a case study, analyzing it in small groups as a method for applying their knowledge of Section 504. By addressing the legal parameters early in the series of seminars, instructors laid the ground for subsequent workshops on self-advocacy and reasonable classroom accommodations.

Several available resources touch upon the area of awareness of the laws. These could be adapted for use in workshops or group discussions facilitated by disability services staff or other staff members, such as counselors. Thompson, Bethea, and Satcher (1994) produced the *Employment Guide for College Students with Disabilities* with sections on understanding the ADA and its impact; when, where, and how to disclose a disability; how to ask for job accommodation; job-seeking and job-keeping skills; and a resource list for job seekers with disabilities. The guide contains many concrete examples to which students can readily relate, such as emphasizing the importance of self-talk that reframes negative statements into positive statements to reduce stress and anxiety during the job search and interview.

Payne (1995) participated in an interactive satellite teleconference sponsored by the University of Georgia that focused on success in the workplace for adults with learning disabilities. She has developed an integrated workplace accommodation model that takes a number of factors into consideration, including the essential functions of a job and the construct of "reasonable accommodation." Latham (1995), an attorney with a broad base of experience in disability and the law, also participated in this conference, discussing legal rights that may facilitate success in the workplace. Postsecondary service providers may want to review resources such as these when planning ways to incorporate awareness activities regarding individual rights and responsibilities under Section 504 and the ADA.

Career Planning

The ability to recognize strengths and weaknesses and focus on the "goodness of fit" between the job and personal attributes distinguished highly successful adults in the Gerber et al. study (1992). There are obvious implications with respect to the importance of career planning. Siperstein (1988) proposed a three-stage model of transition services for college students with learning disabilities, with the third phase to be implemented during their college enrollment. To enhance students' preparation for transition to the workplace, Siperstein suggested that colleges expand their services to include career planning. He described three types of workshops to benefit students: career awareness, job search strategies, and job maintenance skills. Many of the topics he identified parallel suggestions made in this chapter: self-assessment, job exploration, goal setting, interview skills, interacting with fellow employees, and tapping into networks of family and friends to locate jobs.

Ryan and Price (1992) also emphasized the role of career counseling for students with learning disabilities in higher education. They underscored the importance of transition planning that includes training in asking for appropriate accommodations for promotion in the workplace, instruction in how to make informed choices in light of strengths and weaknesses, and disability self-awareness. Similar themes are highlighted by Satcher (1994), who stressed that self-knowledge, knowledge of specific jobs, and self-advocacy are crucial if adults with learning disabilities are to take advantage of the provisions of the Americans with Disabilities Act (ADA).

College LD support services personnel have an opportunity to act as catalysts for collaborative efforts to infuse many of these elements into already existing student services. Siperstein (1988) pointed out that college career services specialists could assume an important role by offering workshops for students with learning disabilities in the areas of career awareness, job search, and job maintenance strategies. Through a number of federally sponsored postsecondary LD career projects, curricular materials have been developed that focus on many aspects of career planning.

For example, the University of Alabama produced a training manual for working with college career counselors in several areas, including information about diagnosis and characteristics, pertinent legislation, career planning and placement issues, and resources for working with this population (Satcher et al., 1993). Another resource is a handbook on job maintenance skills (Harris & Satcher, 1995) that explores key topics important in maintaining successful employment and job relationships, including a positive attitude, commitment, communications skills, social skills, stress management, and job accommodations. At California State University/Northridge, a curriculum was developed to assist campus personnel in providing career services for students with learning disabilities (Goldstein, Chun, Hein, & Kurachi, 1994). An accompanying handbook, designed for consumers, includes sections on discovery as it relates to likes, dislikes, strengths and weaknesses; identifying occupations; presenting and marketing oneself on paper and in person; expectations from the perspective of employers and employees; and facts about the Americans with Disabilities Act (Goldstein, Chun, & Winkler, 1994).

Another federally funded, career-focused project at the University of Massachusetts at Amherst led to development of the Individual Career Plan (ICP), a tool used to encourage self-determination among students with disabilities (Baggett, 1993). Career planning activities culminate in the articulation of a career goal and the steps needed to achieve that goal. The ICP process begins with the disability service provider, but often involves career counselors, academic advisors, and faculty. Students are encouraged to use their plan as a guide that is reviewed on a regular basis. All of these materials lend themselves to use by career center personnel and LD support services staff.

The National Center for Disability Services recently completed a three-year research and demonstration project, "Access to Employment," to improve the employment potential of, and career options for, college students with disabilities in managerial and professional positions. Altschul, Baker, Landers, and Marshall (1995) noted that major obstacles on college campuses are the lack of communication between career services offices and disability offices as well as marginal student response to available programs. Closer working relationships are essential, especially in larger postsecondary settings where decentralization of services is the norm.

Other resources exist that may be pertinent to the development of campus career planning initiatives for students with learning disabilities. Hirshberg (1992) described the emergence of partnerships between business and higher education that can ensure that students are prepared for the demands of the changing workplace. The role colleges and universities play in providing industry with trained personnel cannot be overlooked. In an era when disability rights are assured by the ADA, connections between business and higher education must include access to cooperative programs for *all* qualified students, including those with learning disabilities.

The National Science Foundation (NSF) and the American Association for the Advancement of Science (AAAS), a private, non-profit federation of scientific and engineering societies, have made a major commitment to improving career access in science and technology for individuals with disabilities. On the basis of input resulting from five regional workshops to study issues involved in underrepresentation of persons with disabilities, especially in the fields of science and engineering, a list of strategies for overcoming factors related to limited participation was generated (National Association for Industry-Education Cooperation, 1994). Ongoing efforts to eliminate barriers are under way through projects between the NSF, AAAS, and postsecondary institutions. The American Association for the Advancement of Science (AAAS) has produced a series of four booklets on accessibility including *Barrier-Free in Brief: Laboratories and Classrooms in Science and Engineering* (AAAS, 1991), a resource for professors and laboratory directors on adapted facilities and teaching styles designed to incorporate the needs of students with disabilities. Enhancing the classroom learning environment and tapping into students' strengths contributes to preparation for careers in technical fields that can lead to employment opportunities such as medicine, nursing, and engineering that are predicted to increase at least 80% by the year 2005 (Passell, 1995).

Other colleges and universities such as the University of Minnesota and the University of Wisconsin have received federal funding for projects addressing career planning and students with disabilities. Aune and Baggett (1993) have compiled an extensive annotated bibliography of 31 articles pertinent to college students with disabilities and postsecondary personnel in career centers and disability services offices. Categories include career development/preparation, employment/workplace accommodations, follow-up studies, and policy/professional development. Once again, the underlying theme emphasizes that effective career development should be based upon the construct of self-determination. Resource materials and final products from these sources can be adapted to the needs of individual institutions.

Summary

The field of learning disabilities is advancing into areas seldom considered by professionals and consumers, due, in part, to the "growing up" of children diagnosed in elementary and secondary school settings. One of those areas is postsecondary education and its role in preparing students for transition to and success in the workplace. Given the unique demands of a changing employment market, colleges and universities occupy a pivotal role in preparing students with learning disabilities for their next transition.

Elements of effective strategies are poignantly discussed by the highly successful adults interviewed by Gerber et al. (1992). If postsecondary professionals are to address the transition needs of this population, they would do well to heed the powerful advice of adults who have "made it." The model proposed by Field and Hoffman (1994) should guide efforts at the postsecondary level based upon self-determination, "the ability to define and achieve goals based on a foundation of knowing and valuing oneself" (p. 164). Support services should incorporate a philosophy that respects the rights of students with learning disabilities to make decisions. Brinckerhoff, Shaw, and McGuire (1996) have proposed that "training for independence should become the focus of every activity" (p. 87). Self-advocacy, goal setting, career planning, and problem solving should be reinforced. As postsecondary service delivery models are examined by their coordinators, careful attention should be given to how these elements are incorporated in the overall program model and day-to-day activities. Using a graphic display such as the Continuum of Services (Litt & McGuire, 1989) provides a clear portrayal for students of the mechanism for achieving independence. When developing a model, service providers should bear in mind employers' expectations for the following skills in future employees: (a) basic skills (relating to dealing with information and problem solving); (b) organizational/ leadership skills; (c) self-esteem/goal setting/motivation; (d) interpersonal/teamwork skills; (e) problem solving/creative thinking; (f) oral communication skills; and (g) learning strategies and generalization skills (Carnevale, Gainer, & Meltzer, 1988).

As college students with learning disabilities transition into the workplace, efforts should be initiated to learn from these former students for the purpose of revising or changing approaches to support service delivery and career preparation. Colleges have the unique opportunity to proactively design follow-along data collection methods to systematically implement at multiple points and document outcomes over time. As pointed out by Halpern (1990), this strategy is superior to follow-up strategies that are usually one-shot attempts to gather information.

Finally, adulthood should be conceptualized from a lifespan approach rather than from a "finished product" perspective (Bassett, Polloway, & Patton, 1994). Smith (1996) proposed the use of stage theories of adult development to frame our discussions of the needs of adults with learning disabilities. Although the theories he reviewed vary according to constructs and emphasis, several general assumptions are common across these theories:

1. Everyone passes through life stages in basically the same manner; there is a fundamental universality to the human development experience.
2. Everyone passes through the life stages in the same order; there is a basic sequentiality to the human experience.
3. There are adaptive (positive) ways and maladaptive (negative) ways of going through the sequence of stages. (p. 13)

Smith (1996) wisely pointed out that professionals should consider the values and expectations articulated in the literature defining normal adulthood as a backdrop for examining outcomes for adults with learning disabilities. With a theoretical rationale gleaned from one or more of these adult development perspectives, the model proposed by Cronin, Patton, and Polloway (cited in Patton & Polloway, 1996, p. 7) offers an approach with the potential of capturing the diversity subsumed within the population of adults with learning disabilities. Six domains characterize the major life demands of adulthood: employment-education, home and family, leisure pursuits, community involvement, emotional and physical health, and personal responsibility and relationships. Qualitative methods would appear particularly well-suited to the observation of variables associated with both effective postsecondary service delivery models and the six domains of adult outcomes identified by Cronin et al. (1996). As was so vividly portrayed in the qualitative work of Gerber and Reiff (1991), adults with learning disabilities who have exited postsecondary education and transitioned into employment have a plethora of information and insights that interviews and case studies can capture in a manner not integral to quantitative methodologies. The current void in the literature regarding outcomes for college graduates can be rectified only through systematic efforts to chronicle their life experiences, including their participation in postsecondary education. Studies generating from such a framework could make a substantial contribution to our understanding of adult adjustment.

Resources for Career Planning

California State University, Northridge
    The Career Center
    Students with Disability
    Internship Project
    18111 Nordhoff Street–USU
    Northridge, CA 91330-8241

National Center for Disability Services
    201 I.U. Willets Road
    Albertson, NY 11507

The University of Alabama
    c/o Jamie Satcher
    Box 870231
    Tuscaloosa, AL 35487-0231

The University of Georgia
  Learning Disabilities Research and Training Center
  534 Aderhold Hall
  Athens, GA 30602

University of Massachusetts–Amherst
  Center for Counseling and Academic Development
  123 Berkshire House
  Amherst, MA 01003

University of Minnesota
  Disability Services
  12 Johnston
  101 Pleasant Street, SE
  Minneapolis, MN 55455-0432

University of Wisconsin–Madison
  Center on Education and Work
  School of Education
  1025 West Johnson Street, Room 964
  Madison, WI 53706-1796

References

Adelman, P. B., & Vogel, S. A. (1990). College graduates with learning disabilities: Employment attainment and career patterns. *Learning Disability Quarterly, 13,* 154–166.

Altschul, P., Baker, J., Landers, K., & Marshall, K. (1995, July). *Interviewing skills workshop: Enhancing communication between employers and college students with disabilities.* Presentation at the conference of the Association on Higher Education and Disability (AHEAD), San Jose, CA.

American Association for the Advancement of Science (1991). *Barrier-free in brief.* Laboratories and classrooms in science and engineering. Washington, DC: Author.

Americans with Disabilities Act of 1990 (ADA), P.L. 101-336, 42 U.S.C. 12101, note.

Anderson, P. L., Kazmierski, S., & Cronin, M. E. (1995). Learning disabilities employment discrimination and the ADA. *Journal of Learning Disabilities, 18,* 196–204.

Aune, B., & Baggett, D. (1993). *Career development and employment for college students and graduates with disabilities: An annotated bibliography.* Minneapolis: University of Minnesota, Office for Students with Disabilities; Amherst: University of Massachusetts Center for Counseling and Academic Development. (ERIC Document Reproduction Service No. ED 368 117)

Baggett, D. (1993). *An individual career plan for students with disabilities in higher education.* Paper presented at the annual international conference of the Council for Exceptional Children/Division on Career Development and Transition, Albuquerque, NM. (ERIC Document Reproduction Service No. ED 369 236)

Bassett, D. S., Polloway, E. A., & Patton, J. R. (1994). Learning disabilities: Perspectives on adult development. In P. Gerber & H. Reiff (Eds.), *Learning disabilities: Persisting problems and evolving issues* (pp. 10–19). Stoneham, MA: Butterworth-Heinemann.

Brinckerhoff, L. C. (1994). Developing effective self-advocacy skills in college-bound students with learning disabilities. *Intervention in School and Clinic, 29,* 229–237.

Brinckerhoff, L. C., Shaw, S. F., & McGuire, J. M. (1993). *Promoting postsecondary education for students with learning disabilities: A handbook for practitioners.* Austin, TX: PRO-ED.

Brinckerhoff, L. C., Shaw, S. F., & McGuire, J. M. (1996). Promoting access, accommodations, and independence for college students with learning disabilities. In J. R. Patton & E. A. Polloway (Eds.), *Learning disabilities: The challenges of adulthood* (pp. 71–92). Austin, TX: PRO-ED.

Bursuck, W., Rose, E., Cowen, S., & Yahaya, M. (1989). Nationwide survey of postsecondary education services for students with learning disabilities. *Exceptional Children, 56,* 236–245.

Carnevale, A. P., Gainer, L. J., & Meltzer, A. S. (1988). *Workplace basics: The skills employers want* (DOL Publication No. 0-225-795). Washington, DC: U.S. Government Printing Office.

Chickering, A. W. (1978). *Education and identity.* San Francisco: Jossey-Bass Publishers.

Education for All Handicapped Children Act of 1975 (EHA), P.L. 94-142, 20 U.S.C. § 1401 *et. seq.* (now known as Individuals with Disabilities Education Act [IDEA], P.L. 101-476).

Field, S., & Hoffman, A. (1994). Development of a model of self-determination. *Career Development for Exceptional Individuals, 17,* 159–169.

Gajar, A. (1996). Current and future research. In J. R. Patton & E. A. Polloway (Eds.), *Learning disabilities: The challenges of adulthood* (pp. 195–203). Austin, TX: PRO-ED.

Gerber, P. J., Ginsberg, R., & Reiff, H. B. (1992). Identifying alterable patterns in employment success for highly successful adults with learning disabilities. *Journal of Learning Disabilities, 25,* 475–487.

Gerber, P. J., & Reiff, H. B. (1991). *Speaking for themselves: Ethnographic interviews with adults with learning disabilities.* Ann Arbor: The University of Michigan Press.

Goldstein, T., Chun, M., Hein, V., & Kurachi, C. (1994). *Job seeking skills for people with disabilities.* Northridge: California State University.

Goldstein, T., Chun, M., & Winkler, M. (1994). *Job seeking skills for people with disabilities: A guide to success.* Northridge: California State University.

Halpern, A. S. (1985). Transition: A look at the foundations. *Exceptional Children, 51,* 479–486.

Halpern, A. S. (1990). A methodological review of follow-up and follow-along studies tracking school leavers from special education. *Career Development for Exceptional Individuals, 13,* 13–27.

Halpern, A. S. (1994). The transition of youth with disabilities to adult life: A position statement of the Division on Career Development and Transition. The Council for Exceptional Children. *Career Development for Exceptional Individuals, 17,* 115–124.

Harris, P., & Satcher, J. (1995). *Job maintenance skills.* Tuscaloosa: The University of Alabama, Center for Teaching and Learning, Bridges to Career Success (Grant #H078C20038).

Hirshberg, D. (1992). Higher education-business partnerships: Development of critical relationships. *The ERIC Review, 2,* 7–11.

Individuals with Disabilities Education Act of 1990, 20 U.S.C. 1400 *et seq.*

Information from HEATH. (1995, June/July). *Facts you can use: College freshmen with disabilities* (p. 6). Washington, DC: Author.

Kohler, P. D., & Rusch, F. R. (1995). School to work transition: Identification of employment-related outcome and activity indicators. *Career Development for Exceptional Individuals, 18,* 33–50.

Latham, P. H. (1995, May). *Legal rights in the workplace for individuals with learning disabilities.* Paper presented at satellite teleconference, Success in the workplace: Employability issues facing adults with learning disabilities, sponsored by The Learning Disabilities Research and Training Center. Athens, GA. University of Georgia.

Litt, A. V., & McGuire, J. M. (1989). *Continuum of services.* Storrs: University of Connecticut, A. J. Pappanikou Center on Special Education and Rehabilitation: A University Affiliated Program.

Mangrum, C. T., & Strichart, S. S. (Eds.). (1992). *Peterson's colleges with programs for students with learning disabilities* (3rd ed.). Princeton, NJ: Peterson's Guides.

McGuire, J. M. (1995, September). *Academic status of university students receiving support services from the University Program for College Students with Learning Disabilities* (UPLD). Unpublished data. University of Connecticut, Storrs.

McGuire, J. M., & Apthorp, H. S. (1995). *Connecticut youth with disabilities: An analysis of post high school outcomes for cohort two.* Storrs: University of Connecticut, A. J. Pappanikou Center on Special Education and Rehabilitation: A University Affiliated Program.

McGuire, J. M., & Litt, A. V. (1992). *Learning specialist training manual.* Storrs: University of Connecticut, A. J. Pappanikou Center on Special Education and Rehabilitation: A University Affiliated Program.

McGuire, J. M., Litt, A. V., Silver, B., Hatzes, N., & Madaus, J. (1995, April). *An exploratory study of the effectiveness of a university support program for students with learning disabilities in promoting independence and success.* Paper presented at the annual meeting of the American Educational Research Association, San Francisco, CA.

National Association for Industry–Education Cooperation. (1994). *Improving career access in science and engineering for students with disabilities.* Buffalo, NY: Author.

Passell, P. (1995, September 3). Job advice for 2005: Don't be a farmer, play one on TV. *The New York Times,* Section 3, p. 9.

Patton, J. R., & Polloway, E. A. (1996). Adults with learning disabilities: An emerging area of professional interest and public attention. In J. Patton & E. Polloway

(Eds.), *Learning disabilities: The challenges of adulthood* (pp. 1–10). Austin, TX: PRO-ED.

Payne, N. (1995, May). *Designing workplace accommodations for people with special learning needs and related disabilities.* Paper presented at satellite teleconference, Success in the workplace: Employability issues facing adults with learning disabilities, sponsored by The Learning Disabilities Research and Training Center. Athens, GA: University of Georgia.

Rehabilitation Act of 1973, Section 504, P.L. 93-112, 29 U.S.C. § 794 (1977).

Reiff, H. B., Gerber, P. J., & Ginsberg, R. (1992). Learning to achieve: Suggestions from adults with learning disabilities. *Journal of Postsecondary Education and Disability, 10,* 11–23.

Reiff, H. B., Ginsberg, R., & Gerber, P. J. (1995). New perspectives on teaching from successful adults with learning disabilities. *Remedial and Special Education, 16,* 29–37.

Rogan, L. L., & Hartman, L. D. (1990). Adult outcomes of learning disabled students ten years after initial follow-up. *Learning Disabilities Focus, 5,* 91–102.

Ryan, A. G., & Price, L. (1992). Adults with LD in the 1990s. *Intervention in School and Clinic, 28,* 6–20.

Satcher, J. (1994). Employment, the Americans with Disabilities Act of 1990, and youth with learning disabilities. *Intervention in School and Clinic, 29,* 208–211.

Satcher, J., McGhee, M., Friend, P., Brandt, R. K., Walters-Kemp, P., & Barker, M. (1993). *Bridges to career success: A model for training career counselors serving college students with learning disabilities.* Tuscaloosa: The University of Alabama, Center for Teaching and Learning.

Shapiro, E. S., & Lentz, F. E. (1991). Vocational-technical programs: Follow-up of students with learning disabilities. *Exceptional Children, 58,* 47–59.

Siegel, S., Robert, M., Waxman, M., & Gaylord-Ross, R. (1992). A follow-along study of participants in a longitudinal transition program for youths with mild disabilities. *Exceptional Children, 58,* 346–356.

Siperstein, G. N. (1988). Students with learning disabilities in college: The need for a programmatic approach to critical transitions. *Journal of Learning Disabilities, 21,* 431–436.

Smith, J. D. (1996). Adult development theories: An overview and reflection on their relevance for learning disabilities. In J. R. Patton & E. A. Polloway (Eds.), *Learning disabilities: The challenges of adulthood* (pp. 11–23). Austin, TX: PRO-ED.

Spekman, M. J., Goldberg, R. J., & Herman, K. L. (1992). Learning disabled children grow up: A search for factors related to success in the young adult years. *Learning Disabilities Research and Practice, 7,* 161–170.

Thompson, A. R., Bethea, L., & Satcher, J. (1994). *Employment guide for college students with disabilities.* Mississippi State: Mississippi State University, The Career Development Project.

University of Connecticut Fact Book: 1992–93. (1992). Storrs: University of Connecticut, Office of Institutional Research.

Vogel, S. A. (1993). A retrospective and prospective view of postsecondary education for adults with learning disabilities. In S. A. Vogel & P. B. Adelman (Eds.), *Success for college students with learning disabilities* (pp. 3–20). New York: Springer–Verlag.

Ward, M. J. (1988). The many facets of self-determination. *National Information Center for Children and Youth with Handicaps: Transition Summary, 5,* 2–3.

White, W. J. (1996). The postschool adjustment of persons with learning disabilities: Current status and future projections. In J. R. Patton & E. A. Polloway (Eds.), *Learning disabilities: The challenges of adulthood* (pp. 45–59). Austin, TX: PRO-ED.

Will, M. (1984). *OSERS programming for the transition of youth with disabilities: Bridges from school to working life.* Washington, DC: U.S. Department of Education.

CHAPTER 8

Students with Learning Disabilities in Graduate or Professional Programs: Emerging Issues on Campus and Challenges to Employment

Loring C. Brinckerhoff

According to recent figures, close to 2 million students are now enrolled in graduate and professional schools in United States. In the past 25 years, the number of Americans who have obtained master's degrees has climbed by 60% to 350,000 annually (*U.S. News & World Report*, 1995). Applications to law schools are now gradually dropping, down to 78,000 applicants in 1995, from a peak of 94,000 in 1991. Columbia University Law School, is presently experiencing an 8% decline in applicants; nonetheless, more than 6,000 applicants are vying for 340 spots (Johnson, 1995). For the third year in a row, the number of applicants to the nation's 125 medical schools has reached an all-time high. Boston University School of Medicine was deluged with more than 12,000 applications for admission for just over 100 openings this year. These figures represent more than twice the number of applicants received in 1988. Educators cite two main reasons for this surge of interest in medical school: a renewal of altruism and a belief that despite a changing economy, doctors will always have a job. There are also some very practical and persuasive financial reasons why so many students are choosing to enroll in graduate school. According to the U. S. Bureau of Labor Statistics, the median annual salary of those with a professional degree such as an M.B.A. or a J.D. is nearly double that of those with only a bachelor's degree—$67,131 versus $34,666. The benefits of going to graduate school should not be simply measured in dollars; for many individuals, a graduate degree will provide career opportunities that would have been unreachable without additional course work and specialized training.

The composition and demographics of graduate and professional programs is rapidly changing. For example, nearly half of all applicants to medical schools are female; one out of five applicants represent non-traditional backgrounds; and 8.4% of graduate students report a disability (*U.S. News & World Report,* 1995; information from HEATH, 1994). These findings indicate that, like their non-disabled counterparts, students with disabilities are knocking on the doors of graduate and professional programs in increasing numbers. In some cases, they have been met with skepticism; in other instances, they are welcomed. The Association of Academic Psychiatrists (AAP) stated in a journal article that "medical schools should educate a diverse group of medical students recognizing that in such diversity lies excellence. Included in this group are qualified students who have impairments, functional limitations and/or disabilities" (Recommended Guides," 1993).

One way to get a sense of exactly how many students with disabilities are pursuing graduate study is to review the number of requests for special test accommodations made for the Law School Admission Test (LSAT), Graduate Management Admissions Test (GMAT), and Medical College Admission Test (MCAT)s, as well as for state licensing examinations. In 1988 in the state of California, less than 1% of the test population requested special accommodations in testing for the bar exam. By 1995, more than 4% of the students received accommodations. The majority of these requests involved students with physical disabilities, but an increasing number involved individuals with learning disabilities, particularly dyslexia, and more recently, adult attention deficit disorder (Corneille, 1995). In 1994, the National Board of Medical Examiners reported that it had received nearly 400 requests for alternative testing accommodations for the U. S. Medical Licensing Examinations (USMLE) due to documented disabilities. LSAT administrators experienced more than a threefold increase in requests from 1994 to 1995. On many college campuses, students with learning disabilities (LD) represent the largest consumer group of students with disabilities (Jarrow, 1991).

This upsurge of interest in graduate study by individuals with learning disabilities can be attributed, in part, to greater opportunities that many persons with disabilities are experiencing as a result of the passage of the Americans with Disabilities Act of 1990 (ADA). The ADA clearly articulates that students with learning disabilities have the same rights to instructional and programmatic access as students with physical disabilities. Furthermore, Title II, (Section 202) of the ADA specifically states that, "no qualified individual with a disability shall, by reason of such disability, be excluded from participation in or be denied the benefits of the services, programs, or activities of a public entity . . ." Given these protections under the ADA, job discrimination is less likely, thus increasing the value of a graduate school investment. In addition, the ADA extends coverage to private colleges and universities at both the undergraduate and graduate levels and grants new protections not required previously by the Rehabilitation Act of 1973. For example, individuals who associate with, or care for, a person with a disability cannot be discriminated against on the basis of their association with a disabled individual (Essex-Sorlie, 1994; Kincaid, 1995). A greater awareness of learning disabilities and Attention-Deficit/Hyperactivity Disorders (ADHD) by faculty and administrators at the postsecondary level, and the proliferation of support services on college campuses in general, has encouraged these students to continue their education beyond the undergraduate level (Brinckerhoff, Shaw, & McGuire, 1996; Vogel, 1993).

The intent of this chapter is to explore this new graduate-level frontier by broadening the reader's understanding of this unique cohort of students by (a) defining learning disabilities, (b) highlighting the characteristics of graduate students with learning disabilities, or ADHD or both, (c) addressing graduate admissions requirements, (d) determining academic supports and accommodations; and (e) citing some challenges to employment.

Defining Learning Disabilities

Barbara Bateman (1992), one of the most respected leaders in the field of learning disabilities, noted that, even after a quarter of a century of evolution in this field, we still find individuals who believe that learning disabilities do not exist. Unfortunately, there are still individuals directing universities, graduate schools, medical schools, and corporate training programs who think that a learning disability is just another fancy excuse for getting special attention. Arthur Frakt, dean of Widener University School of Law, is one of the ADA's most vocal critics. He believes that the ADA is too broad and that law schools, in particular, have become too accommodating. He contends that "Everyone who is self-referred to a psychologist or counselor comes back with a diagnosis of a learning disability of some kind" (Cleesattle & Seiberg, 1995, p. 2). At Boston University, Provost and President-elect Jon Westling complained in a speech to the Heritage Foundation that laws to protect students with learning disabilities were being used "to force colleges and universities to lower academic standards" (Shapiro, 1996).

Many higher education administrators and corporate executives are searching for a "medical or scientific" formula for identifying learning disabilities. They have yet to realize that the very nature of the disability makes it impossible to quantify into a neat package. Meltzer (1994) points out that "product-oriented measures including IQ and standardized achievement tests, have been the cornerstone of the diagnosis of learning disabilities . . . but these measures often emphasize the end-product, or learning outcomes while largely ignoring the processes and strategies that students use to approach various learning and problem solving situations." Attempts are underway for developing an operational definition of learning disabilities based on the National Joint Committee on Learning Disabilities' (NJCLD) definition that may help practitioners and diagnosticians with a step-by-step process for sorting out college students with learning disabilities from those who are "underachievers or slow learners" (Shaw, Cullen, McGuire, & Brinckerhoff, 1995).

The NJCLD defines learning disabilities as a

> general term that refers to a heterogeneous group of disorders manifested by significant difficulties in the acquisition and use of listening, speaking, reading, writing, reasoning, or mathematical abilities. These disorders are intrinsic to the individual, presumed to be due to central nervous system dysfunction, and may occur across the life span. Problems with self-regulatory behaviors, social perception, and social interaction may exist with learning disabilities but do not by themselves constitute a learning disability. Although learning disabilities may occur concomitantly with other handicapping conditions (for example, sensory impairments, emotional disturbance) or with extrinsic influences, such as cultural differences and/or insufficient or inappropriate instruction, they are not the result of those conditions or influences (National Joint Committee on Learning Disabilities, 1994, p. 65).

It is important to point out that not all individuals with learning disabilities are affected in the same way or to the same degree. The effects will vary according to the type and severity of the LD; the individual's understanding and acceptance of his or her learning disability; his or her ability to compensate for the LD and the complexity of the learning task at hand. If more postsecondary service providers adhered to the NJCLD definition, we would not be faced with the rampant over-identification and misidentification of college students that we now face. Don Hammill (1990) has been one of the guiding forces behind this definition, and he states that, "The NJCLD never intended to write the perfect definition, only a better one." He adds that, "the NJCLD definition provides a viable definitional umbrella under which all of us may find shelter. It may serve us well during the rainy days ahead" (p. 46).

Therefore, by definition, individuals with learning disabilities are a heterogeneous group who possess a wide array of strengths and limitations. By the time LD students are ready to attend graduate school, they typically have learned how to compensate for their limitations and to capitalize on their abilities. Gerber and Reiff (1991, 1994) have written extensively about successful adults with learning disabilities. They suggest that adolescents and adults with learning disabilities need to be taught to "reframe" their disability in a more positive light. Reframing requires the LD student to reinterpret his or her learning disability experience in a more productive and positive manner. The LD is viewed as just one slice of the student's identity. The research findings of Gerber, Ginsberg and Reiff (1992) indicated that successful adults with learning disabilities often have learned to accept that, despite the learning disability, they can still meet their goals. The implication here is that "if someone doesn't accept that the learning disability is real and that it is something he or she will always have to confront, moving ahead is impossible" (p. 481). By recognizing, understanding, and accepting their LD, students with learning disabilities will be better prepared to advocate for themselves, both on campus and, ultimately, in the world of work.

In employment settings, the determination of whether or not a learning disability is a substantial impairment to a major life activity can be particularly challenging for workers with learning disabilities. For example, management personnel may question whether an employee with an "alleged" learning disability is just looking for a short-cut or requesting a job accommodation that is necessary under the ADA. Employees with learning disabilities may need to assure their supervisors that they are not looking for preferential treatment, but because of a specific learning disability they need a modification in the work environment that will enable them to participate more fully. New professionals in the fields of law or medicine with learning disabilities who have recently graduated from prestigious programs with solid G.P.A.s and strong standardized test scores may discover that they have to prove to a new employer that their learning disability actually "substantially limits a major life activity." This becomes even more burdensome for these talented young professionals who may try and premise their need for accommodations on the fact that they have a significant learning disability. Uninformed employers may challenge such requests for accommodations under the assumption that if the employee with LD could graduate from a professional school with a solid track record, then learning capacity couldn't possibly be limited to warrant an accommodation on the job.

Characteristics of Graduate Students with LD

Given the heterogeneous nature of this population, it is very difficult to characterize graduate students with learning disabilities as conforming to one specific profile. Students with prior histories of learning disabilities who have been fortunate enough to be accepted into graduate or professional programs often have been diagnosed as both learning disabled *and* gifted. Many of these individuals were able to manage an undergraduate education because of their giftedness, meticulous organization, verbal abilities, and work ethic. They often exhibit significant abilities and creative talents despite some fundamental problems with reading, written language, or mathematical reasoning and problem solving. This group of students is often misunderstood, in part, because unique abilities have tended to mask disabilities.

In the world of work, gifted individuals with learning disabilities may appear to be model applicants for a given position in light of superior test scores, letters of recommendation, or grades in a chosen field, or all of these. As a result, employers may falsely assume that such individuals will perform in the superior range across *all* job domains. Given the competitive job market and fear of discrimination, an employee may be reluctant to disclose his or her learning disability, job-related limitations, and any anticipated job accommodations during the interview. In a recent follow-up study of nearly 50 graduates with LD from the University of Maryland, Greenbaum, Graham and Scales (1996) found that of the 46 participants who had been employed at one time or another, only 20% indicated that they had ever disclosed their learning disability when applying for a job. Once hired, employers may come to realize that these employees with LD who interviewed so well may have uneven job performance profiles that result from some type of learning disability. In such instances, the learning disability may directly affect job performance in such a manner that workplace accommodations would be necessary. In the University of Maryland follow-up study, 57% of the participants surveyed indicated that they were still unwilling to reveal their disabilities after being hired. Reasons included fear of discrimination and stigmatization; some respondents indicated they were no longer affected by the disability. This important study showed that, upon entering the workforce, graduates with LD were "unwilling to disclose their learning disabilities, even though such disclosure might result in accommodations that would make them more efficient and effective workers" (p. 172).

Students with LD who have a prior history of learning disabilities are often more ready to self-identify in the admissions process and to seek help before the semester begins. Those individuals with a history of receiving academic accommodations at the undergraduate level often find it easier to access the same accommodations (e.g., additional time, quiet room, and oral exams) since they have a history of success in receiving accommodations. Shaywitz and Shaw (1988) note that gifted students with learning disabilities with the highest probability of success at a competitive institution are those who have "had an opportunity to live with the diagnosis and become comfortable, as indicated by the ability to talk openly about it and accept appropriate help". Regardless of the point at which the learning disability or attention deficit disorder (ADD) is identified, there are some common characteristics that can be noted.

Students with LD who were not formally identified during the undergraduate years are often diagnosed for the first time after performing very poorly on one of the graduate entrance exams. It is not unusual for these students to have "failed" these exams several times before they search in desperation for an answer to the riddle: "How could I score so poorly, given my solid undergraduate record, my preparation, and intellectual abilities?" After a comprehensive diagnostic evaluation, these individuals are often relieved to find out that they have a legitimate disability that directly interferes with their performance on standardized examinations.

To the surprise of many graduate school faculty members and administrators, a large proportion of students with LD and/or ADHD in graduate and professional programs may not be identified until they experience the rigors of the graduate or professional school curriculum. Jordan (1995) recently commented at the 25th-anniversary conference of Curry College's learning disabilities program that "many believe that the term learning disabled graduate or professional student is an oxymoron which just cannot exist." Her point is well taken. Despite their high aptitudes, these students often have a history of performing relatively poorly on standardized tests and in-class exams. This history of uneven test performance is often discordant with written assignments that are completed outside the classroom, such as term papers. Test performance often drops when they feel the pressures of the clock. This, in turn, results in heightened test anxiety, which can magnify the affects of the learning disability. Additional time on exams provides students with LD the opportunity to selectively attend to information, to organize their thoughts, and to retrieve words from memory. At Colgate University, a graduate student with LD recently reflected upon his first year at law school by stating, "I benefited by learning an unsurpassable work ethic because to become successful in law I would have to work much harder and longer than other students. It was seriously disconcerting my first semester when I scored only a 2.24 GPA. I did not finish any of my first semester exams. I was told this was normal" (personal communication, October 1995).

As previously mentioned, IQ scores are often in the average-to-gifted range, with the greatest difficulties noted on tests that tap into language processing abilities. Large discrepancies are often noted between reading and listening comprehension. Students frequently find that they can read technical material, but they don't remember what they have read. In some cases, problems with reading comprehension can be attributed to slow visual processing speed or decoding deficits; in other cases, reading comprehension is directly affected by short-term memory problems. Some students with LD find that their biggest problem with reading comprehension at the graduate level is that they interpret the information too literally. These students are often overwhelmed by the rapid pace of the program, the amount of assigned reading in graduate school, and the amount of lecture material that must be quickly learned and integrated into practice. Written work is often characterized by significant problems with spelling, poor handwriting, and weak grammar skills. Writing a master's thesis or a doctoral dissertation is particularly challenging, because many of these graduate students lack the day-to-day organizational and time management skills needed to budget their time effectively to meet longstanding deadlines. Retrieving and organizing large quantities of technical information from a large university library can be overwhelming. On the positive side, verbal abilities are often a high point for these students. Law students with strong verbal skills often gravitate to the courtroom, and medical students with strong verbal abilities are often praised for their bedside manner and clinical abilities.

Graduate Students with Attention Deficit Disorders

Graduate students with attention-deficit/hyperactivity disorders (ADHD) often have to contend with problems of impulsivity, restlessness, and a short attention span. With adults, an ADHD is often a "hidden disorder," with its symptoms obscured by problems with relationships, staying organized, and holding a steady job. Many adults who are diagnosed as having ADHD are first recognized as having problems with substance abuse or impulse control (Lerner, Lowenthal & Lerner, 1995). Focusing attention in a classroom or in a science laboratory may be hampered by difficulties with selective attention, impulsivity and a tendency to persevere on a given task for too long. For students who do not exhibit excessive motor activity, and who appear inattentive, the ADHD may be limited to problems with controlling the internal distractions of being bombarded with a wellspring of thoughts, facts, and ideas.

Some graduate students with ADHD seem to thrive on the stimulation found in fast-paced graduate programs where juggling multiple tasks is the norm. For others, the biggest challenge is not whether they can pay attention, but rather how can they can effectively sustain attention over time. As a result, more and more students are looking for effective treatments that may include therapy, medication, and counseling. Graduate school may prove to be a better place to find out one's best dosage for a given medication and patterns for use than in the working world where symptoms of dosage irregularities may result in being fired. Taking a stimulant medication, such as Ritalin or Dexedrine, is often a option for these students as they search for a therapeutic method of treatment that will allow them to maximize their talents and abilities without disabling side-effects. Barkley (1990) noted that the success rate for medical treatment is lower for adults than for children—about 50% for adults compared to about 70% for children. In addition, adults have to contend with the fact that the use of stimulant medications may be viewed by graduate school faculty members and peers as a "crutch" As a society, we are often reluctant to accept the fact that people in respected professional fields may need to rely on medication to assist them in traversing the course of their daily lives.

Perhaps the most notable factor that sets graduate students with learning disabilities or those with ADHD apart from their undergraduate counterparts is that they are highly motivated to succeed and often hypersensitive about being "discovered" as having a disability. They don't want to appear "stupid" by asking too many questions in lectures, by depending on peers for assistance, or appearing overly dependent on advisors or clinical instructors for guidance. As a result, they may feel isolated from their classmates. These feelings of isolation and inadequacy can undermine self-confidence and perpetuate feelings of shame and humiliation. They are often fearful that, if they disclose a disability to an academic advisor or dean, the information may be used against them, discounted as not being real, or—worse yet—shared openly in a departmental faculty meeting. One second-year dental student recently commented that a faculty member told him that it would be better if he dropped out of the program "so at least we can get someone with better qualifications." Statements such as these can have a long-lasting and demoralizing impact on students with LD who are enrolled in highly competitive professional programs.

Graduate Admissions Requirements

Given the steep competition in most graduate programs (e.g., law school, medical school, and allied health professions), students with LD are often confronted with the dilemma of deciding whether or not to self-identify during the application process. Even though they may have been graduated from a respectable undergraduate program and earned solid grades, they still have to demonstrate that they are "otherwise qualified" to meet the requisite standards for graduate school admission. Many students fear that graduate school admissions officers will look less favorably on applicants who elect to take their entrance examinations "under non-standardized conditions" versus applicants with a similar profile who do not disclose a disability and who take the exam in the conventional manner. Unlike procedures for admission at the undergraduate level, the admission process for graduate programs often varies widely within a given institution. It is often up to the individual department to determine its own standards and admissions criteria. This decentralized approach makes it difficult for prospective applicants with disabilities to determine the level of understanding and commitment that graduate admissions officers possess about disabilities, and difficult to learn whether or not it is advisable to self-identify.

Graduate school admissions officers may find it especially difficult to assess on paper which applicants with LD are qualified for the rigors of medical or law school. They may realize that "standardized test measures don't tell it all," but they are often unclear as to how a learning disability or attention deficit disorder would affect future student performance in the graduate school curriculum. In such instances, it may be useful for graduate school admissions staff members to confer with a specialist in LD or a psychologist who is knowledgeable and well-versed in working with adults with LD in order to gain further insight about a given applicant's prospects for success. Although admissions officers may not directly ask applicants if they have a disability in the initial stages of the admission process, they may ask an applicant to provide additional documentation of the disability and/or demonstrate how he/she will be able to fulfill essential course requirements with or without reasonable accommodations if the applicant asks for an accommodation (Essex-Sorlie, 1994; Helms & Helms, 1994). For the past several years, many medical professionals, including the Council on Medical Education, have been recommending that admissions committees place more emphasis on personal qualities—such as warmth, concern for the patient and their families, and academic and professional integrity which are so essential to the practice of medicine. For applicants with learning disabilities who may not quite have the requisite MCAT scores, but who possess personal qualities that make them good applicants, this growing perception is reassuring.

Frances Hall, (1995) director of student programs for the Association of American Medical Colleges (AAMC), points out that we need to "evaluate *ability* not their status as being disabled while keeping in mind that we must not fundamentally alter the program or pose a threat to public safety." Ultimately this means that admissions officers, in conjunction with graduate school administrators, have to define their "essential standards" and determine what limits need to be set as they seek to apply standards uniformly to all students. They need to ask: "What can be done to insure that we evaluate a student's true ability without the confines of disability-related factors?" and "What elements of the graduate school curriculum are non-negotiable or viewed as integral to the program of study?"

Once admitted, students with LD may feel compelled to demonstrate for themselves and to others that, with or without accommodations, they can meet legitimate program requirements and professional licensing standards (Kincaid, 1992). Many first-year graduate students believe that, now that they are in their areas of specialty (i.e., international banking, special education, or pediatrics), their learning disabilities won't affect them. Others believe that all they need to do is "buckle down" and study harder to get the results they desire. Students with ADHD may think that, once their prescription medication takes effect, they will be able to handle anything in graduate school. These misguided thoughts often result in students failing to meet performance standards by mid-semester and being referred to the academic support services office.

Providing Academic Supports in Graduate School

Few graduate and professional school programs have direct access to an LD specialist on campus. Similarly, in the world of work, few employees with learning disabilities have the opportunity to work closely with an LD specialist on the job. Although every company must have a human resources manager on site, these individuals are often more concerned about following union rules and company regulations than working with individuals with disabilities. Few employees with learning disabilities are aware of Employee Assistance Programs (EAP) that can assist them in determining work adjustments that will enable them to perform the essential functions of a given job.

Typically, students who are experiencing academic problems are referred to the dean of student affairs, who can determine whether the problems the student is having are minor or, perhaps, more indicative of a pervasive learning disability. If an academic advisor or counselor believes that the presenting problem may be a learning disability or an attention deficit disorder, it may be appropriate to refer the student to a qualified professional for a comprehensive psycho-educational or neuropsychological evaluation. Adelman and Vogel (1991) emphasized that we are now in an "age of accountability"; therefore, evaluation will be increasingly mandated by legislation and government regulations. This need for accountability may encourage institutions to develop on-site diagnostic services. Although the cost of these services is substantial, the resulting consistency in the quality of diagnostic information assures the institution that students receiving specialized support have met clear eligibility criteria. An evaluation conducted by a licensed school psychologist or educational diagnostician will assume that the student receives consistent diagnostic services while also creating a standard that protects the institution (Behrens-Blake & Bryant, 1996).

It may be useful for service providers to establish some guidelines regarding what constitutes acceptable LD documentation and to determine what standards need to be met before an accommodation can be granted. Because of variation in diagnostic procedures, differences in eligibility criteria, and disagreement in the interpretation of test results, there are valid concerns regarding the acceptance of some eligibility statements (Behrens-Blake & Bryant, 1996). It may be advisable to establish a timetable for the recency of documentation. Many institutions follow a three- to five-year limit, given that the unique needs of students can change over time. Most graduate testing services adhere to the more conservative three-year limit and some now request information on the credentials of the qualifying professional who conducted the evaluation. The prevailing practice is to accept documentation from medical doctors, licensed psychologists, neuropsychologists, or learning disability specialists who have histories of reputable practice. Documentation should detail the exact nature of the student's disability and its severity, as well as specifying classroom accommodations or auxiliary aids that may be appropriate. A complete diagnostic report should include measures of cognitive ability, information processing, and academic achievement. All subtest scores should accompany the report. A specific diagnosis of disability should be included; terms such as, *learning differences, slow reader,* or *attention problems* do not signify a documentable disability. If accommodations were not provided in the past, then the diagnostic report should state why accommodations were not necessary and why they are presently warranted.

Documentation of an attention deficit disorder, with or without hyperactivity, should be based on a comprehensive diagnostic interview by a qualified clinician. DSM-IV criteria for the three subtypes of ADHD should be addressed as well as addressing any co-existing mood, behavioral, neurological or personality disorders. A written report should describe and interpret the results of measures of attention, overall intelligence, spatial ability, language, memory, executive functioning, motor ability, and academic skills. The clinician should also make specific recommendations for further treatment, remediation, accommodations, and/or academic counseling based upon the student's profile of strengths and weaknesses.

Academic support staffs in graduate schools are often caught in the position of trying to advocate for students with disabilities while simultaneously being expected to respect a student's right to confidentiality, uphold and maintain rigorous technical standards, preserve core curriculum requirements, and safeguard the public trust. If students with learning disabilities are going to compete equitably in graduate or professional programs, it is essential that academic support personnel understand learning disabilities as well as their responsibilities under the ADA for providing students with reasonable academic adjustments. They may also need to further educate faculty members about these students, how they learn, and their unique needs both in and out of the classroom. Academic support specialists may request invitations to one of the regularly scheduled departmental meetings to discuss learning disabilities. An advantage of this approach is that accommodations and modifications particular to the specific disciplines can be discussed. Tomlan, Farrell, and Geis (1990) have developed a sequenced model for the delivery of faculty inservice training, beginning with large-group training; followed by staff development for individual departments, divisions, or committees; and ending with individual meetings with faculty members whose classes include students with disabilities. Academic support staff can tactfully encourage faculty members to create classroom settings that are more hospitable to learning for all students by sharing a variety of different instructional methodologies and teaching approaches.

Faculty members may need to be reminded to keep regular office hours so they can meet with students to answer questions, clarify material, or give feedback on class progress. It is particularly important that students with learning disabilities receive consistent, regular feedback throughout the semester so that they can utilize available campus resources to their advantage. Access to faculty can be improved if professors have telephone answering machines and e-mail so students can keep in close contact. Faculty members should also make an effort to prepare their course syllabi in advance so that students who need taped materials can secure them in a timely fashion. The syllabus is an essential organizational tool for students with learning disabilities; consequently, it should clearly state the expectations for the course, as well as guidelines with dates for papers, tests, and reading assignments. Faculty members should be encouraged to make a brief statement, during the first class session, that they are happy to meet with students during office hours to discuss any special needs (Brinckerhoff, Shaw, & McGuire, 1993). At several institutions, including Barnard College and Ball State University, professors invite students to share disability-related information by including a brief statement on all course syllabi. A typical statement may read, "If you need course adaptations or accommodations because of a documented disability, or if you have emergency medical information to share, please make an appointment during my office hours."

Brinckerhoff, Shaw and McGuire (1993) pointed out that faculty members and teaching assistants who are on the front lines should be prepared to broach the subject of a suspected disability with students, and to help by referring them to the academic dean or an academic counselor. They may be the first to address the issue by first noting that a student appears to be highly motivated and yet, despite diligent effort, he or she is still performing below expectations. Instructors can assist in this process by describing their experiences with other bright students with LD with whom they have worked in the past, or by offering to connect a newly identified student with a peer who has managed to successfully navigate the graduate curriculum despite a learning disability. Faculty should not trivialize a learning disability to be merely a "learning difference" or a "learning preference". They should emphasize that an LD is a documentable disability influencing how an individual takes in, sorts, retrieves, and expresses information, and does not reflect a lack of intelligence.

Determining Accommodations in Professional Schools

Many graduate school administrators and faculty members are becoming increasingly concerned about how to determine "reasonableness" in accommodating graduate students with disabilities. Hastings College of the Law School employs a full-time staff person who works with students with disabilities and assists in handling all requests for classroom accommodations. At the University of California, Hastings College of the Law, a policy has been developed for all students seeking accommodations. Even though an accommodation may be supported by a school's disability coordinator, some graduate school faculty members feel that they are being stripped of their academic freedom by permitting a student with a learning disability to receive accommodations in the classroom. Some faculty members in graduate programs, unaware of the Americans with Disabilities Act, are reluctant to grant a student with a visual processing disorder additional time on an exam because "all students do better with additional time." Some law school faculty have expressed concerns about whether or not a practicing lawyer needs "split second decision making" in the courtroom or whether is it ethical for an attorney with dyslexia to "double bill" a client because it takes him twice as long to prepare a legal brief. Professor Laura Rothstein (1990) at the University of Houston School of Law challenges those faculty members who think that additional time gives students with learning disabilities an "unfair advantage." She concedes that there should be some limits to the amount of time granted, with only students with the most severe disabilities permitted double time for exams, but notes that unlimited time is unlikely to be granted (Rothstein, 1990).

It is of utmost importance that faculty members maintain their academic standards while also remaining open to listening to students' needs and seriously considering their requests. The students are often in the best position to articulate what types of accommodations they will need and what types of accommodations have been successful in the past. Accommodation amplifies the means for students with disabilities to achieve the desired end or standard required of all students (Jarrow, 1993). On occasion, the agreed-upon accommodations do not serve the student's best interests. Under such circumstances, it is imperative that academic support staff members assist the student in re-negotiating for accommodations that will fill his or her needs effectively. This trial-and-error process can be unsettling to graduate school faculty members, but if a collaborative team approach is used from the outset, it can enhance the knowledge and attitudes of all constituencies. On the other side of the coin, students need to remember that faculty members are not bound to grant every accommodation requested and that, in some instances, students are making a "leap to entitlement" by demanding a laundry list of accommodations that may not be appropriate. Brinckerhoff, Shaw and McGuire (1996) stated that, given the heterogeneous nature of the college population with learning disabilities, requests for testing accommodations must be addressed on an individual basis. To provide blanket accommodations to all students is a disservice both to students, whose strengths may mitigate against a needed accommodation in specific courses, and to faculty members who are pivotal in ensuring access while maintaining technical standards. There should always be a data-based connection between students' strengths and weaknesses and their eligibility for *specific* types of accommodations.

Recently, several graduate and professional programs have developed standard accommodation policy statements regarding services for students with learning disabilities (University of California at Berkeley, 1995). Others have taken a broad, sweeping approach and have developed technical standards that specifically state what skills a matriculated candidate must be able to demonstrate in order to complete a given curriculum (University of Tennessee-Memphis, 1995). Technical standards often focus on specific domains or skill areas that must be mastered in the practice of a given profession. In the field of medicine, for example, standards have been developed around the following areas: observation, communication, motor functioning, intellectual-conceptual, behavioral, and social attributes. For a more in-depth discussion of technical standards, readers should consult the AAMC publication, *The Americans with Disabilities Act (ADA) and the Disabled Student in Medical School: Guidelines for Medical Schools* (1993).

Once admitted, it is the school's responsibility to provide "reasonable accommodations" and, in general, to pay the costs associated with the accommodation unless such expenses would be viewed as an unfair administrative or financial burden (Kincaid, 1995). When determining whether an accommodation presents an undue financial hardship, the entire budget of the institution must be considered. Some accommodations that graduate schools might reasonably be expected to make for students with learning disabilities include course load modification and extended time for the completion of examinations, courses, thesis requirements, and degree(s) (AAMC, 1993; Stone, 1996). Some graduate schools are more willing to experiment with meeting the accommodation needs of students. At Widener University, students have been permitted to use memory-free word processors to type exams; to sit in special chairs or at special tables; to listen to tape-recorded versions of exams; and even to play a "white noise" tape to eliminate distractions during exams (Cleesattle & Seiberg, 1995). This individualized approach to accommodation was exemplified by a Dartmouth Medical School student with a learning disability who stated, "I had also asked for a private place to take the exam, but because every course was different second year, it was hard to ask for this special item with every course director (in fact, I never did the second year but it would have been helpful if I did). What did help me instead was to put ear plugs in and have the space to spread out to take the exam . . ."

The following list of accommodations may be viewed as reasonable under the Americans with Disabilities Act, depending on the nature of the student's disability and the curriculum standards set by the graduate or program.

- readers
- additional time to complete tests, course work, and graduation requirements
- rest breaks between test sessions
- access to a dictionary or spell-checking program
- nonprogrammable calculator
- word processor for essays
- individual testing rooms
- permission to record answers in test booklets rather than on answer sheets
- more than one test day
- oral exams
- proofreader
- calculator with voice output
- tape-recorded version of exam
- tape recorder for note taking
- note taker in course lectures, assistive listening devices, or tape recorder
- adaptations in instructional methods

In addition to the accommodations just listed, Scott (1990, pp. 403–404) has generated a set of questions that may be useful for service providers to follow:

> Can the student with a learning disability meet all the essential program requirements when he or she is given reasonable accommodations?
>
> Will the accommodations provided pose any risk to personal or public safety?
>
> Are the proposed accommodations stipulated in writing, in advance, and do they reflect the purpose of a program or course?
>
> What skills or competencies will be needed for graduation, licensure, or certification?
>
> Which program elements are negotiable and which are not?

Providing academic adjustments to students with learning disabilities at the graduate and professional school level is a complex process that depends on the proactive efforts of administrators, support staff, faculty, and the students themselves. Policymakers need to establish procedures legitimizing the requests for accommodations for students with disabilities (Brinckerhoff, Shaw & McGuire, 1993). Support staff members need to learn more about the unique learning and psychosocial needs of this talented population of students who are often both LD and gifted. Faculty members must acknowledge that students with learning disabilities can and do learn differently, and must be willing to explore alternative ways of determining a student's proficiency with course materials without lowering standards. Ultimately, the key players in this process are the students with learning disabilities, who must be ready to demonstrate their willingness to take risks, to realistically assess their strengths and limitations, and to select academic adjustments that will allow them to effectively compensate for their disability in graduate school and in the world of work.

Challenges to Employment

The future holds tremendous promise for graduates with learning disabilities. These individuals can attain their rightful place in the professions by using their unique skills and abilities. With the passage and implementation of the Americans with Disabilities Act of 1990, more opportunities in the workplace are now available, not only at job entry, but in job advancement and in supervisory and leadership roles (Brown & Gerber, 1994). One sweeping ramification of the ADA may be that workplace accommodations throughout the United States will become an integrated and gradual process continuing throughout the life span of adults with learning disabilities (Payne, 1992). However, in order to take advantage of these protections in the workplace, graduate students with learning disabilities must be diligent at developing and refining employment skills concurrent with their course work. Further exploration of career paths, self-advocacy training, awareness of legal rights and responsibilities, competence in using assistive technology, and a working knowledge of accommodations that will be necessary on the job are essential for students with learning disabilities (Latham & Latham, 1994; Rumrill & Gordon, 1994). A recent graduate of Catholic University Law School, Beth Callahan (1995), reflected on her struggle in earning a law degree.

> I thought about how stressful it had been and how much work and how worth it, it was and how truly proud I was. I had met the challenge. I had ignored the nay sayers and I had taken the discrimination and the disbelievers and I rose above them . . . I was lucky. I was a privileged kid born with the ability to say what I think and feel and I learned how to get what I needed to be successful. Those of us who are successful must keep talking and educating and helping. We can change the world. I know we can. (p. 49)

The next frontier for many college graduates now coming of age, given the protections of P.L. 94-142, is graduate and professional school. The inroads made by students with learning disabilities into graduate and professional programs will bring more diversity to our graduate schools and new challenges to academic school support staffs, faculties, and administrations who will be called upon to listen to students like Beth Callahan. May we listen to her words and become energized by her successes, so that the doors to our graduate schools and corporations will open wider to the next generation of individuals with learning disabilities.

References

Adelman, P. B., & Vogel, S. A. (1991). The learning disabled adult. In B. Wong (Ed.), *Learning about learning disabilities.* (pp. 563–594). New York: Academic Press.

Americans with Disabilities Act of 1990, 42 U.S.C. 12101 *et seq.*

Association of Academic Psychiatrists. Recommended guides for admission of candidates with disabilities to medical school. *American Journal of Physical Medicine Rehabilitation, 72*(1), 45–47.

Association of American Medical Colleges (1993). *The Americans with Disabilities Act (ADA) and Disabled students in medical school. Guidelines for medical schools* Washington, DC: Author.

Barkley, R. A. (1990). *Attention deficit hyperactivity disorder: A handbook for diagnosis and treatment.* New York: Guilford Press.

Bateman, B. (1992). Learning disabilities: The changing landscape. *Journal of Learning Disabilities. 25*, 29–36

Behrens-Blake, M., & Bryant, B. (1996). Assessing students with learning disabilities in postsecondary settings. In J. Patton & E. Polloway (Eds.)., *Learning disabilities: The challenges of adulthood* (pp. 93–136). Austin, TX: PRO-ED.

Brinckerhoff, L. C., Shaw, S. F., & McGuire, J. M. (1993). *Promoting postsecondary education for students with learning disabilities: A handbook for practitioners.* Austin, TX: PRO-ED.

Brinckerhoff, L. C., Shaw, S. F., & McGuire, J. M. (1996). Promoting access, accommodations, and independence for college students with learning disabilities. In J. R. Patton & E. A. Polloway (Eds.), *Learning disabilities: The challenges of adulthood* (pp. 71–92). Austin, TX: PRO-ED.

Brown, D., & Gerber, P. (1994). Employing people with learning disabilities. In P. Gerber & H. Reiff (Eds.), *Learning disabilities in adulthood* (194–203). Austin, TX: PRO-ED.

Callahan, B. A. (1995). Becoming an attorney: From L.D. to J.D. *Their World* [Annual journal], 43–50. New York, NY: National Center for Learning Disabilities.

Cleesattle, J., & Seiberg, J. (1995, Fall). Leveling the playing field? *Postsecondary Disability Network News, 25*, 1,2,7.

Corneille, M. F. (1995, Fall). Testing and disability experts discuss accommodations. *Syllabus. 19*–20.

Essex-Sorlie, D. (1994, July). The Americans with Disabilities Act: History, summary, and key components. *Academic Medicine, 69*(7), 519–535.

Gerber, P. J., & Reiff, H. B. (1991). *Speaking for themselves: Ethnographic interviews with adults with learning disabilities.* Ann Arbor: University of Michigan Press.

Gerber, P. J., & Reiff, H. B. (1994). Perspective on adults with learning disabilities. In P. Gerber & H. Reiff (Eds.), *Learning disabilities in adulthood* (pp. 3–9). Austin, TX: PRO-ED.

Gerber, P. J., Ginsberg, R. J., & Reiff, H. B. (1992). Identifying alterable patterns in employment success for highly successful adults with learning disabilities. *Journal of Learning Disabilities, 25*, 475–487.

Greenbaum, B., Graham, S., & Scales, W. (1996). Adults with learning disabilities: Occupational and social status after college. *Journal of Learning Disabilities, 29*(2), 167–173.

Hall, F. (1995, January). *Students with learning disabilities in medical school.* Presentation at Boston University School of Medicine conference, Boston, MA.

Hammill, D. D. (1990). On defining learning disabilities: An emerging consensus. *Journal of Learning Disabilities, 10*, 39–46.

Helms, L. B., & Helms, C. M. (1994, July). Medical education and disability discrimination: The law and future implications. *Academic Medicine, 69,* 535–543.

Information from HEATH. (1995, June/July). *Facts you can use: College freshmen with disabilities.* (p. 6). Washington, DC: Author.

Jarrow, J. E. (1991, Winter). Disability issues on campus and the road to ADA. *Educational Record, 72,* 26–31.

Jarrow, J. E. (1993, Winter). Beyond ramps: New ways of viewing access. S. Kroeger & J. Schuck (Eds.), *Responding to disability issues in student affairs, 64,* (pp. 5–16), San Francisco, CA: Jossey–Bass.

Johnson, D. (September 22, 1995). More scorn and less money dim law's lure. *The New York Times,* pp. A 1, A 24.

Jordan, C. (1995, September). *Learning disabilities at the graduate or professional school level: Identification, acceptance and accommodation.* Paper presented at Higher Education and Students with Learning Disabilities: Learning Conference, sponsored by Curry College, Milton, MA.

Kincaid, J. M. (1992, July). *Compliance requirements of the ADA and Section 504.* Paper presented at the Association on Higher Education and Disability conference, Long Beach, CA.

Kincaid, J. M. (1995, June). *Legal aspects of accommodating students with learning disabilities.* Farmington, CT: University of Connecticut. Postsecondary Learning Disability Training Institute.

Latham, P. S., & Latham, P. H. (1994). *Succeeding in the workplace—Attention deficit disorder and learning disabilities in the workplace: A guide for success.* Washington, DC: JKL Communications.

Lerner, J. W., Lowenthal, B., & Lerner, S. R. (1995). *Attention deficit disorders—Assessment and teaching.* Pacific Grove, CA: Brooks/Cole Publishing.

Meltzer, L. (1994). Assessment of learning disabilities: The challenge of evaluating the cognitive strategies and processes underlying learning. In G.R. Lyon (Ed.), *Frames of reference for the assessment of learning disabilities: New views on measurement issues* (pp. 571–606). Baltimore, MD: Brookes.

National Joint Committee on Learning Disabilities. (1994). *Collective perspectives on issues affecting learning disabilities.* Austin, TX: PRO-ED.

Payne, N. (1992, June). *Transition strategies: Employment preparation essentials.* Paper presented at the University of Connecticut's Fourth Annual Postsecondary Training Institute, Farmington, CT.

Rehabilitation Act of 1973, 29 U.S.C. 701 *et seq.*

Rothstein, L. F. (1990). *Special education and the law.* New York: Longman.

Rumrill, P. D., & Gordon, S. (1994). Integrated career development services for college students with disabilities. In D. Ryan & M. McCarthy (Eds.), *The student affairs guide to ADA & disability issues, 17,* (pp. 111–124). Washington, DC: National Association of Student Personnel Administrators.

Scott, S. (1990). Coming to terms with the "otherwise qualified" student with a learning disability. *Journal of Learning Disabilities, 23,* 398–405.

Shapiro, J. (1996). Facing a painful dilemma. *America's Best Colleges*. U.S. News & World Report. 37–39.

Shaw, S. F., Cullen, J. P., McGuire, J. M., & Brinckerhoff, L C. (1995). Operationalizing a definition of learning disabilities. *Journal of Learning Disabilities, 28*, 586–597.

Shaywitz, S. E., & Shaw, R. (1988). The admissions process: An approach to selecting learning disabled students at the most selective colleges. *Learning Disabilities Focus, 3*(2), 81–86.

Stone, D. (1996). The impact of the Americans with Disabilities Act on legal education and academic modifications for disabled law students: An empirical study. *The University of Kansas Law Review, 44*(3). 567–595.

Tomlan, P., Farrell, M., & Geis, J. (1990). The 3 S's of staff development: Scope, sequence, and structure. In J. J. Vander Putten (Ed.), *Proceedings of the 1989 AHSSPPE Conference* (pp. 23–32). Columbus, OH: AHSSPPE

U.S. News & World Report (1995). Is Grad School Worth It? *America's Best Graduate Schools*, p. 8–11.

University of California at Berkeley. (1995). *Model for accommodating the academic needs of students with disabilities*. Berkeley, CA: Author.

University of Tennessee-Memphis (1995). Technical standards for medical school admission and graduation. College of Medicine. Memphis, TN: Author.

Vogel, S. A. (1993). A retrospective and prospective view of postsecondary education for adults with learning disabilities. In S. A. Vogel & P. B. Adelman (Eds.), *Success for college students with learning disabilities* (pp. 3–20). New York: Springer-Verlag.

CHAPTER 9

Vocational Rehabilitation: Current Practices for Work Preparation

James R. Koller

M ost individuals would agree that one very basic goal of education is to seek, acquire, and maintain gainful employment. Yet the problem of securing realistic employment for persons with a high school diploma, much less for a college graduate, is becoming increasingly difficult. Furthermore, for individuals with a substantial impediment to employment, e.g., a specific learning disability (SLD), a positive vocational outcome is not guaranteed even when appropriate vocational planning is conducted. Increasingly, each state division of vocational rehabilitation (VR) is serving individuals with a wide variety of different types and combinations of SLD, which manifest themselves in unique ways to significantly impede personal, social, and vocational success. This chapter explores some of the issues which impact on the effective provision of vocational rehabilitation services. It also addresses those factors which are known to facilitate a positive rehabilitation outcome and concludes with specific recommendations to improve existing services.

An Adult Employment Issue

Since the Education for All Handicapped Children Act of 1975, Public Law 94-142, was mandated, SLD has continued to receive increasing recognition as a pervasive and potentially far-reaching disabling condition. Until the mid-1980s, however, the primary focus in schools as well as the research literature was on investigation of the academic residuals that often result from SLD, while the impact SLD has on employment was often not considered (Koller, 1994). A commonly held assumption was that a person's functional limitations accompanying the SLD were considered irrelevant or ignored completely in the non-academic, adult world of work (Berkeley Planning Associates [BPA], 1989).

With the realization that SLD persists into adulthood and that the sequela of the disorder have significant implications for vocational success

(Spreen, 1988; Vogel, 1989), it has only been since the late 1980s and early 1990s that significant recognition has been given to the adult manifestations of SLD (Gerber & Reiff, 1991; Haring & Lovett, 1990; Koller, 1994; Mellard & Hagol, 1992) Furthermore, how SLD impacts upon the ultimate vocational success of adult citizens has only recently been studied (Berkeley, 1989; Reiff, Gerber & Ginsberg, in press; Zigmond, 1990). Assuming that children with SLD eventually become adults with SLD, it is not surprising that this problem constitutes the fastest-growing disability population served by the state and federal VR system (Dowdy & Smith, 1994), as well as the largest of all disability groups in the United States (Gerber & Reiff, 1994). Specifically, the incidence of this disabling condition has continued to grow in our nation's schools and job market (Koller, 1994). The job market increase is due, in part, to a 1981 Rehabilitation Services Administration (RSA) decision to reverse its previous policy, which had recognized SLD as a medical disability and, again in 1985, when RSA promulgated its revised policies with respect to code and definition of SLD.

As Table 9.1 illustrates, a dramatic increase in the number of individuals' cases closed successfully with SLD as a primary disabling condition occurred between 1988 and 1994 and, as a percentage increase, since the early onset of recording SLD as a vocational disability in 1983

TABLE 9.1
Selected RSA Fiscal Year Rehabilitated Characteristics
of Persons with SLD

RSA Fiscal Year	Number of Clients Successfully Closed Nationally with SLD as the Major Disability	SLD Percentage of all Clients Closed Successfully
1994	16,133	7.95*
1993	14,334	7.4**
1992	12,948	6.8**
1989	11,571	5.3**
1988	10,731	4.9**
1983	N/A	1.3***

Source::
* Personal Communication, 1996, RSA Statistician, Rehabilitation Services Administration, Basic State Grants Branch, Dr. Neal Nair
** Personal Communication, 1995, Rehabiliation Services Administration Office of Program Operations, Division of Program Administration, Larry Mars, Chief Statistician
*** Dowdy & Smith, 1994

(Nair, 1996 personal communication). Furthermore, during RSA fiscal year (FY) 1993, the classification of SLD as a secondary disabling condition resulted in 4,420 cases successfully rehabilitated, representing 2.3% of those rehabilitated throughout the state and federal system (Mars, 1995 personal communication). Interestingly, of the 12,948 client cases successfully closed in FY 1992, 77% (8975) were male, continuing the overwhelming preponderance of gender-related incidence referrals into the VR employment sector. The predominance of males served most likely is due to a number of factors, not the least of which might be a gender bias in referral and classification (Shaywitz, Shaywitz, Fletcher & Escobar, 1990; Vogel, 1989). Nonetheless, while VR successful closure rates continue to grow, people with SLD are often unemployed, underemployed, and continue significantly at risk for school dropout or subsequent job failure (Berkeley, 1989; Koller, 1994; Tillman & Abbott, 1992).

Aside from RSA, it is increasingly evident that the rates of individuals with SLD entering the general workforce are also continuing to escalate. In 1993, for example, the U.S. Department of Education revealed that 51% of those students with disabilities in public schools were diagnosed SLD, representing a 200% increase in the student population since 1977 (Coutinho, 1995). It stands to reason, therefore, that if one goal of education is to gain employment, individuals with SLD will continue to present problems as they transition from school to work or from school to any post-secondary training environment—especially with the impact of increasing societal and technological demands.

Etiological, Diagnostic, and Definitional Concerns

Major questions and controversies concerning etiology, assessment, and definition of SLD remain. As Heaton (1988) explains in a review of research involving children with SLD, "a confusing variety of theoretical models, test procedures, and operational definitions are used by different investigators and clinicians, and in many cases, their approaches do not adequately consider the heterogencity of disorders labeled learning disabilities." (p. 787) To complicate the picture, manifestations of childhood patterns of strengths and deficits change as they enter adolescence and adulthood, assessment procedures in methodology change and the diagnosis becomes increasingly complicated as it relates to vocational issues (Koller, 1994). This, in turn, leads to diagnostic problems in distinguishing between primary and secondary deficits as prescribed by the 1994 Diagnostic and Statistical Manual, Fourth Edition (DSM-IV). Public schools follow, for special education placement purposes, a more traditional discrepancy or disparity model that centers around deficits related to the academics, while post-secondary agencies, including VR, follow the RSA (1985) definition, which is broader in scope. As Koller (1994) indicates, the RSA model relates more to adolescents and adults, has wider ramifications for personal, social, and emotional functioning, and centers around issues related to employment and independent living. And, since the nation's secondary schools represent the largest referral source for VR applicants (Berkeley, 1989), it is important to recognize the differences that exist between special education, as defined by school system policy, and VR as a state/federal agency. While school systems have traditionally defined SLD from the perspective of PL 94-142, it should be noted that this definition (reauthorized as PL 101-36, Individuals with Disabilities Education Act of 1990 [IDEA]), addresses only a school-age population through age 21 and does not directly relate to workforce or employment issues. Therefore, for those seeking VR assistance, the federal mandate stipulates that an individual is not eligible for services unless that individual:

1. has a severe physical or mental impairment which seriously limits one or more functional capacities (including mobility, communication, self-care, self-direction, interpersonal skills, work tolerance, or work skills) in terms of an employment outcome.

2. can be expected to require multiple vocational rehabilitation services over an extended period of time.

3. has one or more physical or mental disabilities resulting from . . . specific learning disabilities . . . or combination of disabilities determined on the basis of an assessment for determining eligibility. (Rehabilitation Act Amendments of 1993).

It is not unusual, then, to encounter differences when school personnel, for example, do not understand the VR mandate and assume that any special education student with SLD, regardless of severity, is automatically eligible for VR services within that state.

RSA Definition of Specific Learning Disability

Given the strong emphasis on transition from school to work efforts in the United States, it is important to recognize the RSA definition of SLD, which is mandated by all state and local vocational rehabilitation agencies and is the basis upon which the diagnosis (the first requirement for VR eligibility determination) is established:

> A specific learning disability is a disorder in one or more of the central nervous system processes involved in perceiving, understanding and/or using concepts through verbal (spoken or written) language or nonverbal means. This disorder manifests itself with a deficit in one or more of the following areas: attention, reasoning, processing, memory, communication, reading, writing, spelling, calculation, coordination, social competence and emotional maturity (RSA, 1985).

Thus, all referrals to the state and federal VR system, including those from public school settings, will be expected to comply with the RSA definition. Since passage of the Education for All Handicapped Children Act of 1975, PL 94-142, which established learning disability in the schools as a serviceable disabling condition, was not mandated until 1974, it stands to reason that a substantial number of citizens with SLD who are at least 22 years of age were not identified SLD while in school. Therefore, many of these individuals did not receive appropriate services which prepared them for employment. And, since the mean age of individuals in the U.S. workforce is clearly over 22, it can be further assumed that SLD exists, often undetected, in the current employment sector. Therefore, the number of individuals with SLD receiving services from governmental programs, in addition to RSA, has been on the rise during the last two decades. For example, the U.S. Department of Labor estimates that 50-80% of those in adult basic education programs may have SLD, while 15-23% of all Job Training Partnership Act (JTPA) Title IIA participants and 25-40% of adults in the JOBS program may have this disabling condition (United States Employment & Training Administration, 1991).

In addition to on-the-job difficulties associated with traditional academic deficits, many persons with SLD experience other functional limitations that include various types of memory problems, as well as concerns regarding the processing of visual information, comprehending spoken language, or solving abstract reasoning problems requiring higher-order executive mental processes (McCue, 1995). Personality correlates, including difficulties with interpersonal relationships that often accompany SLD, tend to exacerbate the overall vocational adjustment process of the individual and further promote difficulties on the job (Dunham, Koller & McIntosh, 1996; Gerber & Reiff, 1994). In fact, some researchers have concluded that client personality and social skill deficits create more problems on the job than either academic or vocational deficits alone (Hinkebein, Koller & Kunce, 1992).

Vocational Rehabilitation Determination of Severity

To assist state VR agencies in making decisions regarding severity determination for an individual referred for services, RSA has established
guidelines for a local vocational rehabilitation counselor (VRC) to follow (RSA, 1990). Since only those clients whose disability represents a
substantial impediment to employment are potentially eligible for services, these guidelines assist the VRC in determining whether a client is
severely disabled for program services. The guidelines may be used, for
example, in those states who are under Order of Selection, a process
described later in this chapter.

Because of the nature of SLD, determining the existence of a severe disability is often difficult. Nonetheless, the client's resulting functional limitations may represent a substantial impediment to employment because of
extended services required in order to make the client employable.

Given that SLD presents with a very broad range and heterogeneity
of possible deficits, RSA mandates that the VRC procure and analyze
individual client assessment data within the context of the following
seven functional capacities cited in the RSA statutory and regulatory
definition of an individual with a severe disability (Rehabilitation Act
Amendments of 1993):

1. mobility

2. communication

3. self-care

4. self-direction

5. interpersonal skills

6. work tolerance

7. work skills

Specifically, the VRC is encouraged to secure an accurate assessment of
the client's skills, including achievement, intelligence, perception, language, and behavioral functioning. By determining the client's functional
limitations as they impact these functional parameters, the VRC has taken
an initial step in establishing eligibility for rehabilitation services.

As a result, the determination that an individual with SLD has
a severe disability meeting VR program criteria is made within both
the statutory and regulatory definitions before extended services are
provided.

SLD and the Americans with Disabilities Act

With the establishment of the Americans with Disabilities Act (ADA) in 1990, federal civil rights protection was extended to all people with disabilities, including individuals with SLD. Appropriately, the ADA is not considered to be an affirmative statute. Rather, it seeks to dispel stereotypes and assumptions about the various disabilities encountered in the workforce and is designed to assure "equality of opportunity, full participation, independent living and economic self-sufficiency for disabled people" (ADA Compliance Guide, 1992, p. 3). This legislation guarantees that persons with known disabling conditions, e.g., SLD, have equal access to training and cannot be discriminated against in hiring practices. Legislation, however, does not guarantee vocational success and, obviously, not all persons with SLD require vocational assistance. However, for those entering the workforce through the VR system, specific requirements, including determination of severity, are enforced.

Establishing Eligibility for Services in a Timely Manner

For those individuals with SLD who choose to apply for services through the state division of VR, determination of eligibility may require a comprehensive psychoeducational and/or neuropsychological evaluation and must be completed in an expeditious manner. Therefore, federal regulations require that each designated state unit determine whether an individual is eligible for VR services within a reasonable period of time (Rehabilitation Act Amendments of 1993). Under Section 102 of this regulation, the VRC must determine eligibility for services within 60 days after the individual has submitted a completed application. In situations that preclude a determination due to unforeseen circumstances beyond the control of the agency, or in which an extended evaluation is needed to further clarify the individual's disability, the agency must submit to the individual a request for an extension of time in order to properly determine eligibility.

The Individual Written Rehabilitation Plan and Determination of Reasonable Accommodations

Once an individual is determined eligible for vocational rehabilitation services, an Individualized Written Rehabilitation Plan (IWRP) is jointly developed and agreed upon by the client and VRC. One of the primary

purposes of the IWRP is to design a plan that will "achieve the employment objective of the individual, consistent with the unique strengths,
resources, priorities, concerns, abilities, and capabilities of the individual" (Rehabilitation Act Amendments of 1993, p. 40) Admittedly, not all
individuals with SLD are in need of special accommodations in order to
be gainfully employed. However, if the nature and extent of the client's
disability makes them eligible for VR services, the individual is entitled
to those reasonable accommodations which allow the client with SLD to
enjoy equal employment opportunities. Generally, these accommodations take three forms:

1. to ensure an equal opportunity in the job application process

2. to provide those accommodations that allow the client with SLD to
   perform the essential functions of the job

3. to enable individual employees with SLD the opportunity to participate in employment benefits equal to those of nondisabled
   employees (ADA Compliance Guide, p. 61-63)

Order of Selection

If a situation arises within a state vocational rehabilitation agency, e.g.,
financial exigency, whereby services cannot be provided to all eligible
individuals with known disabilities, federal regulations establish a
process for serving individuals on a priority basis. This process is
known as order of selection, and RSA has established statutory, regulatory and policy requirements for its implementation (RSA Administration Manual, 1992).

Before an order of selection process can be enforced, however, each
state must approve and submit a plan to RSA specifying the parameters
for implementation. Essentially, each state must implement the specific
statutory requirements for serving individuals with those disabilities
determined to be severe or most severe.

For fiscal year 1996, of the 82 VR agencies under the aegis of RSA
(Some states and U.S. territories have general agencies, and some maintain separate agencies for the blind and visually impaired, while others
combine agencies.), a total of 40 agencies have an established preap-
proval endorsement to enter order of selection (Tillman, 1996 personal
communication). While no state agency can institute order of selection
without prior RSA approval, it is possible for those states that have been
approved to enter and exit order of selection status as the needs dictate.

As such, Section 101(a)(5)(A)(ii) of the Amended Rehabilitation Act (1993) states that order of selection for the provision of vocational rehabilitation services shall be determined on the basis of serving first those individuals with the most severe disability. In general, while federal law does not define their status, a state is "required to select, from among those individuals with severe disabilities that combination of disabling factors, functional limitations, and services required that will make such a distinction justifiable and equitable" (RSA Manual, p. 6–7).

Often, during order of selection, the state agency cannot serve all eligible individuals. As a result, officials establish a priority system to determine who must be served first, and which others, although eligible for services, will be served only if available resources permit. Federal regulations also indicate that a state, under an order of selection policy, is prohibited from selecting a specific disabling condition, for inclusion or exclusion, over any other disabling category. Therefore, establishing client eligibility and rehabilitation service provision on the basis of a specific type of disability condition alone is discriminatory (RSA Manual, 1992). Furthermore, establishing an order of selection based upon age, gender, race, creed, and national origin is also discriminatory (RSA Manual, 1992).

Thus, for the individual with SLD to receive eligibility status, it is important to document that he or she has a severe disability which seriously limits one or more of the functional capacities discussed earlier (e.g., mobility, communication, and others) related to employment. Additionally, the serious limiting of client functional capacities and the need for multiple services over an extended period of time will also help to document severity (RSA Administration Manual, 1992).

A Changing National Racial and Cultural Workforce

As the incidence of individuals with SLD seeking gainful employment increases, the nature and composition of the U.S. workforce is also changing. Ethnic and racial minorities tend to have disabling conditions at a rate that is disproportionately higher compared to that of the general population. For example, in terms of incidence rates, Native Americans are approximately one-and-one-half times more likely than the general population to present with work-related disabilities. A similar pattern is present with African Americans who are one-and-one-half times more likely to be disabled than Caucasians and twice as likely to present with a severe disability in employment (Rehabilitation Act Amendments of 1993).

Thus, patterns of inequitable treatment are possible with traditionally underserved minorities such as those of differing racial and cultural backgrounds. And, while a 3.2% census increase is projected for Caucasian Americans by the year 2000, there is an expected 14.6% increase for African Americans, a 40.1% increase for Asian Americans and other related ethnic groups, and a 38.6% increase for Latinos. As we approach the 21st century, the U.S. is projected to have 260,000,000 people, of which one of every three will be either African American, Latino, or Asian American (Rehabilitation Act Amendments of 1993). Clearly, as it relates to employment, the implications for future cross-cultural and racial research and effective service delivery provision for individuals with all disabilities, not just SLD, become magnified.

Vocational Rehabilitation Client Characteristics

Regarding employment as it impacts the RSA system, Berkeley Planning Associates (1989) conducted a seminal nationwide study regarding vocational rehabilitation services provided to individuals with learning disabilities who were referred through the state-federal VR system. Highlights of this research include:

1. Significant discrepancies exist between current educational and vocational definitions, which impact on diagnostic and subsequent service delivery provisions.

2. The average overall IQ level of persons with SLD served (Mean = 86) through the VR system tends to be lower than the corresponding IQ level in the general population of individuals with SLD.

3. Compared to other disabilities, SLD presents a significant national underemployment problem.

4. The average highest grade completed by persons with SLD who were referred to the VR system is the 10th grade.

5. Effective networking with the referring school system is a critical component in predicting the ultimate success of service delivery to clients with SLD.

6. On average, service to clients with SLD tends to be less expensive than the service provided to other VR clients, with, correspondingly, better long-term outcomes.

7. Individuals with SLD often present with significant behavioral features associated with the disability. Thirty-seven percent of those applicants with SLD fail to complete the VR process of eligibility determination, compared to 23% among non-SLD clients. As a result, continued education of both the referring personnel and members of client advocacy groups is suggested.

8. To increase the opportunity for successful employment outcomes, RSA and other state agencies (including the public school systems) are encouraged to enhance existing services by providing additional support for training in SLD, especially as it impacts employment, to all service providers, parents and significant others (Berkeley, 1989).

For all special education students in the United States who were classified with SLD in 1987–1988, Wagner (1989) reported that 52.9% received no support services (e.g., tutoring, life skills training, or personal counseling that included realistic career exploration). Since these individuals ultimately attempt to enter the workforce, many are referred to VR for appropriate vocational services. However, unless they are graduated, most drop out of school unprepared to meet current workforce labor demands. For students who drop out of school prematurely, course failure appears to be one of the most powerful predictors of early exit. Of all dropouts with SLD, 16% received a failing grade in their most recent school year, compared to 5% who had not. Thus, students with SLD had the second-highest dropout rate (32%) of all disability groups in the National Longitudinal Transition Study (Wagner, 1989). Significant questions arise, then, not only as to the dropout's vocational readiness to enter the workforce, but also the impact this will have on underemployment, unemployment, and service provision through both state and federal entitlement and non-entitlement programs.

Even though students in special education are disproportionately represented among school dropouts, few studies reviewed routinely include students in alternative programs designed to keep youth from dropping out. Nonetheless, as individuals enter the workforce through VR, an evaluation of national RSA client caseload data for 1988 indicates:

1. Individuals with SLD typically spend less time in the VR process than clients with all other disabilities—most likely a function of the services provided. To illustrate, 77.3% of clients with SLD spent 4–36 months in VR compared to 53.5% with other disabilities, while 31.4% of the latter spent 49 months or more in VR, compared to 9.1% of those with SLD.

2. The mean cost of rehabilitation for clients with SLD was $1,024 vs. $2,205 for those with other disabilities (Tillman & Abbott, 1992).

While clients with SLD achieved better placement rates (64% vs. 61%), the occupations in which they were placed varied significantly from those of groups with other disabilities. For example, in spite of the fact that most individuals with SLD have average or above-average intelligence, only 3.4% were placed in professional occupations at closure, compared to 12.2% of clients from all other disability groups.

While the research literature is equivocal as to why such a small percentage of individuals with SLD are placed in professional occupations at closure, several hypotheses are possible. These include level of intelligence and achievement commensurate with professional careers, reluctance prior to ADA compliance for institutions of higher learning to provide accommodations for clients seeking post-secondary training, general reluctance of State VR agencies to fund clients into post-baccalaureate training programs, and individual client personality correlates that include discouragement, fear of failure, and frustration in academic and vocational settings.

Compared to professional occupations, by contrast, 44.3% of those clients with SLD were placed in industrial occupations at closure—statistically more than the proportion of clients (28.4%) with all other disabling conditions (Tillman & Abbott, 1992). And, while 95% of persons rehabilitated with SLD were in competitive employment settings compared to 80% of all other disabling categories, 75% of the successful SLD closures were in basic entry-level service positions compared to 51% for all other categories. As a result, job retention rates among individuals with SLD are lower. And, while young adults with SLD appear to find employment at approximately the same rate or better as their same-age peers, employment tends to be entry-level and frequently not satisfying long-term. Therefore, individuals with SLD spend their working careers in a series of relatively short-term, entry-level jobs with few advancement opportunities (Tillman & Abbott, 1992), ultimately exacerbating underemployment problems (Koller, 1994). By contrast, preliminary evidence predicting post-secondary employment success while still in high school for students with SLD reveals that those with high math abilities, who were employed during their high school years and who had proactive parents involved in their educational training, significantly increased their chances of vocational success (Fourqurean, Meisgeier, Swank & Williams, 1991).

Although few studies have critically examined those factors that predict long-term vocational success for individuals with SLD, one study (Berkeley, 1989) nationally examined the potential vocational correlates associated with successful VR intervention. This study, surprisingly, showed only three out of 20 VR client characteristics that demonstrated statistical significance between a closed Status 26 (successful) case file and closed Status 28 (unsuccessful) case file. Those successfully closed were less likely to have an identified secondary disability (43% vs. 57% for Status 28) and, on average, clients "experienced considerably longer tenure on their longest job (22 months vs. 14 months) although the percentage with no work experience was not significantly different for the two groups" (Berkeley, 1989, p. 152–153). However, when controlling for simultaneous effects of the various factors researchers found the differences tended to disappear. Nonetheless, Berkeley (1989) reported that the differences may be significant, but failed to show in the regression analysis due, in part, to data set limitations.

Significantly, the two status groups were not statistically different on the following predictor variables investigated: average grade levels on achievement tests, average full-scale intelligence, and age at the time of application. Also, while other predictor variables initially appeared substantial, they, too, were not found to be statistically significant. These variables included earnings at application (higher for Status 26), the percent competitively employed at application (higher for Status 26), gender status (female only, higher for Status 28), and percentage African American (higher for Status 28). This study, however, did reveal a number of VR service factors which were significantly different between the two status groups. Those factors positively associated with a successful vocational closure included the following: an active involvement on the part of the client with collaborating agencies, VR job referral and/or job placement, and the guidance and counseling services provided by the vocational rehabilitation counselor. However, if guidance and counseling was unaccompanied by the provision of other services, this factor was negatively associated with a 26 closure status.

Nonetheless, and irrespective of Status 26 closures, a significant number of difficult-to-quantify variables is often associated with success of SLD clients in the VR system. Such factors include community service availability, client readiness for workforce entry, the client's motivation, his or her self-awareness, advocacy status, readily available positive role models, rehabilitation counselor style, motivation and time spent with the client, and the support provided from significant others (e.g., parents). Also, it is apparent in national data that the impact of the local economy in which the client resides can often influence individual successful outcomes when other factors are held constant (Berkeley, 1989).

While the BPA study was an initial investigation to study the effects of VR intervention, one point remains dramatically clear: Since schools (of all types) represent the largest single referral source for VR referrals with SLD, the quality of the agency's relationship with the school has a direct bearing on the ultimate and effective service provision to those clients served. Thus, both agencies need to improve the efficiency and effectiveness of the referral process as well as to work on the quality of those factors which will enhance successful employment outcomes.

Functional Limitations Affecting Employment

In part to replicate, yet also to expand, the BPA study, Dunham et al., (1996) reported preliminary results from a major investigation designed to examine predictor variables associated with Status 28 and 26 closures on individuals with SLD served through the VR system. A total of 613 clients were evaluated (361 Status 26 and 252 Status 28). Across all variables investigated, both closure groups differed in terms of individual intelligence, achievement in reading and writing, and other corresponding functional limitations. Five variables were determined to be significantly different among the two status groups. Ironically, those clients who were closed Status 28 had higher verbal, performance, and full-scale IQ scores; this revelation was consistent with the Berkeley (1989) study. Similarly, Status 28 clients also achieved higher writing and reading achievement scores, but demonstrated no differences in math achievement areas.

Following the RSA definition of SLD and the system's established protocol for eligibility determination, the incidence of documented functional limitations (e.g., attention, verbal and visual memory, reasoning, academics, emotional maturity, and others) was compared for both closure status groups.

Individuals with a Status 28 closure (14%) were more likely ($X^2 = 4.42$, $p < .04$) to present with significant affective states of depression compared to those in Status 26 (9%). And, in addition to the diagnosis of SLD, Status 28 closures (18%) were more likely ($X^2 = 8.05$, $p < .005$) to be diagnosed with significant attention and concentration problems resulting in an Attention Deficit Hyperactivity Disorder (ADHD) as well (Dunham et al., 1996). Regarding client emotional status at the time of eligibility determination, Waldo (1995) reported that 20% of a representative state VR sample of clients diagnosed independently with SLD displayed marked elevations on the Minnesota Multiphasic Personality Inventory (MMPI), the

TABLE 9.2

Comparison of "Successful" and "Unsuccessful" Closure
using Demographic, Ability, Achievement, and Outcome Variables

Variable	*Closure Type*		
	Successful *(N = 361)*	*Non-successful* *(N = 252)*	*Statistic*
Mean Age at Application	20.3 SD = 6.3	19.7 SD = 5.5	$t = 1.20$ $p = .230$
Percent male	76%	69%	$x^2 = 2.88$ $p = .089$
Percent female	24%	31%	$x^2 = 2.88$ $p = .089$
Percent Caucasian	95%	95%	$x^2 = .02$ $p = .89$
Percent African American	5%	5%	$x^2 = .02$ $p = .89$
Average Full Scale IQ	92.4 SD = 8.4	95.2 SD = 10.7	$t = -1.66$ $p = .000$
Average Verbal IQ	88.3 SD = 8.8	91.2 SD = 11.2	$t = -3.48$ $p = .001$
Average Performance IQ	99.8 SD = 11.0	101.7 SD = 12.3	$t = -2.05$ $p = .041$
Average reading score*	81.5 SD = 10.2	83.8 SD = 11.8	$t = -2.59$ $p = .010$
Average math score*	84.8 SD = 12.2	86.2 SD = 12.1	$t = -1.44$ $p = .149$
Average writing score*	78.3 SD = 9.9	80.0 SD = 11.1	$t = -2.01$ $p = .045$
Average number of jobs for those who had worked prior to referral	2.1 (N = 253)	2.3 (N = 188)	$x^2 = 2.05$ $p = .56$

Average length in months of
  longest job for those who had
  worked prior to VR referral
	19.9 (months)	17.9	$t = .64$ $p = .523$

Average highest grade achieved	11.0 SD = 1.2	11.0 SD = 1.2	$x^2 = 1.6$ $p = .66$
Average number with vocational training	30%	26%	$x^2 = 1.41$ $p = .234$
Percent receiving college training as VR service	24%	37%	$x^2 = 87.1$ $p = .000$
Percent receiving guidance and counseling as VR treatment	9.4%	16.3%	$x^2 = 6.49$ $p = .01$
Percent with mood disorder 2nd diagnosis	5%	10%	$x^2 = 5.5$ $p = .019$
Percent with anxiety disorder as 2nd diagnosis	2%	1%	$x^2 = .306$ $p = .58$
Selected Functional Limitations:			
Verbal memory	30%	33%	$x^2 = .418$ $p = .518$
Visual memory	6%	8%	$x^2 = .496$ $p = .481$
Depression	9%	14%	$x^2 = 4.42$ $p = .035$
Anxiety	12%	13%	$x^2 = .295$ $p = .587$
ADHD/ADD	10%	18%	$x^2 = 8.05$ $p = .005$
Self-esteem	15%	16%	$x^2 = .046$ $p = .83$
Reasoning	9%	9%	$x^2 = .013$ $p = .9$

*Because of the high number of standard scores listed as "<65" in the original data, standard scores at or below 65 were automatically entered as 65. Therefore, the "true" mean standard score may actually be lower than this value.

Note. From Dunham, M., Koller, J. R., & McIntosh, D. (1996). A preliminary comparison of successful and unsuccessful closure types among adults with specific learning disabilities in the Vocational Rehabilitation system. *Journal of Rehabilitation.*

impact of which was further documented through external validation. This adds additional supporting evidence to the importance of recognizing client social and emotional considerations (Gerber & Reiff, 1994) in effective case management. Thus, personality factors influence the client's overall functioning and both job-seeking and job-keeping skills.

Enhancing a Long-term Positive Vocational Outcome

Traditionally, when reporting intelligence scores, researchers often cite the client's Wechsler Adult Intelligence Scale–Revised (WAIS-R) Full Scale IQ score (Berkeley, 1989; Minskoff, Hawks, Steidle & Hoffman, 1989). Although consideration of the full-scale IQ is often helpful in understanding the overall cognitive level of the VR client, additional, often more realistic information, may be obtained by studying various subtest patterns and the verbal/performance split, which may render the full-scale IQ score misleading. As Dunham et al. (1996) relate, both Status 26 (Verbal = 88.3, Performance = 99.8, and Full Scale = 92.4) as well as Status 28 (Verbal = 91.2, Performance = 101.7, and Full Scale = 95.2) scores displayed significantly higher performance IQs than verbal IQs. However, it was common to observe significant variances which existed within either the verbal or performance subtests themselves. For example, scaled scores ranging from 4 to 16 (Mean = 10) were not uncommon. Thus, by studying the verbal-performance split as well as the subtest patterns within that split, VR client advocates can often secure additional information about possible client strengths as well as deficits. With individuals who present with SLD, the Full Scale IQ score by itself may be misleading since it is, in essence, a composite.

Given that the State Division of Vocational Rehabilitation is neither designed nor mandated to establish eligibility and thus serve all individuals with SLD who seek employment, it is important to recognize those factors that do facilitate the likelihood of vocational success. Those variables which appear to improve the likelihood of long-term, successful vocational outcomes support the need for the following:

- acquisition of effective on-the-job interpersonal skills

- development of specific job-related academic skills

- development of specific vocational skills to perform more than entry-level personal service jobs (Tillman & Abbott, 1992)

Yet typical state VR agencies cite the following services, reflective of these needs, as frequently unavailable:

- peer support system

- provision of post-placement follow-up services

- training in self-awareness and self-advocacy skills

- good remediation specialist (Berkeley, 1989)

Nonetheless, in most cases, SLD necessitates alternative and often creative approaches to provide the client the opportunity to achieve vocational success. As discussed earlier, intelligence often has little direct relation to the degree of disability, and does not predict successful vocational closures. Therefore, referring agencies, including schools, must take a critical look at those academic and programmatic requirements that will better prepare the individual for employment success. Those factors include:

1. The continued development of good communication skills (McCrea, 1991).

2. For a student in transition from school to work, completion of high school is a positive indicator for future job success (Wagner, 1989). And, because students with SLD often lack the basic academic skills necessary for successful employment, it is essential that the student's academic curriculum translates directly to the world of work. Just as employees in the workforce are encouraged to acquire transferable job skills, students entering the workforce could enhance their opportunities for vocational success by ensuring that pre-vocational readiness skills are acquired (Koller, 1994).

3. A wide variety of verbal and language processing skills, including memory and receptive and expressive communication, contribute substantially to vocational success. While some evidence suggests the possibility that individuals within language-deficit SLD subtypes demonstrate a poorer long-term outcome than those with other SLD (Spreen, 1988), and, given that the most common SLD subtype served by VR appears to include those clients whose deficits lie in the verbal/language areas (Berkeley, 1989; Dunham, et al., 1996), field-tested accommodative strategies need to be implemented whenever possible. It is well known that employers rely heavily on interviews as part of the employment application process. Therefore, effective verbal communication skills, both in job seeking and in job keeping, will improve successful vocational outcomes. (Schemmerhorn, Gardner & Martin, 1990).

4. Successful job attainment and job maintenance is often affected by nonverbal communication skills. As well, Wircenski (1986) notes that affective skills, including dependability, initiative, self-confidence, and a good work attitude are necessary for successful job maintenance. These skills and general employer perceptions of overall client work performance are often transmitted to others in a nonverbal manner.

5. Programs in which students receive concurrent classroom and on-the-job instruction and experience have shown success. This, coupled with educating the employer about SLD specifically and disabilities in general, acts to increase the probability that the client will be able to seek and maintain employment (Dickson, 1993). Furthermore, providing employer training, encouraging meaningful employer feedback, conducting realistic performance appraisal, limiting unwanted helpfulness, understanding cultural differences, and promoting client-coworker inclusion on the job will promote job satisfaction and performance (Dickson, 1993).

6. Disability awareness, including self-advocacy and empowerment issues, effect successful vocational outcomes (Koller, 1994). For the student in transition, or for the individual in the workforce, the perception that the disability will "go away" or "not affect me once I get on a job" will easily disillusion the individual. To facilitate client understanding of a disability, effective career counseling must include a realistic appraisal of individual strengths and weaknesses, and a determination as to how the disability will impact the client's life educationally, socially, and vocationally.

7. State interagency communication and cooperation efforts must exist, not just in theory, but in practice at all levels. Specific learning disability is too complex a phenomenon for one individual, one system, one agency, etc., to combat alone. And, since one goal of education is employment, special education and vocational rehabilitation agencies, in particular, must cooperate. Differences in definition, eligibility, and service delivery continue to plague individuals with SLD as they traverse systems in search of gainful employment. Therefore, as these people continue to enter the workforce, policy makers, private sector representatives, and employers, including practitioners in education and human services, must find a common ground for communication (Young, Gerber & Koller, 1994).

8. The relationship between SLD and adult literacy remains unclear. Estimates that 50–80% of those in adult basic education programs may have SLD complicates not only identification but also the

employment outlook. Why so many adults fail to develop functionally adequate literacy skills as a characteristic of SLD is unclear. Nonetheless, SLD "is dramatically higher among adults with low levels of educational attainment or literacy proficiency" (Reder, 1995). Accordingly, among adults with the lowest levels of proficiency in literacy, the SLD incidence rate is projected to be nearly 10% (Reder, 1995).

9. Most adults with learning disabilities enter community life with little confidence that they can get jobs and are often pessimistic about long-term vocational outcomes (Fischer, 1994). As was previously discussed, personality factors play a significant role, not only in job performance, but in job satisfaction. Therefore, counseling is often needed to develop the individual's self-concept and to assist him or her in coping with the ramifications of the deficit. Individuals with SLD must come to the realization that they can develop an internal locus of control (Dane, 1993).

Conclusion

Recognition that SLD is the fastest-growing disability category served by the state and federal vocational rehabilitation system, and that individuals with SLD are at significant risk for both school and job dropout, informs a growing national employment concern for wasted human potential. Given that most individuals assume that one goal of education is to seek gainful and productive employment, it is important to understand those factors which will help facilitate a long-term successful vocational outcome.

As the structure and function of the U.S. workforce changes—due, in part, to racial, cultural, and increasing technological demands as we approach the 21st century—it becomes increasingly important that the individual with SLD focus not just on deficits but on his or her strengths. Undoubtedly, the employee who is able to succeed in the workplace is the one who possesses transferable job skills.

By now, it is quite apparent that SLD is more than an academic deficit. Comments that "it will go away" or "if you would only work harder" no longer hold substance. For those individuals in transition from school to work, the curriculum clearly needs to focus on work-related objectives. We have also learned that personality plays a far greater role in the life of an individual with SLD, both on and off the job, than ever thought possible. Perhaps now we can understand why the incidence rate of affective disturbances, characterized by poor self-concept, frustration, and denial, impact significantly both in school and on the job.

For those individuals whose disabilities represent a substantial impediment to employment, necessitating vocational rehabilitation service delivery intervention, this chapter has focused on factors known to facilitate or impede vocational rehabilitation success. One point is clear: The individual with SLD has the right and obligation to be a self-supporting and contributing member of society. As knowledgeable advocates, vocational rehabilitation professionals can play a pivotal role in maximizing this effort.

References

American Psychiatric Association (1994). *Diagnostic and statistical manual of mental disorders* (4th ed., revised). Washington, DC: Author.

Americans with Disabilities Act of 1990, 42 U.S.C. 12101 *et seq.*

Americans with Disabilities Act: *ADA Compliance Guide* (1992). (p. 3). Washington, DC: Thompson Publishing Group.

Berkeley Planning Associates (BPA) (1989). *Evaluation of services provided for individuals with specific learning disabilities: A final report.* (Vols. I–II). Prepared for U.S. Department of Education (Contract # 300-87-0112).

Coutinho, M. J. (1995). The national profile and recent studies regarding characteristics, integration, secondary school experiences, and transitions of youth with specific learning disabilities: Summary and implications. In Learning Disabilities Association of America (LDA), *Secondary Education and Beyond: Providing Opportunities for Students with Learning Disabilities.* Pittsburgh, PA: LDA.

Dane, E. (1993). Family fantasies and adolescent aspirations: A social work perspective on a critical transition. *Family and Community Health, 16*(3), 34–45.

Dickson, M. B. (1993). *Supervising employees with disabilities: Beyond ADA compliance.* Menlo Park, CA: Crisp Publications, Inc.

Dowdy, C. A., & Smith, T. E. C. (1994). Serving individuals with specific learning disabilities in the vocational rehabilitation system. In P. J. Gerber and H. B. Reiff (Eds.), *Learning disabilities in adulthood: Persisting problems and evolving issues.* (pp. 171–178). Stoneham, MA: Butterworth-Heinemann.

Dunham, M., Koller, J. R., & McIntosh, D. (1996). A preliminary comparison of successful and nonsuccessful closure types among adults with specific learning disabilities in the Vocational Rehabilitation system. *Journal of Rehabilitation, Jan., Feb., Mar.,* 42–47.

Education for All Handicapped Children Act of 1975, 20 U.S.C. 1400 *et seq.*

Fischer, R. J. (1994). The Americans with Disabilities Act: Implications for Measurement. *Educational Measurement: Issues and Practices, 13*(3), 17–26.

Fourqurean, J. M., Meisgeier, C., Swank, P. R., & Williams, R. E. (1991). Correlates of postsecondary employment outcomes for young adults with learning disabilities. *Journal of Learning Disabilities, 24*(7), 400–405.

Gerber, P. J., & Reiff, H. B. (1991). *Speaking for themselves: Ethnographic interviews with adults with learning disabilities.* Ann Arbor: The University of Michigan Press.

Gerber, P. J., & Reiff, H. B. (1994). *Learning disabilities in adulthood: Persisting problems and evolving issues.* Stoneham, MA: Butterworth-Heinemann.

Haring, K. A., & Lovett, D. L. (1990). A follow-up study of special education graduates. *The Journal of Special Education, 23,* 463–477.

Heaton, R. K. (1988). Introduction to the special series. *Journal of Consulting and Clinical Psychology, 56*(6), 787–788.

Heinkebein, J. H., Koller, J. R., & Kunce, J. T. (1992, Oct., Nov., Dec.). Normal personality and adults with learning disabilities: Rehabilitation counseling implications. *Journal of Rehabilitation,* 40–46.

Individuals with Disabilities Education Act of 1990, 20 U.S.C. 1400 *et seq.*

Koller, J. R. (1994, Summer). Improving transition outcomes for persons with specific learning disabilities. *Journal of Rehabilitation,* 37–42.

Mellard, D. F., & Hagel, S. J. (1992). Social competencies as a pathway to successful life transitions. *Learning Disabilities Quarterly, 15,* 251–271.

Minskoff, E. H., Hawks, R., Steidle, E. F., & Hoffman, F. J. (1989). A homogeneous group of persons with learning disabilities: Adults with severe learning disabilities in vocational rehabilitation. *Journal of Learning Disabilities, 22,* 521–528.

McCrea, L. (1991). A comparison between the perceptions of special educators and employers: What factors are critical for job success? *Career Development of Exceptional Individuals, 14*(2), 121–130.

McCue, M. (1995). Assessing vocational rehabilitation services for individuals with specific learning disabilities. In Learning Disability Association of America, *Secondary Education and Beyond: Providing Opportunities for Students with Learning Disabilities,* Pittsburg, PA: LDA.

Reder, S. (1995). *Literacy, education and learning disabilities.* Portland, OR: Northwest Regional Education Laboratory.

The Rehabilitation Act of 1973 as amended by the Rehabilitation Act Amendments of 1993. Congressional Records, Washington, DC: U.S. Government Printing Office.

Rehabilitation Services Administration (1992, March 20). *Order of Selection for Services Policy Manual RSA-MT-92-17.* Washington, DC: Office of Special Education and Rehabilitation Services.

Rehabilitation Services Administration (1985, March 5). *Program Policy Directive RSA-PPD-85-7.* Washington, DC: Office of Special Education and Rehabilitation Services.

Rehabilitation Services Administration (1990, September 28). *Program Assistance Circular RSA-PAC-90-7.* Washington, DC: Office of Special Education and Rehabilitative Services.

Reiff, H. B., Gerber, P. J., & Ginsberg, R. (In press). *Exceeding expectations: Highly successful adults with learning disabilities.* Austin, TX: PRO-ED.

Schemmerhorn, J. R., Gardner, W. L., & Martin, T. N. (1990). Management dialogues: Turning on the marginal performer. *Organizational Dynamics, 18*(4), 47–59.

Shaywitz, S. E., Shaywitz, B. A., Fletcher, J. M., & Escobar, M. D. (1990). Prevalence of reading disability in boys and girls: Results of the Connecticut Longitudinal Study. *Journal of American Medical Association, 264*, 998–1002.

Spreen, O. (1988). Prognosis of learning disability. *Journal of Consulting and Clinical Psychology, 56*(6), 836–841.

Tillman, Z., & Abbott, J. (1992, March). *Transition of youth with learning disabilities* (working papers). Washington, DC: Rehabilitation Services Administration, U.S. Department of Education.

United States Employment and Training Administration (1991). *The Learning Disabled in Employment and Training Programs* (Research and Evaluation Report Series 91–E), Washington, DC: U.S. Department of Labor.

Vogel, S. A. (1989). Adults with language learning disabilities: Definition, diagnosis and determination of eligibility for postsecondary and vocational rehabilitation services. *Rehabilitation Education, 3*, 77–90.

Wagner, M. (1989). *The transition experience of youth with disabilities: A report from the National Longitudinal Transition Study.* Menlo Park, CA: SRI International (ERIC Document Reproduction Service No. ED 303 988).

Waldo, S. L. (1995). *Personality profiles of adults with verbal and nonverbal learning disabilities.* Unpublished doctoral dissertation, University of Missouri, Columbia.

Wircenski, J. L. (1986). School to work transition skills for the disadvantaged learner. *Journal of Industrial Teacher Education, 24*(1), 74–82.

Young, G., Gerber, P. J., & Koller, J. R. (1994, August). The Building Bridges Interagency Conference: Innovative efforts for collaboration on learning disability in adult basic education, literacy and employment. *Learning Disability: A Multidisciplinary Journal, 5*(2), 63–68.

Zigmond, N. (1990). Rethinking secondary school programs for students with learning disabilities. *Focus on Exceptional Children, 23*, 1–22.

CHAPTER 10

Preparation for Employment: Counseling Practices for Promoting Personal Competency

Craig A. Michaels

Treat people as if they were what they ought to be,
and you help them to become what they are capable of being.

—GOETHE

Historically, learning disabilities have been viewed, within the context of education, as ". . . imperfect ability to listen, think, read, write, spell, or do mathematical calculation" (Interagency Committee on Learning Disabilities, 1987, p. 220); and, from the limited vantage point of the individual, as ". . . a disorder in one or more of the central nervous system processes" (Rehabilitation Services Administration, 1985). Even when viewed within a limited context and from a narrow vantage point, we now know that anywhere from 4 to 8% of *all* school-aged children are classified as having a "Specific Learning Disability." In the 1992–93 school year, this translated to roughly 2.3 million students ages 6 through 21 (United States Department of Education, 1994).

Missing from this picture of learning disabilities—when presented within the contexts of education and/or individual central nervous system dysfunction—are the related social-emotional and personality issues, present upon initial diagnosis and possibly changing over time. The roles of parents, educators, rehabilitation professionals, other community members, and society in creating, sustaining, and promoting awareness of learning disabilities and their associated social-emotional characteristics also are not addressed. The significant impact of learning disabilities, within this more broadly defined context, upon work and participation in the "real adult world" has been neglected, as well.

While I will not argue that there exists a tremendous body of research demonstrating that there are clearly real central nervous system differences at the heart of what we choose to label "learning disabilities," we also need to realize that "[w]e create disability" (Higgins, 1992, p. 6) through our beliefs, attitudes, politics, and practices (e.g., see Ferguson, 1987). Minow wrote that "[t]he dominant group's experience in the guise of the 'natural' way of life becomes the standard by which other experiences are evaluated and are said to differ. Thus 'difference is not discovered but humanly invented'—and invented in ways that favor some people over others" (as cited in Higgins, 1992, p. 8).

Glenn's description of his early school years (grades 1–4) in Canfield and Hansen's *A 2nd Helping of Chicken Soup for the Soul* (1995) is representative of the experience and life stories of all too many individuals with learning disabilities:

> I [initially] perceived my world as a wonderful place filled with these shapes called words and developed a rather extensive sight vocabulary that made my parents quite optimistic about my ability to learn. To my horror, I discovered in the first grade that letters were more important than words. . . . So my first-grade teacher called me learning disabled. She wrote down her observations and passed them on to my second-grade teacher over the summer so she could develop an appropriate bias against me before I arrived. . . . Now I was totally intimidated by the learning process, so I developed a stutter. . . . That sealed my fate. . . . My third-grade teacher knew before I arrived that I couldn't speak, write, read or do mathematics . . . I [then] discovered malingering as a basic tool to get through school. This allowed me to spend more time with the school nurse than the teacher or find vague reasons to stay home or be sent home. (Glenn, 1995, pp. 212–213)

While participation in school is a painful experience for many individuals with learning disabilities, the thought of entering into the adult world of employment is often terrifying. West (1991) asserts that, beyond the experience of school as "difficult, painful, and often humiliating. . . . the prospect of real work in the world of adults is a cause for despair and even terror" (p. 54).

Focus on Personal Competency

This chapter takes an ecological look at learning disabilities and addresses the counseling needs of young adults as they prepare to assume their rightful roles as fully contributing members of our society. There is an omnipresent focus on the development of personal competency which I will define as the belief in one's ability to positively effect change in one's own life. Personal competency subsumes such terms as self-determination, self-advocacy, and personal autonomy.

My reason for taking this approach is that in all our lives, the experiences we tend to classify as our *triumphs* or our *successes* are always fewer than the experiences we euphemistically title our *learning experiences*. It seems to be primarily our sense of self, or our belief in our own ability to positively effect change, (i.e., what I am calling personal competency) that allows us to continue trying, if you will, in spite of our all-too-numerous *learning experiences*.

For many adults with learning disabilities, triumphs or successes tend to be even fewer in relation to the proportion of learning experiences. In addition, these learning experiences, in most instances, are labelled by service providers, parents, significant others, and—worst of all—by individuals with learning disabilities as *personal failures*. Each failure is attributed to self (and, all too often, turned against the self, eroding competency) while triumphs and successes are attributed only to luck or some external force or agent (Michaels, Thaler, Zwerlein, Gioglio, & Apostoli, 1988). The result is an individual with a poor sense of personal competency who lacks the will to try in pre-anticipation of failure. Due to the pre-anticipated sense of failure and lack of competency, many young adults with learning disabilities have been described as having difficulties with all the skills necessary for making the transition from dependence to independence. They have been described as having difficulty:

- taking responsibility for oneself
- separating from parental control and values
- separating from the control of the school system
- developing an internal locus of control (Michaels et al., 1988, p. 5)

The counseling needs of persons with learning disabilities can best be addressed within an ecological framework, through the presentation of personal competency from sociological and psychological perspectives. The sociological perspective encompasses the role society plays in promoting and inhibiting the development of personal competency. The psychological perspective includes the impact of the associated cognitive, behavioral, and emotional characteristics of individuals with learning disabilities on the development of personal competency.

The Role Society Plays in Promoting and Inhibiting Development of Personal Competency

Society's role may seem, at first, to lie beyond the scope of this chapter. The results, however, of the biased attitudes, lowered expectations, and limited focus on disability contribute significantly to the personal counseling needs of young adults with learning disabilities. By the time many reach adolescence, their sense of competency, willingness to dream, and ability to actively participate in creating a vision for their future (Mount, 1992) have been severely diminished. Addressing the role of society (and, more specifically, service providers, parents, and the educational system) is a critical *primary intervention* in the prevention of damage to the developing sense of self and competency among individuals with learning disabilities. This type of primary intervention will be, in almost all instances and certainly in the long run, more effective and cost-efficient than providing the *secondary intervention* (i.e., direct counseling) once an individual's sense of self and competency are damaged.

Learning disabilities, and more importantly, the students labeled as "learning disabled," now represent reality instead of being part of our explanation of reality. We tend to forget that "[o]ur descriptions of human differences are artifacts of cultural values and hence of our world view, rather than being definitions of fixed traits in individuals," noted Sarason (as cited in Kronick, 1988, p. 33). Sociologists who subscribe to the notion of symbolic interactionism stress the idea that human beings treat others on the basis of the meaning they attribute to them. "The slow child's [i.e., child with learning disabilities] functioning may be as dependent upon the definition [meaning] given to his condition by those in positions to influence the circumstances of his life as the 'reality' of his 'slowness'" (Bogdan, 1986, p. 348).

Our behavior and treatment of individuals with learning disabilities is determined, to a large extent, by our ideologies and our assumptions about the world (see Covey, 1990; Wolfensberger, Nirjer, Olshansky, Persker, & Roos, 1972). Others have used the term *paradigm* in a manner similar to the way I am using the term *ideology*. Skrtic (1991), for example, defines paradigm as "an accepted way of interpreting the world" (p. 27). Covey (1990) in a similar manner defines *paradigm* as: "a model, theory, perception, assumption, or frame of reference. . . . [i.e.] the way we 'see' the world—not in terms of our visual sense of sight, but in terms of our perceiving, understanding, interpreting" (p. 23).

Snow (1994) challenges our way of conceptualizing disability and logically points out how our current "paradigm" ultimately leads to the internalized "wounded" sense of self possessed by so many persons who we have labelled as LD.

> *Disability is a paradigm* [emphasis in original]. Believing in disability allows us to have certain thoughts and assumptions about people. The whole notion of disability depends on the thought that people can be hampered by limitations. . . . *We have become certain that only young, happy and otherwise perfect people are eligible for fulfillment. Until we attain these three conditions we consider ourselves wounded in our ability to be creative or to make a contribution* [emphasis in original]. (Snow, 1994, pp. 12–13)

But Not Exactly a Rocket Scientist: Embracing the Disability Paradigm

We may say that the motto of our special education and vocational rehabilitation programs is that "we build on strengths." More often, however, it appears that our entire focus and energies are expended on the identification and remediation of skill deficits. This focus only serves to highlight an individual's learning disabilities (West, 1991; Wilson, 1994). Rather than viewing the person as an individual with a whole host of relative strengths and weaknesses, we begin to describe him or her solely based on deficits. West's 1991 book, *In the Mind's Eye: Visual Thinkers, Gifted People with Learning Difficulties, Computer Images, and the Ironies of Creativity* is a notable exception. In fact, West's major hypothesis within this text is that many of the people we classify as *learning disabled* "have achieved success or even greatness not in spite of but because of their apparent disabilities" (p. 19).

Still, researchers and service providers continue to justify this focus on deficits with assertions about the tenacity and pervasiveness of learning disabilities so that the disability, and not the person's ability, is constantly brought to bear (Hoy, 1986). The unfortunate reality of our current approaches (and the embracing of the disability paradigm) is perhaps best expressed by Poplin in her last editorial as editor-in-chief of the *Learning Disabilities Quarterly* (LDQ):

> The horrifying truth is that in the four years I have been editor of LDQ, only one article has been submitted that sought to elaborate on the talents of the learning disabled. This is a devastating commentary on a field that is supposed to be dedicated to the education of students with average and above average intelligence. . . . Why do we not know if our

students are talented in art, music, dance, athletics, mechanical repair, computer programming, or are creative in other nontraditional ways? . . . It is because, like regular educators, we care only about *competence* [emphasis added] in its most traditional and bookish sense. (Poplin, 1984, p. 133 cited in Armstrong, 1994, p. 134)

As I sit in my office in front of my computer I often muse upon a poster of Albert Einstein on my wall.[1] We might debate—as we can with almost any other person labelled as learning disabled—whether Albert Einstein was in fact "LD" (see West, 1991), but the poster's message is succinct: *They said he was a nice enough kid, but not exactly a rocket scientist.* Einstein's unique combination of strengths (and learning differences) has been described frequently. West (1991), for example, presents the following profile:

> Einstein used the most sophisticated mathematics to develop his theories, but often his sums would not come out right. He was a daydreamer who played fancifully with images in his mind, but in the process he created an objective image of the universe that transformed forever our view of physical reality. Einstein had trouble learning and remembering facts, words, and texts, but he was teacher to the world. He was slow to speak, but, in time, the world listened. (West, 1991, p. 129)

Perhaps one of Einstein's saving graces was that he was never officially labelled "a nice enough kid, but not exactly a rocket scientist"—*learning disabled.* In an early address to the Orton Dyslexia Society, titled "The Advantages of Being Dyslexic," Masland (1976) provides an interesting analysis of Einstein's early years, attributing much of his success in life to luck. Masland concludes this address by stating that:

> . . . it almost appears that Einstein's development was made possible only by a series of fortuitous, almost trivial circumstances, occurring primarily outside of the framework of his formal education. How fortunate that his environment made this possible. (p. 17)

We would all agree (at least in theory) that for us, as educators, parents, and rehabilitation service providers, to focus only on deficits and thus limit potential, is problematic. The more insidious and devastating consequence (especially from a counseling and personal competency

---

[1]For more information about this poster, contact the Roanoke Valley Learning Disabilities Association, P.O. Box 20232, Roanoke, Virginia 24018.

point of view), however, is that we, in turn, silence the dreams, goals, and aspirations of young children with learning disabilities before they even begin to engage in self- and vocational exploration as young adults. We also disempower young adults from achieving the personal autonomy necessary to self-actualize and develop a vocational identity (Michaels, 1994a).

The recent findings of national focus group sessions on attitudes and awareness of learning disabilities conducted for the Tremaine Foundation, support the persistence of this unfounded belief (i.e., that a person with learning disabilities is "not exactly a rocket scientist"). Many participants—including individuals with learning disabilities—associated learning disabilities with retardation. "A most disturbing aspect of this misconception is that the LD students and adults believe others view them as mentally retarded, sub par, or dangerous" (Belden & Russonello, 1994, p. 5). Other misperceptions identified by the focus groups include notions equating learning disabilities with "laziness" and "lack of discipline" (Belden & Russonello, 1994, p. 5). The life stories of students and young adults with learning disabilities, as shared in these focus groups, "revealed the enormous pain they have encountered in trying to be 'normal' in the non-LD world—most of the pain [they believe is] caused by a lack of knowledge and understanding by others" (Belden & Russonello, 1994, p. 6).

In the various training sessions for parents, advocates, special educators, and rehabilitation service providers that I conduct around the country, I often begin by putting on an overhead slide with only the words "Learning Disabilities" and/or the initials "LD" on it. I then elicit a whole host of perceptions and associations from members of the audience in relation to these two words or initials. For ease of presentation, the following lists present samples of the typical audience associations which, for the purposes of this presentation, have been artificially separated into three somewhat logical, but by no means mutually exclusive, performance categories: academics, social and independent living, and vocational.

Typical Professional Perceptions of Young Adults with Learning Disabilities

Academic Performance

- terrible spellers
- slow readers

- comprehension difficulties
- poor notetakers
- illegible handwriting
- difficulty with word problems
- poor study skills
- failures
- inconsistent

Social/Independent Living Performance

- extreme frustration
- inappropriate behavior
- learned helplessness
- low self-esteem
- can't stay focused
- hyperactive
- intrusive/disruptive
- unmotivated
- poor communication skills
- poor self-monitoring
- troublemakers

Vocational Performance

- gives up easily
- blames others
- rush through work
- unrealistic
- lacks self-control
- easily distracted

These lists provide only a sample of the typical responses. The fact that all responses can be classified as negative associations and negative personal attributes is no coincidence. Usually, it is only after I point out that all the traits and characteristics generated by audience members appear to be negative attributes that someone will come up with a positive attribute to add. In almost all cases, the positive attribute (added as an afterthought) relates to the unique personality of one individual with learning disabilities that the audience member knows, or knew, on some personal level—rather than the more general and negative attributes and associations which tend to be equated with the disability group in the abstract. One only needs to imagine (without even dealing with any of the internal attributes or psychological characteristics of a given individual) what the counseling and self-esteem issues would be for any young adult who was a member of a group of individuals perceived as the one just described. We can then begin to gain a personal glimpse into the damaged sense of personal competency that so many young adults with learning disabilities possess.

Work currently in progress, creating person-centered planning models that empower people with disabilities to actively take control of their lives and plan for their futures, confronts the service providers' focus on deficits as the critical starting point. The success of these models relies on an ideological shift in the focus of service providers from deficits to a belief in the gifts, capacities, and dreams of the individuals they serve (Mount, 1992).

Snow calls this ideological shift "the expression of giftedness" (1994, p. 20). She speaks in terms of a paradigm shift, indicating that "[e]veryone has gifts—countless ordinary and extraordinary gifts. A gift is anything that one is or has or does that creates an opportunity for a meaningful interaction with at least one other person. Gifts are the fundamental characteristics of our human life and community. . . . *Meaning is only possible because of difference*" (emphasis added, Snow, 1994, pp. 18–19). Covey (1990), in *The 7 Habits of Highly Effective People*, also talks about the need for society and parents to make this paradigm shift. He relates how his wife and he "were consumed with a desire to help [their son]" (p. 17), yet:

> we began to realize that what we were doing to help our son was not in harmony with the way we really saw him. When we honestly examined our deepest feelings, we realized our perception was that he was basically inadequate, somehow "behind." No matter how much we worked on our attitude and behavior, our efforts were ineffective because, despite our actions and our words, what we really communicated to him was, "You aren't capable. You have to be protected." We began to realize that if we wanted to change the situation, we first had to change ourselves. And to change ourselves effectively we first had to change our perceptions. (Covey, 1990, p. 17–18)

The Role of Parents in the Development of Competency: Fostering Giftedness

Mike Green, a parent of a child with a disability, perhaps best captures in words the paradigm shift so necessary if we as a society (and parents) are to fully embrace the giftedness of individuals (and our own children) with learning disabilities.

> When people begin to see gifts and begin to participate in the Giftedness paradigm, it is as though a fog has lifted from their eyes. To see gifts after being conditioned to see only deficits and problems is a wrenching, heart opening experience. This different view leads to a new world, it is as simple as a new pair of glasses. We see what we believe. (Snow, 1994, p. 21)

In addition to assisting young adults develop personal competency by changing our beliefs about people with learning disabilities in general, we must also begin, especially in early adolescence, to assist individuals develop a sense of personal autonomy. Will points out that "separating emotionally and physically from the family remain[s] a critical milestone for all young people with and without disabilities. [Although special education graduates with learning disabilities may progress academically and intellectually, there is still] . . . a frustrating lack of clarity regarding the way these young people [define] themselves as young adults" (Will, 1993, p. 9).

Parents of young adults with learning disabilities tend to exercise a tremendous amount of control over the lives of their sons and daughters.[2] Whether the need to exercise this control is real or imagined, many parents also get involved in serving as teacher and advocate for their children, again whether the need for this service is real or imagined (Michaels, 1994b).

The net result, evoking the old notion of the self-fulfilling prophecy, is that the need does, in time, become real—even if, at one point in the past, the young adult may have possessed the potential to show that the parental belief in that need was indeed imagined. Most devastating for these young adults, when parents assume these additional roles, is that

---

[2]Before taking offense at any statements contained within this section, the reader should at least take note that the author is writing from the personal perspective as a parent of two children with learning disabilities (a 19-year-old son and an 8-year-old daughter at the time of this publication). All comments should be viewed first as self-reflections and then as comments on the general practices of other parents.

it tends to take away time and inhibit parents from serving in their primary and most empowering role: to "give their child as much unconditional love as possible" (Will, 1993, p. 10). The end result of parental overinvolvement may be that sons and daughters with learning disabilities tend to either:

- feel guilty about assuming power (personal autonomy)

- lack the ability and self-advocacy skills to assume power

- lack the confidence (which comes from knowing that they are loved unconditionally) to take this power

- not be empowered (through the feedback they received from parents and their home environment) to assume their autonomy (Michaels, 1994b, p. 13)

Parents must begin to question every action they take for, or on behalf of, their sons or daughters. They must develop the vision which will allow them not only to question the short-term effect, but also the long-term effect, especially on the development of personal autonomy and sense of self. I believe that empowerment, especially in relation to the development of autonomy from parental control, cannot be given. This empowerment must be actively taken by the young adult. In fact, if we were to study how this empowerment occurs *"naturally,"* (i.e., in young adults without disabilities), we would see that adolescence is a time when young adults try on roles and identities while simultaneously confronting the values and beliefs of their parents (Smith, Finn, & Dowdy, 1993). The inner strength (or, to borrow from Erikson, strong sense of *"ego-identity"*) required for young adults to actively seek to take this power and differentiate from their parents, must be predicated on the sense of competency that has been fostered by their parents in the past.

As already stated, parents of children with learning disabilities must be provided with the counseling necessary to view their primary role as the giving of unconditional love (e.g., Will, 1993) while simultaneously creating a safe and nurturing space for *"learning experiences"* to occur. It appears to be part of the soul, or essence, of the parental experience to want to shield the children we bring into this world from as much pain, suffering, and failure as humanly possible. This natural tendency may become overexaggerated in the parents of young adults with disabilities, especially those with learning disabilities.

Society, as well, fosters this role for parents, even to the point that parents are frequently viewed as "bad parents" when they appear to ignore or allow their children to struggle "unassisted." Parents of children with disabilities may even be judged more harshly when they fail to "rescue" their children. Dale Brown (personal communication, February 3, 1996) relates the story of an angered visitor watching as a young boy without arms struggled savagely to put his shirt on. When the visitor could no longer stand it she finally questioned the mother asking "Why don't you help him?" The wise mother calmly replied, "I am helping him!" In truth, the secret of wise parenting is that this shielding (or rescuing) may be unrealistic and, frequently, is counterproductive. In fact, as described in most spiritual philosophies and religious traditions, our life lessons tend to become more painful when these lessons are learned at later opportunities, rather than in earlier ones, during our process of becoming.

The Role of the School System in Promoting Competency

Dudley-Marling and Dippo (1995) suggest that "the field of learning disabilities emerged to contain the perceived failure of society's principal institution for education and socializing its youth [the schools]" (p. 408). One of the underlying assumptions we (as a society) make is that potential (intelligence) and effort (hard work) equal school success. Conservative estimates on prevalence (cited earlier in the chapter) suggest that, for 4 to 8% of the school-age population, this assumption is not valid (United States Department of Education, 1994). In order to maintain the status quo or *"to preserve conventional assumptions about the role of potential and effort in school achievement"* (Dudley-Marling & Dippo, 1995, p. 410, [emphasis in original]), we must, in turn, place the responsibility for school failure on the individual student.

Higgins (1992) argues that we cannot even understand learning disabilities except within the context of society, "how can a student be a slow achiever without some standard of acceptable (i.e., 'nondisabled') achievement" (p. 11)? He goes on to state that we cannot understand special education except within the context of general education, "how typical education sets the context within which education for children with disabilities is made 'special'" (Higgins, 1992, p. 11). Citing Lazerson (1983) and Barton (1988), Higgins comments on society's role in creating special education:

> If "regular" education had been created to speak to the diversity of our youth, rather than as a means to educate advantaged children and too often control or ignore disadvantaged children, then all of it would be special and no "special education" would be developed. (1992, p. 12)

Be this as it may, special education, and services for individuals with learning disabilities, primarily seek to change this anomaly (learning disabilities) by *"changing academic demands to enable students to succeed "* (Michaels, 1994b, p. 15, emphasis in original). Many traditional special education interventions for individuals with learning disabilities consist of some combination of three strategies (or intervention models):

- the provision of less work
- the provision of easier work
- the provision of extra time (Michaels, 1994b)

These types of intervention strategies may make sense at earlier developmental levels, in order to initially build self-confidence and self-esteem. Their successes are short-lived over time, however, and they quickly exert the opposite influence on students. By changing academic demands, we externally control the learner, rather than providing the learner with the tools (internal controls) necessary to negotiate the learning environment (and, ultimately, to achieve personal competency). It is beyond the scope of this chapter to address specific teaching and learning strategies that can equip students with learning disabilities with the skills to keep up with grade-appropriate content materials and grade-appropriate task demands. However, within the conceptual framework of the focus on counseling and promoting personal competency, it is crucial that individuals with learning disabilities compete with their peers in the real world. The Americans with Disabilities Act of 1990 (ADA), which is described as a landmark civil rights act for people with disabilities, speaks only of *the provision of reasonable accommodations to qualified individuals with disabilities* (Americans with Disabilities Handbook, 1991). It is extremely doubtful that an individual who needs to be accommodated by being provided with less work, easier work, or more time than co-workers to complete the work—accommodations most often provided by special education—will be considered "qualified" under ADA.

Within the purview of this chapter's focus on counseling is the role of special education programs, and more specifically, of special education teachers in promoting knowledge of self. Currently, both special and general education programs treat "learning disabilities" as something not to be discussed or acknowledged. Students leave school for college, employment, and/or vocational training with no personal ownership of their learning disabilities or knowledge of how their learning disabilities affect them on a day-to-day basis. More importantly, they also lack self-awareness or strategies they can employ to negotiate successfully in a variety of adult settings.

When counseling or working with special educators, we can conceptualize the development of self-awareness (or ownership) of one's learning disabilities (Michaels, 1994b) as occurring in three somewhat discrete stages. Figure 10.1 graphically depicts the three stages of this conceptual model.

Intellectual Awareness. The bottom portion of the triangle presented in Figure 10.1 is labeled "intellectual awareness." The majority of students with learning disabilities leave school having only achieved this level of self-awareness. At this level of self-awareness, "students can voice that they may have been in special education because they have 'problems,' but they cannot describe their own strengths and weaknesses" (Michaels, 1994b, pp. 17–18).

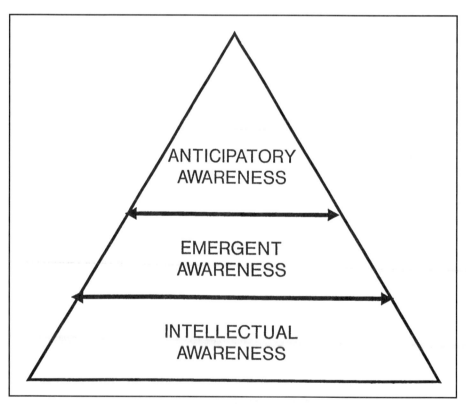

FIGURE 10.1. Conceptual Models of Self-awareness. From "Transition, Adolescence, and Learning Disabilities" by Craig A. Michaels, (1994). In C. A. Michaels (Ed.), *Transition strategies for persons with learning disabilities* (pp. 1–22). Copyright 1994 by Singular Publishing Company, Inc. Reprinted with permission.

Emergent Awareness. The middle portion of the triangle is labeled "emergent awareness." At this level of self-knowledge, which, unfortunately, is only achieved by a small number of students upon exiting special education, students can intellectually state the fact that they have a learning disability and can also usually describe their specific strengths and weaknesses" (Michaels, 1994b, p. 18). Individuals who have achieved this level of self-awareness are usually aware when they are in situations which are problematic, but they do not possess the "bag of tricks," so to speak, to effectively negotiate these difficult situations.

Anticipatory Awareness. The highest level of self-knowledge or awareness, currently achieved by only a small handful of students with learning disabilities upon exiting school, I have titled "anticipatory awareness." Those who reach this stage of self-awareness leave school empowered with the knowledge of self, specific strategies, and the sense of personal competency that will ensure success in a variety of post-school environments. Students who reach the anticipatory awareness stage of self-knowledge can: "(a) describe intellectually that they have learning disabilities, (b) describe their strengths and weaknesses, (c) anticipate problems that may require the application of task-specific strategies, and (d) implement the strategies to be successful" (Michaels, 1994b, p. 18).

The Impact of Cognitive, Behavioral, and Emotional Characteristics on the Development of Personal Competency

So far, this chapter has addressed many of the detrimental affects associated with current societal practices on the development of personal competency among individuals labelled as "learning disabled." Hoping that these practices and beliefs will change drastically in the near future, we now turn our focus to the individual. Since this chapter's primary focus is on the counseling needs of young adults with learning disabilities, it is probably useful to describe the typical presenting personality profile of young adults involved in the federal-state vocational rehabilitation (VR) system. Michaels, Lazar and Risucci (1995) present composite profile information on a sample of 75 subjects referred for vocational services through the federal-state vocational rehabilitation system. All individuals were classified by the VR system as having specific learning disabilities (SLD). Sixty-two of the 75 individuals completed the Millon Clinical

Multiaxial Inventory (MCMI [Millon, 1983]). The MCMI is an objective, self-reporting personality inventory with 20 scales directly related to categories in the DSM-IIIR.

Table 10.1 shows the percentage of participants in the Michaels, Lazar and Risucci study, with scores equaling or exceeding a particular salient feature of the MCMI clinical sample, namely, the percentage of the clinical sample that displayed some of the diagnostic features of a personality type or syndrome disorder without regard to the actual diagnosis of the individuals. The table also presents the percentages of

TABLE 10.1
Personality Characteristic Based
on the Millon Clinical Multiaxial Inventory[a]

Subscale	Observed Percentage of Participants	Comparison Clinical Sample
Dependent	59.7	Higher
Paranoid	29.0	Higher
Paranoid Disorder	29.0	Higher
Schizoid	27.0	Higher
Narcissistic	25.8	Higher
Avoidant	35.5	Similar
Anxiety Disorder	33.9	Similar
Dysthymia	27.4	Similar
Histrionic	24.2	Similar
Somatoform Disorder	22.6	Similar
Passive-Aggressive	21.0	Similar
Drug Abuse	17.3	Similar
Antisocial	14.5	Similar
Manic Disorder	11.3	Similar
Schizophrenic Disorder	9.7	Similar
Schizotypal	1.6	Similar
Borderline	9.7	Lower
Alcohol Abuse	3.2	Lower
Compulsive	3.2	Lower

[a]The percentages of participants at or above the base rate of 75 in comparison to the clinical norming sample.

individuals who scored higher than, the same as, or lower than the percentage of the clinical norming sample.

The individuals in our sample scored similarly to, or higher than, the clinical norming sample on most subscales. This indicates that they had more clinical symptoms than would be expected of a random nonclinical sample (and definitely more symptoms than the non-clinical norming sample). These young adults tended to score higher than anticipated on five of the Millon scales: dependent, paranoid and paranoid disorders, schizoid, and narcissistic; in the range that would be of some concern, although not clinically high on the avoidant scale; and lower than would be anticipated on three scales: compulsive, borderline, and alcohol abuse.

Dependent individuals can be characterized by their marked need for social approval and affection and their willingness to live in accord with the desires of others. In the most extreme cases, these individuals can be devastated by disapproval and they can excessively deny thoughts and feelings that may arouse displeasure in others. They will be unable to draw on themselves for comfort and gratification (Millon, 1981). Overall, this appears to be the most salient personality trait of the young adults with learning disabilities in our sample. In previous sections of this chapter, a strong rationale was presented for how the attitudes and behaviors of parents, educators, and society contribute (and in some cases create) this personality trait (which is tied closely to the special educational concept of "learned helplessness").

Paranoid individuals can be characterized by their mistrust of others and desire to stay free of relationships in which they might lose the power of self-determination. Paranoid individuals are suspicious, guarded, hostile and they tend to misread the actions of others. They are frequently limited in their coping skills (Millon, 1981). The higher-than-would-be-anticipated, self-reported level of paranoid tendency may actually result more from a misreading of social situations and lack of coping skills within social contexts than from traditional paranoid thinking patterns. The samples' scores on this scale may reflect adult manifestations of the social skills processing deficits that have been so often cited in the literature on children with learning disabilities. For example, children with learning disabilities frequently misinterpret social cues and nonverbal communication (e.g., Bryan, 1977) and also tend to be less able than peers to predict consequences or solve social problems (e.g., Schumaker, Hazel, Sherman, & Sheldon, 1982).

The schizoid, narcissistic and avoidant behavior categories seem to be various manifestations of the inability to form meaningful relationships with others. Schizoid individuals tend to be socially detached. These individuals display emotional and cognitive deficits that hinder the development of close or warm relationships (Millon, 1981). Individuals with narcissistic patterns are independent in their orientation. They turn inward for gratification and learn to rely on themselves. Unfortunately, in the pathological case, weaknesses and dependencies may be threatening. The fear of loss of self-determination may lead to self-aggrandizement and the need to be more important than others (Millon, 1981). Individuals who engage in avoidant type behavior (about a third of our sample) may actively avoid close or warm relationships except with special individuals in their lives, perhaps, specific family members.

Self-Actualization: Personal Autonomy and Meaningful Relationships

Wilson (1994) states that recognition by others contributes to our development of self. Positive recognition, particularly during our formative years, is critical to the development of what Erikson (1968) termed a healthy "ego-identity." Wilson goes on to point out that all social interactions are complex, and that the beliefs and expectations of others frequently influence our interactions. "If the social recognition becomes one that focuses on lack of skills, such as an inability to speak on one's own behalf, rather than on recognition of the individual, the person may be viewed as less competent and the individual's self-view may become distorted" (Wilson, 1994, p. 156). Kohut argues against the traditional Freudian notion of drive theory to say that the object of the self is relatedness, attachment, and connection to others—not tension reduction. "[R]elatedness with others is as essential for [the] psychological survival [of the self] as oxygen is for . . . physical survival" (as cited in Greenberg & Mitchell, 1983, p. 353).

Sullivan felt that disturbances in the ability or capacity to relate to others directly relate to the history of the individual's experiences with others in the environment. "Personality is by definition a temporal phenomenon, a pattern of experiences and interactions over time, and the only way in which personality can be known is through the medium of interpersonal interactions (as cited in Greenberg & Mitchell, 1983, p. 90). As experiences (interpersonal interactions) threaten our sense of self, we begin to separate from the feedback we receive from others, and from the environment, in order to reduce anxiety, thus engaging in narcissistic fantasies.

> Each of us comes to be possessed of a self which he esteems and cher-
> ishes, shelters from questioning and criticism, and expands by com-
> mendation, all without much regard to his objectively observable per-
> formances, which include contradictions and gross inconsistencies.
> (Sullivan, 1938, p. 35 cited in Greenberg & Mitchell, 1983, p. 100)

The first portion of this chapter addressed the all-too-numerous ways
in which parents, advocates, educators, rehabilitation service providers,
and society at large contribute (either willingly or unknowingly) to the
difficulty individuals with learning disabilities have in experiencing "connectedness." As individuals with learning disabilities seek to:
(a) become competent, contributing adult members of their communities
and (b) explore meaningful relationships with others, investigating the
balance between autonomy and relationships with others through counseling becomes essential to the integration of self.

Vocational Counseling Strategies and Suggestions

Young people with learning disabilities must be given control of their
lives. As service providers move towards empowering people with
learning disabilities to actively participate in creating their vocational,
recreational, and social futures, we must act from the ideological perspective that McKnight refers to as a community vision (McKnight, 1987,
cited in Schwartz, 1992). McKnight describes three visions of society in
relation to people with disabilities; each vision carries with it an associated set of ideologies and operating paradigms. The traditional vision in
the fields of special education and vocational rehabilitation McKnight
calls the *therapeutic vision.* This vision is deeply enmeshed in the medical
model and ties the ultimate well-being of individuals with disabilities, in
most instances, to a segregated environment rich in professionals and
their associated services. The *advocacy vision,* conceives of a group of
helpers or protectors defending individuals with disabilities from an
alien, often hostile, community. In the *community vision,* community is
the basic context in which individuals with disabilities and individuals
without disabilities can together contribute to the vitality and the diversity of their community (McKnight, 1987, cited in Schwartz, 1992).

From the ideological perspective of community vision, person-centered
approaches to the delivery of services begin to make more sense. Questions
at the heart of real empowerment come to the forefront (e.g., "How do we
describe people?, How do we think about and plan for the future?, Who
makes the decisions?, [and] Who is in control?)" (Mount, 1992, p. 3).

I have argued throughout this chapter that individuals with learning disabilities must, first and foremost, be treated with the same dignity and respect as their peers without disabilities (which includes the right to fail and the right to learn from their mistakes). At issue, perhaps, is my use of the word *"same"* in the previous sentence rather than the word *"equal."* Being provided with the *same* opportunities as their peers without disabilities probably will not result in creating an *equal* opportunity to learn. As a caveat, I would say that it is important to reconcile the research findings on adults with learning disabilities with the creation/facilitation of equal opportunities for growth and self-exploration. We know that persons with learning disabilities tend to be unrealistic and random goal setters (Tollefson, Tracy, Johnson, Buenning, & Farmer, 1981) and that they also are usually not satisfied with their eventual jobs (Faford & Haubrich, 1981). We also know that, in most instances, young adults without disabilities appear to spontaneously be able to profit (i.e., learn) from their mistakes. In most instances, individuals with learning disabilities need more formal and direct instruction to be able to synthesize the knowledge to be gained from their experiences (e.g., Blalock & Dixon, 1982; Buchanan & Wolf, 1986).

Equal treatment, in this case, may then be to view the vocational counseling relationship as an opportunity to facilitate the capacity of individuals with learning disabilities to learn about themselves and their goals from their mistakes (which, earlier in this chapter, I euphemistically referred to as "learning experiences"). Vocational counseling, then, must become a process of *"controlled learning experiences."* From a community vision and a person-centered operating paradigm, it no longer remains feasible to dismiss the vocational goals or desires of young adults as simply unrealistic without assisting them to actively engage in a process of learning and self-discovery. I have previously described this new role for the counselor as "tenuous, at best" (Michaels, 1994a, p. 126) as we are required to move from our roles as service directors and professionals to become experience facilitators.

Specific recommendations (adapted from Michaels, 1994a) for controlling the learning experiences, serving as experience facilitator, and for actively involving individuals with learning disabilities in the career decision-making process include:

1. *Share psychological and vocational testing results.* This may appear obvious but in most cases (as described previously in this chapter) young adults have little ownership or real knowledge of how their learning disabilities affect them on a day-to-day basis. When shar-

ing test results, stay away from jargon and psychological terms and offer as many concrete examples from the actual testing sessions as possible. Prior to moving on, you should elicit as many examples from the young adult as possible about how this specific trait effects him or her in school, in social situations, in previous jobs or work experience, and so forth. You also need to focus on strengths and particular compensatory strategies you observed in the testing (or that are noted in the evaluation report). Young adults with learning disabilities tend to be better at describing weaknesses than strengths and also tend to have difficulty realizing how a compensatory strategy that was successful in a specific situation can be generalized and utilized more systematically to promote success in other, similar, types of situations.

2. *Explore vocational interests.* Standard fill-in-the-blank vocational interest tests, and even the more sophisticated computerized vocational exploration programs, tend not to be very appropriate for young adults with learning disabilities. In many instances, questions are answered impulsively or in a random fashion. Reviewing answers to the fill-in the blank questions with the individual in a counseling session tends to be more useful than proceeding with the actual scoring of the interest inventory.

   You might also ask the young adult to tell you about a chosen career of interest and have him or her actually describe what a typical day in the life of a *fill-in the blank* would be like. Following this description, you then might want to have the young adult describe how his or her strengths and weaknesses might affect job performance within the specific career of interest. With the information and knowledge gained through the previous steps, you can then have the individual actually research the chosen career in both the *Dictionary of Occupational Titles* (United States Department of Labor, 1991) and the *Occupational Outlook Handbook* (United States Department of Labor, 1990). If possible, for potential career areas still under consideration, you should try to arrange a "job shadowing" experience during which the individual can spend time (preferably the better part of a day) following someone actually working in that career area. As the last step in this process, you should then have the individual recap and synthesize the information gleaned from all sources.

3. *Develop a one- to-five-year plan.* Beginning at some specified end point, either one or five years down the road, have the young adult describe where they want to be in terms of employment, independent living, and within their social life. Working backwards from that point, you begin to help them to set long- and then short-term

goals to reach those specified end points. Within this process, it is important to identify critical milestones along the way.

4. *Explore interests, desires, and dreams and assist in creating a vision for the future.* The development of the one-year or five-year plan is an extremely cognitive task requiring flexible thinking and goal-setting. Some individuals, especially those who have difficulty maintaining two possibilities in mind simultaneously and/or who have had their personal dreams crushed along the way, may have difficulty with this approach. In addition, the development of the one- and five-year plan typically is a solitary activity that does not involve and or empower significant others and the community to take part in the creation and realization of a vision for the future.

While many different person-centered planning models exist for accomplishing this type of community mobilization and individual empowerment (e.g., see Mount, 1992 or Pearpoint, Forest, & Snow, 1992), the Planning Alternative Tomorrows with Hope (PATH) process will be described here (adapted from Pearpoint, O'Brien, & Forest, 1992). PATH requires that an individual or group work together through an eight-step planning process with assistance from two co-facilitators—one eliciting information, the other graphically recording information. The reader is cautioned that only a brief description of the PATH process is provided here and that prior to attempting to facilitate a PATH, additional in-depth training should be pursued.

The eight-steps of the PATH process are:

1. *Identify the dream.* The dream is often described as the "north star" of an individual's life. From this reference point, we are able to orient for the remaining seven steps of the process and in the design and implementation of all future services and interventions.

2. *Develop the goal.* While the dream is frequently "out there" as an almost spiritual ideal, the goal is more concrete and attainable. The goal stems directly from the dream in much the same way as a corporate mission statement might stem from the corporate vision statement. The goal results from having the individual remain focused on the dream while simultaneously "traveling forward" to some specified time (e.g., one year down the road) and should be described in as much detail as possible.

3. *Describe the present.* Traveling back to the here and now, the individual is asked to describe where he or she is today in relation to both the dream and the goal. This step helps to capture exactly where the person is currently in his or her life compared to where

they would like to be. At this point in the process, a natural tension is created between what is and what could be. The individual must be permitted to experience this tension and then make a conscious commitment to beginning the journey to the goal.

4. *Identify people to enroll in creating change.* In this step, the individual works to identify people within the immediate family and the extended circles of support (i.e., neighbors, friends, members of the community, etc.) who can be mobilized to support the individual in creating the future (or at least in minimizing potential roadblocks along the way). This step is particularly important for young adults with learning disabilities who may have difficulty developing relationships or asking for assistance (based upon the personality profile described earlier).

5. *Build strengths.* The individual is asked to identify the skills, knowledge, and relationships (people resources) necessary to move from what is current (Step 3) to the goal (Step 2). Frequently, the need for additional education and/or training may be identified at this stage of the process. It is important to also identify the internal supports, e.g., exercise, meditating, that the individual needs to do for him or herself to remain motivated and vital through the journey.

6. *Set objectives to be accomplished in the next few months.* After reviewing the goal again, the individual begins to describe what concrete steps can be taken in the next three to six months. The individual should describe actions to be taken in concrete terms and make sure that those actions are consistent with both the goal and the dream.

7. *Plan for the next month.* Describe the immediate steps to be taken in the achievement of the objectives just established (Step 6). Eliciting information to answer the question *Who* will do *what* and by *when?* in the next month will help to move the process into action.

8. *Gain commitment to action.* The final step of the process requires that the facilitators get the individual to commit to taking the very first step towards the achievement of the goal. As with almost any other change discussed within a counseling milieu, "breaking the grasp of inertia is critical" (Pearpoint, O'Brien, & Forest, 1992, p. 18).

Conclusion

This chapter focused holistically on the counseling needs of young adults with learning disabilities. The development of personal competency was described from both the sociological and psychological perspectives. I highlighted the roles of families, educators, rehabilitation specialists, counselors and advocates in treating individuals with dignity and respect in order to prepare them to assume their rightful roles as fully contributing members of society. The ideology of service providers was given equal treatment to the actual personality profile and the counseling needs of individuals with learning disabilities, because it was deemed more effective in the long run to create *primary interventions* aimed at the prevention of damage to the developing sense of self and competency among individuals with learning disabilities.

Wolfensberger states that: "Man's [and woman's] behavior is in good part determined by what I want to call his [her] ideologies" (Wolfensberger et al., 1972, p. 7). We must be willing to look at our individual and professional roles in promoting and promulgating incompetency among individuals with learning disabilities. Wolfensberger et al. (1972) affirm that more often than not, we are not aware of the ideologies that shape our behaviors, at other times we simply are not intellectually able to put our ideologies into words. Most insidious however, are the times when "our ideologies are so bad that we cannot consciously face up to them" (p. 10). This chapter is a call for all service providers and individuals interacting with people with learning disabilities (especially those entering into any type of counseling relationship with individuals with learning disabilities) to consciously face their ideologies and work to achieve "good ideologies rather than bad ones; ideologies which either transcend empiricism or at least are not inconsistent with it; and conscious ideologies rather than unconscious ones" (Wolfensberger et al., 1972, p. 9).

References

Americans with Disabilities Act of 1990, 42 U.S.C. 12101 *et seq.*

Armstrong, T. (1994). *Multiple intelligences in the classroom.* Alexandria, VA: Association for Supervision and Curriculum Development.

Belden, N., & Russonello, (1994, November). *Attitudes, awareness, and new concepts of learning disabilities: A report of findings from focus groups for the Emily Hall Tremaine Foundation.* Washington, DC: Belden & Russonello Research and Communications.

Blalock, G., & Dixon, N. (1982). Improving prospects for the college-bound learning disabled. *Topics in Learning Disabilities, 2*(3), 67–78.

Bogdan, R. (1986). The sociology of special education. In R. J. Morris & B. Blatt (Eds.), *Special education: Research and trends* (pp. 344–359). Elmsford, NY: Pergamon Press.

Buchanan, M., & Wolf, J. S. (1986). A comprehensive study of learning disabled adults. *Journal of Learning Disabilities, 19,* 34–38.

Canfield, J., & Hansen, M. V. (1995). *A 2nd helping of chicken soup for the soul.* Deerfield Beach, FL: Health Communications, Inc.

Covey, S. R. (1990). *The 7 habits of highly effective people.* New York: Simon & Schuster.

Dudley-Marling, C., & Dippo, D. (1995). What learning disabilities does: Sustaining the ideology of schooling. *Journal of Learning Disabilities, 28,* 408–414.

Equal Employment Opportunity Commission and United States Department of Justice. (1991). *Americans with disabilities handbook.* Washington, DC: Authors.

Erikson, E. H. (1968). *Identity: Youth and crisis.* New York: W. W. Norton & Company.

Faford, M. B., & Haubrich, P. A. (1981). Vocational and social adjustment of learning disabled young adults: A follow-up study. *Learning Disabilities Quarterly, 4,* 163–169.

Ferguson, P. M. (1987). The social construction of mental retardation. *Social Policy, 18,* 51–52.

Glenn, H. S. (1995). Miss Hardy. In J. Canfield & M. V. Hansen (Eds.), *A 2nd helping of chicken soup for the soul* (pp. 212–215). Deerfield Beach, FL: Health Communications, Inc.

Greenberg, J. R., & Mitchell, S. A. (1983). *Object relations in psychoanalytic theory.* Cambridge, MA: Harvard University Press.

Higgins, P. C. (1992). *Making disability: Exploring the social transformation of human variation.* Springfield, IL: Charles C. Thomas.

Hoy, C. (1986). Preventing learned helplessness. *Academic Therapy, 22*(1), 11–18.

Interagency Committee on Learning Disabilities (1987). *Learning disabilities: A report to Congress.* Washington, DC: Author.

Kronick, D. (1988). *New approaches to learning disabilities: Cognitive, metacognitive, and holistic.* Philadelphia: Grune & Stratton.

Masland, R. L. (1976). The advantages of being dyslexic. *Bulletin of the Orton Society, 26,* 10–18.

Michaels, C. A. (1994a). Employment issues: Transition from school to work. In C. A. Michaels (Ed.), *Transition strategies for persons with learning disabilities* (pp. 119–152). San Diego, CA: Singular Publishing Company, Inc.

Michaels, C. A. (1994b). Transition, adolescence, and learning disabilities. In C. A. Michaels (Ed.), *Transition strategies for persons with learning disabilities* (pp. 1–22). San Diego, CA: Singular Publishing Company, Inc.

Michaels, C. A., Lazar, J. W., & Risucci, D. A. (1995). *A neuropsychological approach to the assessment of adults with learning disabilities in vocational rehabilitation.* Manuscript submitted for publication.

Michaels, C. A., Thaler, R., Zwerlein, R., Gioglio, M., & Apostoli, B. (1988). *From high school to college: Keys to success for students with learning disabilities.* Albertson, NY: Human Resources Center.

Millon, T. (1981). *Disorders of personality DSM-III: Axis II.* New York: John Wiley & Sons.

Millon, T. (1983). *Millon Clinical Multiaxial Inventory.* Minneapolis, MN: Interpretive Scoring Systems.

Mount, B. (1992). *Person-centered planning: Finding directions for change using personal futures planning.* New York: Graphic Futures, Inc.

Pearpoint, J., Forest, M., & Snow, J. (1992). *The inclusion papers: Strategies to make inclusion work.* Toronto: Inclusion Press.

Pearpoint, J., O'Brien, J., & Forest, M. (1992). *PATH: Planning alternative tomorrows with hope—A workbook for planning better futures (Version 1.2).* Toronto: Inclusion Press.

Rehabilitation Services Administration (1985, March 5). *Program policy directive.* RSA-PPD 85-7. Washington, DC: Author.

Schumaker, J. B., Hazel, J. S., Sherman, J. A., & Sheldon, J. (1982). Social skills performance of learning disabled, non-learning disabled, and delinquent adolescents, *Learning Disabilities Quarterly, 5,* 388–397.

Schwartz, D. B. (1992). *Crossing the river: Creating a conceptual revolution in community & disability.* Brookline, MA: Brookline Books.

Skrtic, T. M. (1991). *Behind special education: A critical analysis of professional culture and school organization.* Denver, CO: Love Publishing Company.

Smith, T. E. C., Finn, D. M., & Dowdy, C. A. (1993). *Teaching students with mild disabilities.* Fort Worth, TX: Harcourt Brace College Publishers.

Snow, J. A. (1994). *What's really worth doing and how to do it.* Toronto: Inclusion Press.

Tollefson, N., Tracy, D., Johnson, E., Buenning, M., & Farmer, A. (1981). *Implementing goal setting activities with LD adolescents* (Research Report No. 48). Lawrence: The University of Kansas Institute for Research in Learning Disabilities.

United States Department of Education (1994, October). *Sixteenth annual report to Congress on the implementation of the Individuals with Disabilities Education Act.* Washington, DC: Author.

United States Department of Labor (1990). *Occupational outlook handbook* (1990–91 ed.). Washington, DC: Author.

United States Department of Labor (1991). *Dictionary of occupational titles* (4th ed.). Washington, DC: Author.

West, T. G. (1991). *In the mind's eye: Visual thinkers, gifted people with learning difficulties, computer images, and the ironies of creativity.* Buffalo, NY: Prometheus Books.

Will, M. (1993). The question of personal autonomy. *Journal of Vocational Rehabilitation, 3*(2), 9–10.

Wilson, G. L. (1994). Self-advocacy skills. In C. A. Michaels (Ed.), *Transition strategies for persons with learning disabilities* (pp. 153–184). San Diego, CA: Singular Publishing Company, Inc.

Wolfensberger, W., Nirje, B., Olshansky, S., Perske, R., & Roos, P. (1972). *The principle of normalization in human services.* Toronto: National Institute on Mental Retardation.

PART III

Workplace Issues

CHAPTER 11

Persuading Employers to Hire People with Learning Disabilities

Richard G. Luecking

The field of job development for people with disabilities—particularly for people with learning disabilities—holds both exciting opportunities and distinct challenges. The promise of employment appears greater than at any time previously, due to several recent advancements. First, new protections under the law, specifically Title I of the Americans with Disabilities Act of 1990, prohibit employment discrimination. Second, the states' vocational rehabilitation systems now serve more customers with specific learning disabilities than ever before (Dowdy & Smith, 1994). Third, more than a dozen years of federal policy emphasis on school-to-work transition have brought many effective approaches and educational programs for young people with learning disabilities who are leaving secondary schools for employment and adult life (Gajar, Goodman, & McAfee, 1993). Finally, more is known about how to accommodate specific learning disabilities in the workplace (Brown, Gerber, & Dowdy, 1990).

On the other hand, people with disabilities, as a group, continue to experience extremely high unemployment rates—as high as 79% in some studies (Louis Harris and Associates, 1995). Several researchers have estimated that more than half of all former special education students remain unemployed 1 year after exiting school; for many of these young adults who do secure employment, serious underemployment is typical (Chadsey-Rusch, Rusch, & O'Reilly, 1991; Wagner, 1991). One recent longitudinal study indicated that young people with learning disabilities are only slightly more likely to be employed 3 to 5 years after exiting secondary school than are young people with other disabilities, with the percentage of the employed youth only reaching 58% (Wagner, 1991). Despite comprehensive curricular emphasis on workplace preparation and agreements now commonplace between school systems and vocational rehabilitation systems, young people with learning disabilities are frequently reluctant to participate in a system for which eligibility is contingent on identification as a person with a disability. Thus, referral to vocational rehabilitation to be further assessed, categorized, and labeled is not considered an attractive alternative by many young people (Tilson, Taymans, & Germino-Hausken, 1991).

People whose disabilities are not apparent often find it relatively easy to obtain an entry-level job. However, they face a high probability of failure unless specific and individualized accommodations are provided (Neubert, Tilson, & Ianacone, 1989). Studies of postsecondary outcomes for individuals with learning disabilities who received special education services have shown that, in addition to job failure, the possibilities of poverty, and in some cases, contact with the criminal justice system are notably heightened (Wagner, 1991).

The irony, then, is that in a climate of theoretically better opportunity, unemployment remains a reality for too many people with learning disabilities. To what factors can this dilemma be attributed? Is it that too many people with learning disabilities are not ready for the workplace, or is it that too many places of work are not ready for them? It is likely that the reasons lie as much in the latter circumstance as in the former. Issues addressed in this chapter include soliciting employer interest in hiring people with learning disabilities and minimizing employment barriers inherent in the workplace. Discussion of case studies of job development efforts, particular job development strategies, and suggestions for more effectively engaging employers also are included.

Vocational Adjustment and Employer Perception

The literature is replete with examples of how various characteristics of learning disabilities interfere with successful vocational adjustment. Oral language, perceptual processing, problems with basic literacy, and social problems have all been cited as contributing factors. (Anderson, 1994; Brown & Gerber, 1994; Dowdy, Smith, & Nowell, 1992). Suggestions and case studies about how these characteristics can be mediated abound. Among these are better social skills training (Chadsey-Rusch, 1985; Vaughn, 1985), specific job accommodation strategies (Brown & Gerber, 1994), more opportunities for paid employment or training programs as integral features of secondary school programs (Hasazi, Johnson, Hasazi, Gordon, & Hull, 1989), and job support groups (Neubert, Tilson, & Ianacone, 1989).

Little published material is available, however, concerning how employer perception interferes with successful employment. Some have suggested that employers are less sensitive to learning disabilities than they are to other, more visible disabilities, and therefore more reluctant to accommodate them (Minskoff, Sautter, Hoffman & Hawks, 1987). Minskoff, et. al. (1987) also cited employers' lack of knowledge and limited experience with learning disabilities as reasons, although a similar conclusion could be drawn for many other disabilities. While much has been written about mediating the specific circumstances of disability, precious little is available about how to better relate to and educate employers so that they are more receptive to the idea of hiring people with learning disabilities. There remain gaps in knowledge about how to more effectively develop jobs.

The good news is that employers of every size and description have learned—sometimes merely through trial and error and sometimes with expert advice—how to effectively accommodate and manage employees with learning disabilities. The bad news is that too few do. Successful employment models and effective educational approaches facilitating smooth transition to work represent years of groundwork. Now, the challenge involves strategically relating to employers so as to make employment happen for almost every person with any degree and type of specific learning disability.

Shortcomings of Conventional Job Development

Rehabilitation agencies and special educators only recently began to consider shifting the focus of services to employers. Traditionally, rehabilitation and special education programs have concentrated on assessing individual characteristics, providing a service that in some way mediates the impact of the disability, and counseling individual job seekers on presenting themselves to prospective employers. The task of interacting directly with employers by rehabilitation personnel has traditionally been relegated to a low-status professional endeavor (Schiro-Geist, Walker, & Nerney, 1992) and assigned to individuals who are relatively new to the field.

Complicating this perception of job development as low-status work is the fact that employers have often been solicited through charitable appeals to hire people with disabilities (Fabian, Luecking, & Tilson, 1994). Thus, often the first point of contact that an employer has with rehabilitation agencies is with inexperienced individuals who, in essence, are marketing the human service aspect of their program. "Helping people with disabilities achieve independence" or similar slogans are typical in job development marketing brochures (DiLeo & Langton, 1993). This inadvertently stigmatizes the job seekers as dependent on the goodwill of the employer to "give them a chance."

Rehabilitation/job development personnel and employers often have different perceptions and assumptions about job development and employment. For example, one study (Fabian, Luecking, & Tilson, 1995) found that job development personnel tended to attribute successful job placements to open, flexible, risk-taking employers. They typically were looking for employers who were aware of, and understood the needs of, people with disabilities. Employers in the same study, on the other hand, credited successful placements to job developers who knew and responded to their needs. Contrary to the perceptions of job developers, employers were looking for quality and competent service. In other words, employers are less interested in altruistic appeals than in assurances that they will receive service that meets the needs of their enterprise.

When job placement services present themselves to prospective employers as human service agencies focused on disability issues rather than as potential business partners, they communicate expectations of employers' goodwill gestures. They seem to need employers far more than employers need their services. As a result, job placement programs are most often relegated to a subordinate role in relationships with businesses and employers. Not only does this place job development at a distinct disadvantage, it inadvertently devalues job seekers with disabilities.

Reframing the Message to Employers

Recently, several authors and practitioners have suggested that direct inquiry into the needs of the employer should replace charitable appeals (DiLeo & Langton, 1993; Fabian, Luecking, & Tilson, 1994; Nietupski, Verstegen, & Petty, 1995). In other words, the job developer needs to frame contacts with employers in the context of benefiting the employers' operations. Ideally, the job developer wants to be considered a business resource person rather than simply a representative of job seekers with learning disabilities. The benefits of this approach are evident throughout each phase of job development, including preparation of the job seeker for the job search, marketing, initiating contacts with employers, arranging interviews, and negotiating accommodations.

Preparation for the Job Search

People with learning disabilities often have limited understanding of their disabilities, and, regardless of the degree of understanding, are often reluctant to disclose their disability to employers (Brown, 1994). With the advent of the Americans with Disabilities Act of 1990 (ADA) (P.L.101-336) it is now illegal for employers to discriminate against applicants who, with or without reasonable accommodations, are qualified for available positions. Although it is no panacea for difficulties related to the high levels of unemployment among people with learning disabilities, the ADA provides an avenue for enhancing employment outcomes. Its language contains important implications for job preparation.

First, since employers are prohibited from discriminating in hiring decisions based on disability, the ADA potentially makes it easier, if not advantageous, for applicants to disclose their disabilities and identify potential job accommodations. Thus, as people with disabilities prepare for the job search, it is important that—with assistance from teachers, rehabilitation personnel, or others assisting in the job search—they are prepared in the following areas: (a) self-knowledge, including understanding their disability and its manifestations, functional limitations, personal and functional strengths, and accommodations needed for one's learning style; (b) knowledge of specific occupational areas and specific jobs; and (c) self-advocacy, especially as it relates to presenting skills and strengths to employers and identifying and requesting accommodations.

One individual with whom the author is acquainted was provided with extensive preparation (similar to that just outlined) by his high school transition teacher. In addition, because of his desire to work in some aspect of the communications industry, his preparation included several visits to local television and radio stations. Various jobs were explored during these visits and subsequently discussed with his teacher. Based on his experience during this process, he was ready when the time came for a real job interview to confidently tell the employer about his ability to perform the tasks of an archivist at a television station's library.

During the interview, he asserted that his encyclopedic knowledge of television shows would make his job easier, adding that he would need to ask his supervisor to provide instructions in writing—due to an oral processing disability. With this small accommodation, he informed the station manager, he thought he could do the job quickly, thus making himself available to help out with other tasks, perhaps helping with transcription in case of a backlog. By recognizing his strengths and by clearly understanding what accommodations would be necessary, he was prepared to emphasize that he had skills the employer needed and that, with accommodation, he could even take on more tasks. The message to the employer included information on his disability, but it was framed in the context of how accommodating him would ultimately benefit the employer's operation.

Marketing and Initial Employer Contacts

Effective marketing to prospective employers emphasizes service, not disability. In the example above, the teacher first approached the station manager by identifying herself as a high school teacher who worked with students interested in communications careers (as opposed to identifying herself as a special education teacher who worked with students with disabilities). She informed the manager that she wished to visit the station to better learn the types of jobs in the field and the specific requirements for performing them. During the visit to the station, the teacher learned from the manager that archivist positions were open. Disability was not mentioned except in the context of the employment interview, when the student and manager discussed potential accommodations. Her relationship with the employer was based not on her role as a special education teacher, but as someone who was able to help recruit for an open position.

Similarly, many organizations that represent job seekers with disabilities are positioning themselves to be perceived more as human resource firms rather than as rehabilitation agencies, adopting such program names as "Workforce Connections" and "Employment Resources" (DiLeo & Langton, 1993). The message of their promotional materials and the basis of their contacts with employers is the potential service their programs have to offer, rather than their role as disability service organizations. They present the skills and abilities of particular applicants as they relate to the essential functions of the job, while being prepared to identify needed accommodations.

Interviews

Preparing the job seeker for an employment interview is an essential aspect of the job development process. Putting one's best foot forward requires the type of self-knowledge and training described earlier. However, Inge & Tilson (1994) recommend that, in addition to helping the jobseeker to develop his or her interviewing skills, the job developer consider preparing the employer as well. They relate an example where an employer was informed, with permission from the applicant, of a difficulty with oral instructions prior to an interview. The developer assisted the employer in preparing a set of written questions and instructions as a guide for the applicant during the interview. The employer, in this circumstance, gained an effective method for getting a true picture of an applicant's suitability for a job, and reduced the risk often taken when interviewing walk-in applicants.

Negotiating Accommodations

In the example cited the teacher and the young job seeker presented the station manager with options for accommodating his disability which potentially would make life easier for the station manager. It was not necessary to tout the applicant's rights under the ADA to reasonable accommodation. In another case with which the author is familiar, an individual secured a job as a convenience store manager position after it was arranged for the applicant, who has a reading disability, to take the prerequisite test orally and untimed. The ADA now requires such accommodations; in this case, though, the job developer worked with the employer after the employee passed the test to determine how the employee learns, areas in which the employee may have difficulty, and strategies for capitalizing on strengths while minimizing limitations. In this fashion, the job developer again was looking for more than a quick placement; she became a valued consultant. The subsequent success and continuing job tenure of the employee has made the employer an advocate of the employment service. In every respect, employers are customers of the job developer. Employers should have every reason to expect quality and responsive and value-added service. Designers of effective employment programs weave this message into their operations and regard it as critical to the entire employment process. In this way, employment program representatives present and prove themselves as partners with employers, offering tangible services.

Components of Developing Meaningful Relationships with Employers

The most effective and lasting partnerships have similar characteristics, whether they link businesses to businesses or between special education/ rehabilitation programs to employers. Fabian, Luecking, and Tilson (1994) identify characteristics of such partnerships as including mutual trust, mutually beneficial objectives, assumed long-term relationships, service competence, and orientation to mutual customer service. They describe these characteristics as follows:

1. Trust. Avoid the trap of overpromising and underdelivering. In its simplest form, this means: Do what you say you are going to do, do it right the first time, and do it on time. Trust will result.

2. Mutually Beneficial Objectives. While, on the surface, it may seem that a satisfactory job match benefits the employer as much as the employee, on closer examination it means much more than that. The case studies that follow will illustrate that benefits to each party are enhanced when other services are part of the relationship.

3. Being in it for the Long Haul. Quick job placements for the case closure hurts relationships with employers because trust never gets established. Long-term relationships with employers not only enhance mutual trust, but also provide excellent means of marketing employment services as word travels to other employers.

4. Service Competence. This means making a worthwhile contribution and meeting the specific needs of the employers through offering and following through with expertise in job matching, job accommodations, employer consultation, or enhancing employee performance.

5. Customer Service Orientation. Regarding employers as customers requires a shift in orientation that many educators and rehabilitation agencies are making (Albin, 1992). It entails adding value to the service encounter to meet the employer's needs beyond merely providing a good employee. Additionally, a satisfied customer's comments to others about the service can generate more customers and make future employer contacts easier.

For job developers and employment programs, relationships with employers boil down to one basic question: "How will these programs benefit the employer's enterprise?" When programs are ready to offer several tangible examples to answer this question, meaningful relationships with employers are likely to ensue. Consider the following examples.

Case Studies in Job Development

Michael

Michael is a 20-year-old recent high school graduate with dyslexia and consequent reading disability. His learning disability also manifests itself in the area of written expression, including spelling. He has difficulty in meeting new people. Prior to his job search, his communication skills were very deficient; he would respond to questions with one-word answers and would avoid eye contact. Throughout high school, Michael received special education services, alternating between special classroom programs for children with significant learning disabilities and occasional inclusion in general education classes with the assistance of resource teachers.

He has a longstanding interest in arts and crafts and is very good at creating drawings and three-dimensional arrangements. A large arts-and-crafts franchise store was located within easy commuting distance of his home, and he expressed interest in working there. An employment specialist with a rehabilitation agency learned of a job opening for a clerk. Knowing that the interview would be difficult for Michael, she worked with both parties. She helped Michael develop answers to potential interview questions and better ways of projecting his answers. She helped the store manager set up a series of common tasks so that Michael could perform them as part of a "working interview." In spite of a poor oral interview, when the employer saw that Michael could perform the main tasks, he hired him.

With assistance from the employment specialist, the store manager was able to successfully teach Michael various clerk tasks, including operating the cash register. As his confidence increased, he eventually began helping to arrange displays, and wait on customers. Because of his skill in crafts and arrangements, many customers began to ask for him, and the manager was ready to promote him to supervisor. However, his reading disability made it difficult for him to pass the brief written test the franchise required. The employment specialist helped the store manager set up an oral test, which Michael passed easily.

The employer, by making this relatively simple accommodation, gained some important expertise that the franchise was later to use in its hiring and promotional procedures. In a region where there are many individuals for whom English is a second language, the idea of an oral test and other such accommodations for this single employee with a learning disability benefited the franchise in recruiting and hiring in significant ways. In fact, the employment specialist was frequently consulted concerning human resource procedures. Her willingness to help and her expertise became a boon to the employer, who later hired other job seekers represented by the agency and recommended its services to other store managers. All of this occurred over a period of several months, but with a significant payoff in terms of a long-term relationship with an employer.

Wanda

Wanda, age 25, has severe dyslexia as well as difficulty processing oral instruction and social cues, especially subtleties such as sarcasm and ordinary kidding. She also becomes very disoriented and frequently gets lost. She has tried several jobs, but lost each one after only a few days because of repeated errors and seeming inability to follow instructions. She was fired from one job as a fast food restaurant cashier because she lost her temper and swore at a customer who complained about the food. Her high school teachers and, later, rehabilitation agency staff members, were very skeptical of her ability to complete vocational training; they recommended entry-level work in retail with certain accommodations such as straightforward customer interaction requiring little complex social interaction.

Her stated interest, however, was criminal justice. She was fascinated by the court system and legal processes and wanted to be in a job where she would somehow interact with this system. She was discouraged from this tack because most positions required a college degree, and college, for Wanda, seemed a remote possibility to the teachers and professionals that knew her.

At her parents' insistence, she was eventually referred to a local agency, known for having well-established employer networks, for job search assistance. One of the agency's employment specialists, after getting to know Wanda and learning of her interest in criminal justice, made several contacts with people she knew in the court system, including a lawyer who she met through mutual service on a local chamber of commerce committee. The lawyer referred her to a private firm that had a contract with the courts to maintain remote court-ordered electronic contact with non-dangerous felons, sentenced to home confinement. The employment specialist made a call on this company and, after a series of contacts and an on-site visit, learned that they had a backlog of daily reports to file and process. She offered her assistance in addressing this problem, as she knew a young woman wanting very badly to work in this field and who could be taught to do what was necessary to catch up on the backlogged work.

Because of the significant backlog, the firm agreed to create a position in the company for all of its filing and report processing. A trial employment period was arranged. The employment specialist worked closely with Wanda and her employer to organize the tasks, which were only haphazardly arranged, as well as develop a series of accommodations. These accommodations included setting up a sequence of directions on a checklist, adding written versions to accompany all supervisor instructions, and advising her co-workers to be very literal in their communication and to avoid joking and teasing. Prominent labels were also attached to the offices and file cabinets to assist in orienting her to the office layout. With the help of the employment specialist, the company found a way of getting the backlogged work done. It also received value added service in that the employment specialist, in helping to organize the accommodations for Wanda, also helped organize this aspect of the company's operation. And, of course, Wanda had the first job she really liked and in which she succeeded.

In both examples, the employers were approached by job developers who showed genuine interest in their enterprise and offered effective ways to help solve problems. In both, there was an element of "service after the sale." Also, developers added value to the encounters over and above merely helping the employers hire another employee. In the case of the arts-and-crafts store, assistance translated into generally improved human resource practices and, in the case of the home confinement firm, included help in organizing its work load. The employers were treated as customers of a competent employment service. In essence, the employers perceived job developers as consultants who diagnosed problems, offered solutions, and helped execute the solutions. In the eyes of the employers, they were far more than human service workers with a good cause.

Lessons from One School-to-Work Program

Opportunity to experience working for pay has been cited as an desirable aspect of secondary education, enabling youth with learning disabilities to better prepare for the challenges of adult employment (Gajar, et al, 1993). In fact, there is evidence to suggest that such opportunities not only lead to better post-secondary employment outcomes, but that employers who are involved in these programs are more receptive to hiring and accommodating employees with disabilities. Marriott International and the Marriott family, in 1989, decided to share the corporation's experience with other employers by establishing the Marriott Foundation for People with Disabilities (MFPD) and developing its signature program, *Bridges . . . from school to work* (Donovan, 1990).

Operated in select cities nationally, *Bridges* is a business-driven model that works with young people with disabilities during their final year in high school and partners with local employers to develop paid, time-limited internships that last between two to six months. The amount of time spent on the internship varies according to the school schedule of the student and the needs of the employer, averaging is slightly more than 20 hours per week.

Bridges members simultaneously undertake activities designed to recruit employers and to prepare the students. Pre-internship training events are held for both students and employers, *Bridges* specialists then work with both the students and the employers to develop internships that match their mutual needs. Students participating in the program represent all disability categories and severity-of-disability levels. The proportionate representation of each disability very nearly reflects the prevalence of these disabilities in the population of students receiving special education services nationally. Almost 50% of *Bridges* students are identified as having a specific learning disability (Tilson, Luecking, & Donovan, 1994).

Bridges administrators encourage virtually every size and type of employer to participate. They use several approaches to recruit and support participating employers who provide internships. Among these are:

- CEO Events: Richard Marriott, as Chairman of Host Marriott International and Chair of the MFPD, invites business leaders from the local community to attend an informational breakfast meeting introducing *Bridges*. This has the advantage of a direct business-to-business appeal.

- Manager/Supervisor Training: Key supervisory staff members from area employers are invited to complimentary seminars that provide information on recruiting, hiring, and accommodating youth with disabilities.

- Employer Networking and Intensive Job Development Activities: *Bridges* personnel make continuous contacts with the business community, including on-site visits and participation in business organizations such as chambers of commerce.

- Business Advisory Councils (BAC): Key members of the business community, especially those whose companies have hired *Bridges* interns, comprise this advisory body in each *Bridges* location. The BAC acts to advise *Bridges* staff members as to the needs of the employers in the area, develops suggestions for employer contacts, and provides a referral to other potential employers of students participating in *Bridges*.

In its first three years of operation, *Bridges* served over 700 students in five localities (Chicago, IL; Washington, DC; San Francisco, CA; Los Angeles, CA; and Montgomery County, MD) (Tilson, Luecking, & Donovan, 1994). *Bridges* has recently expanded to Atlanta, GA, and Fairfax County, VA. More than 86% of the students referred were assisted in obtaining an internship. This figure compares very favorably to national employment rates of people with disabilities overall and according to more recent data, the internship placement rate has improved to more than 94% (Marriott Foundation for People with Disabilities, 1995). For interns with learning disabilities, the placement rate is slightly higher.

Another encouraging outcome is that, of the internship completers (82% of those in internships), more than 75% are offered long-term employment with their host companies. This suggests, among other things, that employer exposure to disability, as well as the receipt of support and training, removes many of the barriers that otherwise inhibit positive hiring behavior. Not only does a work-based learning program such as *Bridges* introduce youth with learning disabilities to work, but it also introduces employers to youth with learning disabilities. The fact that more than 75% are offered long-term employment at the conclusion of the internship indicates that long-term employment relationships are likely once the employee is in place, effectively accommodated, and contributing to the employer's enterprise.

School-to-work transition programs such as *Bridges* indicate that, while it is important to mediate for removal of employment barriers endemic to various manifestations of learning disabilities, it is at least as important to lift the barriers that make it difficult for employers to willingly and skillfully accommodate learning disabilities in their workplace. By learning firsthand how to make accommodations and manage workers with learning and other disabilities, employers who participate in these work-based learning programs are overwhelmingly willing to continue the relationship.

The Future of Job Development

Several significant shifts in the provision of employment services and job development for people with disabilities are occurring (Albin, 1992; Luecking, 1995). While perhaps not yet commonplace, they do represent the movement toward a more businesslike approach—that is, a desire to create partnerships characterized by mutualism rather than charity—intended to establish enduring employer comfort with disability in the workplace.

Some of these shifts, and their implications for job development for persons with learning disabilities, are summarized here:

1. From hiring incentives to value-added service. In rare circumstances, when extensive accommodation is needed, it may be useful to "sweeten the pot" with such incentives as tax credits,

training subsidies, or similar, commonly used inducements to hire people with disabilities. For the most part, however, initially approaching employers with the promise of such incentives usually serves to reinforce the notion that it is difficult, costly, and time-consuming to hire people with disabilities.

By contrast, giving employers service over and above what is expected, as in the case study of Michael, will go much farther in convincing employers to work with job developers to hire people with disabilities than well-meaning, but generally ineffective, incentives. Employer customers, as with any customers, will do business with those services that "underpromise and overdeliver."

The implication for job seekers with learning disabilities is that employer perception is influenced by good service received, not "what's wrong with this applicant." Promoting service over disability reduces the stigma that people with learning disabilities may associate with special education or rehabilitation employment services.

2. From 'placement' to 'hiring.' Statements about being "placed" in a job imply that the job seeker is a passive recipient of employment service rather than an empowered consumer. Potentially, albeit unconsciously, such phrasing reinforces a message to employers that people with disabilities are in need of extraordinary assistance in order to become employed.

Effective job developers help employers "hire" to meet human resources needs. They should leave employers with the impression that their enterprises are as much the ultimate beneficiaries of the employment service as are the job seekers, as seen in the preceding case studies. Presenting a subtly different characterization of the employment process is part of the developer's approach.

The implication for job seekers with learning disabilities is that if employers see themselves as ultimate beneficiaries of the employment service, they are likely to be more open to applicants who willingly disclose their disabilities and request specific accommodations. Applicants, in turn, will be less reluctant to do so.

3. From 'paternalism' to 'choice.' Well-meaning professionals often take charge of the employment process because it may seem that the job seeker—because of inexperience or the nature of the disability—is not as prepared to direct his or her job search. Many consumers of rehabilitation services have objected to this assumption and have demanded more control over the process (Hearne, 1991).

Informed choice, on the other hand, means that the job seeker takes the lead role in identifying occupational areas, types of employers to contact, and the parameters of the job search such as wage range, location, etc. It may be necessary for the job developer to provide information and guidance upon which choices are based, but the final word is up to the job seeker. Not only does this empower the job seeker to be more actively involved in the job search, but it also enhances the likelihood that better and more enduring job matches are made and that employers' needs are better served.

People with learning disabilities constitute a heterogeneous group. While one individual may be impulsive, another may be extremely passive. Therefore, the type and degree of guidance and information provided job seekers to assist them in making choices will vary dramatically. In the long run, however, the confidence necessary for effective self-advocacy will grow when informed choice drives the job search process.

4. From slogans to action and consultation. Slogans such as "Hiring people with disabilities makes good business sense" are not only examples of marketing disability—the ineffectiveness of which was discussed earlier in this chapter—but they carry the stereotypical inference that more loyal employees and less turnover will result from hiring people with disabilities. The only employment decision that really makes sense to employers is hiring people who will contribute to the success of their operation.

Rather than relying on slogans, effective job developers show employers that skillful management of diversity makes good business sense. Changing workforce demographics require employers to consider wide-ranging accommodations for all employees, including child care arrangements, flexed schedules, job sharing, and even English classes. The successful business leader realizes that, in order for work to get done, services to be delivered, or products to be manufactured, considerable skill is necessary to manage these circumstances. By shaping the presentation of their services to address these issues, job developers are more likely to attract employer interest.

Many employers are already arranging accommodations such as job restructuring, job sharing, and alternative methods of providing instruction and training for non-disabled workers. Workplace diversity's implication for job seekers with learning disabilities is that education programs and employment agencies are in a position to offer their expertise to employers in new ways. Their specialized knowledge about accommodations and job analysis will become more and more valuable to employers. It is also likely that employers, with this guidance, will be more amenable to the types of accommodations needed by workers with learning disabilities.

5. From human service perspectives to customer service perspectives. Relationships with employers, as we have seen, are not likely to be enhanced when an appeal to their altruism is made. Profit, not charity, is the motive behind most business operations, and the success of the operation is more important to employers than whether or not people with disabilities achieve greater independence.

By providing quality service, gauging the satisfaction of employer customers, and seeking to provide value-added service, job developers will, in the long run, advance the employment of people with disabilities more effectively than with any other approach. Business-like methods and focus on the needs of employer customers will be the hallmark of successful employment programs.

When job seekers with learning disabilities are represented and assisted by organizations that operate in a business-like fashion, they are likely to be more valued in the eyes of potential employers. Employers will see job seekers as potentially valuable human capital, not as the recipients of human service or special education programs. The stigma of disclosure will be diminished and requests for accommodation more readily considered.

Conclusion

New methods of vocational preparation and new approaches to minimizing the impact of specific learning disabilities hold promise for a better vocational future for job seekers with learning disabilities. However, employer perceptions and the continuing high unemployment rate among people with learning disabilities reflect persistent barriers to full employment. Ironically, one of these barriers may be the shortcomings of conventional job development approaches. An alternative process of job development focuses on components of marketing to employers and emphasizes service, not disability. Suggestions for framing the message to employers throughout the process—from job search preparation, through initial employer contacts, employment interviews, and negotiating for accommodations—were explored through case studies and anecdotes in this chapter.

Partnerships between employment programs and employers that are characterized by trust, mutual objectives, and customer service orientation are likely to result in long-term relationships so that people with learning disabilities are more likely to achieve meaningful employment. One effective school-to-work transition model, the *Bridges* program, demonstrates that not only is paid work experience in high school a good predictor of post-secondary vocational success, but that such experience exposes employers to the nuances of effective accommodation and management of employees with learning disabilities.

The ADA has improved the environment for job development in that it has raised the general awareness of disability and increased the prospect of equal treatment and nondiscrimination. It is neither a panacea, as some thought it would be, nor a key to all doors. Instead, it is a tool for employer education and a basis for setting the stage for workplace accommodation. It also clears the way for more comfort in disclosing disability to employers. While revealing disability is not always likely to evoke a sensitive response in employers, the ADA at least provides some legal protection for those who take that step.

Trends in the field of job development for people with disabilities include choice over paternalism, value-added service over hiring incentives, and consultation over slogans. These preferences give jobseekers with learning disabilities, and those who assist them, more effective avenues to find and educate prospective employers.

A wide range of characteristics makes the population with learning disabilities a highly heterogeneous group. Likewise, each job and each work environment is unique. It is the uniqueness of each person and each employer that should drive the job development process.

Acknowledgment

The author would like to acknowledge Rachelle Silver and Margaret Leedy of TransCen, Inc., two experienced and effective job developers, for suggesting the case study examples discussed in this chapter.

References

Albin, J. (1992). *Quality improvement in employment and other human services.* Baltimore: Paul H. Brookes Publishing Company.

Americans with Disabilities Act of 1990, 42 U.S.C. 12101 *et seq.*

Anderson, C. (1994). Adult literacy and learning disabilities. In P. Gerber & H. Reiff (Eds.), *Learning disabilities in adulthood: Persisting problems and evolving issues* (pp. 121–129). Boston: Andover Medical Publishers.

Brown, D., & Gerber, P. (1994). Employing people with learning disabilities. In P. Gerber & H. Reiff (Eds.), *Learning disabilities in adulthood: Persisting problems and evolving issues* (pp. 194–203). Boston: Andover Medical Publishers.

Brown, D., Gerber, P., & Dowdy, C. (1990). *Pathways to employment for people with learning disabilities: A plan for action.* New York: National Center for Learning Disabilities.

Brown, D. (1994). Personal perspectives and problems and promises: Adults with learning disabilities in the past and present. In P. Gerber & H. Reiff (Eds.), *Learning disabilities in adulthood: Persisting problems and evolving issues* (pp. 46–51). Boston: Andover Medical Publishers.

Chadsey-Rusch, J. (1985). Identifying and teaching valued social behaviors. In F. R. Rusch (Ed.), *Competitive employment issues and strategies* (pp. 273–287). Baltimore: Paul H. Brookes Publishing Company.

Chadsey-Rusch, J., Rusch, F., & O'Reilly, M. (1991). Transition from school to integrated communities. In P. Kohler, J. Johnson, J. Chadsey-Rusch, & F. Rusch (Eds.), *Transition from school to adult life: Foundations for best practices and research directions* (pp. 1–29). Champaign, IL: Transition Research Institute, University of Illinois.

DiLeo D., & Langton, D. (1993). *Getting the marketing edge: A job developer's toolkit.* St. Augustine, FL: TRN Publishing Company.

Donovan, M. (1990, Summer.). Envisioning links from school to work. *Rehab USA, 3–4.*

Dowdy, C., & Smith, T. (1994). Serving individuals with specific learning disabilities in the vocational rehabilitation system. In P. Gerber & M. Reiff (Eds.), *Learning disabilities in adulthood: Persisting problems and evolving issues* (pp. 171–178). Boston: Andover Medical Publishers.

Dowdy, C., Smith, T., & Nowell, C. (1992). Learning disabilities and vocational rehabilitation. *Journal of Learning Disabilities, 25,* 442–447.

Fabian, E., Luecking, R., & Tilson, G. (1995). Employer and rehabilitation personnel perspectives on hiring persons with disabilities: Implications for job development. *Journal of Rehabilitation, 61,* 42–49.

Fabian, E., Luecking, R., & Tilson, G. (1994). *A working relationship: The job development specialist's guide to successful partnerships with business.* Baltimore: Paul H. Brookes Publishing Company.

Gajar, A., Goodman, L., & McAfee, J. (1993). *Secondary schools and beyond: Transition of individuals with mild disabilities.* New York: Macmillan Publishing Company.

Hasazi, S., Johnson, R., Hasazi, I., Gordon, L., & Hull, M. (1989). Employment of youth with and without handicaps following high school: Outcomes and correlates. *Journal of Special Education, 23,* 243–255.

Hearne, P. (1991). Employment strategies for people with disabilities: A prescription for change. In J. West (Ed.), *The Americans with Disabilities Act: From policy to practice.* New York: Milbank Memorial Fund.

Inge, K., & Tilson, G. (1994). Supported employment: Issues and applications for individuals with learning disabilities. In P. Gerber & H. Reiff (Eds.), *Learning disabilities in adulthood: Persisting problems and evolving issues* (pp. 121–129). Boston: Andover Medical Publishers.

Louis Harris & Associates, Inc. (1995). *The N.O.D./Harris Survey of Americans with Disabilities.* (available from National Organization on Disability, 910 Sixteenth Street, NW, Washington, DC 20006)

Luecking, R. (1995). What's in and what's out for job developers. *Supported Employment InfoLines, 6*(2), 1–6.

Marriott Foundation for People with Disabilities. (1995, Fall). Report on *Bridges* project by site. (Available from Marriott Foundation for People with Disabilities, One Marriott Drive, Department 901.10, Washington, DC 20058)

Minskoff, E., Sautter, S., Hoffman, F., & Hawks, R. (1987). Employer attitudes toward hiring the learning disabled. *Journal of Learning Disabilities, 20,* 53–57.

Nietupski, J., Verstegen, D., & Petty, D. (1995). *The job development handbook: Facilitating employer decisions to hire people with disabilities.* Knoxville, TN: Tennessee Initiative on Employment: University of Tennessee.

Neubert, D., Tilson, G., & Ianacone, R. (1989). Postsecondary transition needs and employment patterns of individuals with mild disabilities. *Exceptional Children, 55,* 494–500.

Schiro-Geist, C., Walker, M., & Nerney, N. (1992). Rehabilitation counseling and placement. *American Rehabilitation, 18*(2), 25–27.

Tilson, G., Luecking, R., & Donovan, M. (1994). Involving employers in transition: The Bridges model. *Career Development for Exceptional Individuals. 17*(1), 77–87.

Tilson, G., Taymans, J., & Germino-Hausken, E. (1991). *A descriptive study of young adults with mild disabilities who participated in a model postsecondary transition project.* (Available from The George Washington University, Department of Teacher Preparation and Special Education, 2201 G Street, N.W., Washington, DC 20051)

Vaughn, S. (1985). Why teach social skills to learning disabled students? *Journal of Learning Disabilities, 18,* 588–591.

Wagner, M. (1991). *Youth with disabilities: How are they doing? The first comprehensive report from the National Longitudinal Study of Special Education Students* (Contract No. 300-87-0056). Washington, DC: U.S. Department of Education.

CHAPTER 12

Employment Testing and the Americans with Disabilities Act of 1990: Court Cases Regarding Learning Disabilities

Ernest Biller

Settled case law regarding employment testing of persons with learning disabilities (LD) is emerging as a result of legislative and judicial action under Section 504 of the Rehabilitation Act of 1973 and Titles I & II of the Americans with Disabilities Act of 1990 (Americans with Disabilities Cases, 1994; Biller, 1993; Grossman, 1994; Nesler, 1993). Along with this increase in established case law, a correspondent increase in the employment activity of persons with LD is apparent. For example, data from the Job Accommodation Network (JAN) indicate that the percentage of requests for job-related accommodations by employees with LD has risen from 5% of the total disability requests in 1992 to 7% in 1994. Such accommodation requests numbered approximately 925 in 1992, 1,185 in 1993, and 1,600 in 1994 (D.J. Hendricks, personal communication, September 22, 1995). Approximately 10% of these requests were for testing accommodations.

The purpose of this chapter is to review the case law and its implications regarding the employment testing rights of individuals with LD. It is important to iterate that it was the intent of the U.S. Congress that the regulations implementing the employment provision of ADA be modeled on the regulations-implementing Section 504 of the Rehabilitation Act of 1973. In fact, the EEOC stated in its final ADA rules and regulations for Title I that the "commission has been guided by the Section 504 regulations and the case law interpreting those regulations." (*Federal Register*, July 26, 1991, p. 35726).

Why Employers Test

According to business efficiency experts, it is possible to increase productivity by using valid tests to select workers (Schultz, 1984). Historical precedence for this theory dates to the turn of the century, when psychologist William James' hand-picked successor to operate his psychological laboratory, Hugo Munsterberg, developed an employment screening test for hiring trolley car operators (Hale, 1982). Employment testing has never been touted as a perfect science, however. It is generally known that persons who score poorly on a job-related test may do great work and that those with high test scores may perform poorly. But on the average, it is calculated that as little as a one-point difference on a valid test significantly increases the probability of efficient work performance (Schultz 1984). The passage of the Civil Rights Act of 1964, with its Title VII provisions regarding nondiscriminatory employment testing, had a dampening effect on traditional employment testing in business and industry and ultimately led to the widespread use of employment assessment centers—an alternative to paper-and-pencil cognitive tests. These centers relied more on actual work performance by using work samples to assess ability. The enactment of the Civil Rights Act of 1964 also marked the establishment of the United States Equal Opportunity Commission (EEOC), which now oversees the employment provisions of the Americans with Disabilities Act (ADA) of 1990, as well as the employment aspects of Title VII of the 1964 Civil Rights Act.

Testing Persons with Learning Disabilities

Accommodating persons with LD presents a special challenge to employers in that a majority of employment selection tests are designed to assess cognitive functioning, the very essence of a learning disability (Duane, 1979; Stanovich, 1988; Swanson, 1988; Torgesen, 1988). Even if the learning disability is not a reading-related one, the information-processing speed of a person with a learning disability is often impaired, necessitating at least the allowance of extra time—the most common form of testing accommodation for a learning-related disability (Nester, 1993). Providing extra time for an employment test, however, presents another dilemma (Biller, 1993). For example, a person with a learning disability has a legal right to request extra time over and above the amount of time for which the test was initially standardized. However, if such a nonstandard test result leads to over-predicting the actual ability of an applicant with LD and the employee fails to live up to the predicted level of capability, neither side is likely to be satisfied. The employer loses because he or she may not actually have identified the most qualified person in the employment pool and the employee loses because he or she becomes frustrated at not being able to work at the level of the employer's expectation, which is based on the employee's score on the test. Essentially, this is a legal and psychometric dilemma that remains unresolved in the testing of persons with learning disabilities (Biller, 1993; Grossman, 1994).

The Americans with Disabilities Act and Employment Discrimination Law

Employment nondiscrimination law, outlined in Title I of the ADA, applies to private employers with fifteen or more employees, as well as to agencies of state and local governments, employment agencies, labor unions, and joint labor-management committees, regardless of the number of persons employed. Complaints of employment discrimination against any of the above entities are to be registered with the EEOC. Quite simply, Title I states that none of the abovementioned employers cannot discriminate against qualified applicants and employers on the basis of a disability (U.S. Equal Employment Opportunity Commission, 1995). The ADA definition of an employer includes persons who are "agents" of the employer, such as managers, supervisors, foremen, or others who act for the employer (e.g., agencies used to conduct background verifications on job candidates). Title I of the ADA, as well as the extension of its employment testing guidelines to Title II of ADA, is unique to all other provisions of ADA. Its terminology and concepts are derived solely from Title VII of the Civil Rights Act of 1964 which, in turn, comprised the majority of the language and provisions of Section 504 of the 1973 Rehabilitation Act—which provided the first civil rights protection law for persons with disabilities. Title I of ADA, therefore, actually has a long history of regulatory and legal review. Executive agencies of the U.S. government are exempt from ADA, but are covered by requirements of the Rehabilitation Act of 1973. Entities totally exempted from the ADA, as well as Title VII of the Civil Rights Act of 1964, are corporations fully owned by the U.S. government, Native American nations, and formally established private membership clubs that are not labor organizations.

Eligibility Under the Americans with Disabilities Act

A qualified applicant/employee, under ADA, is an "individual with a disability who meets the skill, experience, education, and other job-related requirements of a position held or desired, and who, with or without reasonable accommodation, can perform the essential functions of a job" (EEOC, 1995, pp. 1–2). It is timely to note here an important difference under ADA employment discrimination law between a "qualified individual with a disability" and an "individual with a disability." This distinction is critical, as ADA only protects *qualified* individuals with disabilities from employment testing discrimination. An "individual with a disability" is a person who has a physical or mental impairment that substantially limits one or more major life activities such as seeing, hearing, walking, learning, speaking, etc., or has a record of such an impairment (or both), or is regarded as having such an impairment. An individual formally diagnosed as having a specific learning disability under guidelines detailed in The Education for All Handicapped Children Act of 1975 (P.L. 94-142) or Individuals with Disabilities Act of 1990 (P.L. 101-467) would be legally identified as having a learning disability which would, most likely, be formally documented.

Being "regarded" as having a learning disability is a circumstance more difficult to assess. For example, a student who experienced academic difficulty throughout school, despite the absence of factors such as poor home life, an emotional disturbance, poor teaching, mental retardation, or sensory deficits, could be "regarded" as having a learning disability despite not ever being formally diagnosed as such. Because a "qualified" individual with a disability is an applicant or employee who must meet the skill, experience, education, and other job-related requirements of a position held or desired and could, with or without reasonable accommodations, perform the essential functions of a job, a person with an officially diagnosed learning disability under P.L. 94-142 or P.L. 101-476 guidelines may not always be a "qualified" individual with a disability under Title I of ADA. A person with LD must be sure that the job being applied for reasonably matches his or her skills, experience, and education if he or she expects to be protected under Title I of ADA. It follows that persons with learning disabilities would greatly benefit from comprehensive career guidance (Biller, 1985, 1987, 1988).

Employment Testing Rules Under the Americans with Disabilities Act

The essential ADA employment discrimination testing nondiscrimination rule under Title I of ADA posits that employers will not discriminate against a qualified applicant/employee with a disability because of the individual's disability in regard to job application procedures, or in hiring, advancement, termination, compensation, training, and other terms or privileges of employment (P.L. 101-336, Section 102, 1990). ADA guidelines stipulate that discrimination may exist when qualification standards, *employment tests,* or other selection criteria screen out, or tend to screen out, an individual with a disability *unless* that standard test or other selection criteria are shown to be job-related for the position in question and are consistent with business necessity. Testing discrimination, moreover, can occur when an employer fails to select and administer tests concerning employment in the most effective manner. The employer must ensure that, when such tests are administered to a job applicant/employee with a disability, the test results accurately reflect the skills, aptitudes, or whatever other factor of such applicant/employee that such a test purports to measure, rather than reflecting the impaired skills of the applicant/employee or applicant—except when such skills are the factors that the test purports to measure (P.L. 101-336, Section 102 (b)(6)).

For example, an employer wanting to hire a proofreader for a magazine or newspaper may devise a reading sample that has errors embedded in the test. Assuming it is typical that a very short turn-around time exists between the time a story is first drafted and the press deadline, there may also be a time limit in which those errors in the test must be found and corrected. Such a test might very well screen out (discriminate against) a person with a reading disability. But, in this case, the essential skills needed (accurate reading skill and speed) are, in fact, the skills being tested. As such, this proofreading test may not be legally discriminatory, and asking for extra time would not necessarily be a reasonable accommodation. In other words, the proofreading test is "job-related" and also represents a skill that is an essential function within the overall job or classifications of jobs known as "editor" or "proofreader." An important determination in deciding whether an experienced person with a reading disability is "qualified" rests on how quickly the copy would need to be edited and how frequently this was the case. The employer has the burden of validating this proofing activity, and the speed by which it needs to be done is essential.

On the other hand, if the same newspaper or magazine company wanted to hire a salesperson to sell subscriptions for the company and, on occasion, help out with copy editing, a proofreading test may be discriminatory. The test criteria for salespersons should represent the essential skills necessary for selling, not proofreading. Assuming an applicant with a reading disability was "qualified" (i.e., possessed the skills, education, and experience required for the class of jobs known as "salesperson") then such an applicant could ask that he or she be allowed accommodations for testing as well as the opportunity to perform some other task in the organization in lieu of the occasional proofreading task. Proofreading may be a job related to this company's sales operation, but it is probably not an essential function of the job of salesperson. In ADA language, proofreading is most likely a "marginal" job duty for a salesperson, and thus subject to accommodation consideration.

Employment Testing Law and the Courts

Following is an overview of 10 court cases decided between 1983 and 1994 (see Table 12.1). Essentially, these cases span the period just following implementation of Section 504 of the Rehabilitation Act of 1973 and the four years following the implementation of ADA in July of 1990. For the purpose of this LD case review, an employment test will be broadly defined as any aptitude, state board, bar, certification, entrance, or course examination that has a direct link to entering a specific type of employment field. The cases cited in this review represent approximately 90% of the LD-related cases reported in the 1994 and 1995 editions of the *Americans with Disabilities Cases*. At the completion of this overview, a brief synthesis of these cases will be presented.

Stutts v. Freeman (Tennessee Valley Authority [TVA])

Stutts v. Freeman represents one of the earliest Section 504 court cases involving the employment testing of a person with a learning disability (Biller, 1993; Grossman, 1994). As a temporary employee of TVA, Mr. Stutts wanted to enter a company-sponsored apprenticeship program for operating heavy equipment. TVA had required applicants to take the General Aptitude Battery (GATB) as part of the application process for this apprenticeship program. As a result of his aptitude scores on the GATB, Mr. Stutts was denied access to the training program. Mr. Stutts filed a suit against TVA on the basis of failure to provide a reasonable testing accommodation given his learning disability. TVA attempted to arrange for Mr. Stutts to take a nonverbal version of the GATB, but was unable to do so, and a U.S. Court of Appeals stated that attempting to provide alternative testing was not equivalent to providing it. Therefore, Mr. Stutts' case was remanded back to the district court to determine whether he was qualified for provisions to be made for a reasonable alternative to taking the GATB to determine his ability to complete a training program in heavy equipment operations (694f 2nd 666, 1983).

TABLE 12.1
LD and Employment Testing in the Courts

Plaintiff	Defendant	Deciding Legal Component	Setting	Contested Issue	Judgment In Favor Of	Year	Court	Type Test	Law
Stutts	Freeman/TVA	Reasonable Accommodation	Utility Company	Denied Training Program	Plaintiff	1983	U.S. Court of Appeals	GATB	RA*
Pandazides	Virginia Board of Education	Essential Function	School System	Denied Teaching Job	Defense	1992	U.S. Court of Appeals	NTE	ADA
Dearmont	Texas A&M	Reasonable Accommodation	Post-secondary	Extra Time In Testing	Plaintiff	1991	U.S. District Court	Qualifying Exam	RA
Riedel	Kansas Board of Regents	Reasonable Accommodation	Post-secondary	Dismissed from Program	Defense	1993	U.S. District Court	MCAT	RA/ADA
Wynne	Tufts Medical School	Reasonable Accommodation	Post-secondary	Denied Testing Accommodation	Defense	1993	U.S. Court of Appeals	Course Exam	ADA
Pazer	New York State Board of Law Examiners	Qualified Disability	Post-secondary	Denied Testing Accommodation	Defense	1994	U.S. District Court	Bar Exam	ADA
Argen	New York State Board of Law Examiners	Qualified Disability	State Bar Examiner	Denied Testing Accommodation	Defense	1994	State Court	Bar Exam	ADA
Christian	New York State Board of Law Examiners	Reasonable Accommodation	State Bar Examiner	Denied Testing Accommodation	Defense	1994	U.S. District Court	Bar Exam	ADA
Rubenstein	Delaware Bar Exam	Reasonable Accommodation	State Bar Examiner	Extra Time for Testing	Plaintiff	1994	State Court	Bar Exam	ADA
Daniels	Electrical Contractor	Qualified Disability	Electrical Company	Failed Safety Test	Defense	1994	U.S. District Court	Corp Safety Test	TCHR**

*Rehabilitation Act of 1973

**Texas Commission on Human Rights

Pandazides v. Virginia Board of Education

Ms. Pandazides, a first-year special education teacher, was required to take and pass the *National Teacher Examination* (NTE) during the 1988–89 school year in order to validate her provisional teaching certificate — a mandatory requirement for teaching in the state of Virginia. The NTE is published by the Education Testing Service (ETS) and consists of a core battery and specialty area sections. Within the NTE core battery are a communications skills test, a general knowledge test, and a professional knowledge test. Ms. Pandazides was able to pass the latter two tests but, after eight tries, was unable to pass the communications section despite various accommodations of extra time provision, a private testing room, and a multi-speed tape recorder for the auditory listening items. Ms. Pandazides' first-year teaching evaluations were not good and regardless of her passing or failing the NTE, she had been told that she would not be offered a permanent second-year teaching position.

Citing discriminatory action by the Virginia Board of Education as per Section 504 of the Rehabilitation Act of 1973, Ms. Pandazides went to a Federal District Court to contest being denied her teaching job as a result of having to take the NTE without the kinds of accommodations she felt appropriate for her learning disability. Ms. Pandazides' initial effort in this Federal District Court was unsuccessful. However, in 1991, a U.S. Court of Appeals reversed and remanded this decision back to the district court on the basis that, in the process of deciding that Ms. Pandazides was not a "qualified person with a disability," the district court failed to ascertain (a) whether the NTE requirements represented the "essential functions" of a teacher, (b) whether or not Ms. Pandazides could perform the essential functions of the position, and (c) whether a test wavier was a reasonable accommodation. In 1992, the U.S. District Court, on remand, once again ruled against Ms. Pandazides. In this most recent decision on Ms. Pandazides' case, the U.S. District Court stated that: (a) the Rehabilitation Act of 1973 imposes no requirement on educational licensing bodies to lower or modify their standards for persons with disabilities, (b) Ms. Pandazides had failed to establish existence of an impairment under guidelines commensurate with Section 504 of the 1973 Rehabilitation Act, (c) even if Ms. Pandazides were a person with a disability under 1973 Rehabilitation Act guidelines, she did not show that testing accommodations made for her by ETS were inappropriate, (d) the communications section of the NTE does accurately measure "essential functions" of a teacher, and (e) Ms. Pandazides is not a "qualified person with a disability" because she cannot perform the "essential functions" of a teacher as shown by her failure to pass the NTE and because her teaching evaluations indicated an inability to effectively manage her classroom.

Dearmont v. Texas A&M University

In a 1991 U.S. District Court decision, it was ruled that Mr. Dearmont, a graduate student at Texas A&M University, was a qualified individual with a disability who should be permitted extra time to take his qualifying examination in economics. Mr. Dearmont, like Ms. Pandazides, did not have his learning disability diagnosed until after failing his economics qualifying examination. After failing the examination twice, the university assessed Mr. Dearmont and substantiated that he had a learning disability. Even after granting Mr. Dearmont extra time to take the exam a third time, he again failed. However, the qualifying exam grading policy had changed since Mr. Dearmont's first two attempts. The new scoring process led to some activities that were considered quite irregular (i.e., a surprise oral exam for Mr. Dearmont). The results of this new grading system left Mr. Dearmont with a failing grade and a dismissal from the doctoral program.

The qualifying examination at Texas A&M, as at most universities, is a test of basic knowledge in a given field of study—in this case, economics. Viewing this case from the legal perspectives of Section 504 of the 1973 Rehabilitation Act, the district court questioned the relevance of the Texas A&M qualifying exam and offered that "no one ever suggested that the [qualifying] test fairly represented the tasks that make up the work of an agricultural economist." The district court decided in favor of Mr. Dearmont, stating that he should not have been dismissed from the program.

Riedel v. Kansas Board of Regents

Mr. Riedel was dismissed from the State of Kansas Medical School after failing Part I of the National Board Examination four times. Mr. Riedel, 2 years after his dismissal, informed the medical school that he had a learning disability and that this was the reason for his failing the board examination. A request by Mr. Reidel to the medical school to allow him a fifth try at passing the examination was denied. The record states that the Kansas Medical School directors did not feel the documentation Mr. Riedel presented to support his claim for a learning disability was valid. Mr. Riedel then filed a claim of disability discrimination against the school under Section 504 of the Rehabilitation Act of 1973 and Title II of ADA. A U.S. District Court ruled in 1993 that Mr. Riedel did not officially request readmittance to the program—and a requirement from taking Part I at this medical school is having status as an enrolled medical student. Therefore, the Court ruled that Mr. Riedel had no status for requesting a waiver to permit taking the examination a fifth time. The issue of whether or not Mr. Riedel did or did not have a qualified disability was not a factor in the Court's ruling.

Wynne v. Tufts University School of Medicine

At issue in Mr. Wynne's dismissal from the Tufts University School of Medicine was to what extent a training program must go to accommodate a student with a learning disability in altering the testing format of the training courses completed in the medical program (see Biller, 1993, McCusker, 1995). In the final action of the Wynne case, the U.S. Supreme Court refused to review a First Circuit Court's opinion that held that Tufts Medical School did not unreasonably deny Steven Wynne an accommodation by allowing him to take a biochemistry test in a non-multiple choice format (932F.2d at 19). Some particulars regarding Wynne v. Tufts are: (a) Mr. Wynne was not identified as having a learning disability before enrolling at Tufts, (b) Tufts provided testing for Mr. Wynne after he failed most of his first year medical courses, and (c) Mr. Wynne did not request the specific accommodation of a non-multiple choice format until after he filed a suit of discrimination under Section 504 of the Rehabilitation Act of 1973.

The case record shows that Wynne repeatedly failed most of his first-year medical school courses, but was allowed to retake them and was able to pass all of them except the course in biochemistry. Mr. Wynne then asked Tufts to use a testing format other than multiple-choice questions, which Tufts refused to do. Tufts had initially failed to document why a multiple-choice format was "essential" to the work of becoming a doctor, so in the appeal its attorneys made a better case as to why multiple-choice tests are essential to a doctor's duties. Tufts now explained to the court that the thinking process a medical doctor uses in diagnosing patients requires a rapid sorting of alternatives and then a selection of one choice, followed by quick action. Tufts' final claim was that a multiple-choice test format is a valid indicator of making a real-life medical diagnosis. Thus Tufts won its summary judgment on this Section 504 claim, and Mr. Wynne's request for review by the Supreme Court was denied (McCusker, 1995).

Pazer v. New York State Board of Law Examiners

One of the United States Office of Education (U.S.O.E.) definitional criteria for designating a school-age person as having a learning disability has been the existence of a significant discrepancy between a student's predicted achievement level and actual achievement in any of the basic academic subject areas (e.g., reading, arithmetic, written language, etc.) (Biller & White, 1989). The U.S.O.E. definition states that such discrepancies cannot be attributable to such factors as sensory impairments, mental retardation, or emotional disturbances in order to arrive at a diagnosis of learning disability. In other words, LD is a condition that is defined, in part, by eliminating other more obvious factors that can impair learning performance.

A law school graduate, Mr. Pazer was denied his request for an accommodation to take the New York State Bar exam on the basis that his claim for being a person with LD did not coincide with the court interpretation of what constitutes a learning disability. An expert witness for the New York Board of Law Examiners testified that Mr. Pazer's actual achievement, as measured by a standard reading achievement test battery with adult norms, was average to above average for adults his age and that these achievement scores are discrepant, but not significantly discrepant, from his grade-point averages, which were essentially the same when Mr. Pazer had not received any accommodations during his first 2 years of college and the same when he had received accommodation in his last 2 years of college (*Americans with Disabilities Cases*, 1995).

Mr. Pazer took the New York Bar examination and failed it, at which time he again applied for an accommodation and retaking of the examination. This request was again denied and Mr. Pazer filed a complaint under Titles II and III of ADA. Mr. Pazer's request was that he be allowed to take the exam over a period of 4 days rather than within the normal two-day period. He also requested the use of a computer with a word processor that had a spell-checking capability and a quiet place in which to complete the exam.

Specifically addressing the comment of the "disparity" between a person's "inherent capacity and performance on a test," the court indicated that such a disparity "may, in some circumstances, permit the inference that an individual has a learning disability, even though that individual's performance has met the standard of the ordinary person" (p. 363). The Court opinion went on to say that:

> The Court is not persuaded, however, that such a disparity compels that conclusion as a matter of law, especially since that disparity could reasonably be the result of many other factors, such as stress, nervousness,

cautiousness, and lack of motivation . . . Indeed, to hold otherwise would complete the conclusion that any underachiever would by definition be learning disabled as a matter of law . . . (p. 362)

In summary, the Court held that Mr. Pazer did not require or request special testing accommodations in high school or though college and that no disparity in grades existed through college and, therefore, failed to make a sufficient showing of irreparable injury. It is worthy to note that, in this case, each party (the plaintiff and defendant) employed its own learning disability expert to support their respective positions.

Argen v. New York State Board of Law Examiners

This case followed the same course of events as Pazer v. New York State Board of Law Examiners. Mr. Argen had been denied the requested accommodation of double the amount of standard time normally allowed to take the New York Bar examination. In this case, the court specifically cited the fact that Mr. Argen did not meet the federal guidelines for having a "specific learning disability." Moreover, the court stipulated that the ADA's Title II regulations are to be construed consistently with the definition that the U.S. Congress provided under the U.S.O.E. definition for an official designation of learning disability (*Americans with Disabilities Cases*, 1995).

Mr. Argen's story differs from Mr. Pazer's in several aspects, but particularly in level of education he had attained prior to action against New York Board of Law Examiners. Mr. Argen already held two master's degrees—one in logic and one in ethics—and also had completed coursework for a Ph.D. in philosophy.

Mr. Argen failed the law school admission exam (LSAT) three times and, after obtaining an evaluation from a learning disability specialist, was allowed to take the LSAT a fourth time with accommodations. He successfully passed on this fifth try.

When Mr. Argen later requested permission to take the bar examination with accommodations, his request was denied on the advice of the board's learning disability expert. Mr. Argen filed suit under Title II of ADA and, on a subsequent agreement, was allowed to take the bar exam with accommodations on the condition that his test results, if positive, would be certified only if his ADA suit was ruled in his favor.

In ruling against Mr. Argen, the court cited the necessity of following the Federal definition of a learning disability as cited under the Individuals with Disability Act of 1990 (IDEA), as ADA does not specifically define what a learning disability is. After hearing testimony from the two learning disability experts representing Mr. Argen and from the expert representing the board of examiners, the court decided that Mr. Argen's experts conflicted with one another and that the board of examiners' expert had made a credible argument that Mr. Argen did not meet the IDEA guidelines for having a learning disability.

Christian v. New York State Board of Law Examiners

This case was identical to Pazer and Argen. Like Mr. Pazer and Mr. Argen, Ms. Christian had requested a special testing accommodation for her examination under ADA on the basis that she suffered from dyslexia and dysgraphia (reading and writing disabilities). Ms. Christian asked to have extra time to take each section of the examination, be provided with enlarged-type examinations, use of a computer with word processing and spell-checking programs, a separate room, and permission to hand-mark letters on multiple-choice questions rather than making marks on an computer scan sheet. Ms. Christian, like Pazer, employed her own learning disability expert, as did the New York State Board of Law Examiners. It is important to note that Ms. Christian had already been admitted to the New Jersey Bar for practicing law. The U.S. District Court in the Southern District of New York ruled in 1994 that Ms. Christian had not shown "irreparable injury" warranting issuance of preliminary injunction requiring the New York State Board of Law Examiners to grant her these testing accommodations.

Rubenstein v. Multistate Bar Examiners

Following Pazer, Argen, and Christian, a bar examiner denied Ms. Rubenstein a request under Title II of ADA for additional time to take the Multistate Bar Examination (MBE) portion of her bar examination on the basis of her claim that she had a learning disability. However, in contrast to the outcomes of Pazer, Argen, and Christian, a Delaware Superior Court did find the bar examiner's denial of extra time to Ms. Rubenstein to be an arbitrary and manifestly unfair decision. In this case, Ms. Rubenstein had already passed the essay portion of the bar examination with an accommodation of extra time, but had not simultaneously passed the multiple-choice portion. Ms. Rubenstein later passed the multiple-choice portion of the bar exam but failed the essay portion. The court, in its final decision, waived the bar examination rule that holds that both the essay and multiple choice portions be passed at the same time. (*Americans with Disabilities Cases*, 1995).

As with Pazer, Argen, and Christian, Ms. Rubenstein was seeking permission to take the bar examination with special testing accommodations (i.e., extra time, special room, and so forth). However, this is where similarity with the previous three cases ends. Ms. Rubenstein first applied for admission to the Delaware Bar in 1990, but failed both parts of the two-part examination. In 1991, she passed the essay of the examination, but not the multistate bar examination portion. In 1992, Ms. Rubenstein passed the multistate bar examination portion, but this time failed the essay section.

Ms. Rubenstein, since 1989 had been serving as a law clerk to the President Judge of the Delaware Superior Court and, in 1990, was certified under a limited provision of Delaware law to practice law in Delaware Courts. This provision also allowed her to accept employment in the Department of Justice of the State of Delaware as an Assistant Deputy Attorney General. As a result of these experiences, Ms. Rubenstein was able to provide significant letters of support of her ability to practice law when she applied in 1993 to again attempt to pass the Delaware bar examination. She had also consulted with a learning disability specialist and was advised that she did, in fact, have a learning disability. Ms. Rubenstein, in her request to the board of examiners, presented a report that verified a 21-point discrepancy between her measured verbal ability level and her measured performance ability, which, Ms. Rubenstein claimed, showed her to be a primarily sequential learner rather than a primarily simultaneous-type learner. Ms. Rubenstein further noted that if given a test formatted in a "simultaneous" format she would do less well. Ms. Rubenstein claimed that her role as a prosecutor allowed her to develop problem solutions in a sequential style, within her strength area. In reference to her 21-point IQ test discrepancy, Ms. Rubenstein indicated that this was a meaningless average except that it does portend a psychological "overlay" associated with having a learning disability. In other words, for Ms. Rubenstein, as her disability expert stated, this type of a learning disability "would not impair her law practice" (p. 920).

With this supporting documentation about her learning disability, Ms. Rubenstein's request for taking the board examination with accommodation was granted, except that she would not be permitted extra time for the multistate bar examination portion. Given the extra time provision for the essay portion of the examination, Ms. Rubenstein passed, but scored 9 points below her previous passing score of 137 (130 is passing) on the multistate portion and subsequently then petitioned the Board to disregard this two-point insufficiency, which was denied, and then Ms. Rubenstein took this issue to the Delaware Supreme Court. The issue, Ms. Rubenstein protested, was that she was allowed extra time in one portion of the examination but not the other.

Ruling under Title III of ADA, the Delaware Supreme Court cited the lack of any refuting evidence regarding Ms. Rubenstein's learning disability and that "the Board's decision to afford Rubenstein additional time (one-third extra time) to take the essay section, but no additional time to take the MBE Section of the bar examination without any explanation, was "internally inconsistent" (p. 924). The court also suspended the Board rule that both sections of the bar examination be passed during one sitting and concluded that she had passed both portions of the examination.

Daniels v. Allied Electrical Contractors (a Subsidiary of Mobil Oil)

Mr. Daniels was terminated from his job of oil refinery worker for twice failing the company's written safety test. Mr. Daniels contested his firing on the basis of not being able to pass the written test because of a lifelong reading and writing disability and said that he was denied the opportunity to take the test orally. Mr. Daniels' original suit was brought under ADA, but a district court ruled that Title I of ADA was not yet in effect at the time of Mr. Daniels' claim. The court rejected all ADA and Title VII claims against the defendant, but did rule that Mr. Daniels had a right to seek relief against Allied Electrical (a subsidiary of Mobil Oil) through the Texas Commission on Human Rights.

Synthesis of LD Case Law

It would be unwise to attempt any broad generalizations from this handful of law cases. It is evident, however, that the majority of these discrimination suits were filed after the plaintiff failed an examination. Of course, persons with disabilities, including those with learning disabilities, are not required under disability discrimination law to volunteer their need for a testing accommodation (EEOC, 1995). On the other hand, an employer is only required to provide such an accommodation if he or she knows, before administering a test, that an accommodation will be needed. It is the responsibility of the individual with a disability to request any required accommodation for a test (EEOC, 1995). However, employers should always inform applicants, in advance, of any tests that will be administered as part of the application process so that they may request an accommodation, if needed. Under ADA, an employer does have the right to specify the span of time between announcing the need for an accommodation and when the test will actually be given (EEOC, 1995). The employer may also require that documentation of the need (proof of existence of a disability) for accommodation to accompany such a request—a particularly important part of ADA law to remember for those persons with learning disabilities or persons with other types of "hidden" disabilities. Occasions will arise in which a person with a disability may not have realized, in advance, what type or degree of accommodation would be needed. The applicant should immediately stop work on the test, ask to take the exam at another time, and, in the interim, make known to the employer the need to arrange for other types of accommodations. It is important to remember that, as in the Wynne and Pandazides cases, the employer is not required to offer an applicant the exact accommodation requested. The employer is only required to provide an "effective accommodation." More specifically, the employer is only required to provide, upon request, an "accessible test format" for individuals whose disabilities impair their ability to take the test, unless the test is specifically designed to measure those skills (EEOC, 1995). Generally recognized accommodations for persons with LD are extra time (not necessarily unlimited time), a quiet room, a change in test format (but only where format does not represent one of the "essential skills" of the job one is being tested for), and a test given orally instead of a test that requires reading. All these accommodations should be considered carefully by both applicant and employer in light of test validity issues (Biller, 1993; Nester, 1993).

Another consistent problem for persons with learning disabilities, in presenting their cases, was how they defined and identified their disabilities. The only congressionally approved definition for identifying a learning disability was spelled out by U.S.O.E. in 1977 under "procedures of evaluating specific learning disabilities" (Federal Register, 42, 65082-65085). The federal definition of learning disability stipulates that LD is: ". . . a disorder in one or more of the basic psychological processes involved in understanding or in using language, spoken or written, which may manifest itself in an imperfect ability to listen, think, speak, read, write, spell, or to do mathematical calculations. . . ." (U.S. Office of Education, 1977, p. 65083). Determination of a learning disability under U.S.O.E. Guidelines:

> is made based on (1) whether a child does not achieve commensurate with his or her age and ability when provided with appropriate educa-

tional experiences, and (2) whether the child has a severe discrepancy between achievement and intellectual ability in one or more of seven areas relating to communication skills and mathematical abilities. These concepts are to be interpreted on a case by case basis by the qualified evaluation team members. The team must decide that the discrepancy is not primarily the result of (1) visual, hearing, or motor handicaps; (2) mental retardation; (3) emotional disturbance; or (4) environmental, cultural, or economic disadvantage (Fed. Reg., 1977, 42, p. 65082).

This U.S.O.E. definition and determination guidelines must be applied to adult populations using ability and achievement tests normed for adult populations. As shown in Pandazides, Pazer, and Argen, the courts will be looking at this federal guideline in the face of the many and varied types of definitions used over the last 20 years to describe this LD population. The provisions of Section 504 of the Rehabilitation Act of 1973 and ADA Titles I and II were designed to guide individuals with disabilities, to furnish employers with the basic guidelines for preventing unfair hiring procedures, and to insure that employers retain the right to hire only the most qualified applicants. It was to be expected that many discrimination issues would arise following the implementation of ADA's employment provisions. It is now up to persons with disabilities, advocates for persons with disabilities, professionals with LD specialization, and employers to keep current with ongoing interpretations of ADA through the courts, as well as through the many seminars and publications that are available to describe court decisions regarding ADA and Section 504 legal interpretations.

References

Americans with Disabilities Act of 1990, 42 U.S.C. 12101 *et seq.*

Argen v. New York State Board of Law Examiners, District Court of Western New York, August 11, 1994, *Americans with Disabilities Cases,* (1995) 3, pp. 1455–1460. Washington, DC: The Bureau of National Affairs, Inc.

Biller, E. F. (1993). Employment testing of persons with specific learning disabilities. *Journal of Rehabilitation, 59,* 16–23.

Biller, E. F. (1988). *Understanding adolescents and young adults with learning disabilities: A focus on employability and career placement—a guide for rehabilitation counselors.* Springfield, IL: Charles C. Thomas, Publishers.

Biller, E. F. (1987). *Career decision making for adolescents and young adults with learning disabilities: Theory, research, and practice.* Springfield, IL: Charles C. Thomas, Publishers.

Biller, E. F. (1985). *Understanding and guiding the career development of adolescents and young adults with learning disabilities.* Springfield, IL: Charles C. Thomas, Publishers.

Biller, E.F., & White, W. J. (1989). Comparing special education and vocational rehabilitation in serving persons with specific learning disabilities. *Rehabilitation Counseling Bulletin, 33*(1), 4–17.

Christian v. New York State Board of Law Examiners. U.S. District Court, Southern District of New York, February 18, 1994. *Americans with Disabilities Cases,* (1995), 3 pp. 917–918. Washington, DC: The Bureau of National Affairs, Inc.

Civil Rights Act of 1964, Pub. L. No. 88-352, 78 Stat. 257 (Codified as amended at 42 U.S.C. 2000 e-3) (1994).

Daniels v. Allied Electrical Contractors, Inc., District Court of Eastern Texas, March 11, 1994, *Americans with Disabilities Cases,* (1995) 3, pp. 441–446, Washington, DC: The Bureau of National Affairs, Inc.

Dearmont v. Texas A&M University, 2 National Disability Law Reporter (LRP) S. 10 (Office of Civil Rights, May 18, 1991) at 31.

Duane, D. D. (1979). Theories about the causes of dyslexia and their implications. *Pediatric Annals, 8*(11), 12–17.

Education for All Handicapped Children Act of 1975, 20 U.S.C., Sec. 143.

Federal Register (August 23, 1977). Education of handicapped children: implementation of part B of the Education for All Handicapped Children Act of 1975. 42, 65082-65085.

Federal Register (July 26, 1991). Equal employment opportunity for individuals with disabilities, final rule. 29 C.F.R. Part 1630 Section 4630. 11. Administration of Tests, Vol. 56.

Grossman, P. D. (1994). Developing issues for the learning disabled community under employment discrimination laws. In P. J. Gerber & H. B. Reiff (Eds.), *Learning disabilities in adulthood* (pp. 20–45). Boston, MA: Andover Medical Publishers.

Hale, M. (1982). History of employment testing. In A. K. Wigdor & W. R. Garner (Eds.), *Ability testing: Uses, consequences, and controversies* (pp. 3–38). Washington, DC: National Academy Press.

Individuals with Disabilities Education Act of 1990, 20. U.S.C. 1400 *et seq.*

McCusker, C. E. (1995). The Americans with disability act: Its potential for expanding the scope of reasonable academic accommodations. *Journal of College and University Law, 21*(4), 619–641.

Nester, M. A. (1993). *Pre-employment testing and the ADA.* Ithaca, New York: Cornell University, Program on Employment and Disability, School of Industrial and Labor Relations.

Pandazides v. Virginia Board of Education, U.S. District Court of Appeals, Richmond, October 10, 1991. *Americans with Disabilities Cases, 2* (1994), pp. 33–36. Washington, DC: The Bureau of National Affairs, Inc.

Pazer v. New York State Board Law Examiners. District Court, State of New York, April 26, 1994. *Americans with Disabilities Cases,* (1995), 3 pp. 360–363. Washington, DC: The Bureau of National Affairs, Inc.

Rehabilitation Act of 1973, 29 U.S.C. 701 *et seq.*

Riedel v. Kansas State Board of Regents, District Court of Kansas, November 17, 1993, *Americans with Disabilities Cases,* (1994), 2, pp. 1528–1532. Washington, DC: The Bureau of National Affairs, Inc.

Rubenstein, In RE: Delaware Supreme Court, February 28, 1994. *Americans with Disabilities Cases,* (1995), 3, pp. 919–928. Washington, DC: The Bureau of National Affairs, Inc.

Schultz, C. B. (1984). Saving millions through judicious selection of employees. *Public Personnel Management, 13*(4), 409–415.

Section 504. Subpart B. *Federal Register.* 42, May 4, 1977, 22680-22681.

Stanovich, K. E. (1988). Science and learning disabilities. *Journal of Learning Disabilities, 21,* 210–214.

Stutts v. Freeman, 694 F. 2nd 666 (11th Cir. 1983).

Swanson, H. L. (1988). Toward a meta theory of learning disabilities. *Journal of Learning Disabilities, 21*(4), 196–209.

Title I of Americans with Disabilities Act of 1990, § 42 U.S.C. § 12101-12213 (1990).

Torgeson, J. K. (1988). The cognitive and behavioral characteristics of children with learning disabilities: An overview. *Journal of Learning Disabilities, 21*(1), 587–589.

U.S. Equal Employment Opportunity Commission (1995). *Disability discrimination.* Washington, DC: EEOC Office of Communications and Legislative Affairs.

Wynne v. Tufts University School of Medicine, 932 F. 2d 19 (1st Cir. Mass., April 17, 1991), aff'd 976 F. 2d 791 (1st Cir. Mass., October 6, 1992).

CHAPTER 13

Job Accommodations: What Works and Why

Nancie Payne

S uccess in today's marketplace, for an employee with a learning disability, may depend heavily on the development and implementation of effective job accommodations. Over the last decade, two factors have significantly increased the need to address job accommodations for people with learning disabilities: a changing economy and increased knowledge about these hidden disabilities (Brown & Gerber 1994).

Prior to the emergence of the information age, many people with learning disabilities were able to compete for and perform in jobs that accentuated their aptitudes and skills. Even for those who struggled to keep their jobs, there was still an opportunity to maintain employment by working extra hours, accessing support staff, and securing help from co-workers. However, as the economy has shifted from the industrial to the information age, job structure, responsibilities, and competencies have changed significantly resulting in the loss of support staff, less availability of co-workers, and more responsibilities. In many instances, the changes have resulted in disappearing jobs and dislocation (Brown & Gerber 1994).

During this period of economic change, significant progress has been realized in the recognition of learning disabilities as a life-long condition affecting adults in a variety of circumstances including job training and performance.

While there is still fairly limited information about the number of adults in the workplace who have learning disabilities, most research suggests the incidence is between 3 and 14% (Brown, 1988; Brown, 1994). In 1992, the Job Accommodation Network (JAN), a service of the President's Committee on Employment of People with Disabilities, reported that 4.3% of their cases from 1984 to 1991 involved employment accommodation requests for adults with learning disabilities (Jacobs & Hendricks 1992). These numbers are estimated to more than double when adults with learning disabilities also are economically disadvantaged. A U.S. Department of Labor report (Employment and Training Administration, 1991) suggested that 15 to 23% of all Title IIA Job Training Partnership Act (JTPA) terminees may have learning disabilities. The report further cited that 25 to 40% of all adults receiving Aid to Families with Dependent Children (AFDC) support also may have learning disabilities. Additionally, a U.S. Department of Health and Human Services report from the Office of the Inspector General (1992) attempted to identify those functional impairments which were significant among adults receiving AFDC support. The report concluded that learning disabilities and substance abuse were most frequently identified as significant functional impairments.

As America enters what Gingrich (1995) has termed the Third Wave Information Age, scientific and technological advancements will continue to promote constant change in marketplace characteristics. The effect of this change on the workplace can best be represented as a continuous restructuring of organizations and systems to maintain productivity. In turn, this constant restructuring and revitalization to keep up with the changes creates an increasing need for job accommodations for many people with learning disabilities.

Disclosure and Obtaining Job Accommodations

Securing accommodations requires that the employee disclose his or her learning disability. Much debate continues about what to disclose, when and how to disclose it and to whom. Disclosure may result in a meaningful exchange of information, the outcome of which is appropriate accommodations to assist the employee in performing on the job in a satisfactory manner. However, disclosing a disability is not risk-free, as it also may result in negative, antagonistic conditions that breed hostility and distrust. *The choice to disclose a disability or any related information is the right and privilege of the individual.*

To determine whether the organization or company climate is supportive of individuals with disabilities, prospective employees must consider several questions: Are accommodations critical to maintaining acceptable performance? Could accommodations be self-initiated without disclosure? Would the company benefit from information about disabilities and accommodations? Are there other support systems that could assist in the education process? Serious thought should be given to what, if any, repercussions might occur as a result of disclosure.

Disclosure generally occurs *after* the job or promotion has been offered (Payne, 1992) and should only be discussed with those who have a need to know the information. Sometimes an employee feels there is no need to disclose the disability immediately after hire or promotion. If this is the case, then the employee should systematically and carefully monitor his or her progress during job probation or for at least the first 6 months of employment. It can be a very awkward and diffi-cult situation when, during an evaluation, an employee realizes perfor-mance is less than satisfactory and knows poor performance is probably the result of the undisclosed disability. This situation can be avoided if the employee is clear about job responsibilities and requests regular feedback about performance from supervisors and coworkers.

Disclosure may also occur after years of employment due to organi-zational growth, restructuring, or technological advances. These changes may prompt a long-term employee with a diagnosed but undisclosed hidden disability to seek specific job accommodations in order to learn and perform new tasks or skills. An employee may discover that an undiagnosed learning disability has affected performance and may rec-ognize that specific job accommodations would significantly improve productivity. Still, in many cases, poor performance or loss of employ-ment are directly linked to lack of knowledge about learning disabilities and job accommodations on the part of the employer, the employee, or both. The Americans with Disabilities Act of 1990, Section 1630.13, as cited in the Equal Employment Opportunity Commission's and the U.S. Department of Justice's *Americans with disabilities act handbook* (1991), specifies that it is unlawful for an employer who may suspect a disabil-ity to conduct a medical examination or make inquiries as to whether the employee has a disability, or to inquire about the nature or severity of such disability. If this is the case, development of accommodations is dif-ficult until the employee realizes that a possible disability exists and is willing to disclose.

Disclosure should begin with a meeting between the employee and a staff person from the human resources or personnel department. The human resources specialist should assist and guide the employee in iden-tifying specific accommodations and choosing a plan of action. Many employees work in small businesses or companies where such depart-ments or resources are nonexistent. In these cases, deciding with whom to discuss a request for job accommodations is extremely important. The most logical person may be the employee's supervisor, but other options include the person who manages the benefits package or payroll, the union representative, or the owner of the company. The employee should choose a person with some authority or influence, someone who can be trusted to strive for a workable solution. If the employee has difficulty identifying the appropriate person, then he or she should seek advice from outside the work environment. For pre-disclosure consultation, one might contact the Job Accommodation Network (JAN) or advocacy groups such as the Learning Disabilities Association of America, Orton Dyslexia Society, or Children and Adults with Attention Deficit Disorders (CHADD). The local employment office, human rights commission, state vocational rehabilitation agency, employee assistance program (community or company-based), disability information center, state commission on disability issues and employment, or the regional or state disability business technical assistance center also could provide appropriate assistance and information.

Defining Job Accommodations

The equal employment opportunity provisions of the Americans with Disabilities Act of 1990 (ADA), Title I, (Section 1630.2), as cited in the Equal Employment Opportunity Commission's and the U.S. Department of Justice's *Americans with disabilities act handbook* (1991) and the U.S. Equal Opportunity Commission as cited in University of Wisconsin ADA Alliances (1994), defines reasonable accommodations as modifications or adjustments to the work environment, or to the manner or circumstances under which the position held is customarily performed, that enable an otherwise qualified individual with a disability to perform the essential functions of that position. Additionally, reasonable accommodations are further defined as modifications or adjustments that enable an employee with a disability to enjoy equal benefits and privileges of employment as are enjoyed by the other similarly situated employees without disabilities.

Reasonable accommodations should not create undue hardship for the company or organization (U.S. Chamber of Commerce, 1992, as cited in University of Wisconsin ADA Alliances, 1994). In other words, providing an accommodation should not cause significant difficulty or expense. The nature of the accommodation and cost must be considered in tandem with the operation of the company. What impact will the accommodations have on operations? What is the cost of the accommodations compared to the financial resources of the company or organization? Reasonable accommodations should seek to equalize an employee's abilities to perform the essential functions of the job fairly by taking full advantage of the knowledge, skills, and abilities the employee possesses. Essential functions are defined as the fundamental job duties of the position the employee holds. Accommodations should never replace or compromise the knowledge, skills, or abilities required to do the job. Of critical importance is the assurance that job accommodations, when put into place, will neither result in a violation of safety standards nor create safety hazards. Remember, the purpose of providing accommodations is to equalize the employee's abilities to perform, not to rectify a poor job match or compensate for a lack of knowledge, skills, or abilities.

Developing Job Accommodations

A variety of methods and techniques have been designed to assist an employee in identifying and implementing specific job accommodations (Brown & Gerber, 1994; Jacobs & Hendricks, 1992; Payne, 1992; University of Wisconsin, 1994). Sometimes the process is as simple as discussing with a supervisor a better way to complete a task or to minimize a difficulty. For example, a person easily distracted by noise may need a white noise machine, earplugs, or a Walkman to filter out the distractions. Another employee having difficulty using a company computer system may ask the supervisor to identify software that would enhance functional use and, after checking with the systems manager to purchase the software. No matter how complex or simple the employee request for accommodations may be, several factors simply must be addressed.

Assessment

To develop effective job accommodations, management must assess or review two elements: (a) the structure, environment, and management of the company or organization, and (b) the performance and needs of the employee requesting job accommodations. Research or data addressing best assessment practices are scarce. Perhaps the process or methods employed are not as important as the elements themselves.

To address these two critical elements, Payne & Associates of Olympia, WA developed a workplace accommodations assessment model. The model, depicted in Figure 13.1, focuses on the structure, environment, and management of the company or organization through an *employment assessment* and the performance and needs of the employee with the disability through an *employee assessment*. These elements are vital to the development of accommodations that are logical, reasonable, and effective for both the employee and the company or organization.

The workplace accommodations assessment model provides the foundation for a four-phase process: assessment, followed by planning, implementation, and evaluation (Payne, 1992). The assessment phase takes the

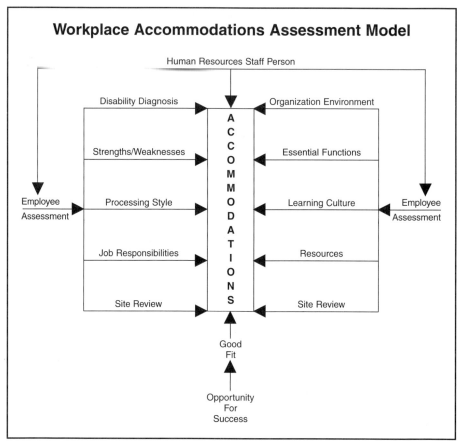

FIGURE 13.1. Workplace accommodation assessment model. From Payne & Associates, 1995. Development of a model of workplace accommodations assessment. Reprinted with permission.

longest time and involves the human resources staff person (if available), the employee, the employee's immediate supervisor, and other significant supervisors or coworkers. Because disclosure of a disability involves the right and choice of the employee requesting accommodations, the human resources specialist must thoroughly discuss with the employee the involvement of any supervisors or coworkers, *even an immediate supervisor.* Directly involving people who do not have a need to know about the disability or the request for accommodations can negatively impact the success of implementation. On the other hand, it is important to involve those key individuals who would benefit from knowing about the disability or the request for accommodations as they will probably be impacted by the accommodations or may be able to contribute to the development or implementation of recommended accommodations. For example, in setting up accommodations for a company repair person, a designated coworker in the billing department may need to know what has been implemented to accommodate for a learning disability that affects the employee's ability to submit completed invoices.

A consultant or the human resources staff person may facilitate the assessment process. If a consultant is used, his or her role is to facilitate the process of assessment, planning, implementation, and evaluation of accommodations, in concert with the human resources staff person. The consultant should provide pertinent information and training so, if modifications or adjustments are required or another request for accommodations is received, the company or organization can implement the protocols with minimal assistance from the consultant. If the company does not have a human resources staff person and a consultant is not feasible, then someone in the company should be identified as the designated staff person to assist in the assessment, planning, implementation, and evaluation of accommodations if and when necessary.

After this person reviews any medical or clinical diagnostic reports (if available), job description, performance evaluations, and any other pertinent information, a team assembles. The team meeting usually involves the human resources person as facilitator, the immediate supervisor, and the employee. If a consultant is involved, the human resources staff person and the consultant share the facilitator role. During the meeting, they work together to plan the process, setting sensible timelines for the four phases and reviewing essential and nonessential tasks of the employee's job—assuming they have been identified—and validating these as accurate and up-to-date. *Remember that the goal of the plan is to develop and implement logical and reasonable accommodations to the essential job functions of the employee who has disclosed a learning disability, maximizing productivity for both the employee and the company or organization.*

In the assessment phase, facilitated by the consultant or the designated human resources staff person, the focus is first on the employee. Five components comprise the employee assessment: appraisal of the employee's (a) diagnostic information, (b) strengths and limitations, (c) processing style, (d) a task analysis of job responsibilities, and (e) a site review. Each of these components, facilitated by the consultant or the human resources staff person, require the employee's active involvement. If the employee does not have recent documentation of the learning disability, it may be beneficial to encourage the employee to seek formal assessment services. Additional diagnostic information, if requested of the employee, should provide more detail about the learning disability as well as how job performance is affected.

Engaging the employee in a discussion of his or her strengths and limitations at work, in classroom and training situations, and in recreational and social settings will foster reflection on his or her experiences in different environments. This is one of the more critical components of the employee assessment phase, as it provides important insight into what has worked and what has not worked. It also reveals specific strengths to be used and developed further—strengths that will provide the underpinnings of any successful accommodations.

The third critical component of employee assessment is the evaluation of the employee's processing style. In this context, processing style refers to the methods the employee uses when receiving and interpreting information (input), combined with his or her preferences and needs for responding or performing the job competencies (output). Simply asking the employee a series of questions about the methods necessary to adequately perform the essential functions of the job, in many cases, elicits enough information to develop accommodations.

The final two components of the employee assessment are a task analysis of the specific job competencies and responsibilities together with an on-site review of the environment. Since the task analysis is usually conducted at the worksite location, these two components can easily be combined. The best way to accomplish a task analysis is to have the employee walk the facilitator (consultant or human resources person) through the steps or processes of each essential function. As this occurs, the facilitator may query the employee about methods or procedures that, if changed or implemented, might enhance or improve the capacity to utilize his or her knowledge, skills, and abilities. At the same time, the facilitator should assess the environment, identifying any aspects that might affect job performance or should be adjusted as part of the accommodations planning. Throughout the assessment phase, the employee's physical, emotional, and social needs merit particular attention. Many times, these factors are overlooked, but they provide valuable insight into the stability and stamina of the employee, as well as the level of support he or she may require during the implementation phase.

Once the employee assessment is complete, attention shifts to the organization or company: the employment assessment addresses structure, environment, and management. The five components in this phase of the assessment are: (a) appraisal of the organizational environment, (b) identification of the essential functions of the employee's job, (c) analysis of the learning culture, (d) inventory of resources, and (e) a site review.

The facilitator plays a pivotal role, working closely with the immediate supervisor and coworkers who may be impacted by accommodations. Coworkers often can offer insight into how various aspects of the job could be changed or enhanced to improve overall performance. However, when involving other employees in the development and implementation of accommodations, the employee's right employee to choose disclosure cannot be stressed enough.

The facilitator begins the employment assessment with a functional or basic review of the organizational environment. This segment includes a review of the internal operations, and of the structure and management of the employee's department or section. It may be minimal or may require a more in-depth look, depending on changes and growth factors that may be affecting employee performance. As organizations continue to grow and restructure in order to compete in the global economy, changes influencing behaviors and organizational environments transpire. All too often, the employee with a learning disability, caught in the organizational growth or restructuring, is unable to control the influencing behaviors that significantly impact his or her performance and productivity (Payne, 1995). The result is a perception that the employee needs accommodations, when in fact the organization needs to manage the growth or restructuring more effectively. In other words, the perceived need for accommodations to assist an employee who has a learning disability achieve a higher level of productivity and effectiveness is just that—a perceived need which has its roots in the effects of organizational growth and restructuring and not the employee's knowledge, skills, or abilities or the limitations of the disability. The facilitator manages the review by conducting individual interviews with each team member to gather information about new procedures and changes in workflow and productivity.

At the same time the organizational environment is being assessed, the site review can be completed. This is really an extension of the site review conducted earlier under the employee assessment phase and should be complete by the end of the organizational review. It should include an examination of the physical layout including lighting, organization of equipment, and work space access. Pay attention to visual and auditory distractions and disturbances. Worksite communication patterns and social interaction should also be observed and strengths and weaknesses noted. This will affect decisions on how to introduce and implement accommodations.

Once the organizational environment and site reviews are complete, the facilitator should interview the immediate supervisor, examining the last three components: essential job functions, learning culture, and available resources. According to the Americans with Disabilities Act of 1990, Title I, Equal Employment Opportunity provisions, the essential functions of the job are the fundamental job duties of the position held by the employee with the disability. A review of specific job tasks and assignments should clarify essential functions and responsibilities, and identify trouble spots. This aspect of the employment assessment is extremely important. Many times, the employee and employer differ in their opinions about essential functions, job responsibilities, and assigned tasks, as well as what has been going well and what needs improvement.

The learning culture component may be defined as an analysis of the way a company, organization, department, or work team globally processes information (Payne, 1992; 1995). The global input and output of an organization can significantly impact an employee with a learning disability who cannot readily shift to the learning culture as a result of the disability. For example, an employee with a visual processing learning disability (one that affects her ability to accurately interpret and act on printed information) was constantly challenged by the presentation of long, detailed memoranda and procedural manuals. Her department's learning culture was a print-oriented environment which exacerbated her learning disability. In evaluating the learning culture, the facilitator should examine the following elements: modalities which are commonly used by, or required of, employees to process the work load; methods typically used to accomplish the work; and expected or established methods of response.

Finally, the facilitator should inventory any company or organization resources that may assist in the development of accommodations. Technology, supplies, training, materials, and staff support should be counted among factors in the planning and implementation process.

Planning

The next phase of the workplace accommodations process, planning, involves the systematic review and evaluation of information collected from all components of the assessment. At this point, it is time to match the needs and priorities of both the employee requesting accommodations and the employee's supervisor and coworkers. The planning process brings the employee's processing style and the company or department's learning culture, the impact of the organizational environment, the employee's physical needs, and the strengths and limitations of both the company and the employee *together* to form a foundation upon which to build accommodations. With this information, combined with the identification of company or organization resources, the facilitator will identify specific, logical, and reasonable accommodations that equalize the employee's competencies—the knowledge, skills, and abilities—creating work power which maximizes efficiency, effectiveness, and finally, overall productivity.

The plan should include techniques and recommendations that are concrete and specific in nature, prioritized in an order of suggested implementation. Built-in flexibility should allow for adjustments and growth. The plan should address the employee's and supervisor's concerns and needs in a succinct and systematic manner. This will promote ease in understanding and implementation as well as monitoring and evaluation.

Implementation

Specific recommendations for logical and reasonable accommodations should be presented in the facilitator's written report. Any recommendations should cite the background and assessment processes conducted to reach the written conclusions. Recommendations for accommodations should be divided into two levels: primary and secondary.

Primary recommendations are those actions and accommodations resulting from the site review, organizational environment evaluation, and learning culture analysis. An example might be a change in the employee's work station arrangement, an enhancement to computer software, a different lighting system, or an efficiency study to determine productivity levels due to recent changes.

Secondary accommodations can be best explained as those strategies, techniques, methodologies, and adaptations which allow for the employee's maximum potential to be realized. Implementation of secondary recommendations and accommodations usually occurs after primary accommodations are underway and positive progress has been noted. Usually secondary divisions are: company or organization responsibilities, employee personal strategies, and shared employer–employee responsibilities.

In a performance evaluation of a customer service employee who had a learning disability affecting visual discrimination and sequencing, the supervisor cited poor oral communication skills. The facilitator found that the employee was providing customers with inaccurate information about products and service, and that she was exhibiting a poor disposition in the customer's presence. The essential job functions specified customer service

and good verbal abilities as fundamental skills. In recommending accommodations, the facilitator cited the employee's disposition as a skill requiring personal strategies for improvement. The facilitator requested the company take responsibility for providing additional training in product
service and information dissemination to customers as well as for furnish-
ing a sequenced outline and script of what to say to customers. In the
assessment rationale, the employee was hired on the assumption she could
meet the essential functions of the job, which included the ability to greet
customers in a pleasant and appropriate manner. The customer service
training originally provided did not include a sequenced outline or script.
The employer and the employee then agreed to work several times per
week, role-playing situations using the outline and script. As this example
portrays, it is important to assign responsibility for accommodations to the
employer, to the employee, and to a joint effort or partnership—along with
implementation timelines.

The facilitator should present recommendations for accommodations in a systematic way that prevents misunderstandings, communicating the information in a clear, concise, and consistent manner. One of
the most effective presentations involves a three- or four-part process. If
a consultant is presenting, the human resources staff person should
review the recommendations to ensure agreement with policy and organization procedures. The consultant or the human resources staff person
schedules several 2-to-2½-hour meetings within the same day: the first
with the employee; the second, to be held within a few hours after the
first, with the supervisor for the purpose of presenting the recommendations; the third, scheduled shortly thereafter, brings the supervisor
and the employee together to review the recommendations; and the
fourth meeting, to be held as soon as possible after the first three meetings and should include the employee, supervisor, and those significant
co-workers who took part in the earlier assessment process. This meeting schedule works very well, allowing the employee to hear and
process the recommendations three or four different times with all
involved personnel. The third meeting is optional, especially if no others were involved in the assessment phases, or if both the supervisor
and the employee indicate they are comfortable enough with the recommendations to move to the full team meeting.

The facilitator disseminates information and recommendations, presenting recommended accommodations during the first two or three
meetings without comment or modification by attendees. At the final
meeting, the team accepts, modifies or rejects recommendations and

makes assignments for task completion, implementation of specifics, and monitoring plans. The team approach reduces negative impacts (feelings of unfair review, special treatment, or misunderstood recommendations) and controls the rumor mill by promoting an open communication process that seeks to recognize diversity and difference while achieving equalization of knowledge, skills, and abilities.

Presentation of recommendations should occur within the outlined format of meetings scheduled within a 1-to-2-day period. While it is important to allow participants (especially the employee) time to think through the recommendations, too much time can create questions and confusion. The team meeting allows for open discussion. If the employee says a recommendation or suggestion doesn't look workable, it can be modified or bypassed. If a supervisor asks for clarity about a resource availability, the response may go on the "to do list" for a future follow-up meeting. The team initiates the process of implementation. Not every recommendation should or will be acceptable, and certainly not every acceptable recommendation or suggestion should be implemented simultaneously. Small, thoughtfully planned steps will provide the best opportunity for review, modification, and success.

Evaluation

Evaluation, the final phase, is truly an essential phase of the process and the one that usually receives the least attention. Each agreed-upon accommodation or personal strategy should have a timeline for implementation and a person assigned for implementation responsibilities. The process of implementing accommodations must be monitored in a very functional way on a weekly or bimonthly basis. A regular team meeting should occur to review the accommodations and the implementation process for effectiveness and efficiency. Employee performance should begin to improve at an acceptable rate as evidenced by consistent increases in productivity. If accommodations are not creating an improved situation, then modifications and adjustments should be implemented until improvements are measurable.

As the accommodations work, the number of meetings can be reduced and eventually scheduled at the request of the team. Even if the company or organization is small, the team meetings are a very important part of implementation as they provide a safe, structured opportunity to evaluate and communicate progress. Feedback is critical to the success of an employee with a learning disability.

Specific Job Accommodations

The Job Accommodations Network (JAN) has evaluated data on the cost of accommodations across the board for all disability requests and has concluded that 31% of accommodations made involve *no cost to the employer*. Other costs are as follows:

19% of the cost of accommodations fall between $1 and $50.

19% of the cost of accommodations fall between $50 and $500.

19% of the cost of accommodations fall between $500 and $1000.

11% of the cost of accommodations fall between $1000 and $5000

less than 1% of the cost of accommodations exceed $5000.

The following are examples of workplace accommodations. Note that they range from index cards to a computer-equipped van.

A secretary with a learning disability that affected visual discrimination was working in a bank and having difficulty compiling information and producing weekly banking reports. Recommended accommodations included developing a guide that defines the terms and vocabulary used on specific reports; providing an acceptable model for each report, noting format, style, and organization of text; developing a checklist of items to prepare or consider prior to writing the report; providing a screen enlarger to make reading and preparation of reports easier; and using a larger type size to prepare the report which, when complete, would then be reduced to the standard size and format.

A repair person with dyslexia had a large, regional service area and was having trouble processing customer calls through the voice mail system, especially when driving. A portable computer with a fax modem, E-mail, and a printer was installed in the repair van. As the request for services came through, it was processed through the computer system and a print-out was immediately available. This allowed the employee to refer to the information several times. It also assisted in preparing invoices and ordering supplies because there was a consistent record of work and materials used.

A forklift driver working in a warehouse had directional disabilities as well as reading problems. To accomodate the directional needs, aisles and bins were assigned color designations and the employee was given a color-coded, pictorial schematic of the warehouse. By placing graphic replicas of items to be shelved in the intended locations, for accuracy when loading and unloading supplies, management compensated for the driver's reading disability.

A clerk-typist with visual processing and spelling difficulties worked in a large import/export store. He was responsible for completing order forms on the computer after orders had been filled. Accomodation involved programming the function keys to help him place the correct information in the appropriate field on the computer screen and minimize his use of codes and terms. This significantly reduced his ordering and shipping errors, thus saving the store costly charges.

A person with an auditory processing disability worked in a manufacturing company where multiple job tasks and frequent change are common. She created a memory log from a small three-ring binder and index cards. As changes or new instructions for product manufacturing occurred, the employee asked her supervisor to write out step-by-step instructions on a card, using key words and phrases to facilitate memory. Relying on the cards in the mini-binder, she completed all steps of new or changed operations.

An employee in an auto parts store was having severe problems pulling the right parts from the storeroom due to visual perception and discrimination difficulties with part code numbers. Since the lighting in the storeroom was poor, the employer agreed to add new lighting fixtures. Prior to the fixtures' installation, the employee kept a miner's hat with a headlamp just inside the storeroom door and donned it each time she entered the storeroom. She also labeled each bin or shelf section with the name and picture of the part stocked there so she did not have to rely totally on part numbers.

A young employee with multiple reading and language memory difficulties started her first job as a kitchen assistant. The employee had difficulty sequencing and organizing the tasks of the job, needing constant reminders. Color-coding on a list of work tasks (using words she could read) and corresponding color-coded numbers on a large wall clock signalled the times for beginning specific job tasks.

An employee who had difficulty taking notes at staff meetings because of visual-motor integration problems that affect writing asked for an electronic white board to be available at meetings. The supervisor agreed to write pertinent facts on the white board. After a meeting, the employee could then run a hard copy directly off the board. This saved money for a notetaker or hours of listening to taped recordings of meeting discussion. A community service organization donated the board in return for free monthly use of the meeting room.

Summary

Job accommodations should be developed through a four-phase process that begins with assessment and finishes with a strong evaluation component. The process identifies empoyee's strengths as well as limitations or weaknesses. Whenever possible, accommodations should be based upon the use and further development of the already intact knowledge, skills, and abilities of the employee with the disability (Brown & Gerber, 1994; Jacobs & Hendricks, 1992). Using these strengths creates learning power by compensating for the limitations and creating a level of self-knowledge that promotes increased employee self-esteem, self-motivation and the ability to self-advocate (Silver, 1995). All of these contribute essentials to employee effectiveness and productivity.

Job accommodations must not be developed in isolation. When a disability is disclosed and accommodations are requested, both the employer and employee need to work toward a productive relationship. Working together to find on-the-job solutions takes time and energy. The model described is not meant to inhibit or complicate the accommodation process. Sometimes developing accommodations is as simple as scheduling some time with a supervisor to discuss a better way to accomplish a task. In doing so, participants cover the elements contained in the model in an informal way. The objective is not just to do something, but to do something that makes sense and works. Job accommodations occur because both parties collaborate to maintain the human resource and increase productivity. As the assessment process unfolds, a partnership forms between employer and employee, increasing communication and support for the development and implementation of accommodations.

Accommodation designs vary from workplace to workplace, even though a job and disability may appear similar. Two individuals may each have a learning disability and hold identical jobs, but will differ in terms of coping, self-advocacy, and the like in other ways, just as work environments differ.

Effective accommodations are developed through a systematically planned process that includes organized assessment, planning, implementation, and evaluation phases. The process seeks to maintain fairness, recognizing the individual diversities and differences of the employee, the supervisor, the coworkers, and the company or organization as a whole.

Resources

Securing current and correct information about job accommodations for employees with learning disabilities is critical in this age of shrinking resources. The following organizations and services, as compiled by HEATH (1994), provide assistance to employers and employees as well as consultants, educators, trainers, and human service providers.

Equal Employment Opportunity Commission (EEOC)
1801 L Street NW
Washington, D.C. 20507
(800) 669-3362

The EEOC voice mail directs all calls from 7 a.m. to 5:30 p.m. Eastern Time (Monday–Friday). Operators accept orders for publications, fact sheets, posters, and a resource directory for people with disabilities, including learning disabilities (LD). They do not answer questions relating to employment, but can give referrals to local EEOC offices.

Job Accommodation Network (JAN)
West Virginia University
809 Allen Hall
Morgantown, West Virginia 26506
(800) 526-7234

JAN operates a free consulting service from 8 a.m. to 8 p.m. (Monday–Thursday) and 8 a.m. to 5 p.m. Eastern Time (Friday) that provides information on equipment, methods, and modifications for disabled persons to improve their work environment. All information is specific to the disability, including learning disabilities.

Learning Disabilities Association of America, Inc. (LDA)
4156 Library Road
Pittsburgh, Pennsylvania 15234
(412) 341-1515   FAX: (412) 344-0224

LDA, a non-profit, volunteer advocacy organization, provides information for parents, professionals, and consumers.

Learning Disabilities Research and Training Center
The University of Georgia
534 Aderhold Hall
Athens, Georgia 30602
(706) 542-1300   FAX (706) 542-4532

The Learning Disabilities Research and Training (LDR & T) Center focuses on employment/transition, functional assessment, and consumer empowerment.

National Adult Literacy & Learning
  Disabilities Center (The Center)
Academy for Education Development
1875 Connecticut Avenue N.W., Suite 800
Washington, D.C. 20009-1202
(202) 884-8185   (800) 953-2553   FAX (202) 884-8422

The Center, established in 1993, is a national information exchange regarding learning disabilities and their impact on the provision of literacy services, including workplace issues.

President's Committee on the Employment
  of People with Disabilities
1331 F Street NW
Washington, D.C. 20036
(202) 376-6200   (202) 376-6205   FAX (202) 376-6859

The President's Committee on the Employment of People with Disabilities is an independent federal agency. Its mission is to facilitate communication, coordination, and promotion of public and private efforts to empower Americans with disabilities through employment.

References

Americans with Disabilities Act of 1990, 42 U.S.C. 12101 *et seq.*

Brown, D. S. & Gerber, P. J. (1994). Employing people with learning disabilities. In P. J. Gerber & H. B. Reiff (Eds.), *Learning disabilities in adulthood: Persisting problems and evolving issues* (pp. 194–203). Austin, TX: PRO-ED.

Brown, D. (1988). *Personal communication.* Washington, DC: President's Committee on Employment of the Disabled.

Brown, D. (1994). *Working effectively with people who have learning disabilities and attention deficit hyperactivity disorder* (Implementing the Americans with Disabilities Act). Ithaca, NY: Cornell University.

Equal Employment Opportunity Commission and the U.S. Department of Justice. (1991). *Americans with disabilities act handbook.* Washington, DC: U.S. Government Printing Office.

Gingrich, N. (1995). *To renew America.* New York: HarperCollins.

HEATH Resource Center. (1994). *National resources for adults with learning disabilities.* Washington, DC: Author.

Jacobs, A. E., & Hendricks, D. J. (1992). Job accommodations for adults with learning disabilities: Brilliantly disguised opportunities. *LD Quarterly, 15*(4), 274–285.

Office of the Inspector General. U.S. Department of Health & Human Services. (1992). *Functional impairments of AFDC clients* (OEI-02-90-0040). Washington, DC: Author.

Payne, N. (1992). Designing workplace accommodations for people with special learning needs and related disabilities. *Journal of the National Association for Adults with Special Learning Needs, 2,* 1, 23–27.

Payne, N. (1995). The connection between learning culture and learning disabilities. *Linkages, 2*(1), 7.

Payne, N. (1995, Fall). Are we managing the right disability? *The LD Link.* Athens, GA: University of Georgia, Learning Disabilities Research & Training Center.

Silver, L. B. (1995). Knowledge of self: The key to self-esteem and self advocacy. In Learning Disabilities Association of America (Ed.), *Secondary education & beyond: Providing opportunities for students with learning disabilities* (pp. 223–233). Pittsburgh, PA: Learning Disabilities Association of America (LDA).

U.S. Chamber of Commerce. (1992). *What business must know about the ADA: A 1992 compliance guide.* Washington, DC: Author.

U.S. Department of Labor. (1991). *The learning disabled in employment & training programs* (Research & Evaluation Report Series 91-E). Washington, DC: U.S. Government Printing Office.

U.S. Equal Opportunity Commission. (1992). *A technical assistance manual on the employment provision (title I) of the americans with disabilities act.* Washington, DC: Author.

University of Wisconsin. (1994). *ADA alliances: Reasonable accommodations.* Madison, WI: Center on Education and Work, School of Education, University of Wisconsin.

CHAPTER 14

Psychosocial Issues of Workplace Adjustment

Lynda Price

J oseph: Joseph is a bright, charming college graduate in his middle 20s who just completed his studies at a small, private college on the East Coast. When he was a child, Joseph had difficulties with writing. spelling, study skills, and following directions, although he was very good at reading and math. His teachers described him as socially imma- ture and shy. When he wrote down or stated his ideas aloud, Joseph often would ramble about things tangential to the main topics at hand.

After he was diagnosed with learning disabilities, Joseph entered a private school, where he received additional tutoring but no specific accommodations for his disability during either grade school or high school. Joseph held two part-time jobs during high school and didn't work at all during college. His postsecondary grades were mostly Cs and Bs. He also spent a great deal of time socializing with his room- mates and dating two or three girlfriends.

When he received his bachelor's degree in history, Joseph was con- fused and concerned about what to do next. Both his parents (who are professors) and his older brother (who was then completing a master's degree in history abroad through a fellowship) encouraged him to apply for graduate education. Joseph took the summer off—living at home, working part-time as a lifeguard, and catching up on his social life while he decided what to do next. Because Joseph had discovered, in college, that he enjoyed being around people and that he wanted to be involved in private industry, he applied to a master of arts program in industrial psychology. He was recently accepted into that program and plans to get his own place on campus in the fall.

Ray: Ray is a middle-aged married man with a son in junior high school. He was a mechanic in the U.S. Navy for about 10 years. Now he does maintenance work and various mechanical tasks in different chem- ical labs for a midwestern Fortune 500 company. Ray has been employed by this same company for over 20 years. Although he was never diag- nosed as learning disabled, he remembers always having trouble in school and still dislikes reading and jobs entailing much written material.

He was always very good with his hands and he is highly creative, especially when it comes to building things and construction work. He has been known to look at a set of blueprints once, memorize them, and conceive the best and cheapest way to build whatever is needed.

Ray is known around his company for his social skills. He is kind-hearted, blunt and outspoken with both his friends and colleagues—attributes which have made him some loyal friends, but also sometimes gotten him into trouble. Ray often says exactly what he thinks. He dislikes rigid, close supervision and prefers the autonomy that he has on his current position where he is given projects to work on independently.

Although Ray has never asked for any disability-related accommodations, he relies on various techniques to compensate for difficulties on the job and in his daily life. For instance, he carries a small notebook in which he writes down ideas and directions so that he won't forget them. Sometimes he will read aloud the steps of projects. Although he never expresses a desire to go back to school for a college degree, he has encouraged both his wife and son to pursue further education.

Maggie: Maggie is a single, middle-aged, former pre-school teacher with bachelor's and master's degrees in education. She was an excellent teacher who supervised a special education classroom for abused children for more than 12 years in a large public school system. However, numerous administrative changes along with an increased, more intensive caseload of preschool children forced her and a few of her colleagues to quit due to job burnout. During this time, Maggie also found herself experiencing severe bouts of depression. Although Maggie s energy and concentration levels had fluctuated widely ever since childhood, she also found that her phases of activity, frustration, restlessness, and lack of concentration were becoming more intense and frequent as well.

Maggie lived off of her savings for awhile after she quit, doing various part-time jobs (teaching in a private preschool, cleaning offices, clerking in a toy store, etc.). One part-time job during this period turned into full-time, permanent work after some initial job-related problems were addressed.

A large toy retailer hired her as a night stock clerk and cashier. Due to her difficulties in processing information and her restlessness, she had significant problems using the computerized cash register with the speed and efficiency necessary to keep the lines of customers moving as fast as possible. However, because Maggie was a highly motivated, dependable employee, her supervisor was willing to work with her. About this time, Maggie was also formally diagnosed with learning disabilities and attention-deficit/hyperactivity disorder (ADHD) after a referral from a therapist she had seen for her depression. Based on this new information, Maggie asked her employer for the following accommodations: shorter but more frequent break times; autonomy to alternate such tasks as stocking shelves, running errands, and using a cash register, and cash register training in a quiet place, with additional time for keyboard practice. Maggie asked to put colored pieces of tape on keys that were especially important. She also volunteered to be a floater and to work extra shifts on short notice.

After this assistance was in place for 6 months, Maggie's work performance improved immeasurably. In fact, her supervisor selected her for the "Most Valuable Employee" award and offered her a full-time job. Maggie was glad to accept the position.

These three people have a number of characteristics in common. They are adults with specific learning disabilities, they have used accommodation or assistance to compensate for their disability, and they have psychosocial characteristics which have had a significant impact on their daily lives as adults, especially in the workplace.

Joseph, Ray, and Maggie also share an even more important characteristic: They are successfully employed in either part-time or full-time jobs. Unfortunately, many of their peers who also have various types of learning disabilities are not so fortunate. Despite all the progress that has been made in the United States in the last few decades with legislation, appropriate educational assistance, and disability awareness, the majority of Americans with disabilities today are still jobless. For instance, in 1991, a Louis Harris National Poll revealed that two-thirds of the 43 million Americans with disabilities were either unemployed or underemployed. Of that group, two thirds of those individuals were actively trying to find jobs (Career Connections, 1992).

Because individuals with learning disabilities constitute the largest subgroup of Americans with disabilities, their stories reflect this trend, but with an interesting twist. Many people with learning disabilities are able to find jobs, but they are often underemployed in entry-level, low-wage positions which do not match their potential (Fourqurean, 1991; Werner, 1993). For example, Herzog and Falk (1991) followed 113 students with learning disabilities who graduated from a local job training program. Seventy-six percent of those students were employed, but 60% were earning less than $10,000 per year. In a secondary analysis of the data from the study on the National Indicators of Youths with Disabilities, researchers found that of the 249 individuals with learning disabilities surveyed who had been out of high school for 1 or 2 years, 37.9% were employed full-time, 19.3 were employed part-time, and 37% were unemployed. Of that sample (N = 142), 36% were making less than $5 per hour, 27.7% were making between $4 and $4.99 per hour, 28.7% were making between $3 and $3.99 per hour, and 7.6% were making less than minimum wage or $3 per hour (Harnisch, Ping, & Shinyoung, 1992).

Many professionals believe that some of the most influential factors in this bleak employment picture for adults with learning disabilities are various types of psychosocially related issues (Gerber, 1991; Manhattan Adult Learning and Resource Center, 1988; Roffman, 1994; Ryan & Price, 1992; White, 1992). As Okolo and Sitlington (1988) strongly assert, ". . . One of the major causes of the reported unemployment and under-employment of handicapped individuals is poor interpersonal skills . . . Studies investigating the vocational adjustment of handicapped adolescents and adults have consistently demonstrated a strong relationship between job success and interpersonal factors such as behavior, appearance, and relationships with peers and supervisors" (p. 294–295). While these situations are not unique to employees with disabilities, adults with learning disabilities may often need assistance in these areas if they are to be successful in the workplace. All material described in this chapter refers to adults for whom a learning disability is the primary disability, and who exhibit related, secondary psychosocial characteristics. The focus of this chapter is to address three important questions that directly influence the lives of individuals with learning disabilities in the workplace:

- What are the psychosocial ramifications of learning disabilities?
- How are they seen in vocational settings?
- What interventions and suggestions can address the psychosocial issues that employees with learning disabilities bring to the workplace?

Critical Assumptions About Psychosocial Issues and Adults with Learning Disabilities

The workplace response to the questions just posed will have an enormous impact on the daily lives of adults with learning disabilities. To truly appreciate their significance, one must be aware of two related trends found in the professional literature. These trends mirror the assumptions underlying the relationship between psychosocial issues and the employment prognosis for adults with learning disabilities.

Children with learning disabilities do not "grow out" of their disability when they become adults.

One critical trend discussed by professionals revises the notion that learning disabilities may be remediated or "fixed" in childhood. In fact, different authors explain that specific cognitive deficits and their related psychosocial problems do not disappear with age, but often continue to have a significant impact on the lives of adults with learning disabilities in different, personal ways (Alley, Deshler, Clark, Schumaker, & Warner, 1983; Cohen, 1985; Cruickshank, Morse, & Johns, 1980; Gehret, 1993; Gottesman, 1994; Maag & Behrens, 1989b; Renick & Harter, 1989; Rourke, 1989; White, 1992). Telander (1994) found, when he examined the most current research discussing the academic, vocational, and psychosocial adjustment of adults with learning disabilities, that individuals still had difficulties in these various areas, but could compensate for these with appropriate accommodations and assistance. Hayes (1993) also concisely sums up this premise in her book, *You Don't Outgrow It: Living with Learning Disabilities*. She emphasizes repeatedly to adults with learning disabilities that they must learn useful strategies and coping techniques to achieve their potential. Their responses to the challenges of adult life, which range from employment to dating and household tasks, will always be influenced by their disability.

There is a strong relationship between learning disabilities and psychosocial issues.

Just as learning disabilities do not disappear when children with learning disabilities grow into adulthood, various professionals posit that there is a strong relationship between learning disabilities and social or psychological disabilities (Anderson, 1992; Brier, 1994; Fisher, 1985; Fox & Forbing, 1991; Learning Disabilities Council, 1991; Lombana, 1992; Maag & Behrens, 1989a; Neuwirth, 1993; Rourke & Fuerst, 1992; VSA Educational Services, 1991; Wilchesky & Minden, 1988). For example, it has been suggested that children with learning disabilities are more vulnerable to emotional disturbances (Bryan, 1989; Epstein, Cullinan, & Neiminen, 1984; Rourke, 1989; Silver, 1984; Weinberg, McLean, Snider, & Nuckols, 1989). Many adults with learning disabilities who received psychological counseling as children have continued it in adulthood.

For instance, Lehtinen and Dumas (1976) reported that of the 90 adults they studied, the vast majority (73%) had received psychological counseling sometime in their lives. As adults, 24% of this same sample were currently attending therapy sessions, and 11% had started therapy, but later stopped. Although it is impossible to determine if these are truly representative samples of all adults with learning disabilities, the trends noted within them clearly warrant further investigation.

Definition of Psychosocial Issues

Not only must we be aware of our own and others' underlying assumptions, we also require a simple, working definition of psychosocial issues. The following definition provides important insights into the ramifications of learning disabilities for individuals in each of the roles they fill in daily adult life.

The term "psychosocial" neatly summarizes two integral areas of the life of every individual. Those areas are: the psychological aspects (i.e., how one perceives and feels about oneself), and the social aspects (i.e., how one relates to and communicates with others in the everyday environment) (Price, 1988b). For greater clarity, various psychosocial characteristics can be grouped in the following categories: (a) self-concept, (b) social skills, (c) dependency or locus of control, (d) stress and anxiety, (e) various negative behaviors, and (f) depression, suicide, and chemical dependency (Price, 1988b). These areas are summarized in Figure 14.1. (For further information about each category, also see: Price, Johnson & Evelo, 1994; Ness & Price, 1990; Price, 1988b, and Price, 1990.)

Three other points must be kept in mind when examining the psychosocial issues of adults with learning disabilities. First, one cannot generalize these characteristics to all individuals, although the literature clearly shows that many adults with learning disabilities may exhibit one or more of them over time (Gerber, 1991; Hayes, 1993; Maag & Behercns, 1989a; Manhattan Adult Learning and Resource Center, 1988; Okolo & Sitlington, 1988; Roffman, 1994; Ryan & Price, 1992; Telander, 1994; White, 1992).

Second, the previous material obviously does not represent the whole picture for the specific strengths and weaknesses of each unique adult with learning disabilities. People with disabilities (and all other people) must be viewed holistically. It is critical to examine both an individual's psychosocial strengths as well as weaknesses when exploring

---

Categories of Psychosocial Characteristics

1. *Self-Concept*—how one perceives oneself or feelings of self-worth (Cohen, 1984; Gerber, 1991; Price, 1988a; Telander, 1994). Example: Persistent feelings of incompetence or insecurity.

2. *Social Skills*—social relationships or how effectively one communicates and connects with others in everyday life (Alley, Deshler, Clark, Schumaker, & Warner, 1983; Denka, 1986; Gottesman, 1994; Kroll, 1984). Examples: Difficulties making friends, decoding social cues, and establishing relationships.

3. *Dependency or Locus of Control*—overdependence or independence from others (Fisher, 1985; Hall & Haws, 1989; Kuncaitus, 1986; Wehmeyer, 1992; White, 1992). Example: Causal attributions to others for personal success or failure.

4. *Stress and Anxiety*—both physical and mental health symptoms (Bryan, 1983; Frels 1969; Gerlach, 1992; Margalit & Heiman, 1986; Silver, 1984). Examples: physical mannerisms (i.e., tics, red eyes, bleeding fingernails); general physical health problems (i.e., long-term colds, coughs, stomach disorders); repeated self-reports of high levels of stress or anxiety.

5. *Various Negative Behaviors and Feelings*—related mental health issues/unhealthy feelings or behaviors that may exist simultaneously with learning disabilities (Brier, 1994; Geist & MacGrath, 1983; Hill Top Preparatory School, 1988; Smith, 1986). Examples: Feelings of intense frustration, anger, hostility, poor impulse control, maladaptive behaviors.

6. *Depression, Suicide and Chemical Dependency*—A new category of additional mental health conditions that may influence or exist with learning disabilities (Anderson, 1992; Hall & Haws, 1989; Hayes & Sloat, 1988; Huntington & Bender, 1993; Karacostas & Fisher, 1993; Maag & Reid, 1994; Wright–Strawderman & Watson, 1992). Example: Varying incidence (e.g., 10%–64%) of depressive symptoms observed in children and adolescents with learning disabilities.

FIGURE 14.1. Categories of psychosocial characteristics.

the complex aspect of learning disabilities. (Gerber & Ginsberg 1990; Gerber & Reiff, 1991; Price, et al., 1994; Sitlington & Frank, 1993).

Third, it is currently difficult, if not impossible, to generalize from qualitative and quantitative data currently available in this area. Most of these data likely contain at least a grain of truth about the complexity and incidence of psychosocial issues in adults with learning disabilities. But, given the state of the current research base on both psychosocial issues and learning disabilities in adults in general, we must proceed with caution into this newly investigated territory.

A Comparison of the (SCANS) Characteristics and Psychosocial Issues for Adults with Learning Disabilities

Joseph, Ray, and Maggie all brought different psychosocial strengths to the workplace. For instance, Joseph has a charming manner that attracted many friends to him at school and the workplace. Ray's honesty was appreciated by some of his colleagues while they were planning various projects remodeling the chemical labs for his company. And Maggie's high levels of persistence and motivation were appreciated by her supervisors, both in the preschool setting and in private business.

All adults, either with or without disabilities, spend a great deal of their lives in some sort of workplace that is shaped by both covert and overt expectations. For instance, the achievement of adulthood in America today is based on the ability to function successfully and independently in two interrelated areas: at home and on the job. To prove this truism, just ask yourself, What is the first question that you would usually ask someone that you are meeting for the first time? You would probably ask a stranger, "What do you do [for a living]?" This question illustrates how we as Americans define one of our major roles in our society by "what we do" or how we are employed. If Americans see their society through this perspective, then vocational achievements may be especially critical hurdles for adults with learning disabilities. Researchers have shown us that these adults may have a low-status, inconsistent, negative employment history, at best. Other researchers, concurring with the testimonials from employees with learning disabilities and their employers, stress that one key reason for this negative pattern is the way psychosocial issues surface everyday in the workplace.

The necessity of psychosocial skills in the workplace was illustrated by a report from the Secretary's Commission on Achieving Necessary Skills (SCANS) (U. S. Department of Labor, 1991). This landmark federal document was written by a task force of employers who were asked to tell the Secretary of Labor about ". . . the level of skills required to enter employment" (U. S. Department of Labor, 1991, p. xv). The commissioners examined various occupations, ranging from manufacturing to government work, through the efforts of six special panels. They asked consultants to interview all types of workers in many occupations. In addition, they held extensive meetings with private business owners, public employers, various union representatives, supervisors, and employees in shops, plants, stores, and businesses around the United States to identify skills needed for employment and levels of proficiency acceptable for success.

From all this information, the commission identified eight skills necessary for entering and keeping jobs in the workplace of the 21st century. Basic skills (i.e., reading, writing, and mathematical computation), as typically taught in U.S. grade schools and high schools, will no longer be enough to qualify all Americans, with or without disabilities, for work by the year 2000, the commissioners indicated.

In fact, basic academic skills constitute only one small component within the requirements of "workplace know-how" as delineated in the SCANS report. Or, as the Commission explains, " . . . This know-how has two elements: competencies and a foundation. This report identifies five competencies and a three-part foundation of skills and personal qualities that lie at the heart of job performance . . . These essential requirements are essential preparation for all students, both those going directly to work and those planning further education" (U.S. Department of Labor, 1991, p. xv).

The competencies are the first part of workplace know-how. They may be similar to the basic academic skills or technical knowledge necessary for jobs in either public or private settings. They are classified into five areas: resources, interpersonal, information, systems, and technology. (See Figure 14.2.) Of special interest is the second area, called interpersonal competencies (e.g., in working with others) which relates to various psychosocial issues discussed earlier in this chapter. For example, the following sub-competencies could be strongly influenced by ineffective social skills or a low self-concept: participating as a member of a team, teaching others new skills, serving clients or customers, exercising leadership, negotiating, and working with diversity.

The competencies are clearly rooted in a three-part foundation defined by the commission as the second part of workplace know-how. These areas of basic skills, thinking skills, and personal qualities provide the knowledge and skills needed for workers to achieve the five competencies in the American workplace. (See Figure 14.3).

These eight essential elements to success in the workplace mirror, in many ways, the psychosocial issues and characteristics discussed earlier in this chapter. As the commissioners explained, ". . . very few of us will

Five Competencies

Resources—Indentifies, organizes, plans, and allocates resources:
  (a) Time
  (b) Money
  (c) Material and facilities
  (d) Human resources (Assesses skills and distributes work accordingly, evaluates performance and provides feedback)

Interpersonal—Works with others:
  (a) Participates as member of a team—contributes to group effort
  (b) Teaches others new skills
  (c) Serves clients/customers—works to satisfy customer expectations
  (d) Exercises leadership—communicates ideas to justify position, persuades, convinces others, responsibly challenges existing procedures and policies
  (e) Negotiates—works toward agreements involving exchange of resources, resolves divergent interests
  (f) Works with diversity—works well with men and women from diverse backgrounds

Information—Acquires and uses information:
  (a) Acquires and evaluates information
  (b) Organizes and maintains information
  (c) Interprets and communicates information
  (d) Uses computers to process information

Systems—Understands complex interrelationships:
  (a) Understands systems
  (b) Monitors and corrects performance
  (c) Improves or designs systems

Technology—Works with a variety of technologies:
  (a) Selects technology
  (b) Applies technology to task
  (c) Maintains and troubleshoots equipment

*From: The U. S. Department of Labor. (1991, June). *What work requires of schools: A SCANS Report for America 2000*. Washington, D.C.: U.S. Department of Labor, The Secretary's Commission on Achieving Necessary Skills.

FIGURE 14.2. Workplace Know-how from the SCANS Report: Competencies.

work totally by ourselves. More and more, work involves listening carefully to clients and co-workers and clearly articulating one's own point of view . . ." (U.S. Department of Labor, 1991, p. xviii). For instance, note in Figure 14.4 how the personal qualities and competencies in the left col-

---

A Three-part Foundation

1. *Basic Skills*—Reads, writes, performs arithmetic and matematical operations, listens, and speaks

2. *Thinking Skills*—Thinks creatively, makes decisions, solves problems, visualizes, knows how to learn, and reasons

3. *Personal Qualities*—Displays responsibility, self-esteem, sociability, self-management, integrity, and honesty:

    (a) Responsibility—Exerts a high level of effort and perseveres toward goal attainment

    (b) Self-Esteem—Believes in own self-worth and maintains a positive view of self

    (c) Sociability—Demonstrates understanding, friendliness, adaptability, empathy, and politeness in group settings

    (d) Self-Management—Assesses self accurately, sets personal goals, monitors progress, and exhibits self-control

    (e) Integrity/Honesty—Chooses ethical courses of action

*From: The U. S. Department of Labor. (1991, June). *What work requires of schools: A SCANS Report for America 2000*. Washington, D.C: U.S. Department of Labor, The Secretary's Commission on Achieving Necessary Skills.

FIGURE 14.3. Workplace Know-how from the SCANS Report: Foundation.

umn are directly related to the psychosocial issues of adults with learning disabilities listed on the right. It is clear from this chart that what employers want from their employees and what adults with learning disabilities bring to their shop or their office are similar concepts, with one important exception—*the personal elements that are needed in the workplace may be exactly the ones where employees with learning disabilities continue to need the most assistance.*

Other Connections Between Psychosocial Issues and the Employment of Adults with Learning Disabilities

The eight essential elements of the SCANS report show only one set of connections between psychosocial issues and workplace adjustment for adults with learning disabilities. Three equally important connections that influence adult life are described below.

Personal Qualities (Foundation):	Psychosocial Qualities:
1) responsiblility and self-management	1) locus of control (dependency/independence)
2) self-esteem	2) self-concept
3) sociability	3) social skills
4) integrity	4) *locus of control
(*Note: Dependency on others can inhibit achieving personal integrity.)	

FIGURE 14.4. A Comparison of psychosocial qualities from Price (1988) and personal qualities from the SCANS report.

'Mary's Little Lamb' and Workplace Adjustment

It is naive, at best, and erroneous at worst, to assume that the psychosocial issues we have examined will only happen in the workplace. Adult Basic Education teachers who serve clients with learning disabilities in Athens, GA, have observed that:

> Problems are not restricted by environment; family and fiscal problems, like Mary's little lamb, often follow wherever you go, including the workplace. Conversely, maladjustments from the job can affect the family routine and life style. Daily living and social skills influence job performance . . . Daily living and personal-social skills are pre-requisites for breaking into and succeeding in the job world. People are hired because the employing person is convinced that they can do the job; and people are fired because they cannot get along with co-workers or the boss, or cannot conform to the routine. . . . Personal-social skills greatly influence the quality of occupational and daily living skill performance. (Clarke County Board of Education, 1985, p. 1–2, as cited in Hayes, 1993)

The Georgia educators' emphasis on personal skills critical for success in adult life mirror both the SCANS report and Maslow's stages of self-actualization discussed in the next section. Psychosocial issues may follow adults with learning disabilities throughout all phases and aspects of their lives. As Dale Brown (1980) describes this holistic perspective,

> The problems that learning disabled adults have with their families foreshadow problems on the job. Someone who leaves possessions all over the house is bound to do the same thing with work tools unless he makes a conscious effort to change. In business, clumsiness and carelessness are costly. The hammer left on the floor can cause a worker car-

rying expensive machinery to trip and break the equipment. An error made in a print shop could result in having to redo the whole job. Beyond the costs involved, these problems exasperate supervisors and coworkers and cause them extra work. (p. 23)

Brown then goes on to list job problems that are ramifications of learning disabilities for adults: inefficiency; tendency to commit frequent errors; accident–prone behavior; difficulty with academic skills; problems in learning a sequence of tasks; tendency to arrive late and miss deadlines and schedules; having to work longer to approach coworkers' productivity; having to choose between carelessness and slowness; and various social problems (i.e., awkwardness in meeting people, reluctance to work with others, often misunderstanding comments, and having to do consciously what comes naturally to others). In addition, she emphasizes that they bring the following strengths, as well, to their jobs: creativity, self-discipline, overcompensation, and inner-directedness (Brown, 1980). She summarizes the hurdles of workplace adjustment for adults with learning disabilities by stressing that "Social skills are usually as important [for adults with learning disabilities] as performing a job well." (Brown, 1984, p. 2)

Psychosocial issues that adults with learning disabilities bring to all aspects of their lives have as far-reaching an impact as ripples in a pond when one stone is thrown into the still water. This impact may be especially powerful in the workplace, as Chadsey-Rusch (1988) said when she asserted that addressing psychosocial issues for individuals with disabilities can keep them from losing jobs, reduce job stress, and decrease the appalling unemployment rate for Americans with disabilities.

Adults with Learning Disabilities as Employees

Another connection between psychosocial issues and workplace adjustment is the mix of attitudes and self-perceptions shaping the workplace performance of adults with learning disabilities. Brown (1980; 1990) has already provided a comprehensive list of job problems that adults with learning disabilities may experience every day. However, psychosocial issues will directly effect the attitudes and subsequent accomplishments of this population in the workplace in two other ways.

First, employees with learning disabilities often further complicate their working lives by trying to hide their "handicap" and appear as normal as possible. They, like their employers, often don't understand their own disability or how it will impact their daily lives. For instance, Murphy

(1992) found that: "The majority of people [with learning disabilities] interviewed leaned toward withholding information on their initial contacts with employers. Reportedly, they did so because they believed that (a) the disability was none of the employer's business; (b) most employers did not know what a learning disability was anyway; (c) the information might be held against them; (d) the disability might not affect their work performance; and (e) it was likely that nothing could be done about their problems anyway." (p. 105) As one woman recalled,

> Before I accepted the position I told him point-blank that I was learning disabled. I wanted him to know so that there would not be questions about it if I had a difficult time integrating information. . . . I also shared with my supervisor, peers, and people around work. . . . that was why it was taking me so long to integrate information. I told the director that I had some special needs, but he didn't want to spend too much time discussing things. . . . There are limited accommodations. . . . My supervisor doesn't have the knowledge, coping skills, or—most of all—patience to deal with this. (pp. 104, 105)

Second, as this illustrates, few individuals, with or without disabilities, work totally alone in the workplace. Adults with learning disabilities interact with a wide variety of people in many different roles during the workday (e.g., friend, colleague, supervisor, supervisee, client, customer, etc.). But we have already seen that many adults with learning disabilities find relating to others especially troublesome, due in part to low self-esteem, dependency, and inadequate social skills. For instance, they may have these difficulties that are detrimental to working relationships: misunderstanding verbal language or nonverbal social cues; problems communicating with supervisors or peers; problems requesting and comprehending feedback or criticism; and difficulty working as part of a team (Ness & Price, 1990; Price, 1990).

These psychosocial difficulties, in turn, become significant barriers to the networking that is so vital for employees to survive in today's workplace where downsizing and change may continue to be the norm into the 21st century. Such problems may also keep adults with learning disabilities from developing alliances and friendships in the workplace.

Employers' Perceptions of Adults with Learning Disabilities

Adults with learning disabilities do not function on the job in a vacuum. Just as they impact the work around them, they are equally influenced by their supervisors and employers. One definite trend in the professional literature about employment and adults with learning disabilities is the fact that employers frequently do not understand learning disabilities or their ramifications (Brown, 1984; Gajar, 1992; Price, 1990). Harte (as cited in Boyd, 1995) eloquently describes how a supervisor can misunderstand an employee with learning disabilities with damaging results:

> No one has found out. You really like this new job, have been giving it your best effort, and feeling confident, for a change, about your future. What you don't know is that at 4:30 this afternoon, your boss will call you in and fire you. 'You're a bright person who seems capable', the boss will say, 'but we just don't feel it's working out.' These words are designed to excuse the fact that the boss is either unaware of the nature of learning disabilities or ill-equipped to compensate for yours. . . . (p. 8e).

Other studies of employers' attitudes support this scenario. For instance, Minskoff, Sautter, Hoffmann, and Hawks (as cited in Career Connections, 1993) interviewed 326 employers to their perceptions of employees with disabilities. They found that many of the employers spoke positively about hiring individuals with disabilities in general, but conveyed more negative beliefs about employing people with learning disabilities. Minskoff and her colleagues postulated three important reasons for this: (a) Employers were more supportive about providing accommodations for physical disabilities than for cognitive disabilities, because the disability was not hidden from them; (b) Most of the employers had no experience hiring employees with learning disabilities; and (c) Most of the employers had limited knowledge about learning disabilities.

This lack of familiarity with learning disabilities also relates to eight commonly held, but erroneous notions shared by employers that have been discussed by Johnson, Aune and Aase (1992):

1. Certain jobs are more suited to persons with disabilities.

2. We should hire one disabled person just to see what he/she can do.

3. Persons with disabilities are better workers than the non-disabled.

4. We need special training to work with people with disabilities.

5. Reasonable accommodations are expensive.

6. We do not have any jobs that a person with a disability can do.

7. Insurance rates go up when a person with a disability is hired.

8. It is important to place people with disabilities in jobs where they will not fail. (Handout 10)

Other employer misconceptions, and how they relate to the Americans with Disabilities Act of 1990, are discussed in greater depth elsewhere in this book. Such stereotypic attitudes, held by employers, can be critical for job success or failure in the psychosocial area for a worker with learning disabilities. As White (1992) explains: ". . . . [psychosocial] skills. . . . as required in the workplace will not be areas of strength for many adults with learning disabilities and may prevent them from maintaining or advancing in employment" (p. 454).

Even if employers have some knowledge about learning disabilities, they still may believe that their company does not have the resources or skills to offer appropriate accommodations to the employee with disabilities. Further complicating factors may include negative employer attitudes based on past experiences with federal guidelines, or different vocabulary and goals within academic and vocational settings (i.e. cost-effectiveness vs. maximizing the individual's potential). Clearly, as Aune and her colleagues assert, ". . . employers' negative perceptions of employees [with disabilities]. . . are more disabling than the disability itself" (Johnson, Aune, & Aase, 1992, p. 5)

Successful adjustment in the workplace for adults with learning disabilities is clearly a complicated, multifaceted phenomenon. It demands a wide variety of assistance options that may be personalized to match the unique profile of each individual with disabilities.

Suggested Psychosocial Interventions and the Workplace

Theoretical Rationale for Psychosocial Service Delivery

So far, most of the discussion in this chapter has been framed as an answer to the first question posed in the introduction: What are the psychosocial ramifications of learning disabilities? The rest will be devoted to answering the two remaining questions: How are they seen in vocational settings? and What interventions and suggestions can address the psychosocial issues that employees with learning disabilities bring to the workplace?

Defining the psychosocial issues of adults with learning disabilities is only the first step in understanding the ramifications of these life-long characteristics. A second, equally important, step is to find a theoretical model upon which to base the assistance for psychosocial issues in the workplace. Integrating Maslow's model of self-actualization into accommodations for people with learning disabilities provides us with a theoretical rationale which is worth further examination.

Abraham Maslow, a leader in the field of psychology, spent a great deal of his work examining the developmental phases of adult life. In 1962, he explored a branch of psychology that he named "the psychology of being." This particular model postulated various stages of human development from childhood to late adulthood. (Maslow created his model for everyone, including individuals with disabilities.) He postulated that the psychology of being was propelled by a developmental process he named "self-actualization" (Cormier & Cormier, 1991).

Maslow suggested that everyone goes through different developmental stages that share certain characteristics. He identified eight characteristics of individuals as they move through the self-actualization process. Those characteristics describe adults who are:

- becoming fully functioning as mature individuals (e.g., self-identity, self-realization, and self-direction);

- being responsible for their own behaviors and attitudes;

- realizing their own unique potential as human beings;

- having a strongly developed sense of integrity based on on a defined personal value system;

- exhibiting high levels of personal creativity;

- being challenged rather than defeated by new events or information in daily life;

- having a sense of humor; and

- showing high levels of motivation and persistence (Cormier & Cormier, 1991, p. 262)

When reading these eight characteristics, it is easy to reject them as too lofty for anyone to achieve. But to view self-actualization in only that way denies us a practical application of Maslow's theory. He stresses, instead, the overriding theme of self-actualization as growth, not completion. Maslow believed that no one will ever truly reach the state where all goals are simultaneously achieved. However, it is the process for each person that is important. Maslow postulated that the central focus of adult development is the continual movement towards personal levels of integration, wholeness, and fulfillment in all life experiences.

Interesting parallels may be drawn between Maslow's stages of self-actualization and the eight requirements for workplace know-how as delineated by employers in the SCANS report (1992). For example, notice that each uses slightly different terms to highlight the same psychosocial characteristic. These are illustrated in Figure 14.5.

Consequently, when addressing the vocational needs of adults with learning disabilities, we should always base our assistance on carefully conceived goals that emphasize the ongoing process of adult psychological development and continually reinforce self-responsibility in the workplace through self-actualization. These stages also have other benefits, as well, for service providers in vocational education or rehabilitation. For instance, self-actualization goals are purposefully open-ended to allow for individual change as the individual with learning disabilities matures. They actively involve the individual as much as possible, instead of encouraging passivity. They have a flexible timeline to encompass all of the changes inherent in the complicated lives of adults in the workplace. And, of special importance, the goals are mutually evaluated periodically (i.e., usually every three to four sessions) to see if the goals and accommodations are still appropriate for psychosocial skill development.

All of this may sound easy to do on paper, but it may be harder to accomplish with adults with learning disabilities in real life. As a result, the rest of this chapter is devoted to practical ways to give psychosocial assistance to employees with learning disabilities in a wide variety of workplaces and educational or vocational settings. All these techniques and ideas can be successful in the workplace, but they are provided as a "smorgasbord" so that each practitioner may choose and refine the mix

Maslow's Stages of Self-Actualization:	*SCANS 8 Essential Elements:*
(a) self-identity, self-realization, self-direction	(a) personal quality—self-esteem
(b) a strongly developed sense of integrity based on a defined personal value system	(b) personal quality—integrity
(c) being responsible for one's own behaviors and attitudes	(c) the personal qualities of responsibility and self-management

FIGURE 14.5. A Comparison of Maslow's Stages of Self-Actualization and the Eight Essential Elements from the SCANS Report.

of ideas and strategies that best fit local needs. Additional changes and adaptations—according to each service provider's own expertise, values and beliefs—also are strongly encouraged.

Using Group Activities, Especially Support Groups, to Address Psychosocial Issues

One service resource that can be extremely beneficial to adults with learning disabilities who are struggling with psychosocial concerns is the group. Support groups and job clubs (Aune & Ness, 1990; Johnson, 1989; Payne, 1992; Price, 1988a; Scheiber & Talpers, 1987) have proven to be a successful way to address a wide variety of psychosocial issues (i.e., inadequate social skills, negative self-concept, problems with communication) for students with learning disabilities (Cooper, 1986; Johnson, 1989; Kuncaitis, 1986; Neault, 1988). Group activities, especially those used in vocational settings, are excellent vehicles to reinforce self-actualization goals (i.e., self-realization, understanding personal strengths and weaknesses) and to practice or model successful group participation as required by the SCANS report.

To facilitate workplace adjustment, these groups should have flexible formats for simultaneously addressing a wide spectrum of related issues with various themes and offering individual or group activities (e.g., exercises in disability self-awareness and self-disclosure, self-esteem, communication skills, giving and receiving feedback from peers and authority figures, friendship skills, job readiness and job-seeking skills). And, perhaps of greatest importance in this era of shrinking financial resources and increasing caseloads of individuals with learning disabilities, they also are a cost-effective way to provide psychosocial assistance to small groups of students (Johnson, 1989; Price, 1988a).

At this time, it is still unclear who is responsible for providing assistance in the psychosocial arena to adults with learning disabilities as they graduate from education to employment. Just as our knowledge and expertise in learning disabilities expands to meet the needs of children with learning disabilities as they mature, creative solutions must be found that will extend services beyond the boundaries of secondary and post-secondary classrooms.

With the ongoing corporate downsizing trend, human resources specialists in both large and small companies may hesitate to provide extra assistance to potential or currently employed individuals with learning disabilities. In that situation, vocational rehabilitation clients may wish to return to their caseworkers for additional assistance. Or postsecondary learning disability specialists may want to expand their accommodations to apply to employment situations. (For instance, if a student with learning disabilities needs a notetaker in a postsecondary class, having a colleague share notes on important directives in a corporate meeting may be equally helpful for effective job performance.) However, few precedents exist that demonstrate how academic and psychosocial accommodations can be successfully generalized from classroom to workplace. Clearly, this is a new frontier for service providers to explore as both clients with learning disabilities and professionals move into the 21st century.

Unfortunately, as many professionals have discovered, establishing and maintaining successful support groups for individuals with disabilities can be challenging. It may be difficult to get adults to attend the initial group session. A large number of individuals may show up for the first meeting, but attendance may gradually fade away until only 2 or 3 people remain. One way to guard against these problems is to lay the proper groundwork for the group from the first meeting, following steps that have maximized the success of group activities (Johnson, 1989; Price, 1988a). The steps are:

1. Determine the purpose of the group.

2. Decide who will facilitate the group.

3. Determine who will be the members of the group.

4. Decide how individuals will be recruited for group membership.

5. Decide when and where the group will meet.

6. Design what will actually take place during group sessions.

7. Build in allowances for the various learning styles of group participants.

8. Evaluate the group when it is finished.

Further information about implementing these steps in postsecondary and vocational settings appears in the articles and book by Johnson (1989) and Price (1988a & 1988b). These references give many valuable details and hints for practitioners, such as sample recruitment materials, support group evaluation forms, examples of various activities that promote self-actualization skills, and specific ideas from community colleges and other institutions that have implemented successful support groups in the past.

Using Individual Counseling to Address Psychosocial Issues

When seeking assistance for successful workplace adjustment, adults with learning disabilities may need many options in a wide variety of settings. Group activities, while helpful, offer only one type of option. For instance, often career counselors and vocational rehabilitation specialists provide most of their services in individual, face-to-face sessions on-site at the workplace, in their offices, or at other convenient locations for the clients and counselors. As a result, the following material provides hints and strategies for making the most of individual sessions and guiding clients through the various stages of self-actualization. (For further information, see Price, 1988a).

1. *Scheduling sessions:* Some counselors utilize regularly scheduled appointments to provide consistency for individuals with learning disabilities. Others agree to see employees in unscheduled sessions on-site, as needed, during a specific crisis. These impromptu sessions may be especially meaningful to some adults with learning disabilities because the practitioner can apply therapeutic ideas or techniques while the problem is actually taking place and include supervisors or coworkers if appropriate. However, no matter when the individual sees the practitioner, the focus must always be on check-in time for both the employee and the practitioner. Consistent check-ins are especially critical for the employee when trying out new accommodations on the job or preparing for important career transitions, whether through promotions or anticipated downsizing.

2. *Focusing on one behavior at a time:* It is also helpful, when coaching or advising some employees with learning disabilities (especially those with memory problems, sequencing problems, or difficulty transferring ideas from one situation to another) to focus on only one behavior, episode, or job accommodation at a time during individual sessions. This allows the employee to focus his or her energy and concentration fully on each problem. When the individual thoroughly understands that situation, discussion may then shift to others.

3. *Summarizing each session:* The counselor must ask the employee with learning disabilities (especially someone with difficulties in short-term memory, auditory memory, or sequencing) to verbally summarize each session as it takes place. Not only does this provide clarification of new knowledge, but it also assists the employee in seeing how one set of ideas is connected to other suggestions or

accommodations. The counselor may also want to write down a clear, practical plan for change, with discrete steps for the employee to use after the session is finished. These written comments may also compensate for auditory memory disabilities. (Copies of all this material may be shared with the supervisor or coworkers, or both, if the employee agrees.) This written record again emphasizes for the individual how diverse ideas discussed during the session connect to a cohesive whole.

4. *Self-monitoring individual behaviors:* To encourage independence, it is vital that the counselor teach the employee with learning disabilities to self-monitor his or her own behaviors as much as possible. This can be done in many different ways. For instance, the adult can be encouraged to watch for, and then count, a certain behavior whenever it occurs during a specific length of time (i.e., hourly, daily, weekly). The adult can make a tally of the incidence of the targeted behavior in a small notebook kept in a purse or pocket. These records, along with any comments or concerns, can then be shared with the counselor during their next meeting, for further feedback. Some counselors teach individuals to develop self-questioning techniques to use when the behavior happens (i.e., The adult can pause with a few self-questions, such as: "What stimuli caused me to say or do that?" "Can I count to 10 before I respond?" "Can I take 5 deep breaths before I answer this?" and so forth). Other counselors ask the individual to analyze his or her own behaviors after participating in informal role plays during group sessions. All this information can then be shared with supervisors or employers, as needed.

5. *Using relaxation activities:* Frequently, the excessive frustration and stress that accompanies coping with learning disabilities in the workplace can significantly disrupt cognitive processing for many employees who already have difficulties in retrieving, understanding, and retaining new knowledge. Relaxation techniques used at the beginning of one-to-one or group sessions are often beneficial for these individuals. These skills can be taught first by the specialist. The employee can then use them independently on-site whenever the work environment becomes too stressful. (Again, self-monitoring is also useful here when necessary.)

Brief individual counseling hints, while originally intended to be used in postsecondary educational settings, apply equally to employment-related objectives in a wide variety of settings. For instance, focusing on one behavior at a time is especially critical during job shadowing. Consistent check-in times with a consultant familiar with the needs of adults with learning disabilities is especially useful to enhance worker productivity, as companies continue to reconfigure themselves with downsizing and corporate buyouts. The creative use of these suggestions can broaden and enrich any professional's current expertise as we continue to explore how to meet the emerging needs of adults with learning disabilities in the changing workplace.

Other Useful Suggestions for the Workplace

There is no doubt that face-to-face sessions and support groups are effective tools for psychosocial skill facilitation. However, two other areas (often overlapping with individual counseling and group support) deserve equal consideration for successful workplace adjustment: career counseling and disability disclosure. (Note that these suggestions may be implemented either as pre-employment strategies or as guided interventions to improve the quality and quanity of job performance after the employee with learning disabilities has entered the workplace.)

Career Counseling

When experts make their projections about the working world of the late 1990s into the 21st century, one challenging idea is clear: U.S. jobs, as we now know them, will not remain the same. In fact, due to the ongoing impact of many factors (e.g., downsizing, the rapid growth of technology, and the continuing importance of the world market), Americans will routinely change jobs between three and five times in their lifetimes (Payne, 1992; Ryan & Price, 1992). This fact clearly changes the role of traditional career counseling for individuals with and without disabilities, from a single, isolated event into a critical, ongoing process that may be accessed repeatedly throughout an employee's lifetime.

This underscores the need for effective career counseling for adults with learning disabilities, especially since they may have a history of unemployment or underemployment. How can this be accomplished? A few professionals have offered hints on this topic. Several authors have discussed in the professional literature how vocational rehabilitation and career counseling can provide assistance for individuals with disabilities, especially learning disabilities (Career Connections, 1993; Dowdy, 1992). Perreira (1992) has asked, "What then can we identify as the specific needs of individuals with learning disabilities when issues of career development are explored?" (p. 1). Adelman and Vogel (1990) answered the question by pointing to successful employees with learning disabilities who had knowledge about their disability and appropriate types of vocational accommodations. Reiff and his colleagues (1992) emphasized the need for goal setting to facilitate awareness of career options and the skills necessary needed to achieve them. Brill and Brown (1986) asserted that psychosocial skills are the keys to successful job seeking and job keeping.

These authors also have provided valuable suggestions for structuring the counseling process. Perreira (1992) created a model for the effective career counseling of adults with learning disabilities, stressing disability self-awareness, goal orientation, values clarification, and recommendations for appropriate on-the-job compensatory strategies. By design, her model should be implemented in four stages while the individual is still in a higher educational setting: assessment, practical experience (including participation in support groups), résumé development, and interviews. The staff of Career Connections (1992), a federally funded research project at the University of Minnesota, has added the following advice: "Students with disabilities benefit from self-assessment and career exploration techniques just as students without disabilities. Where they may differ is in their need to assess an organization's physical or programmatic accessibility. Students with disabilities may also benefit from meeting with a mentor (preferably another individual with a disability) who may share ideas about how to enter a career field and what accommodations may enhance the student's potential for success" (p. 1).

Zambrano (1988) also cautions that individuals with learning disabilities may need support from career counselors after their initial employment starts. She identifies two common problems that required her assistance after her clients were hired: problems getting along with coworkers and staying on a job, even when they didn't like a particular aspect of their employment. As she explains, ". . . for someone with . . . . severe learning disabilities, ... the task of finding and keeping a job can be a long and sometimes painful journey . . ." (p. 365). These ideas can be valuable tools to address the psychosocial characteristics of an individual with learning disabilities in the first, fifth, or last job before retirement.

Disability Disclosure

As already explained, one issue that will emerge repeatedly when providing career counseling to adults with disabilities is that of how and when to disclose one's disability. This area is especially critical for adults with learning disabilities, as their disability is often hidden to others around them—from coworkers, potential employers, and supervisors.

Disability disclosure may be vital for any type of successful workplace adjustment. In fact, as has been emphasized in other articles on psychosocial issues, disability awareness is the foundation for all growth in the psychosocial arena (Price, 1988b; Johnson, 1989, Johnson, Evelo, & Price, 1992). Disability disclosure also has come to have definite legal ramifications in the workplace. As staff from Career Connections (1993) explains:

> Students with disabilities need to know their legal rights. It is up to the student whether the disability is disclosed. But under the Americans with Disabilities Act (ADA), employers have to provide accommodations only for disabilities which are disclosed. Although it is illegal for employers to ask if a candidate has a disability, at times, it may be to the candidate's advantage to disclose a disability. For example, if the candidate has a visible disability, it can be helpful to discuss how they have completed tasks and what accommodations they have used in previous jobs or in school. Candidates with invisible disabilities may consider disclosing after a job offer has been made." (p. 1)

Consequently, the following hints for effective disability disclosure in the workplace are especially important components of this chapter.

For instance, Boyd (1995) provides these suggestions in a "simple how-to outline" that is broken down into the following steps: prepare, pick the right time, disclose, cooperate, and adjust to your new world. Within these steps, she tells individuals to know the answers to these important questions when asking their employers for accommodations: Do you know the employer/employee relationship (e.g., The employer wants the work done. You agree to do the work, if you get paid.)? Do you know your disability and the associated rights protected under the law? and Do you know if you ARE disabled (under the law)? She explains that this definition of disability will entitle someone to assistance in the workplace: "A person with a disability has an impairment that functionally limits a major life activity" (p. 5).

This definition under the law clearly points to the importance of how and when one discloses his or her disability to employers and coworkers. For instance, Boyd (1995) cautions that ". . . The best time to disclose your disability is when you need an accommodation to maintain your ability to meeting the employer's standard of quality. Don't wait until your second or third unsatisfactory progress report, if at all possible" (p. 6). Murphy (1992) supports this position by saying that "The majority of people [with learning disabilities] concluded that the best strategy for revealing their disability to employers was to wait until they got to know their boss, had established a solid work record, or had difficulties carrying out their duties" (p. 105).

But, Boyd (1995) again cautions that other factors will complicate this process for everyone. As she says, "This is a very emotional process. The initial freedom that you feel, by being open, and honest, can be very short lived. . . . Your employer and co-workers are not going to be comfortable with you for a while. You must reduce this fear by being very specific as to how your disability affects your work" (p. 6).

All of these ideas are useful, but it is important to remember that disability self-awareness is one of the most significant parts of the process of self-actualization. As a result, this component may be one of the most dynamic and changeable of all of the psychosocial issues and interventions discussed in this chapter. Because it gets at the very heart of how a person with learning disabilities defines himself or herself, it is vital that personal values, beliefs, and timelines about disability disclosure be respected as much as possible.

Conclusion

In summary, much of this chapter has been devoted to an initial exploration of three questions: What are the psychosocial ramifications of learning disabilities? How are they seen in vocational settings? What interventions and suggestions can address the psychosocial issues that employees with learning disabilities bring to the workplace? As the material throughout this chapter clearly illustrates, there are no simple answers to these questions.

Now we have come full circle. This chapter started with the stories of three individuals who may have seemed familiar. Maybe they reminded you of a boss, a coworker, a friend, a significant other, a relative, a parent, or a sister or brother. They may have reminded you of yourself. An important point to keep in mind is that, even if the psychosocial ramifications (both positive and negative) of learning disabilities do not go away with childhood, there are many ways to address them effectively. We can accomplish this holistically in many different settings—in college, at home, in social and community settings, and in the workplace—to maximize the quality of life for adults with learning disabilities.

If we, as a society, do not provide assistance for individuals with learning disabilities in the world of work, every one of us will lose, both individually and collectively. We all must do everything possible, so that no employee will ever again hear this message: "You're a bright person who seems capable . . . but we just don't feel that it is working out. . . ."

References

Alley, G., Deshler, D., Clark, F., Schumaker, J., & Warner, M. (1983). Learning disabilities in adolescent and adult populations: Research implications (Part II). *Focus on Exceptional Children, 15*(9), 1–14.

Anderson, D. J. (1992, Sept. 15). Learning disabled have a high rate of addiction. *Minneapolis Star Tribune*, p. 8E.

Aune, E., & Ness, J. (1990). *Tools for transition.* Minneapolis, MN: American Guidance Service, Inc.

Boyd, P. (1995, Spring). Don't bite the hand that feeds you or Helping your employer accommodate you. *Rebus Report.*

Brier, N. (1994). Psychological adjustment and adults with severe learning difficulties: Implications of the literature on children and adolescents with learning disabilities for research and practice. *Learning Disabilities: A Multidisciplinary Journal, 5*(1), 15–27.

Brown, D. S. (1990, May). *Pathways to employment for people with learning disabilities: A plan for action. Recommendations of a consensus-building conference* (1990, April 30–May). Washington, D.C.: President's Committee on Employment of People with Disabilities. (ERIC Document Reproduction Service No. ED 345 444).

Brown, D. (1980). Steps to independence for people with learning disabilities. *Closer Look.* Washington, D.C. 23–4.

Brown, D. (1984, May/June). Employment considerations for learning disabled adults. *Journal of Rehabilitation.* 74–77.

Bryan, J. H. (1983, September). The relationship between fear of failure and learning disabilities. *Learning Disabilities Quarterly, 6*(2), 217–22.

Bryan, T. H. (1989, Winter). Learning disabled adolescents' vulnerability to crime: Attitudes, anxieties, experiences. *Learning Disabilities Research, 5*(1), 51–60.

Career Connections. (1993, Winter/Spring). When career counseling students with disabilities, focus on abilities, interests, and skills. *Career Connections Newsletter.* p. 1. Minneapolis, MN: Career Connections, Disability Services, University of Minnesota.

Chadsey–Rusch, J. (1988). *Social ecology of the workplace.* Urbana-Champaign, IL: The Secondary Transition Intervention Effectiveness Institute, College of Education, University of Illinois at Urbana-Champaign.

Cohen, J. (1985). Learning disabilities and adolescence: Development considerations. In S. C. Feinstein (Ed.), *Adolescent Psychiatry, Development and Clinical Studies,* (vol. 12, pp. 177–195). Chicago: University of Chicago.

Cooper, R. (1986). Personal counseling for the learning disabled college student. In Association on Handicapped Student Service Programs in Postsecondary Education (Ed.), *Support services for LD students in postsecondary education: A compendium of readings.* (pp. 109–111). Columbus, OH: Association on Handicapped Student Service Programs in Postsecondary Education.

Cormier, W. H., & Cormier, L. S. (1991). *Interviewing strategies for helpers.* Pacific Grove, CA: Brooks/Cole Publishing Company.

Cruickshank, W. M., Morse, W. C., & Johns, J. S. (1980). *Learning disabilities: The struggle from adolescence to adulthood.* Syracuse, NY: Syracuse University Press.

Denckla, M. (1986). The neurology of social competence. *ACLD Newsbriefs, 16*(5), 15, 20–21.

Dowdy, C. A. (1992). Learning disabilities and vocational rehabilitation. *Journal of Learning Disabilities, 25*(7), 442–47.

Epstein, M. H., Cullinan, D., & Neiminen, G. (1984). Social behaviour problems of learning disabled and normal girls. *Journal of Learning Disabilities, 17*(10), 609–611.

Fisher, E. (1985). Educator examines myths, realities of LD students at the college level. *Hill Top Spectrum, 3*(1), 1–5, 8.

Fourqurean, J. M. (1991). Correlates of postsecondary employment outcomes for young adults with learning disabilities. *Journal of Learning Disabilities, 24*(7), 400–05.

Fox, C. L., & Forbing, S. E. (1991). Overlapping symptoms of substance abuse and learning handicaps: Implications for educators. *Journal of Learning Disabilities, 24*(1), 24–31, 39.

Freils, L. (1969, June). Behavioral changes in students. *Journal of School Health, 39*(6), 405–408.

Gajar, A. (1992). Adults with learning disabilities: Current and future research priorities. *Journal of Learning Disabilities; 25*(8) 507–519.

Gehret, J. (1993, February). *Before the well runs dry: Taking care of yourself as the parent of a LD/ADD child.* Paper presented at the Annual Learning Disabilities of America International Conference, San Francisco, CA.

Geist, C. S., & McGrath, C. (1983). Psychosocial aspects of adult learning disabled person in the world of work: A vocational rehabilitation perspective. *Rehabilitation Literature, 44*(7), 210–13.

Gerber, P. (1991, June). *Being learning disabled, a beginning teacher and teaching a class of students with learning disabilities.* Richmond, VA: The University of Virginia/James Madison University Commonwealth Center for the Education of Teachers.

Gerber, P. J., & Ginsberg, R. J. (1990). Identifying alterable patterns of success in highly successful adults with learning disabilities. Executive summary. Richmond, VA: Virginia Commonwealth University, School of Education. (ERIC Document Reproduction Service No. ED 342 168).

Gerber, P. J., & Reiff, H. B. (1991). *Speaking for Themselves: Ethnographic interviews with adults with learning disabilities.* Ann Arbor, MI: University of Michigan Press.

Gerlach, K. (1992). *Stress in children bibliography.* Seattle, WA: Pacific Training Associates.

Gottesman, R. L. (1994). The adult with learning disabilities: An overview. *Learning Disabilities: A Multidisciplinary Journal, 5*(1), 1–14.

Hall, C. W., & Haws, D. (1989). Depressive symptomatology in learning-disabled and nonlearning-disabled students. *Psychology in the Schools, 26*(4), 359–64.

Harnisch, D. L., Ping, Z., and Shinyoung, S. (1992, June 4–5). *National indicators of youths with disabilities: Lessons learned from secondary analyses.* Presentation at the 7th Annual Project Directors' Meeting, Transition Research Institute at the University of Illinois, Washington, D.C.

Hayes, M. L., & Sloat, R. S. (1988). Learning disability and suicide. *Academic Therapy, 23*(5), 469–75.

Hayes, M. L. (1993). *You don't outgrow it: Living with learning disabilities.* Novato, CA: Academic Therapy Publications. (ERIC Document Reproduction Service No. ED 354 668).

Hill Top Preparatory School. (1988). Learning disabled adolescent viewed at risk for drug and alcohol abuse. *Hill Top Spectrum, 3* (1-4). Hill Top Preparatory School, Rosemont, PA. (ERIC Document Reproduction Service No. ED 309 602).

Herzog, J. E., & Falk, B. (1991). A follow-up study of vocational outcomes of young adults with learning disabilities. *Journal of Postsecondary Education and Disability, 9*(1), 219–26.

Huntington, D. D., & Bender, W. N. (1993). Adolescents with learning disabilities at risk? Emotional well-being, depression, suicide. *Journal of Learning Disabilities, 26*(3), 159–166.

Johnson, J. (1989). *The LD academic support group manual.* Columbus, OH: Association on Handicapped Student Service Programs in Postsecondary Education.

Johnson, D., Aune, E., & Aase, S. (1992). *Putting ability to work: Career development and disability.* Minneapolis, MN: Career Connections, University of Minnesota.

Karacostas, D, D., & Fisher, G. L. (1993). Chemical Dependency in Students with and without Learning Disabilities. *Journal of Learning Disabilities, 26*(7) 491–95.

Kroll, L. G. (1984). LD's—What happens to them when they are no longer children? *Academic Therapy, 20*(2), 133–148.

Kuncaitis, A. (1986). Fostering independence in learning disabled students: A counseling approach. In Association on Handicapped Student Service Programs in Postsecondary Education (Ed.), *Support services for LD students in postsecondary education: A compendium of readings* (pp. 112–115). Columbus, OH: Association on Handicapped Student Service Programs in Postsecondary Education.

Learning Disabilities Council. (1991). *Understanding learning disabilities: A parent guide and workbook. Second edition.* Richmond, VA: Learning Disabilities Council, National Center for Learning Disabilities, Inc. (ERIC Document Reproduction Service No. ED 359 680).

Lehtinen, L., & Dumas, L. (1976). *A follow-up study of learning disabled children as adults: A final report.* Evanston, IL: The Cove School Research Office. (ERIC Documentation Reproduction Service No. ED 164 728).

Livingston, R. (1985). Depressive illness and learning difficulties: Research needs and practical implications. *Journal of Learning Disabilities, 18*(9), 518–20.

Lombana, J. H. (1992). Learning disabled students and their families: Implications and strategies for counselors. *Journal of Humanistic Education and Development, 31*(1) 33–40.

Maag, J. W., & Behrens, J. T. (1989a). Depression and cognitive self-statements of learning disabled and seriously emotionally disturbed adolescents. *Journal of Special Education, 23*(1). 17–27.

Maag, J. W., & Behrens, J. T. (1989b). Epidemiologic data on seriously emotionally disturbed and learning disabled adolescents: Reporting extreme depressive symptomatology. *Behavioral Disorders, 15*(1), 21–27.

Maag, J. W., & Reid, R. (1994). The Phenomenology of Depression among Students with and without Learning Disabilities: More Similar than Different. *Learning Disabilities Research and Practice, 9*(2), 91–103.

Manhattan Adult Learning and Resource Center. (1988). *Project Upgrade. Working with adults who have learning disabilities.* Manhattan, KS: Manhattan Adult Learning and Resource Center, KS. (ERIC Document Reproduction Service No. ED 367 858).

Margalit, M., & Heiman, T. (1986). Learning-disabled boys' anxiety, parental anxiety, and famiy climate. *Journal of Clinical Child Psychology, 15*(3), 248–253.

Murphy, S. T. (1992). *On being LD: Perspectives and strategies of young adults.* New York: Teachers College, Columbia University.

Neault, L. (1988). *Programming for learning disabled college students: Accommodations and autonomy.* (ERIC Document Reproduction Service No. ED245 639).

Ness, J., & Price, L. A. (1990). Meeting the psychosocial needs of adolescents and adults with learning disabilities. *Intervention in School and Clinic, 26*(1), 16–21.

Neuwirth, S. (1993). *Learning disabilities.* Rockville, MD: National Institute of Mental Health. (ERIC Document Reproduction Service No. ED 370 328).

Okolo, C. M., & Sitlington, P. (Summer, 1988). The role of special education in LD adolescents' transition from school to work. *Learning Disability Quarterly, 11*(3), 292–306.

Payne, N. (1992). *Transition strategies: Employment preparation essentials.* Presentation at the University of Connecticut Postsecondary Training Institute, Hartford, CT. Unpublished manuscript.

Perreira, D. C. (1992, Fall). Cooperative career development for postsecondary students with learning disabilities. *Postsecondary LD Network News. 16.* 1–3.

Price, L. (1988a). LD support groups work! *The Journal of Counseling and Human Services Professions, 2*(1), 35–46.

Price, L. (1988b). Effective counseling techniques for LD adolescents and adults in secondary and postsecondary settings. *The Journal of Postsecondary Education and Disability, 2*(4), 19–24.

Price, L. (1990). *A selective literature review concerning the psychosocial issues of LD individuals.* Minneapolis, MN: The LD Transition Project. (ERIC Document Reproduction Service No. ED 315 956).

Price, L. A., Johnson, J., & Evelo, S. (1994). When academic assistance is not enough: Addressing the mental health issues of adolescents and adults with learning disabilities. *Journal of Learning Disabilities, 7*(2), 82–90.

Reiff, H. B. (1992). Learning to achieve: Suggestions from adults with learning disabilities. *Journal of Postsecondary Education and Disability, 10*(1), 11–23.

Renick, M. J., & Harter, S. (1989, December). Impact of social comparisons on the developing self-perceptions of learning disabled students. *Journal of Educational Psychology, 81*(4), 631–638.

Roffman, A. J. (1994). Helping young adults understand their learning disabilities. *Journal of Learning Disabilities, 27*(7), 413–19.

Rourke, B. P. (1989, March). A childhood learning disability that predisposes those afflicted to adolescent and adult depression and suicide risk. *Journal of Learning Disabilities, 22*(3), 169–174.

Rourke, B. P., & Fuerst, D. R. (1992). Psychological dimensions of learning disability subtypes: Neuropsychological studies in the Windsor Laboratory. *School Psychology Review, 21*(3), 361–74.

Ryan, A. G., & Price, L. (1992). Landmarks in the '90's: Addressing the needs of students with learning disabilities. *Intervention in School and Clinic, 28*(1), 6–15, 18–20.

Scheiber, B., & Talpers, J. (1987). *Unlocking potential: College and other choices for learning disabled people: A step-by-step guide.* Bethseda, MD: Adler and Adler, Inc.

Silver, A. A. (1984). Children in classes for the severely emotionally handicapped. *Developmental and Behavioral Pediatrics, 5*(2), 49–54.

Sitlington, P. L., & Frank, A. R. (1993). *Adult adjustment of individuals with learning disabilities: Three vs. one year out of school.* Iowa Statewide Follow-Up Study. Des Moines, IA: Iowa State Dept. of Education, Des Moines. Div. Of Elementary and Secondary Education. (ERIC Document Reproduction Service No. ED 368 132)

Smith, B. K. (1986). *"The wilted flower syndrome."* Paper presented at the 23rd Conference of the Association for Children and Adults with Learning Disabilities, New York City, New York. (ERIC Document Reproduction Service No. ED 270 913).

Swan, R. J. (1983). *Testing a model for promoting academic success of learning disabled students at the university level.* Long Beach, CA: California State University. (ERIC Document Reproduction Service No. ED 241 910).

Telander, J. E. (1994). *The adjustment of learning disabled adults: A review of the current literature.* Unpublished doctoral dissertation. Biola University. (Also see ERIC Document Reproduction Service No. ED 372 586).

U. S. Department of Labor. (1991, April 18). *The SCANS report.* Washington, D.C.: The Secretary's Commission on Achieving Necessary Skills, U.S. Department of Labor.

VSA Educational Services. (1991). *An Overview of Alcohol and Other Drug Abuse Prevention and Disability.* Washington, D.C.: VSA Educational Services, Resource Center on Substance Abuse Prevention and Disability. (ERIC Document Reproduction Service No. ED 346 643).

Wehmeyer, M. (1992). Self-Determination: Critical skills for outcome-oriented transition services. *Journal for Vocational Special Needs Education, 15*(1), 3–7.

Weinberg, W. A., McLean, A., Snider, R. L., & Nuckols, A. S. (1989). Depression, learning disability, and school behavior problems. *Psychological Reports, 64*(1), 275–283.

Werner, E. E. (1993). *A longitudinal perspective on risk for learning disabilities.* Paper presented at the Annual Conference of the Learning Disabilities Association of America, San Francisco, CA.

White, W. J. (1992). The postschool adjustment of persons with learning disabilities: Current status and future projections. *Journal of Learning Disabilities, 25*(7), 448–56.

Wilchesky, M., & Minden, H. A. (1988). A comparison of learning and non-learning disabled university students on selected measures. *Proceedings of the 1988 AHSSPPE conference.* Columbus, OH: Association on Handicapped Student Service Programs in Postsecondary Education.

Wright-Strawderman, C., & Watson, B. L. (1992). The prevalence of depressive symptoms in children with learning disabilities. *Journal of Learning Disabilities, 25*(4), 258–64.

Zambrano, L. C. (1988, March). "What do I do next?" *Academic Therapy, 23*(4), 357–365.

CHAPTER 15

Technology in the World for Persons with Learning Disabilities: Views from the Inside

Marshall H. Raskind
Eleanor L. Higgins
Kenneth L. Herman

Over the last several years, specialists in the field of learning disabilities (LD) have shown an increasing interest in assistive technology to help persons with LD compensate for their difficulties (e.g., Brown, 1987; Bryant, Rivera, & Warde, 1993; Collins, 1990; Higgins & Raskind, 1995; Primus, 1990; Raskind, 1993; Raskind, 1994; Raskind & Higgins, 1995). Literature on assistive technology and LD consists of theoretical papers, philosophical treatises, anecdotal reports, and a few formal research studies. Although varied in approach, these papers have one element in common—they all have viewed technology and LD from the *outside*, imposing the researcher's/writer's preconceived ideas and preexisting language onto the actions, events, and communications of those being studied. In contrast, little has been done to explore technology and LD from an *ethnographic* or *insider's* perspective, with the researcher starting "with a conscious attitude of almost complete ignorance" (Spradley, 1979, p. 4), and seeking to understand technology use directly from the actions and words of those individuals with LD who use technology. Spradley (1979) emphasizes that an ethnographic researcher strives "to understand another way from the native point of view.... Rather than studying people, ethnography means learning from people" (p. 3). This stands in sharp contrast to traditional approaches of studying LD. Several authorities in the field (e.g., Bos & Richardson, 1994; Gerber & Reiff, 1991; Reid & Button, 1995) recently have stressed the importance of focusing on the insider's perspective.

The purpose of the present study was to learn about assistive technology from the insiders—users of technology who have LD. To the greatest extent possible, the investigators refrained from imposing their preconceived views, theories, or hypotheses about how persons with

LD use, or should use, technology. As suggested by Spradley (1979), it was the aim of the investigators to assume the role of students, viewing the insiders as their teachers. Assuming and remaining faithful to these roles was essential (although not always easy for ego- and ethnocentric researchers) for discovering the insider's perspective, which, according to Spradley (1979) "is a different species of knowledge from one that rests primarily on the *outsider's* view. Even when the outsider is a trained social scientist" (p. 4).

The researchers also refrained from approaching and referring to subjects as "subjects." Rather, consistent with an ethnographic approach (and with a commitment to learning from, rather than studying, people), the term "informants" was used. As Spradley (1979) states, "work with subjects begins with preconceived ideas; work with informants begins with a naive ignorance. Subjects do not define what is important for the investigator to find out; informants do" (p. 29).

Methodology

The five informants selected for this research were known to actively use assistive technology in the workplace. All were previously known to the investigators through the informants' participation in prior research projects (Raskind & Higgins, 1995; Spekman, Goldberg, & Herman, 1992; Gerber, Ginsberg, & Reiff, 1992), or the informants' involvement in the field of LD (e.g., LD organizations, conferences, and publications).

All informants were verified as "learning disabled" on the basis of previous formal diagnostic evaluations conducted by qualified psychologists, psychoeducational diagnosticians, neurologists, or university specialists in LD. Three of the informants had been identified in adulthood, the remaining two as school-aged children. All had long histories of academic difficulties that began in elementary school and continued into postsecondary educational settings.

Informants ranged in age from 32 to 60, four of whom were Caucasian males and one Caucasian female. Two informants lived in Southern California, one in Northern California, one in New York, and the other in Washington, DC. All informants were currently employed in "white collar" positions—a software engineer, an attorney, an economist, a leasing operations officer, and a writer/lecturer/business/consultant.

The investigators had (and have) no intention of implying that this small number of informants is in any way representative of the LD population at large. Furthermore, this project should in no way be construed as a formal research study designed to test a specific hypothesis. Again, the researchers wanted to remain as free as possible from preconceived notions of technology use, and had no desire to either prove or disprove a particular theory or idea. The goal was descriptive rather than experimental.

Informants were contacted by telephone to solicit participation in the project. The purpose of the study, the rationale behind the project, procedures for safeguarding confidentiality and what was to be expected of them were discussed with each informant. All agreed to participate and were enthusiastic about the opportunity to "share their stories."

The three authors of this paper conducted the interviews. These ranged from two to three hours, face-to-face and over the telephone. Permission was granted by all informants for audio-recording the interviews.

A 61-question interview protocol, developed for the investigation, was designed to provide informants with a framework to "paint a picture" of their lives and the ways they use technology within their respective work settings. The interviews were structured so as to gather basic information on each informant and elicit their views under the following headings: (a) demographics/current living situation; (b) current employment situation; (c) nature/manifestation of the informant's LD; (d) special abilities/talents; (e) educational history; (f) employment history; (g) technology use; (h) technology experience/expertise; (i) relationship between the LD and technology; (j) benefits/pitfalls of technology use; (k) attitude toward/views of technology; and (l) specific comments to other individuals with LD on the use of technology.

A transcription was made of each interview. The investigators then independently searched for patterns, regularities, and themes from among the five informants' responses, discussed their findings and were able to reach consensus regarding the presence of "common elements" of technology use across the informants.

A predetermined template (following the interview headings just described) was used in writing short vignettes of each informant's "story." Each investigator read each vignette to ensure that it accurately reflected the informant's view; informants reviewed their own vignettes; and changes were made as needed.

Interview Vignettes

The following vignettes afford insiders' views of how technology can be used within the employment setting to compensate for LD. The vignettes are intended to function as snapshots of the full interviews and capture each informant's view in his or her "native language." Verbatim quotes are used extensively in the vignettes to further ensure that the informants' actual language has been captured. Informant quotes have been italicized to differentiate them from those of the authors.

Although a semi-structured interview format was used, each informant focused on, or emphasized, different topics. A general effort was made to maintain the interview protocol; however, interviewers refrained from being overly directive and tried to ensure that the informants were allowed room to take the interviewer "where the informant wanted to go."

Informant 1

Informant 1 is a 32-year-old Caucasian female. For the last 4 years (shortly after her graduation from college), she has worked as an electronics and software engineer (in a civilian capacity) for the U.S. Department of Defense on a North Atlantic Treaty Organization (NATO) project. She holds a bachelor of arts degree in mathematics. She has been divorced for about 5 years and currently shares an apartment with a roommate. She has been romantically involved with a *"special person"* for about 3 years.

She traces a history of learning difficulties going back to early elementary school and continuing through her postsecondary education. She was not formally diagnosed until her third year in college, at the age of 23. She reports that her greatest problems lie in the areas of reading and listening comprehension; and *"just being slow."* She also comments that *"my interpretation of what I read, and what it actually says are two different things . . . the same goes for verbal things."* In addition, she indicated problems with *"focusing"* and attention as well as having Tourette's syndrome.

She describes herself as a *"very social person, very outgoing, making friends with anybody."* Her self-reported strengths are *"patience, determination, "* and being *"very detail oriented."* Writing and math are also strengths. Special talents include her ability to *"look at things differently than most people."* She states that she will often approach a problem by coming in through the

> *side or back door while others come in through the front. . . . I think my learning disability is more an asset than anything and I'm grateful I have it. . . . I think differently than most people and it's that quality of my personality, or characteristics, my abilities, that has opened a lot of doors for me.*

Her job is highly classified and involves considerable international travel. She is responsible for maintaining communications between missile systems located across the globe. She designs, tests, and modifies software that acts as the *"guts"* of these missile systems. Her employer and co-workers are aware of her LD although many don't really *"believe it . . . because it's invisible."*

In addition to her use of highly specialized computer systems associated with the missile systems she maintains, she also uses a number of assistive technologies that help her compensate for the day-to-day manifestations of her LD. These technologies include a 386–DOS-based laptop computer with speech synthesis and screen-review capabilities,[1] a variable speech-control microcassette tape recorder, a microcassette/ transcription system and a wristwatch with personal data and time management capabilities.

She uses the speech synthesis system to read back (via computerized speech) reports and memos she has written (on a word processor) to make sure *"things sound right . . . to see if it makes sense . . . listening helps more than just reading it."* In order to compensate for her reading difficulty, she also uses the system to read back electronic text (on disk) that she has received from her coworkers. She feels that hearing the words spoken aloud enhances her understanding of the written text. She has plans to use the system with a recently installed E-mail system so she can have her mail read to her (via computerized speech).

Her *"number one tool"* is her microcassette tape recorder, which she uses in conjunction with her desktop transcription device.

> *I carry it around [everywhere], meetings, one-on-one, talks in the hallway, talks at the coffee machine, anywhere. Anywhere there's somebody talking to me about something I need to remember or keep abreast of, I record it. And I've got gobs of tape . . . and I keep them because I go back and listen to them later.*

She uses the transcription system to play back the audiotapes. A foot pedal and variable speed capabilities provide her with a convenient way to *'play it, stop it, rewind it and play it again. . . . I'll maybe play it three or four times."* In some instances, (for example *"on instructions on how to do things"*) she uses the transcription system to listen to the tapes as she types what she hears into her word processor or writes it out by hand.

---

[1]The computer reads words aloud from a computer screen, through a computerized/synthetic voice.

There is another piece of technology that she describes as *"very impor-tant;"* this is her combination watch and personal data bank. It is used primarily for its alarm function which "beeps" every 3 hours to remind her to take the medication needed to control her Tourette's and atten-tional difficulties. The device is also used for monitoring "world time" during international travel, scheduling appointments (although she relies primarily on an appointment book), and storing phone numbers.

Although she uses a word processor, she reports that in many instances she prefers to write with a paper and pencil,

> I think it's because when I write [with a pencil and paper], writing is about the same speed as I think. Whereas when I'm typing at a computer, I'm typing faster than my brain is working, and it's too fast. . . . I think because I'm a slow person I opt for the slow version. . . . It [the information] also stays with me better when I write by hand.

She also feels that sometimes new technology and *"peer pressure"* pushes her beyond her own natural pace in using technology. For example, she was raised on DOS, and the move to Windows™ is happening too fast for her comfort level.

Additionally, Informant 1 reports that, in some instances, technol-ogy actually interferes with her work. For example, she reports that it may be distracting to others, or interfering with her ability to listen at that moment, when she has to put a new audiocassette in her tape recorder during a meeting. She also comments that *"some coworkers just think it's a joke, when I show up with my microcassette recorder."*

She emphasizes that her use of technology has positively impacted her employment, stating that technology is

> critical to the quality of my products and processes. I would equate my micro-cassette recorder to my glasses . . . on a scale of one to ten it's an eleven. . . . I feel more confident in my job because of technology—my confidence in what I have produced. . . . It has enabled me to excel . . .

She also believes that technology increases her independence. In regard to her recording/transcription system, she states, *"I don't even have to have a person there, I just do it. . . . It enables me to do it right the first time, without having to go back and ask questions."*

It is important to note that she does not rely solely on technology-based compensatory strategies. She also reports using non-technical strategies such as working at off-hours (late in the day or night, alone). Additionally, she comments,

I listen before I speak. . . . I gather all the information. . . . I'll also make people write things down . . . whatever they have said to me. . . . If I don't have my recorder around . . . my tools to adequately document or record, I put it off on the person I am with.

When asked what she would want to tell other persons with LD about using technology in the workplace she advises, *"find something that works for you . . . experiment . . . try a few different things . . . and stick with it—it will help boost self-esteem."*

Informant 2

Informant 2 is a 48-year-old Caucasian male who has been married for 6 years and has one child. He has worked for the last 21 years as a supervisory government attorney for a civil rights agency. He also has taught at a prestigious private law school for the last 3 years.

He remembers having reading problems as early as the first grade, but did not receive any assistance until his high school years, and *"then it was not on the basis of a learning disability or dyslexia, it was just remedial reading."* It was during high school that he received his first formal diagnosis (dyslexia was suggested); however, he felt *"it was not of any great merit, depth, or substance."*

Problems persisted throughout his postsecondary education (although he stresses that went from a "C+" to an "A" after the first three semesters when courses shifted from multiple choice to essay tests and from an emphasis on memorization to analytical thinking), yet he received no special assistance. It was not until his junior or senior year of high school that he received another assessment which confirmed a diagnosis of "dyslexia." In addition to difficulty with reading, he describes problems with short-term memory, attention, and concentration (that often play themselves out in reading).

He also believes that his LD affects him socially; *"some people think there's something a little awkward or strange about me. . . . I still sometimes miss cues."* He says that he often either forgets or mixes up the names of people he has been working with for 20 years, making some people *"irritated as hell."* He continues, *"I think it's hard for some people to accept the fact that I'm going to have control over their work and yet I can't dial a phone."*

His self-described strengths lie in his

persistence, [being] hard working, a desire to please, and very, very good intuitive thinking skills. . . . I have the analytical skills . . . or the intuitional skill to solve [complex legal cases] that they [coworkers] cannot solve . . . if you come to me with a very complex case that has 16 different, conflicting kinds of issues, and brief me on it orally or schematically, I will be able to cut through the issues very quickly and come to a satisfactory resolution that has eluded lots of people.

He also reports special talents in cooking and photography.

On a day-to-day basis, Informant 2 consults with *"other attorneys and top administrators on the 20% of our caseload that is considered the most sensitive and most difficult."*

His greatest difficulties on the job include dialing a telephone, reading, and writing.

If I have to read 15 cases I haven't read before, it can take me a ghastly long time to get through [them] and really think them through and write a brief. . . . But on the other hand, people can be stuck, unable to resolve a case for months, and they will come to talk to me for five minutes and I will have figured out for them how to resolve it.

His employer is now aware of the disability, *"but was not for a very long time."* Although now aware, the informant does not believe that his supervisor really understands it, *"I don't think he considers it real."*

He personally owns two computers, a desktop 386 IBM clone and a laptop 386 IBM-compatible. In addition, his employer has provided him with a desktop 486 IBM-compatible computer. He uses these technologies primarily for "multitasking" personal data management software and word processing. On a day-to-day basis, he relies extensively on several software programs, including a telephone directory and dialer, a calendar (with prioritization, scheduling, outlining, and notetaking capabilities), E-mail, a tape recorder (for voice mail), and word processing with an integrated outliner and spell checker.

The basis of the technological support system he has created for himself is "multitasking." The idea is to have multiple programs running simultaneously so he can move quickly and easily between programs. This capability is extremely important to him because of his short-term memory difficulties. He states,

for example, to open my phone directory, see a number, shut it down and open up my calendar program and then write down a number in my calendar to remind me who I have to call, I would have forgotten the number. Whereas in multitasking [I have] the ability to instantaneously flip from my phone directory to my calendar. . . .

His computers are set up (at home and at work) so that, when he turns them on, each program is automatically loaded and all are running simultaneously. He uses DOS programs operating within a Windows™ shell. He emphasizes that, while Windows™ allows him to multitask, it is also more difficult for him to use than DOS, *"There are generally more steps that one has to go through for any particular function and in losing that time I may lose my memory."* Pointing and clicking [on an icon] is slower for him than using a function key. He emphasizes that since

part of my disability is lack of understanding of right from left, up and down . . . . I find it [a mouse] extremely frustrating. . . . I may have to move that mouse six or seven times to get it exactly where it needs to be to open the damned thing.

Although he believes that it may take longer to learn to use DOS, it will save time in the long run.

A telephone dialing program allows him to create a dozen content categories, and is *"a good way for me to organize since I don't remember names, but I do remember concepts."* Telephone numbers, along with addresses and short notes, are grouped under such personally created headings as "internal agency," "external-agency related," "law school," etc. Once the number is located, the program will automatically dial the number via modem. During the conversation, he will take brief notes in a telephone directory program or he may multitask to his word processing program or calendar program to schedule an appointment or take notes. He is able to organize all information—telephone numbers, notes on telephone conversations, and appointments through one system. E-mail also is used within this system.

A calendar program also serves as a prioritization, management, and notetaking system. The program functions essentially as an outlining program. The user can set up broad informational categories as well as sub-topic areas. The user can also set priorities and identify a completion date. When he "boots up" his computer in the morning, the program shows him every task he needs to accomplish that day, on which tasks he is late, and all appointments he has made for the day. He also receives his E-mail through this system. However, he stresses that he prefers to use voice mail (over E-mail) when he simultaneously distributes information to other attorneys within his agency. He prefers voice mail because of *"the chance that I will make some kind of grammatical or spelling error."* This organizational system also is available on his laptop computer.

Informant 2 has not yet found a technological solution for his reading problem, *"and maybe that's the reason that's the hardest thing for me."* He comments that his use of "reading machines" (optical character recognition/speech synthesis systems) to compensate for reading problems has been somewhat negative, as he finds the process too slow for his needs. In contrast, he has found technological assistance for his writing problems through the use of word processing with integrated outlining and spell-checking functions. He uses a word processor on a regular basis to write letters, prepare lectures, and develop briefs. He believes that spell checking is *"teaching me how to spell when nothing else ever has . . . my spelling skills have greatly increased."* Although he has tried numerous grammar checkers, he has not found one *"yet that I think is worth using."* He also reports using software that increases the thickness and height of the characters on his computer screen, *"so that they are easier to read."*

He believes that the use of technology has been very important to his job satisfaction and success, *"I suspect that I could have, and maintain the same job without it [technology], but the level of stress I experience would be ten times as great!"* He also points out that compensatory benefits of technology in the workplace have had tremendous impact on his personal and family life, freeing him from reliance on his wife for such tasks as proofreading his work. He states, *"In fact, I just could not have married her if it were not for word processors."* He also believes that technology has made him more self-sufficient and independent. Regarding a past position in which he had no technology available, he explains, *"I was very, very secretary-dependent and dependent on other people. What it has really done is make me more independent. . . . The single biggest thing is that it has made me more self-reliant."*

He reports having also developed non-technological strategies to compensate for his difficulties in the workplace. One is a method of reading he calls *"logic check"* where he reads

> *a line and if it's logical I go on, and if it's not logical I automatically repeat the line and because I've developed a good sense of internal logic I probably catch most misperceptions. . . . I mean there's just this sort of logic circuit and if it doesn't work you go back and rescan.*

His response to questions about what he would like to tell others with LD regarding the use of technology is:

> *I think it would be unfortunate if people put a lot of hope in technology and then because they didn't find it easy the first time they used it, they gave up on it. I think it is like playing the violin— you've got to practice it. And until you do you don't know whether it's going to help you or not.*

Informant 3

Informant 3 is a 60-year-old Caucasian male living in New York City. He is married, with a 43-year-old adopted daughter and two grandchildren. He is an internationally recognized economist working for a renowned economic consulting firm, and has been with his present employer for the last 37 years.

He recalls that his parents took him to Dr. Samuel Orton at Columbia University Teachers College in the third grade, *"I did not speak clearly, wrote the language backward and could not read."* Dr. Orton and his *"day-by-day teacher (Dr Katrina de Hirsch) . . . taught me speech and how to reverse the language."* He states,

> I was remediated very well, by the end of the fourth grade I could read and write very well going from left to right, backwards from my point of view. I had no mechanical problems, my speech was weak under tension, but clear.

It is interesting to note that when he speaks, he feels as if he is speaking a *"second language."*

Although he had been "remediated," he comments that . . . *my school career was very spotted, never agreed with the school system. I don't learn well under the school system . . ."* He continues,

> I flunked out of high school, I flunked out of college, low grades, graduated from high school with a minimal . . . but at the same time I was highly educated because I provided myself with a second educational system I did on my own.

He later returned to college, and received a bachelor of arts degree in political science. He went on to graduate school, but did not complete it.

He stresses that although he had been *"remediated,"*

> I returned back to my native language in 1976. . . . I write mirrored. . . . Language from my point of view should be written from right to left. Either I have a learning disability or the rest of society doesn't. I feel the rest of the world has a learning disability and I'm normal.

He will write from left to right if forced to, *"but it is always a concession."*

He also reports that he was *"out of step"* socially. His greatest problems were in, *"mating . . . I didn't meet my wife until the age of 48, until I started being with my type of person—right-hemisphered."*

He believes his greatest strength is his enormous power to *"put things together, "*

I am very "holistic, I have excellent visualization power. . . marvelous associative thinker . . . that is what I am at the [name of employer]. I can put the world economically, socially and politically together. . . . When it comes to specifics [I'm] not that good. That's where the problem comes, with detail that no one has put into a holistic fashion. If you give me the big picture I have no problems at all. If you don't, I have lots of troubles . . .

He considers this ability a *"special talent."*

As an economist, his primary work involves analyzing economic indicators, and basic general economic and political trends. He disseminates his findings on national television and radio. He is on the air 7 days a week and makes speeches across the country on a regular basis. He travels extensively.

At the moment, he finds *"absolutely nothing"* difficult about his job. *"I am doing work that is completely in my strength . . . I have avoided my weaknesses; I am in my glory."* What he finds most rewarding about his job is that,

I was trying to speak backwards for the first eight years of my life. . . . I have a feeling of how important speech is. Most people take it for granted. . . . I have overcome it. . . The irony is that I now make a substantial living through, and become relatively well-known through, speech.

However, he does comment that, under stress, speech problems may "re-emerge."

He reports that his employer and co-workers are aware of his, *"learning difference. . . . I write everything mirrored except for the IRS and Chemical Bank. I write to my secretary in mirrored fashion. Everything in the office is mirrored . . . this is something you can't keep a secret."*

He uses several technologies to help him on the job. He has a PC notebook with a word processor, and an integrated spell and grammar checker that he carries with him at all times. He also utilizes a mirrored clock, copier transparencies, a phone mail system and the *"technology of the broadcast world ."*

He comments that this technology *"helps me with my weaknesses . . . it makes everything holistic."* He continues,

spelling can be difficult. . . . I love spell checks because I still reverse the "is" and "es" . . . in words. I will still have problems with vowels and the order of vowels and I still reverse numbers here and there if . . . it is not a good day. But again with these kind of checks there is no problem now, or much less of a problem.

He also has a mirrored clock in his office, since he lives in the *"mirrored world"* (right to left). He also occasionally uses transparencies on his copy machine instead of plain paper. Copying with transparencies allows him to write in his *"native language,"* from right to left. He reproduces his writing (using a copy machine) onto transparencies which can then be flipped over so others (like his secretary) can read from left to right.

He uses a phone mail system extensively (which he refers to as a *"big tape recorder"*) to stay in touch, and link up with the broadcast technology,

> . . . it is very important to me. . . . I do use the phone mail system a great deal because I broadcast all over the world. . . . I am broadcasting everyday . . . I mean I am broadcasting everywhere. I've broadcasted from bus stations, train stations, airports . . . . I am really into technology because of the broadcast world.

Informant 3 believes that technology has made a positive impact on his career success and satisfaction. He comments,

> I am considered a weak writer, especially in the economic world. Again, because of the printed word in this atmosphere, I would never had made it. . . . I really had writing problems in the sense of promotions. I would have always been considered a junior person. And I was until this explosion in the business world [broadcasting on television and radio]. Now my sets of skills are the ones that are so good [required].

He continues,

> . . . until the oral world opened up, until we started having business television networks, radio shows, I was pretty mediocre at the [name of employer], and now I am one of their stars. That is the irony of it. . . . The oral world has expanded, and I was the person that could really respond to the oral world. I have been a great success at it . . .

He explains that his primary "non-tech" strategy for dealing with his learning difference is a *"psychological factor."* This psychological factor means *"not being bothered by being different . . . and to depersonalize it."*

Regarding what he would like to say to other persons with *"learning differences,"* he comments, *"I think more than technology, you have to step back and learn about yourself and the society."* He also emphasizes that,

> . . . you have to understand yourself. If you understand yourself and your strengths and weaknesses, how the system is set up, then you can find a strategy to use the technology . . . you can't be helped if you don't know what you

*need help in. . . . You have to do as much as you can about those weaknesses,
but don't forget the strengths.*

He continues, *"The key to understanding your society is to depersonalize [it];
it is not your fault. . . . You are just doing something that is different."*

Informant 4

Informant 4 is a 33-year-old male Caucasian. He is single and has living
arrangements both at his parents and his girlfriend's homes in Southern
California. He has been employed as a leasing operations officer by a
major automobile company for the last several years.

He recounts being diagnosed as "dyslexic" at the age of five. He
attended private special education schools (specializing in LD) until the
ninth grade when he reentered the public school system. He received
special services through junior and senior high school. Self-described
problems in reading and writing persisted throughout his postsecondary education, and he received assistance from LD programs at a
community college and state university. He believes that his strengths
lie in the areas of math and *"verbal communication."* He also describes
"special talents" for mechanical and *"hands-on tasks."*

His work involves leasing automobiles to approximately 500 corporations in the southwestern U.S. and monitoring vehicle maintenance/
repairs until they are returned to his company. Vehicle monitoring is
done from his office, as well as through periodic visits to the companies
leasing the automobiles. His job is *"paperwork intensive"* and requires
him to spend a considerable amount of his day gathering information,
inputting data and writing reports.

He uses a number of technologies to help him compensate for his
difficulties. These include a speech recognition system, a tape recorder,
and a sophisticated cellular phone, voice mail, and speech recognition
system installed in his car. His greatest difficulties on the job occur
"when the computer goes down, and I have to write by hand." He does not
believe that his dyslexia interferes with his work because *"I've got the
computer [speech recognition system]. It makes everything different. If I had to
handwrite all this stuff out . . . forget it, I'd never make it."*

He uses the speech recognition system (which converts his spoken
language to electronic text) to input data (e.g., maintenance, damage,
mileage) into a computer and to generate reports on the leased vehicles.
Using speech recognition enables him to use his "stronger" oral language abilities to circumvent his difficulties with writing. He comments,

I dictate very well. . . . I'm not doing any kind of writing at all. The computer's doing it. You have to imagine that if I didn't have the technology, how hard it would be . . . it would be real hard . . . but now it's great. I don't have any problems.

He uses a "speaker independent" speech recognition system (not dependent on learning the voice profiles of individual users). The system is connected to a mainframe computer and is used by approximately 1,500 other employees. Words are displayed on a computer monitor as he speaks into the computer through a microphone. The system has an on-screen menu that lists a number of other possible words (words the computer thinks the user said) that can be selected by the user. If the system completely fails to recognize a word, *"it will not let you continue;"* at that point, words have to be typed in from the keyboard.

At times, when the speech recognition system is unavailable, (computer system down, he is away from his office), he will use an alternative technologically-based strategy to write his reports. He states,

I will dictate into a cassette recorder. Then I will hand it to a secretary. She will type it up. We will go back over it. She will give it to me all completed. I will listen to my own cassette [while reviewing the typed report] . . . I'll follow it that way. Sometimes, when I have done a couple dozen . . . she will read them back to me.

He also uses technology "on the road." He has a specially equipped prototype car featuring technology that enables him to tap into his self-described stronger oral language and listening abilities. These technologies include a sophisticated cellular phone, speech recognition, and voice mail system. His cellular phone has speech recognition capabilities that permit him to call someone through speech, *"I just say someone's name and the system automatically dials it for me."* The system stores about 30 numbers. He also uses the speech recognition system to "call himself" in the car and leave reminders or create a permanent record of important information. The system is connected to a voice mail/computer system in the trunk of his car. In addition to accessing the voice mail system by cellular telephone, he may also reach it via speech recognition by simply speaking into a microphone installed in the automobile, *"I just say 'record'."* He also uses the system to call himself in the office and leave reminders. Although he does not believe he has memory or organizational problems, he comments that *"it is a very handy thing to have."*

Finally, he has recently begun to use satellite navigation technology to assist him with his driving. The system (which interfaces satellite systems with a computer/CD ROM in the trunk of his car) automatically shows a driver (via an electronic display) the best route to reach a destination, and reroutes the driver as necessary (for instance, in the case of an accident or traffic jam). Maps are available for a number of different cities. According to Informant 4,

> *If you make a right turn, but should have gone left, it tells you that you made a mistake . . . in a voice . . . if a person has difficulty reading street signs, the system will at least tell them if they are going in the right direction.*

When asked how important technology is to his job success and satisfaction, he replied, *"If I didn't have it I would be pretty miserable."* Similarly, when asked if he could do the job without it, he replied,

> *No! I think . . . people with dyslexia have to use technology . . . I could not have taken the job at [name of company] if I didn't have the technology . . . if there wasn't any technology there and I had to do this all by hand, and didn't have this system, it would be back in the cave man days for me.*

Technology is not the only way he compensates for his difficulty at work. His secretary proofreads reports, even when they have been generated on the speech recognition system.

When asked about what he would advise persons with LD about technology, he replied, *"Use it! Younger ones should be taught immediately how to dictate into tape recorders and then boost their way up to computers."*

Informant 5

Informant 5 is a 52-year-old Caucasian male. For the past 5 years, he has been an author, lecturer, and consultant, dealing with conceptual abilities as they relate to emerging technologies such as computer graphics and information visualization. He holds a master's degree in international relations and is married with two sons, both currently in college.

The informant reports not being able to read until 9 or 10 years of age, *"And ever after it was a matter of catching up, compensating however I could."* He attended rural schools and was *"treated as an average student would be."* There were no special programs or assistance available. He states,

> *As a result, I was forced on my own resources. I developed strengths in visualization and the organization of abstract ideas to assist me in the areas where I was not able to function such as rote memorization. In my senior year of high school, I found out to my surprise that I could deal with high level conceptual*

material more easily than my classmates. I found I could deal with a wide range of topics and since then this ability is something I have been able to rely on. I found that if I could get around the reading and go directly to writing itself, I seemed to excel at the very things I thought I would not be able to do. When I finally did go to college I became an English literature major. So that shows you the puzzle of dyslexia. Neither I nor my teachers could ever predict what would happen next. For instance, I was poor at arithmetic, but did surprisingly well at higher-level mathematics such as Boolean algebra.

He found that mathematical concepts often came easily, but *"the special care I had to take to calculate properly, to not get tripped up along the way, prevented me from reaching what I may have been able to do with it."* In college, foreign languages were *"a disaster."* Long after college and graduate school, *"when the struggle was essentially complete,"* at the age of 41, he was finally diagnosed as having an LD.

Gradually, I became aware of the paradoxical pattern familiar to many dyslexics. The "easy" things in the early school years were hard, but the "hard" things in the later years were remarkably easy. When things were less demanding than I expected, it didn't make me happy, but it did clarify my understanding of why it was that I had been struggling in a system that was not flexible in its approach to learning. And on the other hand there was a positive reaction to areas where I had not been aware of the degree of my ability.

To his surprise, Informant 4 found that he had developed a talent for oral communication, perhaps, because it involves visual and performance aspects that *"many, if . . . others do not possess."* He found himself developing over time a *"sensitivity to the audience, to what links them,"* such that he is able to form a bridge and translate ideas *"into something of value for such diverse groups as neurologists, educators and computer programmers."*

He believes his success has been, to some extent, a matter of finding the right "niche," *"between the cracks"* of other disciplines. He has found that bringing several specialty areas together and communicating with each in a way that is unique to them suits his own mix of strengths and preferences. He comments,

Often, I haven't the inclination to work out the details [of a problem] fully. I prefer to leave that to those who are better suited to that task. This allows me to contribute something that the specialists often cannot do themselves, really.

As a consequence of the informant's unique "niche," it is crucial that he maintain communication with a broad range of formal and informal organizations, individuals from various disciplines, publishers, journal and newsletter editors, corporate managers from several industries, and computer hardware and software manufacturers. Additionally, he tries to remain current on developments in a variety of fields of endeavor. He has developed his use of the computer to meet these demands by intensive use of Internet communication, including bulletin boards, mail boxes and chat lines for outgoing communication via electronic mail. The informal written communication that is generated in such an *"instant media"* seems to the informant to be tailor-made to his own writing style. Electronic media also offer the possibility of communicating directly with images and with computer graphic professional organizations; this allows him to tap into one of his perceived areas of strength, visualization.

He is aware of such computer organizational aids as calendars, "address books," "mind mapping" and outlining programs, but he does not use these on his own computer. For these, he often finds paper and pencil easier. He states,

> You see, I had been drawing diagrams like those, the circles and arrows for years. I had become eventually an accurate key word note-taker. And much to my delight, my diagrams and notes appeared to others to be easier to understand as well, those who seemingly did not possess the difficulties I had, but also were without these visualization abilities. I found that this was just one more example of the struggle in private that drove me on, until, unbeknownst to myself, I sometimes surpassed my peers. It had become a positive driving force in my life. My weakness had become my strength. I find that these visual representations allow me to simplify or reduce great amounts of information and sometimes would allow me to relate whole fields of study in such a way that has not occurred to those in the specialist field who had used traditional rote learning.

Informant 5 makes extensive use of word processing to compose, reorganize, and revise his correspondence and publications. Although he is *"a two-finger"* typist, he can rapidly and efficiently translate his thoughts into words using the computer. He finds graphic-oriented Macintosh programs liberating to his writing processes, since no commands need be memorized or sequential steps executed in order to effectively operate them. He stresses that early attempts to use command-line programs—such as DOS —as assistive devices failed. He employs the integrated spell check function of his word processor, as well as the cut-and-paste functions to reorganize early drafts in his efforts to *"get the words out."*

He describes the major difficulties he experiences in his present work as having to *"check it, recheck it and have someone else check it, too, for careless errors."* When complicated tasks are encountered, he is likely to make mistakes, *"but is willing to put in the time to correct them."* Most people with whom he works are aware of his *"dyslexic traits"* because he incorporates reference to them in his presentations, being careful to point out the concomitant strengths in visual conceptualization, which he believes characterize many individuals with dyslexia.

Personally speaking, he believes computer technology has made day-to-day writing tasks much easier for him and, furthermore, has allowed him to tackle larger projects such as books which otherwise would have been extremely difficult. His extensive networking via electronic communication has permitted the formation of many professional connections, more broadly and rapidly than would have been possible previously. He believes that the use of computer technology offers a special opportunity for persons with LD, not only to circumvent their difficulties, but to actually excel due to strengths in visual organization and other areas. He also states that, *"The new technologies can amplify strengths as well as remediate weaknesses."*

This informant actively seeks projects that play to his strengths in abstract analysis, visualization, and oral communication. He has also developed compensatory skills such as notetaking, time management and organization, which, when combined with talents in making connections across diverse academic disciplines, have allowed him to excel.

When asked what he would like to say to others about technology, he replied,

> A lot of our education has revolved around words and I think that new technologies can be used not only as remediation to relieve a problem, but what I think is far more interesting is that new technologies open up new areas of need in the marketplace. People who have difficulty with the old educational system have many traits and nonverbal abilities that will be construed as increasingly valuable over time. So I think change is on our side. These machines will take over the low-level clerical functions that have always been hard for this group of people. Spell checking is only the beginning. What will really be important in future writing (and multi-media) will be those things they are good at: how to communicate with people, how to evoke images or emotions, not the mechanics of writing. So I think time is on the side of change in favor of those who currently have difficulties with words.

Discussion/Conclusions

The informants in this study reflected a broad spectrum of learning difficulties, strengths, and special talents, and functioned within a number of diverse employment settings. Informant 1, an electronics engineer, reported difficulties in reading, listening, and attention. She also emphasized strengths in social relations, in being "detail oriented," and in the ability to "look at things differently." Informant 2, a federal attorney, described difficulties with reading, memory, attention/concentration and social relations, while reporting strengths in persistence and analytical thinking. An economist, Informant 3, reported "learning differences" in reading, writing, speaking, and social relations. He also described himself as having special abilities in "putting things together," "seeing the big picture," holistic and associative thinking, oral language (a weakness that became a strength) and visualization. Reading and writing were the primary problems reported by Informant 4, a leasing operations officer. Informant 4 expressed the belief that he possesses particular strengths in math, oral language, and mechanical tasks. Finally, Informant 5, an author, lecturer, and consultant, recounted a history of problems with reading, mathematic calculations, rote memorization, and learning foreign languages. At the same time, he characterized himself as having talents for oral communication, writing, mathematical abstractions, "audience sensitivity," visualization, and "the organization of abstract ideas."

The informants used wide variety of technologies. These included personal computers (desktop and laptop), word processors, spell checkers, grammar checkers, outliners, telephone dialers, personal data organizers, tape recorders, speech synthesizers, speech recognition and transcription systems, satellite/computer maps, voice mail, E-mail, cellular telephones, "mirrored materials" and broadcast technology. This broad range of technology appeared to be the result of a number of factors including (a) the informant's particular difficulties, strengths and special abilities, (b) the requirements and contexts of the specific jobs, (c) availability of resources on the job (including the technology supplied by employer), and (d) the informant's financial situation.

Despite the diversity of the informants' specific difficulties, strengths, special talents, employment requirements, and resources, several "themes" were common to all the informants' use of technology. First, all stated they believe technology helps them circumvent specific areas of difficulty. For example, Informant 1 uses a tape recorder to assist with listening difficulties; Informant 2 employs a telephone dialer to compensate for memory problems; and Informant 4 utilizes a speech recognition system to bypass difficulties with writing. Furthermore, the technology used by the informants not only circumvents difficulties, but generally allows them to simultaneously take advantage of their strengths and special talents. For instance, Informant 3 works around a written language "difference" by using broadcast technology that plays to his strengths in oral language; Informant 4 takes advantage of his stronger oral language abilities with speech recognition; and Informant 5 uses graphic-based word processing to tap into his special talent in visual conceptualization.

Secondly, every informant reported that using technology has been instrumental in achieving job satisfaction and success. For instance, Informant 1 stated that technology is *"critical to the quality of my products and processes,"* while Informant 2 commented that he could have maintained the same job without technology, but the level of stress would be *"ten times as great!"* Informant 3 emphasized that he *"would never have made it"* without technology; and Informant 4 stressed that *"I could not have taken the job . . . if I didn't have the technology."* Finally, Informant 5 indicated that technology has allowed him to tackle larger projects that otherwise would have been extremely difficult.

Although not explicitly stated by each informant, there was a general sense that all believed that technology had enhanced their ability to function independently. For example, Informant 1 stated that she can now *"just do it, "* without having to have another person around, and Informant 2 emphasized that the *"single biggest thing is that it has made me more self-reliant."* In addition, all informants stressed that they had portable technological support systems that allowed them to work independently in multiple settings.

As discussed, a wide variety of technologies was used by the informants, ranging from "broadcast technology" to tape recorders. Use of specific technologies was dependent on the informant's specific difficulties, strengths, special talents, employment requirements and resources. Despite differences in the types of technology utilized, a pattern of preference emerged. All informants used computers with word processing capabilities, and three of the five informants reported using integrated spell checkers. (During their interviews, the other two implied that they also used spell checkers.) Additionally, four of the five informants reported carrying laptop computers with them as they moved between settings. Finally, three informants used portable tape recorders.

All informants acknowledged reading difficulties. However, none reported using a "reading machine" (an optical character recognition/ speech synthesis system) to compensate for reading problems. In fact, Informant 2 commented that his experience with "reading machines" has been somewhat negative and that he found the process too slow for his needs. Only Informant 1 made use of compensatory reading technology, and this did not involve the reading of hard copy text. Rather, she used a speech synthesis/screen review system (without optical character recognition) to review text she had generated on her word processor, or electronic text (on disk) given to her by her co-workers.

Although some informants used "high technologies" (e.g., speech synthesis, speech recognition), "lower technologies" also played an important role in helping informants compensate for difficulties in the workplace. For example, despite the fact that Informant 1 had access to a speech synthesis/screen review program, she regarded her tape recorder as her *"number one tool."* Additionally, although Informant 4 relied primarily on speech recognition technology, he also depended on a "low-tech" tape recorder, which became particularly important when the "high-tech" system was unavailable. Finally, Informant 3, who utilized broadcast technology, also had to ensure that he had a mirrored clock available in his office. Similarly, although each informant used technology to compensate for difficulties, non-technological strategies also were used. For example, Informant 1 works at "off hours," Informant 2 employs "logic check" when reading, Informant 4 relies on a secretary for proofreading, and Informant 5 uses pencil and paper to organize information.

It should be emphasized that only one of the five informants reported that her LD interfered with her use of technology. Informant 1 reported that using a word processor sometimes forced her to write *"faster than my brain is working, faster than my brain can think."* Similarly, four out of the five informants stressed that technology did not create any particular problems for them, with only Informant 1 reporting that the use of her micro-cassette recorder may be distracting during a meeting or that *"some co-workers just think it's a joke when I show up with my microcassette recorder."*

Several of the informants asserted that their learning difficulties were actually advantages. Informant 1 believed that her LD enabled her to see the world differently, while Informant 2 felt it enabled him to think holistically, and Informant 5 believes that his ability in the area of visualization is the "other side of the same coin [dyslexia]." Informants 2 and 5 also emphasized that technology had actually enabled them to turn their weaknesses into their greatest strengths.

Although the interviews revealed a number of "commonalities of technology use" among the informants, it should be noted that the interviews also uncovered some distinct differences. For instance, Informant 5 emphasized that he finds the graphic-based Macintosh programs (as opposed to DOS) particularly well-suited to his needs, since no commands need be memorized or sequential steps executed in order to effectively operate them. In contrast, Informant 2 stressed that graphic-based programs such as (Macintosh and Windows™ are more difficult for him to use than DOS programs.

> *There are generally more steps that one has to go through for any particular function and in losing that time I may lose my memory . . . part of my disability is lack of understanding of right from left, up and down . . . I find it [a mouse] extremely frustrating . . . I may have to move that mouse six or seven times to get it exactly where it needs to be to open the damned thing*

In addition to preferences regarding general operating platforms (e.g., Macintosh versus DOS), informants varied in their feelings toward specific programs. For instance, Informant 2 believes that the use of his calendar software program is crucial to his job performance, while Informant 5 prefers pencil and paper approaches to time management and scheduling. Similarly, Informant 3 finds grammar checkers very helpful in working around his weaknesses, and in contrast, Informant 2 has not found a grammar checker *"that I think is worth using ."*

The purpose of this study was to learn about assistive technology and LD from the inside. To this end, the authors believe that this exploration was successful. The ethnographic method of inquiry used to investigate assistive technology in the workplace provided a richness and depth that might not have been achieved through more traditional quantitative approaches. As a result of the informants' willingness to share their personal experiences and perspectives, we have been able to move far beyond our own preconceived views, theories, and hypotheses regarding how persons with LD use, or should use, technology. We are very fortunate to have gained an opportunity to learn many highly creative, intelligent, innovative, and effective ways that technology can be used to compensate for learning difficulties. Most assuredly, the informants in this study have helped us gain, in the words of Spradley (1979), "a different species of knowledge" (p. 4). We hope this study has also demonstrated the utility of gaining the insider's perspective and that it will help set the stage for future ethnographic investigations in the field of LD.

Authors' Note

The authors would like to express their heartfelt gratitude to the informants in this study, whose generosity, openness, and sincerity taught us so much.

References

Bos, C., & Richardson, V. (1994). Qualitative research and learning disabilities. In S. Vaughn & C. Bos (Eds.), *Research issues in learning disabilities: Theory, methodology, assessment, and ethics* (pp. 178–201). New York: Springer-Verlag.

Brown, C. (1987). *Computer access in higher education for students with disabilities.* Washington, DC: Fund for the Improvement of Postsecondary Education, U.S. Department of Education.

Bryant, B., Rivera, D., & Warde, B. (1993). Technology as a means to an end: Facilitating success at the college level. *LD Forum 19*, 13–18.

Collins, T. (1990). The impact of microcomputer word processing on the performance of learning disabled students in a required first year writing course. *Computers and Composition, 8*, 49–68.

Gerber, P. J., Ginsberg, R, & Reiff, H. B. (1992). Identifying alterable patterns of vocational success in highly successful adults with learning disabilities. *Journal of Leaning Disabilities, 25*, 475–485.

Gerber, P. J., & Reiff, H. B. (1991). *Speaking for themselves: Ethnographic interviews with adults with learning disabilities.* Ann Arbor: University of Michigan Press.

Higgins, E. L., & Raskind, M. H. (1995). An investigation of the compensatory effectiveness of speech recognition on the written composition performance of postsecondary students with learning disabilities. *Learning Disability Quarterly, 18*, 159–174.

Primus, C. (1990). *Computer assistance model for learning disabled* (Grant No. G008630152-88). Washington, DC: Office of Special Education and Rehabilitation Services, U.S. Department of Education.

Raskind, M. H., & Higgins, E. L. (1995). Reflections on ethics, technology and learning disabilities: Avoiding the consequences of ill-considered action. *Journal of Learning Disabilities, 28*, 425–438.

Raskind, M. H. (1994). Assistive technology for adults with leaning disabilities: A rationale for use. In P. J. Gerber & H. B. Reiff (Eds.), *Adults with learning disabilities.* Stoneham, MA: Butterworth-Heinemann.

Raskind, M. H. (1993). Assistive technology for persons with learning disabilities: A blueprint for exploration and advancement. *Learning Disability Quarterly, 16*, 185–196.

Reid, K., & Button, L. (1995). Anna's Story: Narratives of personal experience about being labeled learning disabled. *Journal of Learning Disabilities, 28*, 602–614.

Spekman, N. J., Goldberg, R. J., & Herman, K. L. (1992). Learning disabled children grow up: A search for factors related to success in the young adult years. *Learning Disabilities Research & Practice, 7*, 161–170.

Spradley, J. (1979). *The ethnographic interview.* New York: Holt, Rinehart, and Winston.

PART IV

Experiences in the Workplace

On the Front Line: Thoughts from Persons with Learning Disabilities in the Workplace

Henry B. Reiff

"It Don't Come Easy"

T he employment picture for individuals with learning disabilities is brightening. With data collected in 1987 and 1990, the National Longitudinal Transition Study of Special Education Students (NLTS) (Blackorby & Wagner, 1996) determined within 3 to 5 years after leaving school, 71% of youths with learning disabilities were employed, actually surpassing the 69% employment rate of the general population. Moreover, nearly half of the youths with learning disabilities, 45%, were earning more than $6 per hour, again comparing favorably with their peers in the general population. Nevertheless, youths with learning disabilities were less likely to attend postsecondary schools than were many others with disabilities. Blackorby and Wagner (1996) speculated that youths with learning disabilities may have success entering the workforce, but with a lack of postsecondary education and advanced training, they may quickly plateau in their ultimate vocational progress.

Other sources, however, suggest that we may not need to look for grey clouds inside this silver lining. The NLTS followed youths for only 5 years after leaving school. In another longitudinal study, Werner (1993) opined that if her investigation had concluded at the threshold of adulthood, the prognosis would have been fairly negative. By following adults with learning disabilities into their 30s, Werner (1993) observed considerable improvement; 75% of these adults with learning disabilities had made a successful adaptation to work, marriage, and family life, comparing favorably to a non-disability control group. The further individuals with disabilities get away from school, and the longer they remain in the world of work, the better things get.

Why do adults with learning disabilities fare relatively well in the workplace? Through questionnaire responses from 65 supervisors in human service agencies and through 27 interviews conducted with employers and supervisors in business and industry, Reisman and

Reisman (1993) concluded that employees with learning disabilities compare favorably to the general population in terms of attendance, punctuality, positive work attitude, ability to accept criticism, and long-term dependability. Nevertheless, we cannot overlook the reality that persons with learning disabilities do encounter major problems on the job. The Reisman and Reisman (1993) survey identified insecurity about work roles, low self-esteem, distractibility, inability to transfer learning, difficulty following directions, reluctance to ask for help, repetition of verbalizations and behaviors, impulsiveness, and poor judgment as issues that affect performance of employees with learning disabilities.

Moody (1995) provided a concise analysis of how the same difficulties that plague individuals with learning disabilities when they are in school may undermine their employment efforts. Poor literacy skills, such as failure to follow written instructions or to read or write reports quickly and efficiently, are probably the most obvious. Learning disabilities are not limited to language processing problems. Commonly identified characteristics such as weaknesses with memory (e.g., remembering messages, instructions, telephone numbers, what was said at meetings), sequencing ability (e.g., filing documents in the correct sequence, writing down numbers correctly, looking up entries in dictionaries or directories), visual orientation (e.g., getting lost in strange or even familiar surroundings, dealing with maps, tables and charts), hand–eye coordination (e.g., slow and untidy handwriting, poor presentation of written work or figures, and inaccurate keying on a word processor or calculator), speech (e.g., talking too little or too much, blurting out things impulsively, not being able to say what is meant), and organizational skills (e.g., missing appointments, getting the times and places of meetings wrong, failing to meet deadlines) can and do present treacherous obstacles for adults with learning disabilities in the workplace. The frustration of dealing with such inefficiencies, as well as the effect on self-esteem and others' perceptions, may lead to feelings of despair, anger, embarrassment, anxiety, lack of confidence, and defensiveness or aggressiveness.

Similarly, McCue et al. (1994) have detailed an extensive list of the vocational problems that tend to result from the nonacademic characteristics of learning disabilities. This list focuses on the impact of specific behavioral deficits in the cognitive domain, including (a) executive functioning (e.g., scheduling problems, unrealistic expectations, difficulty with change); (b) attention (e.g., losing track of what is supposed to be done); (c) language and communication (e.g., problems with reading and writing memos, telephone use, catching on to "hints"); (d) sensory and perceptual skills (e.g., getting lost, problems understanding blueprints or diagrams); (e) motor skills (e.g., messy work, accidents, or injuries); and (f) social/emotional skills (e.g., conflicts with supervisors or coworkers, inappropriate interactions).

The View from the Front

So far in this book, the reader has encountered a variety of perspectives from professionals about learning disabilities and employment. These views represent the cutting edge of research experience on this subject of ever-increasing importance. Yet we have not heard much from individuals who are most intimately acquainted with the most critical issues— employees with learning disabilities and their employers. Of course, relying on personal recommendations and experiences carries the risks of subjectivity and idiographic perspectives. On the other hand, no source could be more empirical than direct, firsthand observation. Additionally, regardless of the merit of an individual suggestion or piece of advice from an individual with learning disabilities, simply listening to the voices of those who deal with the world of work—sometimes succeeding, sometimes failing, oftentimes persevering, occasionally giving up, and almost always struggling—is essential for understanding what adults with learning disabilities perceive they face in the workplace. Whether we do or do not decide that their advice is worth following, we should at least improve our understanding, and perhaps our empathy, because we have walked a mile in their shoes.

There are other reasons for listening to these personal voices. Individual experiences may suggest individual strategies. Developing highly individualized approaches may hold the greatest promise for employment success. The population of adults with learning disabilities is, both by definition and observation, heterogeneous. Consequently, adults with learning disabilities may find the best suggestions for achieving in the workplace not from general "how-to" recipes but rather from picking and choosing among a range of unique recollections. What may be idiosyncratic for many may be "just the ticket" for others. Further, research has indicated the limited usefulness of generic vocational–technical training programs for students with learning disabilities (Shapiro & Lentz, 1991). Instead, offering students a chance to sample occupational trades and focusing on personal career choice may provide more effective vocational preparation (Shapiro & Lentz, 1991).

A Model for Employment Success

A particularly intriguing source of wisdom is the counsel of highly successful adults with learning disabilities. These individuals have proven conclusively that some persons with learning disabilities have the wherewithal and talent to succeed in the workplace in spite of serious difficulties with processing information. Gerber, Ginsberg, and Reiff (1992)[1] conducted in-depth ethnographic interviews of 71 successful adults with learning disabilities. The adults in this study had managed to gain a considerable amount of control over their professional lives. "Taking control" has particular import for persons with learning disabilities. The experience of living with learning disabilities often means a loss of control, with much attention focused on what the individual cannot do. The autonomy of persons with learning disabilities may be undermined, especially as they find they have great difficulty with tasks that others take in stride. They feel "out-of-control."

The adults in Gerber et al.'s (1992) study developed attitudes and behaviors that put them back in control and facilitated their achievements. They clearly articulated reasons for their success in the workplace:

They developed a *desire* to succeed: "You've got to have that inner sense that you're going to do it, want to do it. If you don't want to do it, you are not going to be successful. You might have to do one step at a time and go slower. But . . . you have to be determined in life if you are going to make it."

They adopted a clear sense of *goal orientation:* "Successful people have a plan. You have to have a plan, goals, strategy, otherwise you are flying through the clouds and then you hit the mountain."

They engaged in a process of *reframing* (in a sense, redefining) the learning disabilities experience during which they recognized, accepted, and understood the meaning of their learning disabilities, and consequently developed a sense of how to use their unique abilities, mindful of both strengths and weaknesses: "You have to look within yourself. Accept that your brain may be mechanically handicapped, but you can optimize or give up. Try to look at success around you . . . you have brain power . . . use it."

They exhibited extraordinary *persistence and resilience:* "I'm a real believer in determination. It is three quarters of the battle. There are tons

---

[1]The quotations from the Gerber et al. (1992) study used in this chapter may be found in Reiff, H. B., Gerber, P. J., & Ginsberg, R. (in press). *Exceeding expectations: Successful adults with learning disabilities.* Austin, TX: PRO-ED.

of geniuses in the world who never make it and there are lots of people with personality who don't. The difference between making it and not is determination . . . you absolutely have to stick with it."

They found a *goodness of fit* between their abilities and their work environments: "Capitalize on your strengths . . . Look at what you can do best and enjoy most."

They developed and relied on many kinds of *learned creativity* to cope with, compensate for, and overcome the challenges their learning disabilities presented: "Other people don't seem to look at the possibilities available to accomplish a task. When I have been able to handle tougher jobs, it has always been because I could approach a problem in a different way, a little easier way. I have always tended to think of ways to do things that are a little unusual."

They formed *favorable social ecologies* or interpersonal and interdependent support networks: "You need other people to help . . . to help you believe in yourself. But you must be willing to accept some help, from a secretary or anyone. Otherwise, you will waste too much time. You must learn to depend on others to a certain extent."

As adults with learning disabilities incorporate these characteristics, they increase the likelihood of attaining employment success. Nevertheless, the proportions, sequencing, and interactions of the components of the model for employment success will vary with each individual. There are no absolute "how to's" in the workplace. There are, however, some helpful guidelines for "do's and don't's." Based on their experiences and successful outcomes, the adults in this study offered specific advice to other individuals with learning disabilities in the workplace. To a great extent, they exhorted others to develop and capitalize on the characteristics described in the model of success.

Gerber, Reiff, and Ginsberg (1996) have termed reframing the *trigger mechanism to adaptability*. Surely, a clear sense of self, of one's strengths and weaknesses, must liberate and motivate one to determine goals effectively; to develop goodness of fit; to devise compensations, modifications, and strategies to cope with employment demands; to self-advocate; and to build an interpersonal support network.

> Whatever you do, just go for it! Don't worry about people who try to tell you that you can't do it. In order to get where you want to go sometimes you can't make it on the route you want to take. It's the same with anybody. So you have to accept the fact that you might have to start all over again. If you really want to do it that much, you are going to do it.

> Take the hard work to be your friend. You will be able to think, to function, to succeed at a level a normal person could never reach for. When you are faced with adversaries, forgive them, for they know not what they do. Accept them and move forward. Don't give up!
>
> Be all that you can be. Like yourself. Desire to be happy. The price one pays is worth the reward. And stand up and say, "I failed." So what! Don't worry about what everyone else thinks. It's so hard to climb out of it. You still have to. Because of those experiences, what a great asset you can be to to others that hurt. If you can use dyslexia or LD to your advantage, use it. You can't blame anyone else for how you feel.

We must place these exhortations within the context of reframing. As much as adults with learning disabilities emphasize the importance of perseverance, success tends to result from knowing when to apply this attribute. Sometimes sticking with it does lead to victory; at others, it simply intensifies frustration (Spekman, Goldberg, & Herman, 1993). The successful adults with learning disabilities confronted their strengths and weaknesses, adapted to demands put upon them, and decided to expect positive outcomes. A neurologist (and former physicist) with dyslexia explained:

> The biggest thing is my adaptability and the fact that frustrations or problems haven't gotten me down. Probably the reason I didn't quit is because I wasn't programmed with expectations about what I ought to do . . . It's the adaptability and not feeling bad about yourself that gives you the strength to make use of what you have . . . I am probably the least lonely and least insecure person you'll ever meet.

The desire to succeed, the willingness to persist, to work harder and longer than colleagues, and an indefatigable sense of resilience surfaced repeatedly in the interviews. Successful adults with learning disabilities have gone beyond the notion of simply accepting that hard work is necessary. They have set out to demonstrate unequivocally that their learning disabilities will not hold them back. "Just tell me I can't do it, and I'll do it," proclaimed one individual. Another revealed, "If you want me to finish something, challenge me and say you can't do it . . . I'll be damned to prove you wrong, (to show) that I really can do it." Herein lies the special gift that some persons are able to find within their learning disabilities. Thus, we should expect successful adults with learning disabilities to develop a ferocious work ethic. Simply put, nothing can replace a concerted and unrelenting effort to get the job done:

Start early in the morning and stay up late at night to get the job done. Set up checks and balances for yourself.

Take work home and stay after work. Work harder and do better and you will stay in business. Life is not fair so be thankful for the positive things you have.

Work harder than the average person and figure out what parts of the job you can do better than others and focus in on them. There are no shortcuts.

Work hard and try not to get (in) over your head because repeated failures make you anxious . . . Start off slowly, and as you get confidence, you can tackle more difficult things.

There is no way around the fact that to be equally successful, you're going to have to work harder.

The message could not be simpler. Yet it may be easier for highly successful people to subscribe to an almost fanatical belief in the power of "good old-fashioned hard work." After all, their hard work paid off handsomely. Are such comments merely the product of a rose-colored retrospective? Do less successful adults with learning disabilities recognize the virtue and utility of drive, determination, and perseverance, often in the face of seemingly insurmountable odds?

Interestingly, many other employed adults with learning disabilities reveal a similar perspective. I offer a graduate seminar in special education for which the final project involves interviewing an adult with a learning (or other) disability. Over the years, several graduate students, who tend to be teachers, have interviewed colleagues with learning disabilities. These colleagues are successfully employed, but we would not likely term them as "highly successful." Instead, they are like most of us—individuals of modest ambitions who try to do their best but do not expect to set the world on fire. One graduate student interviewed J, an assistant principal at a middle school, a "lifer" at the middle-management level of public education. He has found his niche by applying this principle of persistence: "Keep hanging in there. It can be overcome . . . Just be persistent. That's the only way I succeeded, because I was persistent."

Similarly, D is a special education teacher in a public high school. He struggled to get through college. He struggles with much of the day-to-day routine of teaching. But his comments could have come from one of the participants in the highly successful adult study:

I don't want to be a different person. I like what I've done with my life and how I've gotten here. It's given me a good work ethic, how to deal with failure and appreciate success. Helped my teaching . . . I have a strong work ethic—work, work, work! The problem with most LD kids is that they're not workaholics and don't have a work ethic . . . You've got to confront the problem. A lot of teenagers bend away from it and don't want to deal with it. It causes a lot of problems later in front of your employer or a group of people . . . You never lose that disability . . . If you don't deal with it, you pretty much become a prisoner to the problem. You never get out of that box if you don't open the door and let others things in. New information. Being afraid of how the world sees you . . . I think LD kids have to go through a period of grieving. 'Hey, I'm different! I do things different.' But you can't drown in your own self-pity. You have to go on with life because life's going to go on whether you do or not.

D's comment also integrates the theme of reframing, urging persons with learning disabilities to recognize, accept, and understand who they are, and then to move on proactively with their lives. Again, D sounded the same call as those from highly successful adults, which validates the critical importance of reframing the learning disabilities experience. From different walks of life, adults with learning disabilities have voiced belief in the power of an unadulterated gut-check.

The specific components of the success model surfaced in specific suggestions to employees with learning disabilities. Some comments focused on the issue of finding a good fit between one's strengths and weaknesses and the type of career or work environment:

Realize your limitations. Know what you can do and you can't do. Interview for the job you can do. Accentuate your abilities and not your disabilities.

Be yourself. Don't be false. Build on your strengths and push your weaknesses aside.

Don't go into a work situation in which you will have to perform in your area of disability. Your employer will think you are stupid, and you'll feel stupid . . . Emphasize strengths and be dedicated.

Find out what kind of work you are suited for.

You can't worry about problems. Don't ignore them, but find something you like doing. If you work hard at it, you will succeed.

You have to find out exactly what your weak points are. Work to improve them completely. Be realistic. Don't choose a profession that stresses your weaknesses. You'll make yourself miserable . . . Be honest with yourself.

These highly successful individuals are not the only persons with learning disabilities who recognize the importance of goodness of fit. Gerber and Reiff (1991) interviewed adults with learning disabilities whose employment outcomes ranged from successful to marginal. The adults who had found success had been able to match their particular talents with their jobs. They had made necessary adaptations, both within themselves and to the work environment. Conversely, the individuals who were having significant difficulties adjusting to the demands of the workplace had been unable to establish a good fit.

One young adult had a history of a quick succession of job failures. G had had problems with mechanical work: "Mechanic work is not too good a job for me to be in . . . . You read a work order, and you have to remember everything on it, everything to do . . . . So many things to do that I'd leave a few things and forget them and not even know they were there. And somebody would say, 'What about this?' Pressure is, like, work orders" (p. 64). He also had trouble matching his penchant for perfection with the realities of the workplace. "Every job I have, I put pride into it. And I figure I did a good job, and the guy says, 'You took so long!' Like okay, man. And I'm sitting here trying to be perfect and he says, 'You're taking too long doing it.' And I've been taken off the jobs. I'll be doing something great, but I'll be doing it too slow" (p. 64).

The inability of G to find goodness of fit was not simply a matter of landing the right job. He would have fared better if his employers had been willing to help him; employers are often in a position to fine-tune a job description that will promote the strengths and not emphasize the weaknesses of the employee. Thus, successful adults with learning disabilities recognize the role employers can play in hiring individuals with learning disabilities for jobs that fit their capabilities:

Find a place where LD people can fit. If a person is willing to put forth the effort, he deserves a chance to try in different areas.

Interview to see if you can match the situation to the talent. Place them in a job where you can optimize their strengths.

Keep them away from what they cannot do. You can hire an acute dyslexic, but not for a job requiring reading.

Match skills with the job. Don't set up that person for what he cannot do.

The employer should see the strengths during the interview process and should put the person with LD into a job that emphasizes their strengths. Push people's talents.

> Realize that LDs have tremendous capabilities in many different areas. Be flexible in the types of job assignments.

> The employer should realize that learning disabled people will be better employees than most people as long as employers understand what they can do. They tend to be more conscientious. They are on time and dependable. You just have to be careful not to put them in a job they cannot do. It may take longer for them to adjust to a task at hand, but once they do, they'll do a great job for you.

Responsive employers surely would have increased the likelihood for G to fit his jobs better. However, another factor contributed to G's difficulty with developing goodness of fit. He did not devise the kinds of coping mechanisms that might have allowed him to demonstrate his skills without exacerbating his weaknesses. Thus, it is not surprising that highly successful adults with learning disabilities encourage employees with learning disabilities to develop and use compensations, modifications, and strategies to meet the demands of the workplace.

> Be a military strategist. Find out exactly where your weak points are and work to improve them or figure out ways around them.

> Be flexible; learn . . . Don't keep yourself on a track leading to disaster.

> Recognize what your limitations are, strengths and weaknesses. Then *deal* with them.

> Identify strengths and weaknesses at an early age so accommodations can be made.

Studies of other adults with learning disabilities have highlighted the advantages of learned creativity on the job. D, the assistant principal, has learned to compensate for his writing deficiencies in a variety of creative ways:

> You always have to be aware. If I'm going into a situation where I might have to write something down, I always think, "Is this going to be a situation where I'm going to have to write something down, do a lot of writing?" If it is, I try to think through what I might have to say and are there words I need to use. I learn how to spell them before I go into the situation. Or, if I'm going into a business to write a check, I'll always make sure I can spell the name of the business. The hardest thing I probably had to do was when I had to take the assessment to become an administrator. You had to write for about four hours, and that about killed me. I think they told me I had 14 misspelled words.

What they didn't know was there were more misspelled words but my writing was so poor. They said my writing was very poor. Well, of course it was; that's how I disguised my misspelled words. They weren't smart enough to figure it out. I sat there and smiled at them and thought, 'You jerks.' I actually got a real high score on that.

J devised clever internal coping mechanisms. Learned creativity, however, is not limited to what a given individual can devise; it can encompass the entire scope of assistive technology. As Raskin, Higgins, and Herman have described in Chapter 15 of this book, employees and employers with learning disabilities may profit substantially from using assistive technology. At the outset, adults with learning disabilities in the workplace need to be aware of the existence of such technologies. Many individuals are aware of what have become commonplace technologies: word processing, spell and grammar checks, talking calculators, audio memo gadgets, and so forth. Fewer individuals have familiarity with the burgeoning software industry that is constantly making everything—from speech synthesis to complex, conceptual written language organizers—available and financially feasible to anyone with a contemporary personal computer. One of the quickest (and most fascinating) ways to increase knowledge of available technologies, particularly software, is to "surf the Internet" or explore the World Wide Web. For example, entering the terms "learning disabilities" and "technology" on any number of web search engines will unleash a veritable fount of potentially relevant information. (In a 10-minute search, I came across a number of sites devoted to assistive technology for persons with disabilities, including Assistive Technology Online, a particularly useful link.)

Knowing what is available is merely a preliminary step in utilizing assistive technologies. The usefulness of any accommodation, modification, or adaptive device directly depends on the the ability to assess one's own needs accurately. Once again, reframing takes on paramount importance in choosing effective technologies. Moreover, the individual with learning disabilities must incorporate goodness of fit into this decision-making process, for the need and impact of various technologies varies from workplace to workplace.

Employees with learning disabilities will be more likely to devise creative coping mechanisms if their employers are aware of their needs and willing to help. Success in the workplace will be quite difficult without an employer who is open to compensatory strategies for successful performance (Gerber, 1992). Consequently, these successful adults recognize the efficacy of employers working collaboratively with employees with learning disabilities:

> Eventually LD people get to a point where their disability is overtaxed. Provide them with support or provide opportunities to use their talents to a maximum.

> Reach out and help them realize what their contributions can be. Help them discover how their personal style and skills can contribute to the organization.

> If disability is unrelated to the task but may come up, be clear about whether assistance will be available or if it doesn't matter.

> Have inservices and brochures . . . help educate them.

> Realize they may need some special guidelines like extra time spans to work at their own pace.

> Provide for reasonable accommodations.

The final component in the model of success, favorable social ecologies—the proactive development and building of interpersonal support systems—also received attention in the advice from highly successful adults with learning disabilities. Building favorable social ecologies not only includes a willingness to get help when needed, but also a determination to assert one's strengths. The first step in this process usually begins with self-disclosure, a particularly thorny issue for persons with learning disabilities. In spite of assurances of nondiscrimination in the era of ADA, many employees fear, perhaps rightly in some situations, that disclosure of learning disabilities may have negative repercussions. S. Arnold (personal communication, March, 1996) developed a 12-hour seminar designed for adults with learning disabilities who are transitioning to either postsecondary education or new jobs, addressing the issue of whether, when, and how to self-disclose. These decisions vary with each employment situation. A number of adults with learning disabilities have difficulty knowing when and how to self-disclose because they do not pick up on social and other environmental cues. S. Arnold (personal communication, March, 1996) asserted that role-playing various scenarios has helped adults with learning disabilities in the program make informed decisions. Moreover, adults with learning disabilities in Arnold's program often have created a formal and structured mechanism for self-disclosure, in the form of a letter or brochure about themselves. Obviously, each was individually oriented, but Arnold (personal communication, March, 1996) has identified the following common ingredients:

1. Why I am writing/doing this?

2. My strengths

3. My weaknesses

4. How I am going to compensate?

5. What will I need from someone else (accommodations)?

6. Why I am a good risk anyway!

At some level, self-disclosure will only be truly effective if the employer and colleagues really want to help. In some cases, it may be necessary to educate others in the workplace about the contributions individuals with learning disabilities can make. A colleague of mine from Great Britain has offered some useful insights about developing support systems in the workplace (M. Radford, personal communication, March, 1996):

> Most people underestimate people with disabilities and try to think for them. They have brains of their own and usually know best how to cope with their disability. If you tell them the end result you want, they will find their own way of getting there. Make sure someone is on hand to help them find another way, usually someone with a creative mind, like the "arty" person in the department or someone who has suffered the loss of limb or sight or whatever at some time in their past. If the person allocated to include the person with the disability in the department is not receptive then it is a no-win situation, and you might as well not attempt it.

Advice from highly successful adults with learning disabilities paralleled the preceding thoughts on self-disclosure and self-advocacy. They recognize that the employer must not only be aware of the needs of employees with learning disabilities but be prepared to address those needs proactively. A responsive employer will need to understand the paradoxical manifestations that learning disabilities may present:

> You have to give LD people equal treatment. But that may also require extra patience sometimes.

> You have to be understanding. Competition can be hard. You have to understand that an LD person can look brutally stupid but actually be quite brilliant. He can look stupid at one point then carry the day on an important issue.

> Learn their strengths and forgive their weaknesses.

Highly successful adults with learning disabilities also recognize that the responsibility for effective self-advocacy ultimately rests squarely on the shoulder of the individual with special needs:

> Make your fellow employees aware that there are certain areas that you are weak in, and you have other areas that you are dynamite in. Don't forget to tell them that it may take longer for you to catch on, but once you do, you'll have a great co-worker.

> The less defensive you are, the more help you can get. The more support systems you can use, the more easily you will develop.

Keeping Work in Perspective

Western culture tends to place great emphasis on success in the workplace. Certainly, as adults with learning disabilities achieve employment success, they will develop and display a sense of worth and competence both to themselves and others. Nevertheless, we should remain circumspect about emphasizing the workplace as the sole area that can provide personal validation. Adulthood presents a slew of critical life events. Supportive relationships, interests and hobbies, and religious and community involvement all present opportunities for adults with learning disabilities to find fulfillment, a sense of purpose and meaning, a profound source of satisfaction with adult outcomes (Werner, 1993). Even highly successful adults with learning disabilities frequently define "success" in personal terms far removed from their career achievements. Consider the following perspectives:

> My definition of success is a life that is balanced, a life that is satisfying. It's not a life that I'm compulsively striving after. It's a life in which I'm moving at a pace which is both healthy and satisfying and productive. But the priorities and goals of my life are clear—those goals being maintaining loving, good, functional relationships with my family members. It means maintaining a level of my health.

> At one time in my life I would have defined success strictly from a financial standpoint. Now, at the age of 45, I feel that there is more— such as family, success, success with people, and success with communication. A successful person is one who has a good mix of business, family and recreation. He is a person who has gotten his life together.

Conversely, in spite of successful employment experiences, individuals who do not find other sorts of engagement may find adulthood to be less than satisfying. Success may carry a hefty price tag. Clearly, for successful adults with learning disabilities, desire, determination, perseverance, and resilience represent a kind of aphorism. Is there such a thing as working too hard? Can one become obsessed with work? Can the demands of one's career diminish one's overall quality of life? Or, specifically in the case of learning disabilities, can the drive to prove that learning disabilities will not hold one back become all-consuming? Many of the successful adults pointedly stated that the basis of their desire was to show the world they were not "idiots."

We probably all know individuals whose work has taken over their lives; at times, we may only have to look in the mirror. Many adults with learning disabilities do share this concern; the issue is exacerbated by the credo that working harder than anyone else is simply a means to level the playing field. Thus, one adult with learning disabilities in the Gerber and Reiff (1991) study described himself as "constantly anxious" because he pushed himself so hard. He harbored some regrets about the toll his determination exacted: ". . . It was determination so rabid that sometimes I might even step on people in the way. . . . Sure, it's great to succeed. It's great to excel. It's fine to have determination. But you don't have to step on people" (p. 109). As a result, his present goal is to reconnect with some of the pleasures that life offers: "The last 4 or 5 years, I believe, I'm beginning to learn how to play and relax a little more" (p. 107).

The importance of balance in one's life cannot be overemphasized . Shessel (1995) interviewed 14 adults with learning disabilities who had found varying degrees of success in the workplace. The summary of their advice to people with learning disabilities recapitulated much of the model for employment success generated by highly successful adults. Shessel's participants encouraged others to "be tenacious," "develop self-discipline," "set goals for yourself," "learn to take risks," "believe in yourself," "like who you are," "understand 'who you are,' your strengths and weaknesses," "take responsibility," "make the right career match," "learn to work through your strengths," "be creative and flexible in problem solving (look at alternatives)," "develop a good support network," "ask for help when you need it," and "learn to 'speak for yourself' (self-advocacy skills)" (p. 177). Equally important, these adults with learning disabilities recognized that there is more to life than work. They also suggested that adults with learning disabilities "develop good stress management strategies," "strive for balance in your life," and "learn to laugh at yourself" (p. 177).

In sum, by listening to the thoughts of persons with learning disabilities, we are reminded that they are people first. They do not live in a vacuum circumscribed by disability. In much of their lives, learning disabilities are simply not an issue. They do strive to lead full and productive lives in the broadest sense. Employment success is important, but it is only one component of successful adult adjustment.

The author acknowledges the contributions of Paul Trask and Jacqueline Wisnauskas, two graduate students whose interview projects added much to this chapter.

References

Blackorby, J., & Wagner, M. (1996). Longitudinal postschool outcomes of youth with disabilities: Findings from the National Longitudinal Transition Study. *Exceptional Children, 62,* 399–413.

Gerber, P. J. (1992). Personal perspective—at first glance: Employment for people with learning disabilities at the beginning of the Americans with Disabilities Act era. *Learning Disability Quarterly, 15,* 4.

Gerber, P. J., Ginsberg, R., & Reiff, H. B. (1992). Identifying alterable patterns in employment success for highly successful adults with learning disabilities. *Journal of Learning Disabilities, 25,* 475–487.

Gerber, P. J., & Reiff, H. B (1991). *Speaking for themselves: Ethnographic interviews with adults with learning disabilities.* Ann Arbor, MI: The University of Michigan Press.

Gerber, P. J., Reiff, H. B., & Ginsberg, R. (1996). Reframing the learning disabilities experience. *Journal of Learning Disabilities, 29,* 98–101, 97.

McCue, M., Chase, S. L., Dowdy, C. A., Pramuka, M., Petrick, J., Aitken, S., & Fabry, P. (1994). *Functional assessment of individuals with cognitive disabilities: A desk reference for rehabilitation.* Pittsburgh, PA: Center for Applied Neuropsychology Associates.

Moody, S. (1995). *Dyslexia in the workplace.* Kensington, G. B.: The Adult Dyslexia Organisation.

Reiff, H. B., Gerber, P. J., & Ginsberg, R. (in press). *Exceeding Expectations: Successful Adults with Learning Disabilities.* Austin, TX: PRO-ED.

Reisman, E. S., & Reisman, J. I. (1993). Supervision of employees with moderate special needs. *Journal of Learning Disabilities, 26,* 199–206.

Shessel, I. (1995). *Adults with learning disabilities: Profiles in survival.* Unpublished doctoral dissertation. Toronto, Canada: University of Toronto.

Shapiro, E. S., & Lentz, F. E. (1991). Vocational-technical programs: Follow-up of students with learning disabilities. *Exceptional Children, 58,* 47–60.

Spekman, N. J., Goldberg, R. J., & Herman, K. L. (1993). An exploration of risk and resilience in the lives of individuals with learning disabilities. *Learning Disabilities Research and Practice, 8* (1), 11–18.

Werner, E. E. (1993). Risk and resilience in individuals with learning disabilities: Lessons learned form the Kauai longitudinal study. *Learning Disabilities Research and Practice, 8*(1), 28–34.

CHAPTER 17

Slow Words, Quick Images— Dyslexia as an Advantage in Tomorrow's Workplace

Thomas G. West

*I've always felt that I have more of an ability to envision,
to be able to anticipate where things are going, to conceive a solution
to a business problem than people who are more sequential thinkers.*

> —CHARLES SCHWAB, explaining that his struggle with his
> own dyslexia has helped him to develop other abilities,
> "The Schwab Revolution," cover article, *Business Week*,
> December 19, 1994.

*I don't read long articles period. I don't like to read. I am dyslexic
and I find it hard. When people send me long [e-mail] messages,
I ignore them. The only print medium I read every day
is the front page of the* Wall Street Journal, *which
I scan for news of the companies I am interested in.
All the rest of my reading is on screens, and often not
very good screens, because I travel so much.*

> —NICHOLAS NEGROPONTE, "Being Nicholas—
> The [MIT] Media Lab's visionary founder . . .
> is the most wired man we know (and that is saying
> something)," cover interview, *Wired* magazine,
> November 1995.

*Back in the days when I was growing up, nobody knew
what dyslexia was . . . . So everybody thought you were lazy
or stupid or both. And I didn't think I was, but I wasn't sure.
I had a lot of drive, and if somebody told me I was stupid,
that usually helped—it really helped me take a lot more risks.
For someone that everybody thinks is going to grow up to pump gas,
you can take all the risks you want. Because if you fail, it doesn't matter.*

> —JOHN R. (JACK) HORNER, who flunked out of the
> University of Montana six times; later, "his brilliant
> synthesis of evidence . . . forced paleontologists to
> revise their ideas about dinosaur behavior, physiology,
> and evolution," "The Iconoclastic Fossil Hunter,"
> cover article, *The Chronicle of Higher Education*,
> November 16, 1994.

Over the lifetime of today's students, many of the basic verbal and clerical skills that have long dominated education at all levels will cease to be important in an economy and marketplace where these tasks will be increasingly taken over by semi-intelligent machines. With these changes, the visual–spatial talents, global thinking, mental models, pattern recognition, creative problem solving and other non-verbal abilities often associated with dyslexia are expected to become increasingly important in tomorrow's workplace, as greater use is made of data visualization, computer graphics, and interactive multi-sensory technologies to understand and communicate information about complex systems and discontinuous trends. As everyone struggles to accommodate themselves to deep changes in thinking and working, some dyslexics will doubtless play, once again, their oft-repeated role—working creatively at the edge of the new frontier, reading little but learning much, experimenting, innovating, establishing a path forward—learning from direct experience, anticipating where things are going, taking risks.

In the long view, ideas of ability and talent in the workplace are conditional and depend on the context of the times. After decades of rapid change in many areas but remarkable continuity in others, it now appears that we are going through a new period of major change—turning upside down conventional ideas of what is worth doing, what is worth learning, and who is considered intelligent. The kinds of education that prepared our generation and our parents' generation for their work may be entirely unsuitable for our students and our children, whether or not they are dyslexic.

Some 50 years ago, Norbert Weiner in his book *Cybernetics* (1948, 1961) predicted a sequence of events that we can see unfolding today. He also set forth the context in which we might usefully think about education and work in a rapidly changing world. According to Weiner, we are seeing a repeating cycle. In the last century, muscle power was taken over by machines and no one could make a living wage in competition with the new machines. Similarly, in the near future, those with clerical skills or even those with pedestrian academic, managerial, or professional skills may find it increasingly difficult to find buyers for their services in the marketplace. We know that machines have replaced assembly line workers and bank tellers, and we may not be surprised to see an erosion of opportunities for those with certain manual or clerical skills. However, many of us still may not be ready to adjust our fundamental thinking based on unprecedented changes in many managerial and professional roles—as with the unrelenting elimination of middle management, for example.

Weiner, one of the fathers of computing and control systems, saw it all coming long ago. Writing from The National Institute of Cardiology in Mexico City in 1947, he explained: "Perhaps I may clarify the historical background of the present situation if I say that the first industrial revolution, the revolution of the 'dark satanic mills,' was the devaluation of the human arm by the competition of machinery." Once this form of competition was in place, there would be "no rate of pay at which a . . . pick-and-shovel laborer can live which [would be] low enough to compete with the work of a steam shovel. . . ."

In the next phase, which is currently unfolding all around us, "the modern industrial revolution is similarly bound to devalue the human brain, at least in its simpler and more routine decisions." There are likely to be some exceptions: "Of course, just as the skilled carpenter, the skilled mechanic, the skilled dressmaker have in some degree survived the first industrial revolution, so the skilled scientist and the skilled administrator may survive the second." However, the overall trend is clear: ". . . Taking the second revolution as accomplished, the average human being of mediocre attainments or less has nothing to sell that is worth anyone's money to buy" (Weiner, *Cybernetics,* 1961).

We can easily see the prescience of Weiner's observations, as machines have increased in power by many orders of magnitude since his day—and as his second revolution moves closer to completion with increasing rapidity. We now know that many of the most routine functions of the copy editor, the bank clerk, and bookkeeper are already being done more rapidly and more cheaply by machines. In similar fashion, we may soon be seeing the beginnings of a less-expected trend: "expert" computer systems and artificial life "agents" learning to reliably replicate the more routine professional judgments of attorneys, engineers, accountants, architects, physicians, and investment bankers. This is no longer a matter of distant speculation. Referring to the work of Stanford University economist Paul Krugman, *The Economist* magazine has carried this observation: "Lawyers and accountants . . . could be today's counterparts of early-19th-century weavers, whose incomes soared after the mechanisation of spinning only to crash when the technological revolution [finally] reached their own craft" (*Economist,* 1995).

In the half-century since Weiner's sobering appraisal, much has come about that was unexpected, but the basic form and direction of this relentless and accelerating trend has remained unchanged. It has become increasingly clear that not only clerical and other "low-level" functions are subject to threat—but also, in time, many functions and jobs are threatened which formerly were thought to require high intelligence and advanced degrees. These changes force us to rethink the fundamentals of education and work. The rules of the game are changing in dramatic and unexpected ways. We will all need to adjust our ideas of talent and intelligence. And, in this world turned upside down, we may expect that many of the students who are at the bottom of the class in the old word-dominated system will rise to the top of the class in a new world where the real work will involve the manipulation of visual–spatial patterns—traditional areas of strength for many dyslexics. Most of us are so accustomed to the old ways that we find it hard to see in this new way. However, we might be persuaded that this new way of thinking is correct, to some extent, when we consider that, among the most creative leaders and visionary innovators in these new technology areas, it is not hard to find individuals with varied dyslexic traits along with their high visual–spatial abilities.

Word Bound

Written language is only a technology. In the long history of human survival, technologies change—and some inborn traits may help or hinder proficiency in the particular technologies dominant at one time or another. As technologies change, the kind of brain that lends itself poorly to an old technology may be just what is wanted with a new technology.

Reading and writing are only adaptations to a particular technology. Dyslexics have long been plagued with the mismatch of their abilities to the requirements of education and employment—the requirements of this particular technology. Sometimes, one who is surprisingly slow with certain verbal tasks—making them appear to be of low intelligence—may be strikingly fast and proficient in certain high-level, visual–spatial, non-verbal tasks. For some, this pattern has long been recognized. But for many others—schooled to assume, deep down, that intelligence is unitary (and largely verbal)—this is a new and revolutionary idea.

It is remarkable to see how many very well-educated people can be totally unaware of the one-sidedness of their views on verbal intelligence. They may argue, for example, that it is impossible to think clearly without words. Of course, those who make such statements often work in heavily word-bound occupations. However, much also depends on the culture of the workplace. In some organizations, there must be endless memoranda before anything can be done. Many still assume that one is not intelligent if one does not use words skillfully and often—a frequent assumption, especially in academic circles. In others, most communication is oral and is oriented to action; memos are almost never written. When it comes to a really successful design or strategy or the forward-looking decision that allows an organization to survive, the skill of writing may be seen as unimportant or irrelevant.

The peculiarity of overemphasis on words in the larger context of human development interests Stephen Jay Gould, who has observed: "Primates are visual animals. No other group of mammals relies so strongly on sight. Our attraction to images as a source of understanding is both primal and pervasive. Writing, with its linear sequencing of ideas, is a historical afterthought in the history of human cognition. Yet traditional scholarship has lost this root to our past. Most research is reported by text alone, particularly in the humanities and social sciences. Pictures, if included at all, are poorly reproduced, gathered in a center section divorced from relevant text, and treated as little more than decoration" (Gould, 1993).

The importance of the underused visual side also is acknowledged by Howard Gardner. Although he argues for several forms of intelligence, he readily recognizes a special status for visual–spatial intelligence in contrast to verbal intelligence. "In the view of many, spatial intelligence is the 'other intelligence'—the one that should be arrayed against, and be considered equal in importance to, 'linguistic intelligence.' . . . For most of the tasks used by experimental psychologists, linguistic and spatial intelligences provide the principle sources of storage and solution" (Gardner, 1983).

We are not trying, of course, to underrate the value of the written word. Its power is obvious and pervasive in literature, politics, religion, history, science—indeed, in almost every sphere of knowledge—and in every means of transmitting knowledge across the generations. Its power is so great, however, that many have been in danger of believing that it is all that there is. Most of our institutions are built around it. The role of language will always be extremely important, whether written or recorded or transmitted in some other manner. But the case we are trying to make is that the new visual technologies will promote a greater balance between words and images—involving a gradual shift to using non-verbal capacities in doing high-level and high-value work. With these changes, the words will be used to comment, to point out, to discuss. But the real center of the work—the real application of talent—will be in understanding the images, not the words. If our expectations are correct, those who wish to do this kind of high-level work will need to be as comfortable with images as they are with words. They will no longer be allowed to work in the one-sided manner now commonplace in many fields.

Appearances can be deceiving. A storyteller was once asked how it was possible to remember all the words for his many traditional stories. His reply was that he rarely remembered any words, as such. Rather, he saw a story or he would see a movie in his mind's eye—and merely related in words what he saw in images (C. Kleymeyer, personal communication, 1985). This process is entirely different from that of memorizing text. Yet, to some extent, in the end, they are both doing the same thing. Accordingly, we may argue that the old system of education and work paid too much attention to the words alone—partly because words are so powerful, so relatively cheap, and so linked to the dominant media of paper and books. However, with the new visualization technologies and techniques, we might expect to find that the process of rendering ideas visually may be made sufficiently rapid and inexpensive to allow a shift toward broader use of this additional mode of communication—permitting more of us to understand and communicate concepts about areas of life and thought that do not lend themselves readily to the world of words.

Many professionals who deal with those with dyslexia and academic learning disabilities assume that career options are limited for this population in a world long dominated by words. They start with the assumption that the main task is to remediate areas of weakness to come up to the standard required in a word-oriented world. They rarely look for non-verbal strengths—and they almost never focus on the development of these strengths. Similarly, many seem to feel that it is hard to gain appropriate accommodations for their clients. However, resourceful dyslexics are already (and have always been) involved in demanding educational programs and demanding occupations—often having constructed accommodations invisible to teachers, employers, and almost everyone around them. It may be argued, further, that many dyslexics are leaders in a range of demanding occupations mainly because of special abilities common among dyslexics, not mainly because of their cleverness in overcoming dyslexic difficulties. We might expect that the current direction of technological change will progressively favor the talents that many dyslexics have while their difficulties are likely to become less and less important over time.

Accordingly, we might consider asking not how dyslexics can be fixed to fit within a word-bound culture. Rather, we might wish to consider how we might be able to follow the lead of dyslexics who are already highly successful—to move beyond a word-bound culture. We should try to find out how successful dyslexics have been able to identify and develop areas of special talent—as ideas of special talent change over time. Skill in reading and writing was once vocationally less important—for farmers, sailors, shipbuilders, mothers, weavers, merchants, warriors, craftsmen, and kings. Now, we assume that the need for conventional literacy is almost universal; soon, we may consider the growing need for a new form of visual "literacy." It may not be long before visualization technologies and techniques spread into many areas that formerly were regarded as the exclusive domain of words. Thus, in this new more balanced world, we might expect a higher regard for a range of abilities—and a higher regard for the needed contributions of people who are unusually good with images, despite their trouble with words.

The MIT Disease

In order to understand what the possibilities may be in a transformed world of education and work, it is useful to look at examples from a range of fields, including the famous and the not-so-famous. It is hard to predict what will actually unfold, but we should expect to see patterns of strengths and weaknesses as varied as the dyslexics themselves. New economic conditions suggest that all of us will have to learn to work at very high levels of effectiveness. This means that all of us will need to find and develop areas of strength and talent consistent with new realities—areas, perhaps, quite different from those we would have selected only a short time ago.

It is not surprising that some of our exemplary dyslexics are to be found at the leading edge of technological change. One example is Nicholas Negroponte, founding director of the Media Lab at MIT. Early in 1995, he was touring the U.S. promoting his new book, *Being Digital*—a compilation of articles he had originally written for the highly successful and innovative new magazine *Wired*. Although the title of his book is *Being Digital*, remarkably, the first sentence on the first page of the introduction is not about computers. It says: "Being dyslexic, I don't like to read." (Negroponte, 1995, p. 3). It is important that Negroponte started his book with this oblique but telling observation. It is important because it encapsulates for us the paradox that we frequently observe: that—contrary to what we have been taught to believe—some of the most brilliant and forward-thinking individuals in our culture have had trouble with words. Sometimes, a great deal of trouble.

As we have suggested, this apparent paradox may be no accident. It is now becoming increasingly clear that often people with great visual–spatial or other non-verbal talents have "extraordinary brains"—brains that seem optimized to do tasks *other than* those normally called for in conventional word-dominated educational systems (Benbow, 1986; Galaburda, 1993; Gardner, 1983; Geschwind, 1982; Geschwind, 1984; Geschwind & Galaburda, 1987; West, 1990, 1991, 1992, 1994, 1995, 1996). It is also worth noting that Negroponte observed on radio talk shows during his book tour that dyslexia is so common at MIT that it is known locally as "the MIT disease." Moreover, it is evident that Negroponte does not avoid references to dyslexia in many different contexts, such as in the *Wired* interview quoted at the beginning of this article. We are a bit surprised to read Negroponte's statement: "I don't read long articles period. I don't like to read. I am dyslexic and I find it hard" (Bass, 1995).

More and more of those working at the edge of new technologies, in the sciences as well as business and the professions, are coming to recognize these surprising trends. For example, Dr. Larry Smarr, a physicist, astronomer, and director of a supercomputer center, recently commented, "I have often argued in my public talks that the graduate education process that produces physicists is totally skewed to selecting those with analytic skills and rejecting those with visual or holistic skills. I have claimed that with the rise of scientific visualization as a new mode of scientific discovery, a new class of minds will arise as scientists. In my own life, my 'guru' in computational science was a dyslexic and he certainly saw the world in a different and much more effective manner than his colleagues. . . ." (L. Smarr, personal communication, E–mail, September 1994) (See also Kaufmann & Smarr, 1993).

As the usefulness of computer data visualization continues to develop, the same visual–thinking abilities that have long served the most brilliant mathematicians and scientists, as well as the artists, craftsmen and mechanics, may increasingly come to serve the most creative and highest-level thinkers in business and other fields. Often, these visual thinkers will see emerging trends and new developments that their conventionally-trained competitors will not see. For some, this extra edge may make all the difference.

Seeing the Rhythm

Other examples of successful dyslexics are not hard to find in the computer industry. One young programmer/engineer's story is especially revealing. He said that he had been diagnosed as dyslexic in high school, but had nonetheless been able to make his way through college studying computer science. For some years, he has been working for a major manufacturer of advanced graphic systems, helping to design computer graphics hardware. In systems involving moving graphics, speed is extremely important. These graphic systems have to be extremely fast to recalculate the positions of all the colored dots in each quick frame of a moving image. In this context, this young man told how a special ability that his coworkers do not have seems to accompany his dyslexia. (R.M., personal communication, August 1993).

He could see the design of an entire graphics system in his mind's eye, he said. He could run the system in his head and see the pulsing and the rhythm of the data coursing through the circuits. Using this mental model, he also could see where the bottlenecks and the bugs are. He could say, for example, that if the loads of a certain set of chips were balanced differently, then the system would go 20% faster. His coworkers felt that it was impossible to know this without doing extensive simulations. Several weeks later, with simulations complete, they found that the corrected designs yielded exactly the performance increase that he had predicted.

In viewing this case, one should consider that this particular computer graphics company may have a considerable national and international competitive advantage, partly because they are making use of the special talents of one key dyslexic worker—one who is using talents that no one yet really understands. Indeed, one could say that this company emerged as a world leader in its industry in part because of an employee who still has a lot of trouble with reading, writing, and spelling.

Dying Spiders and Mental Models

The new mix of talents and skills needed in various parts of the computer industry seems to provide a natural opportunity for many dyslexics. The following long passage from a programmer in Britain provides an elegant profile of a pattern that might be much more common than we would expect. It serves to show a range of classically dyslexic difficulties and their interaction with family situations (described with artful humor) along with a most interesting set of special capabilities which, although little understood, are ideally suited to the novel requirements of this particular workplace.

> About 2 months ago the BBC showed a program in the Q.E.D. [popular science] series about dyslexia and learning difficulties . . . in which you were featured. I had before heard of various famous people being linked to dyslexia, especially Einstein and Churchill. But until seeing

your piece in the show, I think I generally assumed, like most people, that they were great men who had [just] overcome their difficulties to lead distinguished lives. I had not heard before the theory that their abilities could be a result or side effect of their dyslexia. I must say I find [this theory] most interesting. I do not work in any field of research associated with dyslexia but have suffered with the problem all my life.

As you can probably see, my spelling leaves a little to be desired and if you could see it you would know my handwriting is closer to spiders dying than text. However, I have never had any problem expressing myself verbally and have always been told I am very creative. I read very slowly and find new words difficult to read. . . . I avoid reading aloud as I tend to read very slowly and with little expression which generally gives the impression I am unintelligent. I can never be sure to get left and right correct first time.

Unfortunately, my mother used to be an English teacher and so finds all that kind of thing second nature. For a long time, she did not really believe that dyslexia existed but put my problems down to the usual sort of things—lazyness, doesn't concentrate, late developer, etc. My father has the same sort of problems as myself and it is a family joke that my mother used to send his (love) letters back to him with the spellings corrected! My education was mainly at boarding schools and my letters home got much the same treatment. The English teacher at school had the same attitude as my mother and the Headmaster was convinced that beating me enough would knock the laziness out of me. . . .

Anyway, that is just some background. Now back to the subject of your theory (and book). I have bought your book and am reading it (slowly!). I studied, and work in, computers and have done since I was 16. I have always found the subject extremely easy and can produce quite complex systems in very short time scales to a great degree of accuracy and relia-bility. This is based around an "intuition" I have for the way computers work. Once I know the different aspects of a system I can understand all the implications of a single change on the whole, in a way I find that my colleges cannot. They have to analyse each part of the system trying to work out the effect a change will have on that part before going on to the next part and analysing that, etc. This "higher" ability over my peers is something I have only realised more recently and your theory came at just the right time to help me explain the situations I was being faced with (J.S., personal communication, E-mail, September 7, 1995. Confirmed with specific permission, 1996). (E-mail informalities and spelling errors have been slightly corrected. British spelling has been preserved.)

It is especially significant that this programmer finds that, once he has internalized a mental model of the whole system, he can quickly see the effects of any change. This working method differs entirely from the step-by-step analysis of conventional usage and education. Yet one finds the same method in discussions among and about highly creative people.

Envisioning Solutions and Baby Dinosaurs

Another example, from a very different sphere, is Charles Schwab, the founder of a highly innovative and successful stock brokerage company. Like Negroponte, he might be called a "public dyslexic." Schwab often refers to his own dyslexia in press interviews. Also, he and his wife have established a foundation concerned with dyslexia and have worked for years to help parents in their local area understand the problems that he experienced himself and have been experienced by other members of his family (Robins, 1992).

Schwab had classic dyslexic difficulties in his school and university experience. However, Schwab—in cover articles in *Business Week* and elsewhere—attributes his business success in part to the special perspectives that seem to *come with* his dyslexia. As he says in the quotation at the beginning of this article, he is aware that he seems able to "envision" solutions and "anticipate" trends and customer desires better that his competition, while he innovates by using new technologies to serve larger numbers of clients at reduced cost. His coworkers and associates describe him as a big-picture thinker who sees what is needed and leaves the details to others—a combination that seems to be working quite well to keep his company a leader in the industry (Schwab, quoted in Mitchell, *Business Week*, 1995).

Another example from a quite different sphere is John (Jack) Horner, the source of the third passage quoted at the start of this article. Horner is especially interesting in his history of dramatic and persistent academic failures coupled with his correspondingly dramatic influence on the development of an entire field of study. His story forces us to reconsider, in deeper inquiry, what is really important in one's work and what is not. Horner proved to have extraordinary difficulties with activities that are largely peripheral to the discipline (reading, composition, test taking), but proved to be unusually gifted in those functions that lie at the heart of the discipline (being unusually observant while looking for fossils, being able to interpret the surprising patterns that emerge from fossil evidence, thinking his way beyond his associates, developing original and persuasive agruments based on the evidence).

Horner never earned an undergraduate degree. "He flunked out of the University of Montana six times, failing just about all his science courses, and never completing his undergraduate work." He had difficulty passing his courses, but all the time he was really learning, gaining the knowledge and experience needed to revolutionize a field. According to the curator of the museum of vertebrate paleontology at the University of California at Berkeley: "A lot of people have tended to underestimate Jack because he hasn't come through the traditional academic route. But he is, without question, one of the two or three most important people in the world today studying dinosaurs." Horner sees things differently and he sees things others do not see. For example, he feels that it is of little interest to find the fossil bones of a big adult dinosaur. What he wants to find is many dinosaurs of many sizes, in context, to try to understand the life of the animals and the ways they interacted with each other. Horner is known not only for his different perspectives, but also his remarkable ability to see in the field the tiny fossils of baby dinosaurs that other experts cannot find. According to another researcher: "He has a gift. . . . He can see things the rest of us don't see" (McDonald, 1994).

Seeing With Different Eyes

Seeing differently. Seeing the unseen. Understanding patterns with incomplete information. Comprehending the complex whole. In the past, some of the most original scientific thinkers have used their own special powers of imagination and visualization to build models within their own mind. Conversion to words and mathematical formulas followed, so they could be communicated to others. In most cases, however, it seems that the greatest interest has been in the resulting formulas that could then be memorized and tested—rarely in the visual modes of thought employed to arrive at these formulas. Recently, all this has begun to change. A number of trends in several fields are converging to revive long-dormant visual approaches.

During the past few years, with the development of new tools and techniques associated with graphic computers, the methods previously accessible to only a few highly gifted individuals (through imagination) are becoming available to much larger sectors of the less gifted population. What only a few highly visual thinkers could see in their minds' eyes now can been seen by many on the screens of these increasingly powerful and inexpensive machines.

In recent years, various research centers and the computer industry at large have been greatly stimulated by the rapid development of sophisticated graphics capabilities, especially those affording "scientific visualization"—that is, new techniques that allow scientific concepts or extremely large sets of data to be converted into moving color pictures on computer screens. According to one report, "with the advent of graphics, researchers can convert entire fields of variables . . . into color images." With these new techniques, "the information conveyed to the researcher undergoes a quantitative change, because it brings the eye–brain system, with its great pattern-recognition capabilities, into play in a way that is impossible with purely numeric data" (West, 1991).

These same technologies and techniques are finally finding their way into the world of business, trade, and finance as well—sometimes known as "Business Visualization" or for some "Biz Viz." Although there are still few companies using these techniques, evidence indicates that mainstream business users are just now beginning to take visualization techniques seriously. For example, in 1995 an issue of the *Economist* magazine carried an article about visualization of financial and trading data, featuring the products of a small Canadian company providing an "entire portfolio encapsulated as a three-dimensional moving picture." The article refers to the increased capacity of the New York Stock Exchange to handle complex information visually: "We're drowning in lots of data and we need ways of making sense of it." More significantly, the *Economist* article also suggested that the use of such software could have saved Barings Bank, the British bank that collapsed early in 1995 because of the actions of a rogue trader in their Singapore office. Uncovering the machinations of such a trader "is often a matter of luck rather than judgement." However, "with a 3-D view of what traders are doing, strange strategies or dangerous positions jump right out of the picture" (*Economist,* 1995).

Increasingly, specialists in many fields are coming to appreciate the power of visual approaches. However, at the same time, some are becoming aware of the curious fact observed by neurologists—that great visual talents do seem to come at some cost—that is, those who have very high visual talents sometimes seem to have corresponding areas of weakness, often in verbal areas.

Playing With Images

Historically, this pattern of high visual talents mixed with verbal weaknesses is evident in the lives of several extraordinarily creative thinkers. Albert Einstein was a strong visual thinker who, as many are aware, had notable difficulties in his early schooling. His school record at times seemed erratic and self-contradictory, showing areas of great strength combined with areas of substantial weakness. This long-term pattern is evident in a letter Einstein's father wrote to one of his teachers: "with Albert I got used a long time ago to finding not-so-good grades along with very good ones" (West, 1991)

Much of Einstein's most original work involved "thought experiments" that relied upon his highly visual imagination. As he himself said, words or language, "as they are written or spoken, do not seem to play any role in my mechanism of thought." Rather, the "psychical entities" which served as major elements in his "productive" thought were not words at all, but rather "certain signs and more or less clear images" that could be "voluntarily reproduced and combined." And it is only with the greatest difficulty, and in a separate stage of thought, that these visual images were translated into words that could be communicated to others.

Although some find this pattern of mixed talents and weaknesses to be difficult to believe and to understand, there are those who see no inherent incompatibility. Gerald Holton, a historian of physics and an expert on Einstein, observed that "an apparent defect in a particular person may merely indicate an imbalance of our normal expectations." In the "exceptional person," an area of special difficulty "should alert us to look for a proficiency of a different kind." Consequently, Holton observes that "the late use of language in childhood" or "difficulty in learning foreign languages" may show a "polarization or displacement in some of the skill from the verbal to another area." According to Holton, in the case of Einstein, "that other, enhanced area is without a doubt an extraordinary kind of visual imagery that penetrates his very thought processes" (Holton, 1972).

Thinking in Pictures

A similar pattern of mixed abilities is also evident in two visual thinkers greatly respected by Einstein: Michael Faraday and James Clerk Maxwell—English and Scottish scientists of the early and middle parts of the 19th century. Einstein's regard for these two men was so high, in fact, that he had framed pictures of them on his study wall. (Only one other scientist received this honor: Isaac Newton.)

Faraday, a blacksmith's son, had virtually no formal education. However, after 8 years as an apprentice bookbinder, he started work as a junior laboratory assistant. Through years of intensive laboratory work and self-education, he eventually earned a reputation for being the greatest experimental scientist of his time—eventually formulating, after many other accomplishments in chemistry and physics, the basic idea of the electromagnetic "field."

Maxwell, a university-trained mathematician and physicist, was and is most famous for his development of what are still called "Maxwell's equations." These equations (which deal with the basic nature of electricity, magnetism, and light), however, were not entirely Maxwell's—for, as he repeatedly explained, they were mainly Faraday's visual ideas, recast into a mathematical form that could be understood by other professional physicists and mathematicians.

When we look to scientific historians to characterize the thinking styles employed by these two scientists, we find that, like Einstein, "an important characteristic feature" shared by both Faraday and Maxwell was "the habit of thinking in terms of physical pictures." Indeed, although an accomplished mathematician, it was "remarked by many" that Maxwell relied "more on diagrams and geometrical notions than on symbols" (West, 1991).

Visual Gifts and Language Problems

All three of these extraordinarily talented visual thinkers gave some evidence of the pattern that interests us as we contemplate the possibilities in a transformed world of work. They all had visual strengths together with varied verbal difficulties. Einstein experienced no difficulty with reading, although he did have delayed development of language as a child—as well as life-long difficulties with foreign languages and an especially poor memory for texts and certain factual data.

Faraday also showed no difficulty in reading. However, he did struggle with an early speech impediment, along with an extremely poor memory and characteristically poor spelling and punctuation skills. He also seemed to have great difficulty in handling mathematical symbols—although his basic ideas were, as Maxwell repeatedly asserted, essentially mathematical in clarity of conception. He simply had not set them out in conventional mathematical symbols and terminology.

Maxwell's verbal problems took a different form. He was a life-long stutterer—which severely limited the success of his career as a university professor. But, perhaps more important, Maxwell had difficulty with several subtle peculiarities of language commonly recognized among children with "specific language disability." One is called "demand language deficiency." Some dyslexic children puzzle parents and teachers because they can speak with great fluency when they are prepared to speak ("spontaneous language"), but are surprisingly inarticulate when they are required to answer a question on demand or address a topic for which they are not prepared ("demand language") (West, 1991). Although Maxwell was known as an exceptionally clear writer—when he had plenty of time to find the right words—he was thought remarkable by his associates for his pronounced inability to give sensible responses when he was surprised by a new question for which he was not prepared. As they said, he would make "chaotic statements," at least initially. However, when he had time to think a subject over—time to find the right words— his answers and comments were considered clear, keen and perceptive.

Tissue Slides and Weird Daydreams

This pattern of mixed talents is also apparent in the case of a dyslexic physician known as "Marcia." Marcia's experience is especially helpful in showing us the complex interaction of these mixed traits in education and work situations. She first heard of dyslexia and learning disabilities during a lecture on the subject as part of her medical school training. During her early education, she knew nothing of the problem, but had long been aware that something was wrong. She could not really read at all until she was about 14 years old. However, because of an exceptional auditory memory, she was able to retain easily everything that she heard in class and she was able to bluff her way through elementary school and high school while reading almost nothing.

In medical school, she rarely read textbooks, relying primarily on lectures. By then she was able to read, but with great difficulty. She found that she could cope by limiting her reading to short passages in order to memorize certain material for examinations. While in training (as well as later professional life), an extraordinary visual memory helped her. She recognized that she had "an incredible memory for some things, like tissue slides." In one example, she performed 100 autopsies, taking "only brief notes." However, in these, she was able to remember "accurately for years the specific details" (Whitmore & Maker, 1985; West, 1991). Marcia's remarkable long-term memory for anatomical and visual information is accompanied by an unreliable memory for numerical data. Her especially poor memory for numbers and her propensity to confuse sequences were major continuing problems. In these areas, she needed the assistance of staff and coworkers to avoid errors.

What may be most interesting and significant for those trying to see a connection between Marcia's learning difficulties, visual proficiencies, and scientific creativity is her favorite pastime: Her "recreation" is to engage in "weird daydreams" in which she "manipulates scientific facts to come up with scientific answers to problems and needs." In a manner reminiscent of Einstein's "thought experiments," she has stated that she also believes that "living in the quiet, isolated environment" of her own self-sufficient farm would permit her "to let her imagination go, experiment in her private laboratory, and fulfill her potential as an innovative scientist."

Heresy of Learning

We have seen examples of strong visual thinkers with some dyslexic traits. The reverse case can also be observed—that is, comparatively severe dyslexics with unexpected propensities to deal with things in a visual manner.

In her autobiography, the British actress Susan Hampshire has told of her difficulties growing up as a dyslexic and discusses a number of misconceptions about dyslexia and dyslexics. She referred to those who continue to believe that dyslexia is really mainly a psychological problem or that it is merely an excuse for parents who refuse to admit that their child is really not very bright. Then she explained that there is "yet another prejudice that dyslexics, and those who try to help them, have to combat." This prejudice is the "deep-rooted idea" that "all learning, all education, any expression of ideas, must be done through language, through words" (Hampshire, 1983; West, 1991).

She noted that the "idea that it is possible to learn and communicate *visually*, through colour and shape, seems to be a heresy," although she asserted that this idea is one that "naturally occurs to dyslexics." She argued that the rigid application of conventional literacy rules may very well have stamped out much of the potential in dyslexic children. Indeed, she pointed out, some "very impressive intelligences" have appreciated "the value of visual learning and communications." As an example, she notes that Leonardo da Vinci explained, in connection with his anatomical drawings, that "no one could hope to convey so much true knowledge without an immense, tedious and confused length of writing and time, except through this very short way of drawing from different aspects." Given the new visualization technologies that we are now considering, Hampshire's observations were remarkably forward-looking.

It may be no accident that Leonardo himself had difficulty with learning Latin—normally required of all educated and professional people of his time—and thus considered himself "a man without letters." An examination of his manuscripts and journals by an Italian neurologist has identified distinctive patterns in spelling and handwriting errors that document neurologically-based language difficulties similar to those experienced by dyslexics. Acknowledging his own verbal difficulties, Leonardo pointed out that "you should prefer a good scientist without literary abilities than a literate without scientific skills" (Satori, 1987; West, 1991).

From Lectures to Simulators

These examples should serve to suggest that there is something about current developments in technology and changes in the workplace that could transform the way we think of talent and capability—that those who seem to be poorly fitted for an old-fashioned world of traditional subjects and memorized texts may be remarkably well-suited for the coming world of technological change and complex visualization.

Most notable among the newly appreciated areas of talent will be the brain's ability to use new computer graphic and data visualization technologies to recognize patterns and invent creative and innovative solutions to problems. These require, mainly, visual–spatial capacities rather than memorized, rule-based analytical instructions. Accordingly, one may argue that the skills and talents that will be seen as most important in the coming decades will be those most difficult for a machine to replicate: creative and inventive pattern recognition and problem solving, employing visual and spatial capabilities.

With these changes, past ideas of desirable talents and skills could be transformed, gradually but dramatically. Of course, the conventional verbal, clerical, and managerial skills will always be needed and valued to some extent, but these will not be considered as important or as useful in themselves as they were previously. Before too long, that semi-intelligent machines may be more "learned" and better read, with more complete and accurate memories, than even the most experienced and most conscientious of the traditional scholars and experts in any field.

Consequently, in the near future, instead of the qualities desired in a well-trained clerk or traditional scholar, we might find it far more valuable to develop the qualities associated with visual thinkers such as Leonardo da Vinci: a facility with visual–spatial perspectives and modes of thought instead of mainly verbal (or symbolic) fluency; a propensity to invention by making connections among many diverse fields; an ability to learn directly through experience (or computer-simulated experience) rather than primarily from lectures and books; a habit of continuous investigation in many different areas of study; the more integrated approach of the global thinker rather than the traditional narrow specialist; and an ability to move quickly through many phases of research, development, and design using mental models and imagination, incorporating modern three-dimensional, computer-aided design systems (Ritchie–Calder, 1970; Satori, 1987; West, 1991).

Thus, it seems that we might be in a position to come full circle, using the most advanced technologies and techniques to draw on some of the most old-fashioned human capacities. We could simulate reality by computer rather than describe it in words or numbers. Students could learn, once again, by doing rather than by reading or listening to lectures. They could learn, once again, by seeing and experimenting rather than by following memorized texts and algorithms. In so doing, all of us will learn greater respect for the nonverbal abilities and intelligences that were always vitally important—but have been generally eclipsed by a disproportionate emphasis on the verbal abilities most valued by traditional teachers and professors in the higher-prestige academic tradition. Sometimes, the oldest pathways and most primitive capacities can be the best guides into unexplored new territory.

Reversals in the Workplace

After centuries of continuity, there may be need for fundamental change. In recent decades, the prestige of the verbal academic approach was largely overwhelmed by the long tradition of hands-on multisensory learning. This presented a problem for many, but most especially to dyslexics. Perhaps, we will now see an unexpected movement back the other way, moving forward by seeming to move backward. For today's students and workers, many of the basic verbal and clerical skills that have long dominated education at all levels will cease to be as important as they once were. In the new economy, these tasks will be increasingly taken over by semi-intelligent machines, as predicted by Norbert Weiner some time ago.

With these changes, the attention moves from what challenges dyslexics to areas in which they generally excel. In the new economy and marketplace, the visual–spatial talents, global thinking, pattern recognition, creative problem solving and other nonverbal abilities often associated with dyslexia are expected to become increasingly important. Recognition of this trend will accelerate as greater use is made of data visualization, computer graphics, and interactive multi-sensory technologies to understand complex systems and predict unexpected trends.

To survive, many employers will find that they need to adjust to new categories of thought and new rules of practice. In a similar fashion, educators will need to adapt to new realities, as they try to free themselves from an almost universal preoccupation with written symbols, the instruments of the old technology. Accordingly, as we all struggle to adapt ourselves to deep changes in thinking and working, some dyslexics will doubtless play once again their oft-repeated roles. We should expect to find them working creatively at the edge of the new frontier, reading little but learning much, experimenting, innovating, establishing a new path forward—learning from direct experience, anticipating where things are going, taking risks.

Based in Washington, DC, Thomas G. West is the author of *In the Mind's Eye*, now in its seventh printing in English (Prometheus, 1991) and fifth printing in Japanese (*Geniuses Who Hated School*, Kodansha Scientific, Tokyo, 1994). Mr. West has worked with engineering and consulting organizations involved with computer software design, energy research and international trade. These activities and related work have involved periodic travel to the Middle East and the Far East. The author holds graduate and undergraduate degrees in international relations, literature, and philosophy. He learned of his own dyslexia at the age of 41. From a family of artists and engineers, he has long been interested in the connections between mixed abilities, technological innovation, and visual thinking in various occupational and cultural settings. Mr. West has recently established the Visualization Research Institute, Inc. He may be reached at 4139461@mcimail.com or visualres@aol.com.

References

Note: Parts of this article have appeared in different form in *In the Mind's Eye* and other articles and talks by the author.

Bass, T. A. (1995, November). "Being Nicholas: The [MIT] media lab's visionary founder Nicholas Negroponte is the most wired man we know (and that is saying something)." *Wired*, 3.11, 146 ff., 204. [Cover interview.]

Benbow, C. P. (1986). "Physiological Correlates of Extreme Intellectual Precocity," *Neuropsychologia*, 24, 719–725. Oxford, UK: Pergamon.

Economist, The (1995, August 19). "Seeing Is Believing," p. 71

Economist, The (1995, February 11–17). Technology, the Future of Your Job and Other Misplaced Panics, p. 13, A World Without Jobs? pp. 21–23.

Galaburda, A. M. (Ed) (1993). *Dyslexia and Development: Neurobiological Aspects of Extra-Ordinary Brains.* Cambridge, MA: Harvard University Press.

Gardner, H. (1983). *Frames of Mind: The Theory of Multiple Intelligences.* New York: Basic Books.

Geschwind, N. (1982). "Why Orton Was Right." *The Annals of Dyslexia, 32,* Orton Dyslexia Society Reprint No. 98.

Geschwind, N. (1984). "The Brain of a Learning-Disabled Individual." *Annals of Dyslexia, 34,* 319–327.

Geschwind, N., & Galaburda, A. M. (1987). *Cerebral Laterialization: Biological Mechanisms, Associations and Pathology.* Cambridge, MA: MIT Press.

Gould, S. J. (1993). *Eight Little Piggies: Reflections in Natural History.* New York: W.W. Norton & Company.

Hampshire, S. (1983). *Susan's Story: An Autobiographical Account of My Struggle with Words.* London: Sphere Books Limited.

Holton, G. (1972). "On Trying to Understand Scientific Genius." *The American Scholar, 41,* 95–110.

Kaufmann, W. J., III, & Smarr. L. L. (1993). *Supercomputing and the Transformation of Science.* New York: The Scientific American Library, a division of (HPHLP).

McDonald, K. A. (1994, November 16). "The Iconoclastic Fossil Hunter." *The Chronicle of Higher Education,* pp. A9–A17.

Mitchell, R., et al (1995). "The Schwab Revolution." *Business Week,* December 19.

Negroponte, Nicholas. (1995). *Being Digital.* New York: Knopf.

Ritchie–Calder, P. (1970). *Leonardo & the Age of the Eye.* New York: Simon and Schuster.

Robins, C. (1992, March 8). "One man's battle against dyslexia—How financier Charles Schwab is helping others whose kids have learning disabilities." *San Francisco Examiner,* pp. D–3, D–10.

Satori, G. (1987). "Leonardo Da Vinci, Omo Sanza Lettere: A Case of Surface Dysgraphia?" *Cognitive Neuropsychology, 4*(1), 1–10.

Weiner, N. (1948, 1961). *Cybernetics: Or Control and Communication in the Animal and the Machine.* Cambridge, MA: MIT Press.

West, T. G. (1990, November). "Visualization in the Mind's Eye." *IRIS Universe: The Magazine of Visual Processing,* 14.

West, T. G. (1991). *In the Mind's Eye: Visual Thinkers, Gifted People with Learning Difficulties, Computer Images, and the Ironies of Creativity.* Buffalo, N.Y.: Prometheus Books. Seventh printing, July 1996 (The title of this article, Slow Words, Quick Images, is also the title of the first chapter of *In the Mind's Eye,* although the contents are quite different.)

West, T. G. (1992). "A Future of Reversals: Dyslexic Talents in a World of Computer Visualization." *Annals of Dyslexia,* vol. 42, pp. 124–139.

West, T. G. (1994). "A Return to Visual Thinking." In Wittenburg, P., & Plesser, T. (Eds). *Proceedings, Science and Scientific Computing: Visions of a Creative Symbiosis. Symposium of Computer Users in the Max Planck Gesellschaft, Göttingen, Germany, Nov. 1993.* (Paper published in German translation: "Rückkehr zum visuellen Denken," *Forschung und wissenschftliches Rechnen: Beiträge anläßlich des 10. EDV-Benutzertreffens der Max-Planck-Gesellschaft in Göttingen, November 1993.*)

West, T. G. (1995, November). "Forward into the Past: A Revival of Old Visual Talents with Computer Visualization." In Sullivan, K. (Ed). *Computer Graphics,* 29(4), 14–19.

West, T. G. (1996, January–February). "Upside Down: Visual-spatial Talents and Technological Change." *Understanding Our Gifted,* 8(3), 1–11.

Whitmore, J. R., & C. J. Maker (1985). "Intellectually Gifted Persons with Specific Learning Disabilities—A Case Study: Marcia." In *Intellectual Giftedness in Disabled Persons.* Rockville, Md.: Aspen Systems Corporation.

CHAPTER 18

Lifespan Employment and Economic Outcomes for Adults with Self-Reported Learning Disabilities

Stephen Reder
Susan A. Vogel

In 1989, The National Council on Disability urged that the focus on transition for secondary education students with disabilities in the 1990s should shift from assessing processes and procedures to the nature and quality of student outcomes (National Council on Disability, 1989). Impetus and funding for such efforts, provided by the United States Congress, resulted in the awarding of a contract from the Office of Special Education and Rehabilitation of the U.S. Department of Education to the Stanford Research Institute International. This authorized the Stanford group to conduct the National Longitudinal Transition Study of Special Education Students (NLTS) (D'Amico, 1991; Wagner, 1991; Wagner, D'Amico, Marder, Newman, & Blackorby, 1992; Marder & D'Amico, 1992). In addition, federal discretionary dollars were allocated to encourage states to conduct similar follow-up studies. To date, the major studies have been conducted in Washington State (Affleck, Edgar, Levine, & Kortering, 1990; Levine, 1993; Levine & Edgar, 1994), in New Hampshire (Nisbet & Lichtenstein, 1992), and in Iowa (Sitlington & Frank, 1990). These studies addressed a wide variety of labor market outcomes for adults with learning disabilities as well as the question of gender differences; for the most part, there has been a considerable degree of consistency among these studies. In this chapter, we will review briefly highlights relating to the focus of the present chapter. For a review of other aspects of the cited studies, readers are referred to Chapters 1 and 4 in this volume.

The NLTS, the most comprehensive study to date regarding employment outcomes of adults with learning disabilities (LD), was based on a national sample of more than 8,000 youth between the ages of 13 and 23 who were enrolled in special education programs during the 1985–86 school year (D'Amico, 1991; Wagner, 1991). Subjects included youth with disabilities identified by the schools they attended—either public secondary schools or state-operated special schools—and, therefore, would be categorized as a school-identified (in contrast to a research-identified or a self-reported) sample. Follow-up data were collected 2 years or less after the subjects left school and then, 3 5 years after leaving (Wagner et al., 1992), on a subgroup of 1,800 of the original 8,000 participants.

Data on labor force participation revealed that there were no differences in employment rate when the LD group was compared to the general population. However, the picture changed dramatically when these subgroups were subdivided by gender. Although there was no significant difference in the rate of employment among males with LD in comparison to the general population (63.2% vs. 65.4%) the employment rate among females with LD was significantly lower than the employment rate for females in the general population (37.3% vs. 49.1%). As can be seen, the employment rate for males with LD exceeded by 20 percentage points higher than that of the females with LD. Three to 5 years after leaving school, the same trends were apparent, although the overall employment rate had increased.

With regard to occupational status, about 70% of the adults with LD were employed in low-paying, low-prestige jobs. Of these, 7% were employed in clerical jobs such as those of postal clerks; 14.2% held auto mechanics or other craft worker positions; 19.9% were employed as service station attendants or in other operative jobs; and 38.7% were laborers or service workers—such as gardeners, maids, or janitors. It is, therefore, not surprising that when hourly wages were examined within 2 years after exiting school, more than half (54.9%) earned $6 per hour or less, indicating that many of these young adults, though employed, were living near or below the poverty line.

In contrast to the NLTS, the Washington State series of followup studies (Affleck et al., 1990; Levine, 1993; and Levine & Edgar, 1994) collected relevant outcome data periodically over a 10-year period after high school graduation. In New Hampshire (Nisbet & Lichenstein, 1992) and Iowa (Sitlington & Frank, 1990), less than 5 years had elapsed between exit from high school and the study. In an extensive review of the research literature on issues of employment, Adelman and Vogel (1993) identified age at follow-up as an important variable in interpretation of outcome research. In fact, instability in employment among adults in their 20s led Halpern (1992) to refer to the years following high school exit as the "floundering period" because of the difficulty young adults with disabilities often experience in decision-making regarding employment.

As in the NLTS, the three state studies revealed similar employment rates for adults with LD as compared to the general population, significantly higher employment rates for males than females, low wages, and low-prestige jobs. They also reported that many more males with LD were employed full-time, and that significantly more females were employed part-time, with females earning lower wages than males.

In summary, it appears that although recent high school graduates with LD are employed at the same rate as their nondisabled peers, their wages and occupational status are considerably lower than those of their peers. In contrast, females are unemployed more often than males and are more often in part-time and in lower-paying jobs when compared to males with LD and nondisabled females. From the studies reviewed above, however, it is not possible to determine how the restricted age range of the samples studied and the restricted number of years following exit from high school may have impacted on these results. Only one study to date has included adults with LD across the lifespan and, although this group had attained relatively high levels of education, its constituents nevertheless experienced significant difficulties and a high level of need related to employment issues. Thus, although there are indications that adults with LD may have lifelong problems in terms of employment and economic status, there is little data available on the point. This chapter will therefore present and analyze a potentially valuable new data set containing employment and economic outcomes for a nationally representative sample of adults with and without self-reported learning disabilities (SRLD) across the lifespan who participated in The National Adult Literacy Survey (NALS). This allows us to compare the employment attainments, occupational status, and wages of the SRLD group with those of the general population.[1]

Our inquiry will focus on two specific aspects of these issues:

1. The patterns of labor market outcomes—i.e., labor force participation, employment, wages, earnings and occupational status— among adults with LD and the general adult population; and

2. The interaction between gender and LD in the above labor market outcomes to determine if men and women are equally impacted by learning disabilities.

[1] This research was supported by contract R117Q0003 to the National Center on Adult Literacy from the U.S. Department of Education, Office of Educational Research and Improvement, and by the ACLD Foundation. The findings and opinions expressed here are those of the authors, and do not necessarily reflect the views of any institution or agency.

Method

The data presented here are based on secondary analyses of the data collected in the recently conducted NALS survey (Kirsch, Jungeblut, Jenkins, & Kolstad, 1993). The NALS utilized an assessment framework that combined the methodologies of item response theory and large-scale population surveys. These assessment methods were used to profile the literacy proficiency distributions of various subpopulations of adults on *prose, document* and *quantitative* scales. Survey respondents carried out a series of simulated everyday functional literacy tasks such as completing a form, locating information on a map, summarizing information from newspaper articles, processing quantitative information from graphs and diagrams, and so forth. Based on their performance of these tasks, individuals were assigned literacy scores on the three 0-500 point proficiency scales.

The NALS survey and assessment was administered during in-home interviews to a stratified random sample of adults 16 years and older. In addition to performing the simulated functional literacy tasks, survey respondents answered questions from an orally administered background questionnaire. Questionnaire responses provided information about participants' demographic characteristics, educational experiences, employment and training experiences, economic status, perceptions of and uses of literacy and various languages spoken in the home, and other background information. Technical details about the survey design, assessment techniques and instruments and administration procedures are described in detail by Kirsch et al. (1993).

Identification of Learning Disabilities

The background interviews also inquired about various physical, mental and health conditions, including the following yes/no question:

Do you currently have a learning disability?

For this paper, individuals are designated as having a learning disability in terms of their responses to the above question. Individuals thus *self-identify* as having learning disabilities. Although self-identification of learning disabilities is clearly a distinct process from school identification, or clinical identification, or research identification, the use of self-identification in the reporting and study of learning disabilities is not uncommon. The incidence of learning disabilities among entering freshmen in 4-year colleges, for example, is typically reported on the basis of self-identification (e.g., HEATH Resource Center, 1992; Henderson, 1992). Despite the frequent use of self-identification as an indicator of learning disabilities, the false-positive and false-negative rates of misclassification of this indicator with respect to the other assessment techniques in the general adult population is unknown. Nor have the reliability and validity of the measure been established.

Target Population

The data examined here come from the *household sample* of the NALS, which included 24,944 individuals randomly selected from the U.S. non-institutionalized population of age 16 and above. The target population for analyses reported here is defined as a subpopulation of individuals living in the United States age 16 and older who meet 4 additional conditions: (a) born in the U.S.; (b) spoke English before entering school; (c) did not report having mental retardation; and (d) were not students at the time of the survey.[2] The target population is restricted to native-born individuals who spoke English before entering school because of the concern that individuals who first attended foreign schools or who did not speak English at the time they started school in the U.S. may well have been treated differently with regard to school identification of learning disabilities. To understand better the incidence and impact of learning disabilities apart from mental retardation, it was decided not to include individuals reporting mental retardation in the study. Finally, individuals who are currently students are excluded from the study because many labor market and economic outcomes of interest are patterned differently among individuals currently in school (e.g., occupational choice and wages among students whose employment options are voluntarily limited). Of the 24,944 NALS household survey respondents, 18,170 satisfied these criteria. The corresponding 1990 U.S. Census[3] population from which this target subsample of NALS is drawn numbers 141,253,694. We shall hereafter term this the *target population*.

---

[2] This is the same target population considered by Reder (1995).

[3] NALS sample and weighting designs actually included corrections for estimated undercount in the 1990 Census, which totalled approximately 3 million adults (U.S. Bureau of the Census, *Report of the Committee on Adjustment of Postcensal Estimates*, dated August 7, 1992).

Statistical Analyses

Because of the complex sample design used in the survey, survey case weights provided in the public use data files were used to generate population estimates in all descriptive and inferential statistical analyses. The clustered, multistage sample design underlying NALS makes the realized sample less efficient than a similarly sized one produced by simple random sampling. Rather than estimating standard errors of sample statistics with computationally intense jackknife procedures, estimates were produced as if simple random sampling had been utilized, applying a *design effect* to reduce the effective sample size. Following the recommendations of Rock,[4] a design effect of 2.0 was used in these analyses, halving the effective sample size of the household survey from 24,944 to 12,472. Analyses in subpopulations similarly used renormalized design-weights that are proportional to sampling case weights and which sum to an effective subsample size of half the number of cases involved. Analyses based on these weighting assumptions are termed *design-weighted* analyses. Design-weighted analyses of the study's target population used case weights proportional to those supplied in the public use data files, but normalized to sum to half of the target sample size, or 9,085.

Other Research on the SRLD Population in NALS

Kirsch et al. (1993) noted 3% of the adult population reported having a learning disability. The first in–depth look at characeristics of the SRLD population was presented by Reder (1995), who examined the same target subpopulation of the NALS being examined here. In his preliminary depiction, Reder estimated that 3.1% of the target adult population was in the SRLD group. The SRLD population was highly overrepresented among the undereducated, those with low levels of little proficiency, the nonparticipants in the labor force, the unemployed, and among the poor. Among the SLRD more than a quarter (27%) had less than 9th grade education, compared to only 8% of the non-SRLD population. More than half (53%) of adults with SRLD did not have a high school diploma or equivalent, compared to 22% of adults without SRLD (Reder, 1995).

Vogel and Reder (in preparation) looked closely at the literacy proficiencies and educational attainments of SRLD and non-SRLD groups of the target adult population, particularly the interaction of gender and

---

[4]In the forthcoming *Technical Report* on the NALS, by Kirsch, Rock et al.

SRLD on the literacy and educational outcomes of adults. They focused on the age range of 25–64 for their analyses. They looked closely at the distributions of literacy and education separately among men and women with and without SRLD. The pattern of results they found contrasts sharply with previous research on gender differences in youth and adults with learning disabilities. The present paper therefore will look more closely at employment and other labor market outcomes, paying close attention to the interactions between gender and SRLD.

These researchers, in discussing their findings about adults with SRLD, discuss some of the ways in which self-identification of LD differs from other techniques of identification, such as school identification, clinical identification, and research identification (Reder 1995; Vogel & Reder, in preparation). Although the incidence of self-identified LD in the adult population may not be inconsistent with historical rates of school identification, the variation of SRLD with age in NALS is not consistent with the idea that adults self-identify only because schools have previously identified them when they were schoolchildren (Reder, 1995). Vogel and Reder (in preparation) noted that the nearly 1:1 gender ratio in SRLD is quite distinct from the gender ratios typically reported by schools for LD (in which males are as much as 3 times as likely to be identified by schools). Until concurrent identification and cross-validation studies are undertaken, it will be difficult to synthesize research findings based on varying methods of identification. These problems notwithstanding, the NALS data do offer the first nationally representative data in which to compare lifespan employment and economic outcomes for adults with and without (self-identified) learning disabilities.

Results

Labor Force Participation

Figure 18.1 displays adults' labor force status for the week prior to the NALS survey. Each of the two bars in the figure shows the percentage of individuals in 1 of 4 categories: *out of the labor force, unemployed, employed part-time, and employed full-time.*[5] The bar on the left shows the population distribution for individuals who did not report having learning disabilities, whereas the bar on the right shows the population

---

[5]A rarely used category in NALS, "Employed, but not at work last week," was grouped with *employed part-time* for the purposes of this study.

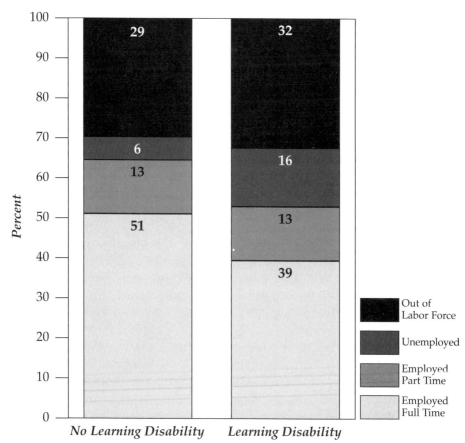

FIGURE 18.1. Labor force participation of target population with and without learning disabilities.

distribution for those who did report having learning disabilities. Percentages shown in the figure are estimates for the target population.

The overall difference between these distributions for the SRLD and non-SRLD groups is highly significant when tested with a design-weighted logit likelihood analysis: likelihood ratio $\chi^2 = 33.60$, df = 3, p < .00001. The major differences between the two groups appeared to be in the percentages of individuals who were unemployed (but in the labor force) and in the percentages of individuals employed full-time. A much smaller percentage of individuals was employed full-time among those having learning disabilities (39%) than among those not having learning disabilities (51%). The percentage of individuals who were unemployed was much higher in the population with learning disabilities (16%) than in the population without learning disabilities (6%). To estimate the corresponding unemployment rates, these percentages had to be adjusted to exclude individuals not in the labor force. When these corrections were made, the unemployment rates became 8.4% for the population without learning disabilities and 23.5% for the learning disabilities population. The two groups appeared not to differ substantially in the percentages of individuals working part-time or those outside of the labor force.

To examine these differences between the groups' patterns of labor force participation more closely, the data are shown separately for men and women in Table 18.1 and Table 18.2, respectively. The well-known overall differences between men's and women's patterns of labor force participation were evident again here (comparing the right-hand columns of the two tables); a substantially higher percentage of men than women worked full-time (63.6% vs. 39.4%), and a much higher percentage of women than men were not in the labor force (37.9% vs. 19.6%). SRLD group membership and gender appeared to exert significant effects on labor force participation. But did these effects interact? That is, did self-reported learning disabilities affect men's and women's labor force participation differently?

To answer this question, a loglinear analysis was conducted to test the null hypothesis that there was no interaction between SRLD and gender in the observed design-weighted $4 \times 2 \times 2$ frequency matrix (4 categories of labor force participation $\times$ 2 categories of gender $\times$ 2 categories of SRLD). In this analysis, labor force participation was considered the dependent variable, and a model evaluated that predicted (logit) frequencies of labor force participation for each combination of

TABLE 18.1

	Men with Learning Disabilities	Men without Learning Disabilities	All Men
Employed full-time	50.2	64.1	63.6
Employed part-time	10.1	9.7	9.7
Unemployed	20.4	6.6	7.1
Not in labor force	19.3	19.6	19.6

Labor force participation of men with and without self-reported learning disabilities. Numbers shown are percentages of target population estimated to be in each category of labor force participation at time of interview. Each column thus sums to 100% (except for rounding error).

TABLE 18.2

	Women with Learning Disabilities	Women without Learning Disabilities	All Women
Employed full-time	25.6	39.8	39.4
Employed part-time	17.3	16.3	16.3
Unemployed	10.9	6.2	6.3
Not in labor force	46.3	37.7	37.9

Labor force participation of women with and without self-reported learning disabilities. Numbers shown are percentages of target population estimated to be in each category of labor force participation at time of interview. Each column thus sums to 100% (except for rounding error).

gender and SRLD, using only the marginal gender and SRLD frequency distributions (i.e., it assumed there is no interaction between gender and SRLD in predicting labor force participation). The fit of these predicted frequencies with the observed frequencies was evaluated by calculating a logit likelihood ratio, which had a chi-square distribution. The calculated logit likelihood ratio was 4.06, which for 3 degrees of freedom had a p-value of 0.25, indicating that we should accept the null hypothesis that there was no interaction between gender and SRLD. Although both gender and SRLD substantially influenced patterns of labor force participation, there was no significant evidence in these data that SRLD differentially impacted women's labor force participation.

Employment

The measure of labor force participation reported above is a "snapshot" of individuals' status at the time the NALS interviews were conducted. Another measure of employment activity was collected in the survey: the number of weeks individuals were employed (part-time or full-time) during the year preceding the interview. This measure ranged between 0 for individuals who were unemployed or out of the labor force for the entire preceding year up to 52 for individuals who had at least some compensated employment during each week of the preceding year. Table 18.3 displays the mean number of weeks individuals with and without self-reported learning disabilities were employed during the year preceding the NALS survey. Adults with self-reported learning disabilities worked fewer weeks per year on the average (24.7) than do adults who did not have learning disabilities (31.5). Men worked more weeks per year

TABLE 18.3

	Adults with Learning Disabilities	Adults without Learning Disabilities	Total
Men	30.8	36.4	36.2
Women	17.4	27.2	26.9
Total	24.7	31.5	31.3

Mean number of weeks employed during year preceding interview in adult target populations with and without self-reported learning disabilities.

(36.2) than did women (26.9). A design-weighted analysis of variance indicated that both main effects of gender ($F = 61.2$, df = 1, $p < .001$) and SRLD ($F = 28.3$, df = 1, $p < .001$) were highly significant, but that the gender $\times$ SRLD interaction ($F = 2.02$, df = 1, $p = .155$) was not significant. As found for labor force participation, SRLD did not appear to impact the quantity of employment differentially for men and women.

Occupational Status

Individuals who had worked at some point during the 3 years preceding the NALS survey were asked to describe their current or most recent occupation. These occupational descriptions were coded into standard occupational categories. Figure 18.2 displays the distribution of occupational categories among individuals with self-reported learning disabilities (right bar in the figure) and those without SRLD (left bar). There was a sharp overall difference between these distributions for the SRLD and non-SRLD groups, which a design-weighted logit likelihood test (likelihood ratio $\chi^2 = 56.87$, df = 3, $p < .001$) indicated to have a high degree of statistical significance.

Individuals in the SRLD group were more highly concentrated in the lower-paying and lower-status occupations held by laborer and service workers, and far less represented in the higher-paying and higher-status sales and professional/technical/managerial occupations. Nearly half (45%) of the workforce with SRLD worked in the service sector, compared to slightly more than one-quarter (28%) of the workforce that does not have SRLD. Workers having SRLD are half as likely to be employed in the sales or technical/professional/managerial fields as are workers not having SRLD.

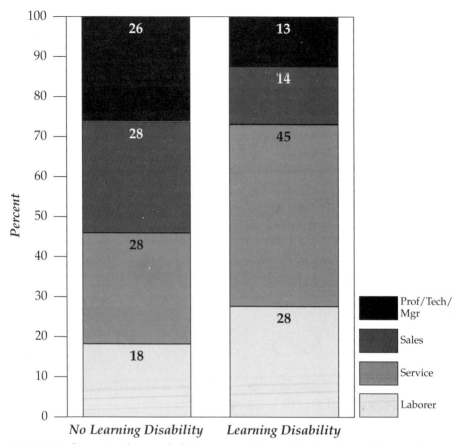

FIGURE 18.2. Occupational status of adult target population with and without self-reported learning disabilities. Excludes those who had not worked at all during previous three years.

Table 18.4 and Table 18.5, respectively, display the estimated pro-portions of the target population of men and women in these four major occupational categories; each table displays the proportion of adults (men or women) with or without self-reported learning disabilities in each of the four categories.

Looking first at the marginal distributions of occupations among working men and women (i.e., the right hand columns of Table 18.4 and Table 18.5), we see two very large differences according to gender: a far greater percentage of men worked as laborers compared to women (26.5% vs. 9.8%), and a much larger percentage of women worked in sales occupations than did men (40.1% vs. 16.5%). It thus appears that there are major differences in occupational patterns in terms of both

TABLE 18.4

	Men with Learning Disabilities	Men without Learning Disabilities	All Men
Prof./Tech./Mgr.	11.0	27.1	26.6
Sales	5.8	16.8	16.5
Service	45.5	30.0	30.5
Laborer	37.8	26.1	26.5

Occupations of men in target population with and without self-reported learning disabilities. Excludes men who have not worked in past three years. Numbers shown are percentages of target population estimated to be in each occupational category. Each column thus adds to 100% (except for rounding error).

learning disabilities and gender. To examine the interaction of SRLD and gender on occupation, a design-weighted loglinear analysis was conducted, similar to the previously described analysis of gender and SRLD effects on patterns of labor force participation. The resulting logit likelihood test statistic ($\chi^2 = 5.29$, df = 3, p = .152) indicates there was no significant interaction between gender and SRLD on occupation.

By assigning these occupational categories to a four-point scale (technical/professional/managerial = 4; sales = 3; service = 2; laborer = 1), we can examine these occupational distributions in terms of an occupational status scale.

TABLE 18.5

	Women with Learning Disabilities	Women without Learning Disabilities	All Women
Prof./Tech./Mgr.	16.3	25.0	24.8
Sales	27.4	40.4	40.1
Service	44.1	24.8	25.2
Laborer	12.2	9.8	9.8

Occupations of women in target population with and without self-reported learning disabilities. Excludes women who have not worked in past three years. Numbers shown are percentages of target population estimated to be in each occupational category. Each column thus adds to 100% (except for rounding error).

Table 18.6 displays the mean occupational scale value for men and women workers who had and did not have self-reported learning disabilities. Consistent with the above occupational distributions, there appeared to be overall differences in occupational status in terms of both gender and SRLD status, with women and individuals without SRLD tending to work in higher-status occupations. A design-weighted analysis of variance indicated that the main effects of gender ($F = 34.00$, $df = 1$, $p < .001$) and SRLD ($F = 30.00$, $df = 1$, $p < .001$) were highly significant, whereas the gender $\times$ SRLD interaction ($F = 1.90$, $df = 1$, $p = .168$) is not statistically significant. Once again, the impact of SRLD on occupations appeared to be parallel for men and women.

Wages

Given the overall differences observed in labor force participation, employment and occupational status between individuals who did, and did not, report having learning disabilities, differences in the wages of the two groups might be expected, as well. Table 18.7 displays the average weekly earnings (for the year preceding the NALS survey interview) in dollars for individuals who reported, and did not report, having learning disabilities. Individuals who did not work at all during the year were excluded from this analysis. Data are presented separately for men and women as well as for all adults. For each group, two measures of central tendency of weekly earnings are shown in the table: mean and median. Since wage distributions were positively skewed, medians could give a better impression of typical wage levels than could means. Regardless of which measure is used, however, the comparative result

TABLE 18.6

	Adults with Learning Disabilities	Adults without Learning Disabilities	Total
Men	1.90	2.45	2.43
Women	2.48	2.81	2.80
Total	2.11	2.62	2.61

Mean occupational status (on a four-point scale) of men and women in target population, with and without self-reported learning disabilities.

TABLE 18.7

	Adults with Learning Disabilities		Adults without Learning Disabilities		All Adults	
	Mean	Median	Mean	Median	Mean	Median
Men	528	300	650	475	589	465
Women	273	204	379	280	344	280
All Adults	327	255	478	360	474	360

Mean and median weekly wages of men and women workers in the target population, with and without self-reported learning disabilities. Wages are dollars earned per week, averaged over those weeks in the preceding year in which workers were employed. Excludes individuals who did not work at all during the preceding year.

was the same: individuals with SRLD tended to earn far less than individuals without SRLD, and women tended to earn far less than men.

Let's consider wages first in terms of self-reported learning disabilities, displayed in the bottom row of Table 18.7. Those with SRLD earned a weekly wage with a mean value of $327, whereas those without SRLD earned a mean of $478 per week. Those with SRLD thus earned only 68.4% of that earned by those without SRLD. Looking at median wages, one can see a similar difference. Median weekly earnings for the two groups were $255 and $360. The median weekly wage of a worker with SRLD were only 70.8% of the median wage of workers without SRLD.

Comparing the rows of the table showing women's and men's earnings, we see that, as is typically found, women earned substantially less than men. The mean women's weekly wage was $344 compared to $589 for men; the mean women's wage was 58.4% of the mean men's wage. The median women's wage, $280, was 60.2% of the median men's weekly wage of $465. A design-weighted analysis of variance of log wages[6] by SRLD and gender was carried out to investigate these wage patterns. The analysis indicated that highly significant main effects of both SRLD ($F = 28.7$, $df = 1$, $p < .001$) and gender ($F = 31.0$, $df = 1$, $p < .001$). The SRLD $\times$ gender interaction also was significant at the .05 level ($F = 6.04$, $df = 1$, $p = .014$). Interaction between the effects of SRLD and gender indicated that learning disabilities have more impact on women's wages than on men's

---

[6]The natural logarithm of weekly wage was used to normalize the postively skewed wage distribution for analystic purposes.

wages; the mean weekly wage of the SRLD group was 72.0% of the mean wage for the non-SRLD group among women, whereas the corresponding figure among men was 81.2%.

Annual Earnings

Table 18.8 displays the corresponding mean and median annual earnings of the two groups for the year preceding the NALS survey interview. Annual earnings were the product of average weekly wage over the year and number of weeks worked during the year. Individuals who reported not working at all during the year were excluded from the analysis.

Looking at the bottom row of the table, one may examine the earnings of those with and without self-reported LD. The mean annual earnings of individuals with and without SRLD were $14,958 and $23,131, respectively. Individuals with SRLD earned less than two-thirds (64.7%) of what individuals without SRLD earned. A similar picture emerged from comparing the median values of the groups' earnings distribution. The median annual earnings for individuals with SRLD ($10,400) was only 58.1% of the median earnings of those not having SRLD ($17,886).

Women's and men's earnings also differed dramatically. Looking across the rows of the table for men's and women's earnings, it is evident that women in all groups earned substantially less than did men. Overall, women's mean annual earnings ($16,272) were 56.5% of men's mean annual earnings ($28,811). A design-weighted analysis of variance of log earnings on SRLD and gender was carried out to look more closely at these results. The ANOVA indicated both main effects of SRLD

TABLE 18.8

	Adults with Learning Disabilities		Adults without Learning Disabilities		All Adults	
	Mean	Median	Mean	Median	Mean	Median
Men	16,205	12,961	29,214	22,984	28,811	22,360
Women	12,369	8,704	16,339	13,000	16,272	13,000
All Adults	14,958	10,400	23,131	17,886	22,930	17,680

Mean and median annual earnings of men and women workers in the target population, with and without self-reported learning disabilities. Earnings are dollars earned per week times number of weeks employed during the preceding year. Excludes individuals who did not work at all during the preceding year.

(F = 35.01, df = 1, p < .001) and gender (F = 22.06, df = 1, p < .001) to be highly significant. Although it approached significance at the .05 level, the SRLD × gender interaction was not statistically significant (F = 3.76, df = 1, p = .053). Although there was a significant interaction between learning disabilities and gender on log weekly wages, the interaction here for annual earnings was not quite statistically significant.[7]

Discussion

The results of our analyses clearly indicate there are major effects of self-reported LD on a wide variety of employment and economic outcomes. Individuals with SRLD were less likely to be employed full-time, more likely to be unemployed, work substantially fewer weeks per year, and work for lower wages and in lower status jobs than their nondisabled peers. They also earned substantially less over the course of a year than did members of the general adult population. The mean annual earnings (among those who work at least at some point in the year) of adults with SRLD, for example, was 64.7% of that earned by their nondisabled peers. These differences, of course, went well beyond mere statistical significance—they signal the serious impact that learning disabilities have on adults' lives. Consider, for example, that when family size and income were used to determine whether families were living below or near the federally defined poverty level, 42.2% of the families of adults with SRLD were living in or near poverty, compared to only 16.2% of the families of their nondisabled peers (Reder, 1995).

These findings, based on a nationally representative sample of adults, partially confirmed previous findings from studies of the experiences of high school students during the first few years of transition from school. Like those studies, the present data indicate that adults with self-identified LD tended to work in lower-status occupations for lower wages than did their non-disabled peers. In contrast to the earlier studies, however, the present findings indicated that adults with SRLD worked fewer hours and weeks than did their peers in the general population. The decrease in quantity of work, combined with the lower rate of pay, translates (of course) into greatly reduced earnings and substantially increased risk of living in poverty.

---

[7] This result is probably not surprising, given we found no significant interaction (among those who worked at some point during the year) on the number of weeks worked during the year.

We also found persistent effects of gender in these data, with women tending to participate less in the workforce, to work more in part- and less in full-time jobs (when they are employed), and to work in lower-paying and lower status jobs than do their male peers. Just as SRLD had a significant negative effect on each measure of adult employment and economic outcomes we examined, so, too, did gender affect each measure. As frequently found in studies of gender differences in labor market activity, female adults exhibited distinct patterns of occupational access or preference or both, due in part to characteristic differences in intrinsic job values and social rewards derived from work (Marini, Fan, Finley & Beutel, 1996).

When we examined the interaction between SRLD and gender on the employment and economic outcomes, we found little evidence of statistically significant interactions. Such interactions would be expected if LD were differentially affecting men's and women's labor market activities, as previous studies have suggested. The SRLD by gender interaction reached significance at the .05 level only for one variable: weekly wages. The interaction for that variable was such that women with SRLD received wages that were more depressed relative to the wages of non-SRLD women than were the wages of SRLD men relative to non-SRLD men. Self-reported LD thus appeared to have a larger negative impact on the wages of women than on those of men. Such interactions were not significant for either annual earnings or occupational status. Although a gender $\times$ LD interaction is suggested by the annual earnings data, the interaction did not quite reach statistical significance at the .05 level. Neither did the measures of occupational choice we examined. Thus, we should reserve judgment on the breadth of measures of employment activities for which gender and LD interact.

This lack of a consistent, overall gender interaction is of considerable significance, given that it contradicts most of the previous research. The significant gap between male and female employment rates reported in earlier studies may be related to differences in sampling. In an extensive review of the literature, Vogel (1990) found that, in order to be identified in school, females with LD must (a) be significantly lower in intelligence, (b) be more severely impaired in their reading and written language abilities, and (c) have a greater aptitude-achievement discrepancy than their male counterparts. In fact, the mean IQ in the SRLD in general was reported to be 87 and 8.7% had an IQ of < 70 (Wagner et al., 1992). Therefore, it is not surprising to find less favorable outcomes for females than for males in the NLTS school-identified sample. As a result, gender differences found in longitudinal studies on samples of school-identified males and females with LD may stem from bias of ascertainment and must, therefore, be interpreted cautiously.

The NALS data has provided the opportunity to revisit the question of gender interactions in a self-identified sample of males and females rather than a school-identified sample, and has suggested that we seriously question the validity of earlier findings regarding gender differences in the impact of learning disabilities on adults.

Implications

The findings that adults with SRLD were more frequently unemployed, employed more frequently in part-time jobs, and at significantly lower wages and occupational status as compared to the general population have important implications for transition planning, vocational/career education, counseling, vocational rehabilitation services, gender equity efforts, and employers education programs. First, because the NALS data indicate a high dropout rate of 52% among adults reporting LD (Vogel & Reder, in preparation) and because other findings indicate that many students with LD drop out of school before 10th grade (Wagner, 1991; Zigmond & Thornton, 1985), it is critical that transition planning begin in the junior high/middle school years. We have witnessed considerable increases in the number of adolescents who have taken vocational education courses since the reauthorization of the Individuals with Disabilities Act of 1990 (IDEA; P.L. 101-476). The IDEA mandates the provision of transition services for any student with disabilities ages 16 years and older, who has an individual educational plan (DeStefano & Wermuth, 1992). This increase may be seen quite dramatically by comparing the participation in vocational education of the respondents to the LDA Adult Issues Committee Survey (1996) with the NLTS sample of younger individuals with disabilities (Wagner, 1991).

Among the 332 adults with SRLD who responded to the LDA survey, only 2% took a vocational education course while in junior high school, and 14% while in high school (Payne, 1996). However, another opportunity for these adults to receive vocational education came while students were enrolled in a postsecondary education setting. Seven percent reported having some vocational counseling while enrolled at a 2-year college, 5% while enrolled in a special vocational school, and another 12% as recipients of vocational rehabilitation services. Interestingly enough, only 51% of the respondents answered this item. However, of those who had responded, 28% reported that vocational and postsecondary education led to long-term jobs or careers (Payne, 1996).

In contrast to the very low percentages of adults with LD who had taken vocational education courses in the group responding to the LDA Survey, many more of the NLTS sample of school-identified young adults ages 16–23 indicated having taken a vocational education courses in junior high and high school. Wagner (1991) reported that 39% of 7th and 8th grade youth with LD had taken a vocational education course while 67% of 11th and 12th graders had taken such a course. Given the dropout rate of between one-third and one-half, many of these students might not have benefited from these courses. Therefore, one implication of these findings—and those of the two follow-up studies reviewed earlier—is that extending vocational/career counseling beyond high school years is important because it provides another opportunity for those adults who were not provided, or did not enroll in vocational education courses while in high school to enroll at a time in life when such services become more relevant.

Fourqurean (1994) has elaborated on the importance of effective transition planning in high school and two-year colleges by incorporating information on careers and jobs that do not require a 4-year degree such as careers in law enforcement, fire fighting, the U.S. postal service, and the military—all of which provide adequate salaries, opportunities for advancement and good benefits. Young adults with LD, especially those with limited work experience, also need information about work standards and assistance in developing a strong work ethic (Evers, 1996). Career awareness education and providing information on career and job options should not be limited to only one level or type of job, however. It is also important to keep in mind that 8% of the adults with SRLD in the NALS data base and as many as 37% of the respondents to the LDA Survey (Adult Issues Committee, 1996) earned a 4-year or graduate degrees. Therefore, career/transition planning should be individualized for those with different levels or severity of LD and at different levels of intellectual ability who may be attending, or are enrolled in a special vocational education program, a 2-year college, a 4-year college, or a university.

All students and adults need to be active participants in the career decision-making process and to be involved in planning their educational programs, whether in junior high, high school, postsecondary, or informal adult education settings. They also need to set goals appropriately so as to enhance motivation to improve their reading, writing, and math skills sufficiently to enable them to be successful in post-

secondary education, to expand their career options, and to be successful on the job.

Rosenthal (1985, 1989) was one of the first to develop a vocational/
career counseling curriculum for individuals with LD in a community
college setting that included self-evaluation leading to increased understanding of abilities, strengths, interests, and awareness of career options.
In fact, 3 to 5 years after exiting high school, 30.5% of the NLTS adults
interviewed had enrolled in some type of postsecondary institution (Wagner, 1991). Therefore, career services centers (CSC) on campuses could
provide an important service to students with LD. deBettencourt, Bonaro,
and Sabornie (1995) surveyed postsecondary institutions to determine the
level of awareness and understanding of the career counseling staff in colleges and universities regarding learning disabilities in adults and the
level of collaboration between those staff and the disabled student services (DSS) staff. Their findings indicated that very few students with LD
used CSC services, 80% of the staff had no special training regarding LD,
70% of the respondents had no contact with the staff of the DSS office, and
there were no specific services for students with LD in the career planning
offices. This landmark study identified an important staff development
focus in order to improve the effectiveness of the CSC offices on campuses, and thereby to prepare students with LD for the transition from
school to work while they are enrolled in postsecondary institutions.

The present results confirmed previous reports of gender by-LD-
interactions for at least *some* employment outcomes. Further research is
needed to clarify the extent to which and ways in which gender and disability issues interact. Regardless, a concerted effort is needed to assure
greater gender equity among adults with disabilities as well as in the
general population. Although some of the employment outcome data
examined here indicated that gender inequities may not be greater
among adults with LD than are gender inequities in the general population, special efforts may nevertheless be needed to achieve gender
equity among adults with LD.

Other research provides some starting points for such efforts. Wagner
(1991) investigated enrollment in vocational courses by males and
females and found that gender and ethnic background had an effect on
accessibility to vocational courses. Though males and females were
equally likely to enroll in vocational courses, males spent significantly
more time than females in occupationally-oriented courses. Another clue
as to the disparity in outcomes for males and females was provided by
Fourqurean (1994), who recommended that students with disabilities be
encouraged to take vocational courses that capitalized on their strengths

rather than traditional sex-role stereotypical courses (e.g., child care, secretarial courses, and home economics courses for adolescent girls and auto mechanics, highway construction, and law enforcement for adolescent males). He suggested that adolescent girls who have severe deficits in reading and written language should be discouraged from taking secretarial courses, recommending that instead they consider law enforcement or careers in the military. Lastly, he noted that women with LD who have experienced sexual harassment on the job often have difficulty recognizing and dealing appropriately with these situations. He recommended that vocational education for adolescent girls and women should include instruction and training regarding appropriate and inappropriate behavior and alternative strategies for dealing with inappropriate situations. Professionals involved in transition planning, curriculum development, and career/vocational counseling should be cognizant of these gender-related issues, evaluations of transition programs and career/vocational counseling should include objective assessment of gender bias.

One possible method to accomplish such assessment would be to develop a student database to conduct periodic follow-along studies to determine continuing educational endeavors, employment status, occupations, wages, needed assistance, quality of life, marital status, etc. In this way, program effectiveness may be determined and monitored, and data-driven recommendations for new or modified programs and services may be justified.

Lastly, and of paramount importance, employers need to be informed about learning disabilities in adults. The implementation of the Americans with Disabilities Act of 1990 has increased the likelihood of adults with LD disclosing their disabilities and requesting accommodations on the job. Employers need to understand the nature of LD and how they may affect job performance. Both employees and employers need to know their rights, responsibilities, and reasonable accommodations that may assist the employee with LD to be successful on the job. Knowledge is the first step toward creating an environment that will be attitudinally receptive to employees with LD so that they are not only employed, but are employed full-time, remain employed, are promoted and well compensated, and find fulfillment in their chosen careers.

References

Adelman, P., & Vogel, S. A. (1993). Issues in employment of adults with learning disabilities. *Learning Disability Quarterly, 16,* 219–232.

Adult Issues Committee (1996). *They speak for themselves: A survey of adults with learning disabilities.* Pittsburgh, PA: LDA of America.

Affleck, J. Q., Edgar, E., Levine, P., & Kortering, L. (1990). Postschool status of students classified as mildly mentally retarded, learning disabled, and nonhandicapped: Does it get better with time? *Education and Training in Mental Retardation, 25*(4), 315–324.

Buchanan, M., & Wolf, J. S. (1986). A comprehensive study of learning disabled adults. *Journal of Learning Disabilities, 19*(1), 34–38.

DeStefano, L., & Wermuth, T. R. (1992). Chapter 29 IDEA (P.L. 101-476): Defining a second generation of transition services. In F. R. Rusch, L. DeStefano, J. Chadsey-Rusch, L. A. Phelps, & E. Syzmanski (Eds.), *Transition from school to adult life* (pp. 537–549). Sycamore, IL: Sycamore.

Evers, R. (1996) The positive force of vocational education: Transition outcomes for youth with learning disabilities. *Journal of Learning Disabilities, 29*(1), 69–78.

Fourqurean, J. M. (1994). The use of follow-up studies for improving transition planning for young adults with learning disabilities. *Journal of Vocational Rehabilitation, 4*(2), 96–104.

Halpern, A. (1992). Transition: Old wine in new bottles. *Exceptional Children, 8,* 202–211.

Haring, K. A., & Lovett, D. L. ((1990). A follow-up study of special education graduates. *The Journal of Special Education, 23*(4), 463–477.

HEATH Resource Center. (1992). Unpublished data from the 1991 Cooperative Insitutional Research Program (University of California at Los Angeles). Washington, DC: American Council on Education.

Henderson, C. (1992). *College freshmen with disabilities: A statistical profile.* Washington, DC: American Council on Education.

Individuals with Disabilities Education Act of 1990, 20 U.S.C. 1400 *et. seq.*

Kirsch, I. S., Jungeblut, A., Jenkins, L., & Kolstad, A. (1993). *Adult literacy in America: A first look at the results of the National Adult Literacy Survey.* Washington, DC: National Center for Education Statistics, U.S. Department of Education.

Kranstover, L. L., Thurlow, M., & Bruininks, R. H. (1989). Special education graduates vs. non-graduates: A longitudinal study of outcomes. *Career Development of Exceptional Individuals, 12*(2), 153–166.

Levine, P. (1993). Gender differences in postschool outcomes for youth with mild mental retardation, learning disabilities, and no disability? Myth or reality? Doctoral dissertation.

Levine, P., & Edgar, E. (1994). An analysis by gender of long-term postschool outcomes for youth with and without disabilities. *Exceptional Children, 60*(4), 334–343.

Marder, C., & D'Amico, R. (1992). *How are youth with disabilities really doing? A comparison of youth with disabilities and youth in general.* Menlo Park, CA: SRI International.

Marini, M. M., Fan, P.–L., Finley, E., & Beutel, A. M. (1996). Gender and job values. *Sociology of Education, 69*(1), 49–65.

National Council on Disability. (1989). *The education of students with disabilities: Where do we stand?* Washington, DC: Author.

Nisbet, J., & Lichtenstein, S. (1992). *Gender differences in the postschool status of young adults with mild disabilities. Fact Sheet: Following the lives of young adults.* (Institute on Disability at the University of New Hampshire) 4(1), 1–5.

Payne, N. (1996). Interventions reported by adults with learning disabilities in *They speak for themselves: A survey of adults with learning disabilities.* Adults Issues Committee, Pittsburgh, Pa: LDA of America (pp. 26–32).

Reder, S. (1995). *Literacy, education and learning disabilities.* Portland, OR: Northwest Regional Educational Laboratory.

Rosenthal, I. (1985). A career development program for learning disabled college students. *Journal of Counseling and Development, 63,* 308–310.

Rosenthal, I. (1989). Model transition programs for learning disabled high school and college students. *Rehabilitation Counseling Bulletin, 33*(1), 54–66.

Sitlington , P. L., & Frank, A. R. (1990). Are adolescents with learning disabilities successfully crossing the bridge into adult life? *Learning Disability Quarterly, 13*(1), 97–111.

Scuccimarra, D. J., & Speece, D. L. (1990). Employment outcomes and social integration of students with mild handicaps: The quality of life two years after high school. *Journal of Learning Disabilities, 23*(4), 213–218.

Vogel, S.A. (1990). Gender differences in intelligence, language, visual-motor abilities, and academic achievement in students with learning disabilities: A review of the literature. *Journal of Learning Disabilities, 23*(1), 44–52.

Vogel, S.A., & Reder, S. (in preparation). *Literacy proficiency and educational attainments of adults with self-reported learning disabilities.*

Wagner, M. (April, 1991). *The benefits of secondary vocational education for young people with disabilities.* Paper presented at the Vocational Special Interest Group/American Educational Research Association , Chicago.

Wagner, M., D'Amico, R., Marder, C., Newman, L., Blackorby, J. (1992). *What happens next? Trends in postschool outcomes of youth with disabilities.* Menlo Park, CA: SRI International.

Zigmond, N., & Thornton, H. (1985). Follow-up on postsecondary age learning disabled graduates and drop-outs. *Learning Disabilities Research, 1*(1), 50–55.

Index